# School Psychology and Social Justice

School psychology practice does not exist in a vacuum and is not value-neutral. As the role and function of the school psychologist continues to evolve and expand, social justice provides a needed real-world framework for school psychology students, practitioners, supervisors, and professors to guide their efforts. Culled from years of experience by experts working in a vast array of applied environments and appropriate both for practitioners and for graduate courses in multicultural school psychology and/or the role and function of school psychologists, this book takes the reader through a tour of common school psychology topics and functions through the lens of social justice. Utilizing case examples and concrete suggestions, a critical yet hopeful vision of ways in which school psychologists can work to achieve positive outcomes for students, families, schools, and society is provided.

**David Shriberg**, Ph.D., is an Associate Professor of School Psychology at Loyola University Chicago. Dr Shriberg is the Editor-Elect of *Journal of Educational & Psychological Consultation*, a recent president of Trainers of School Psychologists, and the founder and former co-chair of a national network of school psychologists committed to social justice. His scholarly work focuses on topics related to social justice, leadership, bullying, and ways in which families, schools, and communities can collaborate to support the academic and social–emotional development of students. A former practitioner, to date Dr Shriberg has edited five books, guest-edited two special topic journal issues on the subject of social justice and school psychology, authored over two dozen articles and book chapters, and has made approximately 100 presentations at the local, regional, national, and international level on topics related to cultural responsiveness and social justice.

**Samuel Y. Song**, Ph.D., NCSP, is an Assistant Professor and the Director of the School Psychology program at Seattle University. He has consulted with diverse schools in various regions of the USA and in the Republic of Korea on bullying, mental health issues, and diversity. His social justice scholarship demonstrates a passion for serving vulnerable populations within diverse communities focusing on school climate and bullying prevention in low-resource schools, children exposed to violence, immigrant populations in urban Head Start programs, and training pre-service school psychologists in social justice practice. He is the co-chair of the Social Justice Interest Group of the National Association of School Psychologists (NASP), and the 2012–13 President of the Trainers of School Psychologists (TSP). Dr Song is a member of the Editorial Boards of two professional journals in school psychology: *Journal of School Psychology* and *Journal of School Violence*.

**Antoinette Halsell Miranda**, Ph.D., is an Associate Professor and former director of the school psychology program at The Ohio State University. Dr Miranda has extensive experience working in urban areas and has been involved in a number of collaborative projects with Columbus City Schools during her tenure at The Ohio State University. Before coming to OSU, she worked as a school psychologist in New York City Public Schools. Since her work in NYC Public Schools, Dr Miranda has been committed to issues of social justice, especially equality of opportunity for marginalized students in school settings. Her research is focused on issues of diversity such as: developing effective interventions with at-risk children in urban settings, consultation services in urban settings, and the development of racial identity and its relationship to academic achievement. She has a chapter in *Best Practices in School Psychology–V* entitled "Best practices in urban school psychology," and coauthored a chapter entitled "Privilege in America". She was instrumental in restructuring the school psychology program at The Ohio State University to have a specialty focus and a commitment to social justice in the practice of school psychology. She is a past president of Trainers of School Psychology.

**Kisha M. Radliff**, Ph.D., LP, is an Assistant Professor in the school psychology program at The Ohio State University teaching the mental health and school neuropsychology courses. Dr Radliff completed her internship at the Children's Hospital of Philadelphia and a postdoctoral residency in private practice, primarily working with children, adolescents, and their families and collaborating with teachers and other professionals to address mental health issues. She is committed to social justice issues, particularly in the context of mental health and school psychology training. Dr Radliff is on the Editorial Board of the *Journal of School Violence* and an ad-hoc reviewer for *School Psychology Review*. She has authored various articles and book chapters related to bullying, relational aggression, and social justice. She has also provided numerous paper and poster presentations locally, regionally, and nationally at various professional conferences related to child and adolescent mental health issues.

# School Psychology and Social Justice

## Conceptual Foundations and Tools for Practice

EDITED BY

DAVID SHRIBERG
Loyola University Chicago

SAMUEL Y. SONG
Seattle University

ANTOINETTE HALSELL MIRANDA
The Ohio State University

KISHA M. RADLIFF
The Ohio State University

NEW YORK AND LONDON

First published 2013
by Routledge
711 Third Avenue, New York, NY 10017

Simultaneously published in the UK
by Routledge
27 Church Road, Hove, East Sussex BN3 2FA

*Routledge is an imprint of the Taylor & Francis Group, an informa business*

© 2013 by Taylor & Francis

*Library of Congress Cataloging in Publication Data*
School psychology and social justice : conceptual foundations and tools for practice /
David Shriberg ... [et al.].
    p. cm.
    Summary: "This book will provide an introduction to social justice from the
    perspective of the major topics that affect school psychology practice"—Provided
    by publisher.
    Includes bibliographical references and index.
    1. School psychology—United States. 2. Social justice—United States.
    3. Education—Social aspects—United States. 4. Educational sociology—
    United States. I. Shriberg, David.
    LB1027.55.S38 2012
    370.15—dc23
    2012026580

ISBN: 978–0–415–52267–0 (hbk)
ISBN: 978–0–415–66041–9 (pbk)
ISBN: 978–0–203–12124–5 (ebk)

Typeset in Minion
by Swales & Willis Ltd, Exeter, Devon

# Contents

List of Contributors ............................................................................................... vii

Acknowledgments ................................................................................................ xiv

CHAPTER 1—Introduction .......................................................................................1
DAVID SHRIBERG, SAMUEL Y. SONG, ANTOINETTE HALSELL MIRANDA, AND KISHA M. RADLIFF

PART 1—Foundations .............................................................................................13

CHAPTER 2—Social Justice in School Psychology: A Historical Perspective ...................15
TERRY B. GUTKIN AND SAMUEL Y. SONG

CHAPTER 3—School Psychology and Social Justice in the Global Community ................29
BONNIE KAUL NASTASI AND KRIS VARJAS

CHAPTER 4—What Do We Mean When We Say *Social Justice* in School Psychology? ....53
MARY M. CLARE

PART 2—Major Issues that Affect Practice ..................................................................71

CHAPTER 5—Understanding and Addressing Inequities in Special Education ................73
AMANDA L. SULLIVAN

CHAPTER 6—Systemic School Discipline: Issues of Equity from a Social
Justice Perspective ...................................................................................91
AMITY NOLTEMEYER AND PAMELA FENNING

CHAPTER 7—Paving the Way for Cosmopolitan Resilient Schools: Promoting
        Resilience and Social Justice in Urban, Suburban,
        and Rural Schools ..................................................................................118
GERALDINE V. OADES-SESE, MARK KITZIE AND WAI-LING RUBIC

CHAPTER 8—Institutional Barriers: Poverty and Education ...........................137
STACY A. S. WILLIAMS AND DEBORAH PEEK CROCKETT

CHAPTER 9—Social Justice in the Air: School Culture and Climate ...............155
SAMUEL Y. SONG AND KELLY MARTH

PART 3—Roles and Functions of School Psychologists ..............................171

CHAPTER 10—A Social Justice Approach to Assessment ............................173
MARKEDA L. NEWELL AND GINA COFFEE

CHAPTER 11—Promoting Social Justice by Addressing Barriers to
        Academic Success ..................................................................189
JENNIFER I. DURHAM

CHAPTER 12—Behavioral Issues in the Classroom ......................................206
ANTOINETTE HALSELL MIRANDA AND CHARLOTTE RISBY ESCHENBRENNER

CHAPTER 13—Consultation and Collaboration ...........................................225
JANAY B. SANDER

CHAPTER 14—Mental Health Issues: Non-academic Barriers to Success in School .....244
KISHA M. RADLIFF AND JENNIFER M. COOPER

CHAPTER 15—Family, School, and Community Partnerships ........................270
JANINE M. JONES

CHAPTER 16—The School Psychologist as Social Justice Advocate .............294
ALISSA BRIGGS

CHAPTER 17—Graduate Education and Professional Development ...............311
DAVID SHRIBERG

CHAPTER 18—Moving Forward ...................................................................327
DAVID SHRIBERG, SAMUEL Y. SONG, ANTOINETTE HALSELL MIRANDA, AND KISHA M. RADLIFF

Index .........................................................................................................332

# Contributors

**Alissa Briggs**, Ph.D., a former teacher and Teach For America alumnus, is a school psychologist in Lincoln County (Kentucky) Schools. Her research interests are in the areas of applied social justice and systems change. The title of her dissertation is "A case study of school-wide positive behavior support from a social justice perspective." Dr Briggs has presented and published widely on topics related to school psychology and social justice.

**Mary M. Clare**, Ph.D., is Professor of Counseling Psychology and Director of the Psychological and Cultural Studies Program in the Counseling Psychology Department of the Graduate School of Education and Counseling at Lewis & Clark College. From the initiation of her scholarly program in the early 1980s her primary areas of focus have been diversity, decolonization and consultation in schools and communities (from the classroom to the board room). She is the author of *Responsive Assessment: A New Way of Thinking about Learning* (Jossey-Bass). Her latest book, *100 Voices: Americans Talk about Change*, was published by Loud Mouth Press in October 2011.

**Gina Coffee**, PhD, is an Assistant Professor in the School Psychology program at Loyola University Chicago. Prior to joining the faculty at Loyola University Chicago, she provided psychological services to children in grades K-12. Currently, in practice, teaching, and research, she focuses on the prevention of academic, behavioral, social, emotional, and health difficulties in children by collaborating with educators and parents in individual and systems-wide consultation. In 2010, she was awarded an Early Career Research Award by the Society for the Study of School Psychology. She earned a PhD in Educational

Psychology, with a specialization in School Psychology, from the University of Wisconsin–Madison in 2007.

**Jennifer M. Cooper**, M.A., a former program manager with the Court Appointed Special Advocate (CASA) program and Big Brothers Big Sisters, is an advanced doctoral student in the school psychology program at The Ohio State University. She is currently participating in advanced practicum with the Center for Intervention Research in Schools (CIRS) through Ohio University and completed her practicum experience in the Columbus City Schools in Columbus, Ohio. Her research interests include system-level change, social justice, school-based mental health, interventions for secondary students, dropout prevention, and home–school collaboration. Jennifer currently serves as President-elect of APA, Division 16's Student Affiliates in School Psychology (SASP) and is a member of the National Association of School Psychologists' (NASP) Student Development Workgroup.

**Deborah Peek Crockett**, Ph.D., NCSP, is a retired school psychologist residing in Atlanta, Georgia. She has supported social justice, multiculturalism, diversity and issues of equity throughout her career. Dr Crockett has lectured at local, national, and international conferences and universities on issues of culture, diversity and tolerance, cultural perspectives of crisis intervention, as well as consultation and culturally appropriate student assessment. In July 1998, she served on President Clinton's expert panel that developed *Early Warning, Timely Response: A Guide to Safe Schools*. In 2000, she was invited by the Department of Education, Office of Safe and Drug Free Schools, to respond to the first school shooting in New Orleans, Louisiana. In February 2009, she published a chapter (with J. Brown), "Multicultural Practices and Response to Intervention," in *The Psychology of Multiculturalism in the Schools: A Primer for Practice, Training, and Research*. She is the founder and chair of the NASP Minority Scholarship Program which provides funds for needy ethnic minority students and supports their scholarly efforts in the field of school psychology.

**Jennifer I. Durham**, Psy.D., began her work in school and community psychology as an intern at The Consultation Center of Yale University Medical School. She left Yale in 1992 to do direct service work as a school psychologist for the Teaneck Board of Education. In 1999 Dr Durham was hired as the Executive Director of Communities in Schools of Newark, Inc. Her work in the areas of social justice, culturally competent services, and racial disparities within health and educational settings has resulted in numerous awards such as the Donald Peterson Prize and the Communities In Schools Baldwin Fellowship. Currently Dr Durham is an Assistant Professor at The Derner Institute of Advanced Psychological Studies at Adelphi University in Garden City, New York. She consults and presents to professional and direct service organizations.

**Charlotte Risby Eschenbrenner**, M.A., is a doctoral candidate in the school psychology program at The Ohio State University. In addition to teaching introductory psychology courses at Columbus State Community College, Charlotte has presented nationally and regionally on social justice and on teacher consultation, published in Student Affiliate in School Psychology's online journal *From Science to Practice*, and plans to complete her dissertation by studying the relationship between in-school mentoring and hope in urban high school students. Charlotte is a member of the National Association of School Psychologists (NASP)'s Professional Growth Workgroup and co-chair of the NASP Speakers Bureau.

**Pamela Fenning**, Ph.D., is an Associate Professor and co-director of the School Psychology Program at Loyola University Chicago. She is a certified school psychologist and licensed clinical psychologist (Illinois). Her research interests and publications focus on designing and evaluating universal systems of behavior and academic support and alternative approaches to suspension in urban high school settings.

**Terry B. Gutkin**, Ph.D., is a Professor in the Counseling Department at San Francisco State. He has served as a Professor in the Department of Educational Psychology at the University of Nebraska–Lincoln and received tenure there. Dr Gutkin was Director of the APA approved doctoral and NASP-NCATE approved specialist School Psychology Programs at the University of Nebraska–Lincoln. He has many honors including an Appointment to the National Advisory Committee for the Buros Center for Testing from 2005 to 2009. Dr Gutkin was cited as the 11th most productive published scholar in the four premiere school psychology journals from 1991 to 2003, and was a Charter fellow for the American Psychological Association, Society of Clinical Child and Adolescent Psychology in 2001. He is also co-editor of *The Handbook of School Psychology*, now in its fourth edition.

**Janine M. Jones**, Ph.D., NCSP, is an Associate Professor and Associate Director of the School Psychology Program at the University of Washington. She is also a licensed psychologist in private practice. Dr Jones has been involved in research, teaching and clinical work since 1992. Her professional settings include community mental health centers, private practice, schools, and universities. Her professional experiences include providing child and adolescent therapy, psychological assessment, and teaching and supervision of graduate students. Dr Jones specializes in providing culturally responsive treatment to children suffering from depression, anxiety, exposure to violence, and trauma. Her research focuses on multicultural counseling and resilience in children from a cultural perspective. She has received early career awards from the National Institutes of Mental Health (2008), Society for the Study of School Psychology (2007), and the National Association of School Psychologists (2011 Presidential Award). Dr Jones has published in journals including *School Psychology Quarterly, Journal of Black Psychology, and Developmental Neuropsychology*. In addition, she edited the book *The Psychology of Multiculturalism in the Schools* in 2009.

**Mark Kitzie**, Psy.D., is a licensed psychologist in private practice specializing in children and adolescents and an Adjunct Professor at Montclair State University in the Forensic Psychology Certificate Program. He directed the psychology department at a residential facility for adolescents with histories of delinquency and trauma and currently is the supervising psychologist at an outpatient clinic that serves children and their families in Newark, New Jersey. Part of his practice includes clinical and forensic assessment of children and their parents for protective services and the family court. His research interests include internal, family and school environment factors that support resilience in children and the effects of trauma on children's development. He has coauthored publications related to the assessment of minority children and resilience in at-risk children.

**Kelly Marth**, Ed.S., is a recent graduate of the school psychology program at Seattle University and a school psychologist in Lake Washington School District, WA. She has been the project director for the Protective Peer Ecology program, which provides schools with assessment and intervention strategies aimed at promoting positive peer relationships and mobilizing peers to prevent bullying. She is also a member of the Social Justice Interest Group of NASP and, based on her academic performance and commitment to social justice issues, was inducted into Alpha Sigma Nu, the honor society of Jesuit colleges and universities. She has coauthored one book chapter, and presented nationally and regionally on social justice and school psychology as well as on the Protective Peer Ecology bullying prevention program. In general, she is interested in the role that school psychologists can play in advocating for preventive and proactive, evidence-based policies that better support all students' socio-emotional and academic development.

**Bonnie Kaul Nastasi**, Ph.D., is a Professor in the Department of Psychology, School of Science and Engineering, at Tulane University. Dr. Nastasi's research focuses on the use of mixed methods designs to develop and evaluate culturally appropriate assessment and intervention approaches for promoting mental health and reducing health risks such as sexually transmitted infections (STIs) and HIV, both within the US and internationally. She has conducted work in New Orleans and Sri Lanka on development of school-based programs to promote psychological well-being, and is currently directing a multi-country study of psychological well-being of children and adolescents with research partners in 12 countries. She is active in promotion of child rights and social justice within the profession of school psychology, and is an Associate of the International Institute of Child Rights & Development (IICRD), Centre for Global Studies, University of Victoria, British Columbia. She directed development of a curriculum for training school psychologists internationally on child rights, *School Psychologist as Advocate for Child Rights*, a joint effort of International School Psychology Association (ISPA), IICRD, and Tulane University's School Psychology Program. Dr Nastasi is a past-president for Division 16 (School Psychology) of the American Psychological Association.

**Markeda L. Newell**, Ph.D., is an Assistant Professor in School Psychology at the University of Wisconsin–Milwaukee. Her research focuses on multiculturalism in school psychology. Specifically, she examines how pre-service and practicing school psychologists make cultural considerations during problem-solving consultation in school-based settings is examined. Dr Newell also identifies and analyzes the multicultural content pre-service school psychologists should be taught as well as how this content should be taught to increase their multicultural competence. Dr Newell has received grants to support her research, and she has been recognized as an Early Career Scholar for School Psychology Research Collaboration.

**Amity Noltemeyer**, Ph.D., NCSP, is currently an Assistant Professor in the School Psychology program at Miami University in Oxford, Ohio. Previously, she acquired experience as a school psychologist and educational consultant in diverse settings. Dr Noltemeyer has published and presented on topics including disproportionality in special education identification/school discipline, educational equity, response to intervention, systems change, resilience, and literacy intervention. She is co-editor of a book titled *Disproportionality in Education and Special Education: A Guide to Creating More Equitable Learning Environments* and serves as President Elect of the Ohio School Psychologists Association.

**Geraldine V. Oades-Sese**, Ph.D., is an Assistant Professor of Pediatrics at the Institute for the Study of Child Development, Robert Wood Johnson Medical School. She is the founder/director of the Research Center for Resilience and Early Childhood Development and the CREATE (Childhood Resilience & Early Achievement Toward Excellence) Clinic. Dr Oades-Sese is a nationally certified school psychologist. Her longitudinal research study examines the social–emotional and academic resilience of at-risk Hispanic American preschool children. She also examines resilience among African American children exposed prenatally to drugs and alcohol. She has authored a number of empirical articles and book chapters on resilience, early childhood development, assessment, and culturally sensitive interventions, and coauthored a book titled *Culturally Sensitive Narrative Interventions for Children and Adolescents*. She authored and served as a guest editor for *Psychology in the Schools: Special Issue on Resilience in the Schools* released in 2011. Dr Oades-Sese is a 2011 SSSP Early Career Scholar and the recipient of the 2010 *NJDEC Lucille Weistuch Early Childhood Special Education Leadership Award*. She is currently a board advisor and Principal Investigator for *Sesame Street Workshop's* Initiative on Childhood Resilience.

**Wai-Ling Rubic**, M.A., is a graduate of Pacific Oaks College (known for its advocacy in social justice) in Pasadena, California. Currently, she is the Mental Health and Disabilities Coordinator for Community Development Institute Head Start Serving Northern San Diego. She is also an Adjunct Faculty at Grossmont Community College in Child Development. She directed the Early

Head Start and Head Start programs at the A.B. Polinsky Children's Center, a 24-hour shelter for abused and neglected children, for eight years and created a developmentally appropriate social–emotional curriculum targeted specifically for traumatized children. Her research interests include the bicultural and bilingual identity formation of people of color, social justice, cultural diversity, developing resilience in young children, and evidence-based interventions for children in crisis. She has coauthored a number of publications on resilience of at-risk bilingual preschoolers and culturally sensitive interventions for young children.

**Janay B. Sander**, Ph.D., is a graduate of the school psychology doctoral training program at The University of Texas at Austin and was a faculty member of that program for eight years. She is a licensed psychologist (Texas) and is now an Associate Professor for the School Psychology Training Program in Teacher's College at Ball State University. She teaches academic assessment and interventions, consultation, ethics, law and multicultural issues, adolescent development, and supervises practicum experiences in school and juvenile justice settings. Her research is in the areas of disruptive behaviors and mental health, juvenile delinquency, and the role of schools and family systems in addressing the academic, emotional, and behavioral needs of youth.

**Amanda L. Sullivan**, PhD, is an Assistant Professor of School Psychology at the University of Minnesota. Her research examines issues of risk and equity, particularly for students with disabilities, within a socioecological framework. She is also interested in professional, ethical, and legal issues related to the provision of psychoeducational services for diverse learners. Dr Sullivan has presented extensively on topics related to disproportionality in special education and the appropriate identification of educational disability. Her research has appeared in numerous scholarly journals in school psychology and education.

**Kris Varjas**, Psy.D., serves as an Associate Professor at Georgia State University in the Department of Counseling and Psychological Services and is a research faculty member of the Center for Research on School Safety, School Climate, and Classroom Management. She has served as the Co-Chair of the National Association of School Psychologists GLBTQ Committee for the past two years. Dr Varjas has received numerous awards, including the Outstanding Faculty Research Award (Georgia State University), Outstanding Service (Division 16: APA), and the Early Career Scholar award (Society for the Study of School Psychology). Her research interests include investigation of bullying, cyberbullying and school climate; mental health prevention and intervention; and research on issues related to lesbian, gay, bisexual, and questioning youth.

**Stacy A. S. Williams**, Ph.D., is a Clinical Assistant Professor and Director of Field Training in the Department of Educational and Counseling Psychology, Division of School Psychology, at the University at Albany, State University of New York. She is also a Licensed Psychologist in New York State. Her years of working with groups of K-12 at-risk learners in both urban and rural communities have provided her with clear insights into the frustrations, challenges and joys of working as a school psychologist with limited resources. She currently consults with Instructional Support Teams (IST) in upstate New York, working closely with school psychologists, general educators, administrators, and support staff in integrating RTI initiatives at the IST level. Additionally, Stacy has also consulted internationally, bringing RTI strategies to rural classrooms in Jamaica. She has extensive experience collecting and managing systems data and developing whole class or individual interventions based on the data. Stacy's area of research focuses on how to effectively communicate research findings to teachers.

# Acknowledgments

We wish to acknowledge former Routledge Senior Editor Dana Bliss for believing in this book and working with us until the chapters were submitted, and we thank current Routledge Editorial Assistant Sam Rosenthal for his efforts in picking up the ball and bringing us through to publication. We also wish to thank Brendan O'Brien for his wonderful copyediting, as well as all others at Routledge whose efforts have been less visible to us as editors but who nevertheless have made important contributions to this book's production and distribution.

Each of us had the benefit of the support of many others over the past few years as this book moved from an idea, to a proposal, to a final product. In the following paragraphs, each editor provides her or his specific acknowledgments.

**Dave Shriberg:** While I like to think I play a role in most positive events that happen for me personally and professionally, I have learned that we are all interconnected and that it is critically important to have work colleagues and family and friends who believe in you. In this sense, I have been incredibly blessed both professionally and personally. Professionally, I am so fortunate to work at a university—Loyola University Chicago—that is based on a social justice mission. I also work with an incredible group of school psychology faculty and students. All of the Loyola school psychology students push me and each other to be a better agent of social justice and all have contributed to this book in this way. In particular, I would like to acknowledge Loyola school psychology graduate students Sofia Flores, Schevita Persaud, and Rachel Pitt for their thoughtful reviews of book chapters. I would also thank my school psychology faculty colleagues Michael Boyle, Gina Coffee, Pamela Fenning, Lynne Golomb, Adam

Kennedy, Diane Morrison, Ross Pesce, and Martie Wynne for being such a wonderful social justice team.

Regarding this book, having admired Antoinette and her work for many years, it was a particular thrill and honor to work with and learn from her on this project. Sam and Kisha were also incredible, going above and beyond at every step and providing sharp yet supportive feedback to authors and to the rest of the editorial group alike. I cannot imagine a better trio to work with and I am so happy to be linked with all of you in this first-ever book on school psychology and social justice. All of you are trailblazers and, even more importantly, just incredible human beings.

I would also like to thank my parents, Arthur and Marjorie Shriberg, for their love and guidance. By word and example they both embody the spirit of *Tikkum Olam*—a Hebrew phrase describing our individual and collective responsibility to make the world a better place. Anyone who grew up with my parents would emerge believing that we have an important responsibility to do our part to be an agent of social justice. Finally, I thank my wife Amy and my children Emma and Nathan for their daily love, support, and inspiration. Editing a book like this is a sustained effort not just for the editors, but for their families. They were with me every step of the way and I love them all.

**Sam Song:** In true ecological fashion, I would like to acknowledge all the people who have interacted with and supported me to help produce this work. Working with such great co-editors and authors on this book made it a lot of fun. While my co-editors are all brilliant, I wanted to highlight Dave's leadership on this effort, Antoinette's wisdom, and Kisha's optimism. I also wish to thank my coauthors Terry Gutkin and Kelly Marth for their work and collaboration. It was fun. I thank the school psychology students at Seattle University (SU) for teaching me a lot about social justice through class discussions. I appreciated the support of my SU school psychology colleagues (Kay Beisse and Ashli Tyre) and Dean Sue Schmitt for her support on this project. Thanks go to Manivong Ratts who is always willing to talk with me about social justice at work, and my graduate assistant Jenn Truoung for her hard work in supporting me. Most importantly, I would like to thank my parents Joseph and Young Song for their sacrifices as immigrant parents and my life partner and wife, Soomie and son Soly for their love, support, and understanding while I was "away" working on this project.

**Antoinette Halsell Miranda:** Throughout my career, in both the public schools and academia, I have been committed to equity and social justice issues for marginalized youth and adolescents. I want to acknowledge the many graduate students, K-12 students, parents, and educators whom I have had the pleasure of interacting with on this almost three decade journey and from whom I have learned so much. It was an honor to be part of a stellar group of professionals who feel equally passionate about social justice issues. I can't say enough about my co-editors. David, whom I have always admired for his commitment to social justice, continues to demonstrate leadership in bringing the issue to the forefront in school psychology. His leadership on this book has been invaluable. Sam brought insight and guidance to the project and always made me smile with his wonderful sense of humor. I have been blessed to have Kisha as a colleague who shares my passion, vision, and sense of advocacy for social justice. She challenged us to think in deeper ways about social justice. And finally to Charlotte, my coauthor and advisee, who demonstrated her strong social justice advocacy early in the program. Hands down, this was the best collaboration project I have been a part of in my career.

A special thanks to my parents, A. C. Halsell and the late Charlotte Halsell, who gave me the gift of education and the belief that I could do anything in life. And finally, I want to acknowledge the most important people in my life who keep me grounded; my husband Jim, my beautiful daughter Michelle, and my courageous son Jimmy, whom I often call my miracle baby. They constantly remind me that family is the most important asset we have in life.

**Kisha Radliff:** I am truly honored to have been invited to be a part of this project and to work with such amazing colleagues. I have found a wonderful colleague and mentor in Antoinette and have learned so much from her; each collaboration with her has been a wonderful experience that pushes me to grow as a professional. It was inspiring to work with Dave, someone who is a leader in integrating social justice language into the field of school psychology. It was great to have the opportunity to collaborate with Sam, a former classmate whom I still consider a mentor. He can be counted on to bring humor and wisdom to the conversation. I also wish to thank my coauthor and advisee, Jennifer, for her dedication and passion for social justice. I thoroughly enjoyed working on the mental health chapter with her. I would also to thank the students in the school psychology program at The Ohio State University for embracing our social justice mission, engaging in dialogue, and supporting the faculty as we continually make changes to strengthen the social justice emphasis throughout the program.

I would also like to thank my mother, Naomi Haye, for her love and encouragement, and my grandparents, June Schmitz and the late Albert Schmitz, who taught me what it means to truly be selfless, to believe the best in others, and to always lend a helping hand. Finally, I would like to thank my wonderful husband Phil and my little sunshine, Alexander, for their love and support throughout the process of working on this book. And to my twins, thank you for taking it easy on me so that I had the energy to work on this project!

one
# Introduction

## David Shriberg,
## Samuel Y. Song,
## Antoinette Halsell Miranda,
## and Kisha M. Radliff

The ultimate measure of a man is not where he stands in moments of comfort and convenience, but where he stands at times of challenge and controversy.

(Rev. Dr Martin Luther King Jr)

School psychology is a field with a long and storied tradition. Inherent in the idea behind the need for school psychologists is the notion that all children have a right to an education and that it is the responsibility of adults such as school psychologists to bring their professional expertise and personal talents to bear to help all students to develop and achieve to their full potential.

At the aspirational level, this fundamental premise of school psychology (why have school psychologists if we are not committed to seeing children reach their full personal and academic potential?) is hardly controversial and to many it is likely inspirational. However, where the rubber often meets the road is not in the broad aspiration, but in translating this aspiration to practice. School psychology does not occur in a vacuum. School psychology is practiced in the United States—and throughout the world—within a context where some children, through no choice of their own, are advantaged and others are disadvantaged. We school psychologists work within a context where all of us are raised with our own personal biases and preconceptions that shape how we view others. We also work with other educators and with families that have their own personal and professional biases that work to some children's benefit and other children's disadvantage. Additionally, we school psychologists work within a societal context where entire communities are often left to suffer from a lack of adequate resources and a lack of political will to support these suffering communities, whereas other communities have an abundance of resources. School psychologists in the United States work within a context where racism, classism, sexism, homophobia, transgendered oppression, ageism, ableism, and religious intolerance abound at all levels. On the positive side, school psychologists in the United States also work within a context where anything is possible and where there are numerous examples of individual, local, state, and national movements towards a more just society.

Contemporary school psychology is not for persons who have a narrow vision of practice. The field of school psychology sets a bold and broad agenda—promoting a vision of school psychologists as systemic change agents covering many specialty areas. Indeed, a quick perusal of the definition of school psychology put out by leading organizations in the field makes clear that school psychologists seek to have a broad impact on behalf of children in many areas. Consider, as one example, the following text taken from the website of the National Association of School Psychologists (NASP) on May 14, 2012 (www.nasponline.org/about_sp/whatis.aspx), under the heading "What Is a School Psychologist?"

> School psychologists help children and youth succeed academically, socially, behaviorally, and emotionally. They collaborate with educators, parents, and other professionals to create safe, healthy, and supportive learning environments that strengthen connections between home, school, and the community for all students.

The website then continues (under the heading "What Do School Psychologists Do?") to spell out 22 different ways that school psychologists work with students, families, teachers, school administrators, and/or community providers. There are numerous other examples across organizations of documents that describe a similarly expansive view of school psychology. As four school psychologists, we like that the field takes such a broad view of practice. It is this kind of thinking that has led the movement away from a reactive test and place model towards a model of practice that emphasizes prevention, systemic thinking, and leadership. However, all movements and change efforts come with potential opportunities and pitfalls. The primary opportunity that we see is the promotion of the view that schools have many needs and that school psychologists are therefore obligated to maximize their positive impact across a variety of domains related to the academic, behavioral, and social development of students. However, a potential pitfall is that if school psychology practice consists of 22 core tasks (or 30, or 40) covering so many different domains, it is vitally important that these domains of practice are linked to an overarching framework that ties these domains to a common purpose that reflects the social, cultural, educational, economic, and political realities of practice. This is why a social justice perspective is critical.

It is perhaps for this reason that over the past several years the major organizations connected with school psychology in the US (the American Psychological Association (APA) and NASP) have incorporated social justice in their organization's practice expectations. For example, in 2003 APA published its "Guidelines on Multicultural Education, Training, Research, Practice, and Organizational

Change for Psychologists" (APA, 2003). The philosophical framework of these guidelines encourages psychologists to view themselves as leaders in social justice and as advocates for multiculturalism. Specifically, Principle 5 of the guidelines begins by stating, "Psychologists are uniquely able to promote racial equity and social justice" (APA, 2003, p. 382) and Principle 6 concludes by stating, "Psychologists recognize that organizations can be gatekeepers or agents of the status quo, rather than leaders in a changing society with respect to multiculturalism" (APA, 2003, p. 382). These guidelines have been followed by a flurry of scholarship on this topic, particularly within counseling psychology. Additionally, in 2010, Division 16 (School Psychology) of APA formed a "Social Justice and Child Rights Working Group" and the Presidential Address at the 2011 APA conference was titled "Psychology and Social Justice: Why We Do What We Do" (Vasquez, 2011). Within NASP, in 2007 a "Social Justice Interest Group" was established. In 2010, social justice was referenced multiple times as an aspiration in the four *NASP Standards* documents. Social justice was also the theme of featured NASP podcasts in June 2010 and June 2011.

There has also been increasing scholarship in school psychology related to social justice. First, in 2008 a special topic issue of *School Psychology Review* on "Promoting Social Justice" featured an opening piece by the journal's editor identifying social justice as a positive direction for school psychology (Power, 2008). Power's article was followed by two full-length empirical articles (McCabe & Rubinson, 2008; Shriberg et al., 2008) and two commentaries from leading multicultural/social justice scholars in school psychology (Nastasi, 2008; Rogers & O'Bryon, 2008). In 2009, a chapter on social justice (Shriberg, 2009b) appeared in NASP's *The Psychology of Multiculturalism in Schools: A Primer for Practice, Training, and Research* (Jones, 2009). We also saw in 2009 the publication of two special topic issues related to social justice in journals widely read by school psychologists. First, *Journal of Educational & Psychological Consultation* published a special topic issue entitled "School Consultants as Agents of Social Justice: Implications for Practice." This issue contained an introductory piece by the guest editors (Shriberg & Fenning, 2009), four core articles related to the intersection of consultation and social justice (Clare, 2009; Li & Vazquez-Nuttall, 2009; Pearrow & Pollack, 2009; Roach & Elliott, 2009), and a commentary from two leading social justice scholars in counseling psychology focused on ways in which school psychology might pursue a more robust social justice agenda (Speight & Vera, 2009). Also in 2009, the peer-reviewed journal *Trainers' Forum*, published by Trainers of School Psychologists, published a themed issue entitled "Teaching for Social Justice in School Psychology Graduate Programs: Strategies and Lessons Learned" (Shriberg, 2009a). This issue contained three examples (Briggs, McArdle, Bartucci, Kowalewicz, & Shriberg, 2009; Li et al., 2009; Radliff, Miranda, Stoll, & Wheeler, 2009) of ways in which school psychology graduate programs incorporate social justice into their training. Finally, in 2011 the results of a national study of school psychologists regarding their perspective on social justice were published in a leading school psychology journal (Shriberg, Wynne, Briggs, Bartucci, & Lombardo, 2011).

This recent recognition of the import of social justice to practice and to scholarship reflects the continuing evolution of multicultural movements that seek to situate the goals of applied fields within the broader societal context in which this applied work is practiced. However, despite the recent work described above and despite the efforts of numerous individuals who have pushed a social justice agenda for decades, school psychology is clearly lagging behind related fields in terms of the depth and scope of its social justice efforts (Shriberg, 2009a). This is a missed opportunity. Given the unique combination of psychological training and access to the broader ecology of a school that school psychologists often have, and given the myriad justice issues (resource allocation, biased and/or outdated assessment procedures, overrepresentation of minority group members in special education and school discipline procedures, and institutionalized racism, sexism, classism, and homophobia, to name but a few) prevalent in schools that directly impact practice, there seems to be a natural connection between school psychology and social justice (a point that is further developed in all chapters of this book). Whereas recent years have seen multitudes of primers on social justice in related fields (e.g., Adams et al., 2010; Frattura & Capper, 2007; Marshall & Oliva, 2009; Toporek, Gerstein, Fouad, Roysircar, & Israel, 2006), to date there are no comprehensive books that speak directly to school psychology practice from a social justice perspective. This book seeks to fill this critical void—and in the process to further school psychology's voice in the emerging social justice paradigm.

## Defining Social Justice

Social justice is not easily defined, but is associated in education with the idea that all individuals and groups must be treated with fairness and respect and that all are entitled to the resources and benefits that the school has to offer (North, 2006). To date, there have been two studies seeking to define social justice from a school psychology perspective. First, Shriberg, et al. (2008) conducted a Delphi study with 17 multicultural experts in school psychology. The participants in this study most strongly endorsed a definition of social justice centered on the idea of "protecting the rights and opportunities for all."

More recently, Shriberg et al. (2011) surveyed 1000 randomly selected NASP members regarding their opinions related to social justice. As one component of this study, participants ($n = 214$) were asked to respond to the statement, "The primary goal of this study is to obtain information about how school psychology graduate students and professionals define social justice. Seven possible components that may contribute to the definition of social justice are listed below. Please rate the following seven elements on the scale below with (1) indicating 'unimportant to the definition' and (7) indicating 'critical to the definition'." As seen in Table 1.1, respondents rated *ensuring the protection of educational rights and opportunities* and *promoting nondiscriminatory practice* significantly more critical to the definition than all other items, except each other ($p < 0.001$).

**TABLE 1.1.** Respondents' mean ratings regarding possible components of the definition of social justice

| Item | M | SD |
|---|---|---|
| Ensuring the protection of educational rights and opportunities for all students* | 6.70 | 0.66 |
| Promoting nondiscriminatory practice* | 6.67 | 0.67 |
| Advocating for individuals or groups of students who may not be able to advocate for themselves | 6.47 | 0.81 |
| Being culturally responsive in service delivery | 6.36 | 0.87 |
| Preventing the over identification of minority groups for special education | 5.98 | 1.22 |
| Working to eliminate the achievement gap | 5.66 | 1.50 |
| Connecting students and families to community resources | 5.50 | 1.36 |

Notes 1 = unimportant to the definition, 7 = critical to the definition. *Items rated significantly higher than all others (except each other), $p < .001$. Reprinted with permission.

In terms of the application of social justice principles to educational practice, based on their findings from a qualitative study with children involved in the juvenile justice system, their mothers, and professionals involved in the juvenile justice system, Sander et al. (2011) offer the following operational definition:

> Social justice is an advocacy-related construct that includes three specific, but not always distinct, ecological system qualities that promote educational success and psychological well-being: *access* to necessary and appropriate resources, experiences of being treated with *respect*, and *fairness*. (emphasis in original, p. 311)

For this book's purposes, Sander et al.'s definition was used as the definition of social justice that chapter authors were asked to consider. However, while definitions provide a framework, practice drives reality. What does a vision for socially just school psychology practice look like? This is the driving question for this book. While every author will have her or his own view of social justice and how it relates to the focus in her/his chapter, there are some overarching ideas that reflect our perspective as book editors, as follows.

- Working towards social justice is and should be an aspirational goal of school psychology practice.
- Social justice is a verb—while "achieving full social justice" may be an ideal, in order to be an effective agent of social justice one must be willing to actively work towards this vision.
- Social justice is as much a process as it is an outcome.
- We will not "sugarcoat" issues. That is to say, we believe that true learning and growth comes from examining issues as they are in real life (or, in the

case of a book, how they are perceived by the editors and authors). Sometimes this means shining a bright light on harsh societal practices and the
role of school psychology in perpetuating these practices.

- Just as psychology is increasingly challenging the value of placing such a
  strong emphasis on deficit model thinking, so also does applying a social
  justice lens require a consideration of wellness and resiliency. A person
  cannot achieve his or her full wellness potential—and hence his or her full
  capacity as a learner—if he or she is living within an inherently unfair and
  unjust situation (Prilleltensky, 2011).
- A key step towards being an agent of social justice is knowing oneself.
  Knowing oneself is a continual process that requires an awareness of values, beliefs, and biases. While it is not possible for anyone to be a "perfect"
  agent of social justice (indeed, this type of thinking can be quite debili-
  tating to personal growth), it is incumbent upon all those who are working towards a social justice aspiration to be vigilant in their self-reflection
  regarding personal strengths and areas for growth.
- A major strategy towards combating social injustice is advocacy, including
  the idea of doing things with and not to others and the idea of having the
  courage to be an ally to those being oppressed in cases and topics where
  you hold unearned power.

Subsequent chapters explore these themes and, in the aggregate, this book provides a comprehensive model of what "socially just school psychology practice"
might look like. This is accomplished through writings in three primary areas.

The first part of the book ("Foundations") provides the reader with a thorough
grounding in the social justice literature as it relates to school psychology practice, tracing the field's historical roots and promoting a national and international
vision of socially just school psychology practice moving forward. Specifically, in
Chapter 2 Terry B. Gutkin and Samuel Y. Song describe how school psychology
has historically had a strong social justice orientation and how school psychologists are in a unique positive to positively affect social justice moving forward. In
Chapter 3, Bonnie Kaul Nastasi and Kris Varjas discuss how an international perspective can help to inform the definition and practice of social justice in school
psychology. These authors then present a model for culturally responsive and
socially just ' *global-community school psychology*' practice. In the third and final
chapter in this section (Chapter 4), Mary M. Clare delves into "What Do We Mean
When We Say *Social Justice* in School Psychology?" In this chapter, she grapples
with this term and its potential implications, including sharing some of her own
story as a female making her way in academic school psychology.

The second part ("Major Issues that Affect Practice") takes the reader through
a tour of cutting-edge topics that provide the context for the work that school
psychologists do. In Chapter 5, Amanda L. Sullivan tackles the critical issue of
disproportionality in special education. Dr Sullivan first provides a context for
understanding disproportionality in special education as a social justice issue and

then describes recommendations for engaging in school psychological practice to ensure that struggling learners are provided with appropriate educational services and supports. Along similar lines, as documented by Skiba, Michael, Nardo, and Peterson's (2002) classic "The Color of Discipline: Sources of Racial and Gender Disproportionality in School Punishment," research has shown for decades that there is severe disproportionality (particularly as relates to minority youth generally and African American males specifically) in school discipline procedures. In Chapter 6, Amity Noltemeyer and Pamela Fenning detail this phenomenon from a social justice perspective. Moving away from traditional punitive approaches that have been shown to be ineffective and often discriminatory in application, they offer recommendations for school psychologists that are conceptualized and delivered from a social justice perspective, including prevention-oriented practices that are intended to meet the needs of all students.

Concurrent with the expansion of social justice scholarship and advocacy in psychology and education have been the recent movements within psychology away from purely deficit-oriented approaches to understanding wellness and resiliency factors that promote optimal health. In what we believe is the first book chapter linking resiliency, social justice, and school psychology, in Chapter 7 Geraldine V. Oades-Sese, Mark Kitzie, and Wai-Ling Rubic write eloquently about the new concept of "cosmopolitan resilience" and how this perspective has the potential to transcend culture, language, and other dimensions of diversity in rural, suburban, and urban schools.

In research conducted to date on school psychology and school justice (e.g., Shriberg et al., 2008, 2011), institutional barriers are frequently cited as a leading obstacle to school psychologists achieving their social justice potential individually and collectively. In Chapter 8, Stacy A. S. Williams and Deborah Peek Crockett provide a full description of these barriers, and ways school psychologists can work to overcome them. In particular, these authors directly address ways in which poverty can impact children and families at multiple levels. In the final chapter in this section (Chapter 9), Samuel Y. Song and Kelly Marth propose that social justice is "in the air". In their thought-provoking chapter on school climate and social justice, they discuss the current state of the school climate and school culture literature, articulate a vision of social justice practice, and then describe what this vision might look like in practice.

The third and final part, titled "Roles and Functions of School Psychologists," takes the reader on a tour of common school psychology duties and practices seen from a social justice lens. First, in Chapter 10 Markeda L. Newell and Gina Coffee describe their vision of a social justice approach to assessment. Specifically, readers will learn their perspective on how social justice applies to assessment, why a social justice approach to assessment can improve equity, and how a social justice approach can be applied to systems and individual-level assessment in schools. In Chapter 11, Jennifer I. Durham describes multiple barriers to academic success. Using an ecological framework, Dr Durham provides comprehensive strategies for overcoming these barriers at the individual and systemic levels.

In Chapter 12, Antoinette Halsell Miranda and Charlotte Eschenbrenner focus on behavioral issues that occur in the classroom, with special attention given to how marginalized students are disproportionately affected by the administration of discipline and punishment. These authors provide an overview of behavioral problems, especially in urban classrooms; review the literature on teachers and classroom management; discuss issues of diversity in classroom management; and describe ways to rethink classroom management utilizing socially just practices with diverse students.

Earlier in this chapter, we provided a definition of social justice (emphasizing the concepts of access, equity, and respect) developed by Janay B. Sander and her colleagues. In Chapter 13, Dr Sander describes the foundational school psychology role of consultation and collaboration utilizing this definitional framework. She provides several leading models of consultation and then, utilizing case studies, describes how these models might be applied using a social justice framework.

While the current *Zeitgeist* in public policy and debate is to focus exclusively on academic performance, as school psychologists (or school psychologists in training, whatever the case may be for you as a reader) we know that there are many "non-academic" factors that can play a major role in positive student development, particularly factors related to mental health. As school psychology advances as a field, it is important for practitioners to have a strong grounding in prevention and treatment strategies related to school mental health. Accordingly, in Chapter 14 Kisha M. Radliff and Jennifer M. Cooper provide both a brief history of school mental health and examples of contemporary school mental health models viewed from a social justice perspective. They give strategies for school psychologists to consider in moving toward adopting a more socially just school-based mental health service delivery model that addresses mental health issues across the tiers (e.g., prevention, screening, small group intervention, and individual intervention).

Throughout every iteration of models of school psychology practice and national policy agendas for school psychology is the cornerstone idea that effective practice involves collaboration between educators, students, families, and communities. Similarly, as the social justice literature in school psychology has developed, the idea that socially just practice involves collaboration (can a practice that purposefully excludes and/or devalues families be considered socially just?) between all key stakeholders is omnipresent (e.g., Li & Vazquez-Nuttall, 2009). In Chapter 15, Janine M. Jones presents a social justice framework for viewing the interaction between families, schools and communities. After providing a historical framework, she discusses common barriers to family/school/community collaboration and provides practical strategies for overcoming these barriers at the individual and systemic level.

Chapter 16 begins with author Alissa Briggs noting that the most recent NASP Standards document (NASP, 2010)—a document that has tremendous influence in defining the primary roles and functions of school psychologists—takes a clear position that school psychologists should aspire to act as change agents. Reflecting the idea that social justice not only is an aspirational goal for society but also is a verb, something school psychologists *do*, Dr Briggs takes the change agent charge several steps further by describing a framework of social justice advocacy. Providing suggestions for social justice advocacy across the tiers, this framework builds on and is consistent with public health and prevention frameworks that are increasingly prominent and valued in school psychology training and practice.

As all teachers have learned, it is one thing to read about a topic and it is quite another thing to teach and/or inspire others on this same topic. If social justice is a widely shared aspiration, then what does it mean to train others to be agents of social justice? David Shriberg grapples with this question in Chapter 17. In this chapter, key components of social justice training are offered, and a case example is provided that highlights this author's attempt to bring social justice ideas to practice with the students with whom he works.

This section closes with a synthesizing chapter (Chapter 18) written by the book's editors, highlighting main themes, lessons learned, and next steps. While this book is intended as a foundational source that will be a springboard for much future advocacy and research, in this chapter we grapple with what it has accomplished, as well as what it may not have accomplished in terms of the need for additional works that can help school psychologists at all levels and of all (assuming a commitment to ethical practice) personal and professional beliefs become ever more sophisticated and effective in their social justice efforts.

As mentioned, while social justice is a wonderful and critical aspirational goal, it is our position that social justice is also a verb—it is something that practitioners, students, and professors *do*. Accordingly, case examples are provided throughout the book in order to further bring chapter ideas to life. Additionally, while of course we hope that readers review every chapter and this book is organized in such a way that reading the chapters in order takes the reader through a clear and comprehensive voyage, we recognize that for various reasons some chapters may be more relevant and/or meaningful to you than others. If this is the case, you will find that each chapter stands on its own as a comprehensive and thought-provoking resource.

Regardless of your approach, as you read, we strongly encourage you to think about your own practice (if you are a student, we strongly encourage you to think about your own intended practice). None of us are perfect social justice beings, if such a thing even exists. However, all of us can find ways to improve our skills and capacities as social justice agents. It has been our honor to edit this work and it is our hope that this book can be a critical tool towards your development as an agent of social justice. If we have helped you in this regard, then this book has been a success.

## References

Adams, M., Blumenfeld, W. J., Castañeda, C., Hackman, H. W., Peters, M. L., & Zúñiga, X. (2010). *Readings for diversity and social justice* (2nd ed.). New York, NY: Routledge.

American Psychological Association (2003). Guidelines on multicultural education, training, research, practice, and organizational change for school psychologists. *American Psychologist, 58,* 377–402.

Briggs, A., McArdle, L., Bartucci, G., Kowalewicz, E., & Shriberg, D. (2009). Students' perspectives on the incorporation of social justice in a school psychology graduate program. *Trainers' Forum, 28* (4), 35–45.

Clare, M. M. (2009). Decolonizing consultation: Advocacy as the strategy, diversity as the context. *Journal of Educational & Psychological Consultation, 19,* 8–25.

Frattura, E. M., & Capper, C. A. (2007). *Leading for social justice: Transforming schools for all learners.* Thousand Oaks, CA: Corwin Press.

Jones, J. M. (2009). *The psychology of multiculturalism in schools: A primer for practice, training, and research.* Bethesda, MD: National Association of School Psychologists.

Li, C., Kruger, L., Mulé, C., Lippus, K., Santora, K., Cicala, G., et al. (2009). Including social justice in the training of school psychologists. *Trainers' Forum, 28* (4), 24–34.

Li, C., & Vazquez-Nuttall, E. (2009). School consultants as agents of social justice for multicultural children and families. *Journal of Educational & Psychological Consultation, 19,* 26–44.

Marshall, C., & Oliva, M. (2009). *Leadership for social justice: Making revolutions in education* (2nd ed.). Upper Saddle River, NJ: Prentice Hall.

McCabe, P. C., & Rubinson, F. (2008). Committing to social justice: The behavioral intention of school psychology and education trainees to advocate for lesbian, gay, bisexual, and transgendered youth. *School Psychology Review, 37,* 469–486.

Nastasi, B. K. (2008). Social justice and school psychology. *School Psychology Review, 37,* 487–492.

National Association of School Psychologists. (2010). *Model for comprehensive and integrated school psychological services.* Retrieved August 27, 2012 from www.nasponline.org/standards/2010standards/2_practicemodel.pdf

North, C. E. (2006). More than words? Delving into the substantive meaning(s) of "social justice" in education. *Review of Educational Research, 76,* 507–536.

Pearrow, M. M., & Pollack, S. (2009). Youth empowerment in oppressive systems: Opportunities for school consultants. *Journal of Educational & PsychologicalConsultation, 19,* 45–60.

Power, T. J. (2008). Editorial note: Promoting social justice. *School Psychology Review, 37,* 451–452.

Prilleltensky, I. (2011). Wellness as fairness. *American Journal of Community Psychology, 49,* 1–21.

Radliff, K. H., Miranda, A. H., Stoll, N., & Wheeler, A. (2009). A conceptual framework for infusing social justice in school psychology training. *Trainers' Forum, 28* (4), 10–22.

Roach, A. T., & Elliott, S. N. (2009). Consultation to support inclusive accountability and standards-based reform: Facilitating access, equity, and empowerment. *Journal of Educational & Psychological Consultation, 19,* 61–81.

Rogers, M. R., & O'Bryon, E. C. (2008). Advocating for social justice: The context for change in school psychology. *School Psychology Review, 37,* 493–498.

Sander, J. B., Sharkey, J. D., Groomes, A. N., Krumholz, L., Walker, K., & Hsu, J. Y. (2011). Social justice and juvenile offenders: Examples of fairness, access, and respect in educational settings. *Journal of Educational & Psychological Consultation, 21,* 309–337.

Shriberg, D. (2009a). Teaching for social justice in school psychology graduate programs: Strategies and lessons learned: Introduction to the special topic issue. *Trainers' Forum, 28* (4), 5–9.

Shriberg, D. (2009b). Social justice and school mental health: Evolution and implications for practice. In J. M. Jones (Ed.), *The psychology of multiculturalism in schools: A primer for practice, training, and research* (pp. 49–66). Bethesda, MD: National Association of School Psychologists.

Shriberg, D., Bonner, M., Sarr, B., Walker, A., Hyland, M., & Chester, C. (2008). Social justice through a school psychology lens: Definitions and applications. *School Psychology Review, 37*, 453–468.

Shriberg, D., & Fenning, P. A. (2009). School consultants as agents of social justice: Implications for practice: Introduction to the special issue. *Journal of Educational & Psychological Consultation, 19*, 1–7.

Shriberg, D., Wynne, M. E., Briggs, A., Bartucci, G., & Lombardo, A. (2011). School psychologists' perspectives on social justice. *School Psychology Forum: Research in Practice, 5* (2), 37–53.

Skiba, R. J., Michael, R. S., Nardo, A. C., & Peterson, R. L. (2002). The color of discipline: Sources of racial and gender disproportionality in school punishment. *Urban Review, 34*, 317–342.

Speight, S. L., & Vera, E. M. (2009). The challenge of social justice for school psychology. *Journal of Educational & Psychological Consultation, 19*, 82–92.

Toporek, R., Gerstein, L. H., Fouad, N. A., Roysicar, G. S., & Israel, T. (2006). *Handbook for social justice in counseling psychology: Leadership, vision, & action.* Thousand Oaks, CA: Sage.

Vasquez, M. (2011). And social justice for all . . . *Monitor, 42* (9), 30.

# Part 1
# **Foundations**

two
# Social Justice in School Psychology: A Historical Perspective

Terry B. Gutkin and
Samuel Y. Song

It is the central tenet of this chapter that school psychology is, always has been, and always will be in a position to do more for social justice agendas than any other mental health profession (e.g., psychiatrists, psychotherapists, clinical psychologists, counselors, social workers). Although most of the field's practitioners, researchers, and theoreticians have failed historically to conceptualize their work along these lines, this is a seemingly immutable reality that is "built into" our field given the way it is structured. Today, having moved through the first decade of a new millennium, the social justice role of school psychologists is coming into increasingly clear focus and gaining substantial new momentum. In this chapter we will document the historical journey of school psychology, as our field struggles with ever-greater determination to fulfill the social justice potential that has always been "hiding in plain sight."

To be blunt, school psychology is in a uniquely strong position to promote social justice. Even though nothing could be more obvious to us as authors of this chapter, this has been a pretty well-kept secret for nearly half a century. Hopefully, after the publication of this book, and this chapter within it, this will no longer be the case.

## The Structural Realities of School Psychology: Grasping Our Potential to Promote Social Justice

Before "pulling back the curtain" on our own field of school psychology, it is important to first consider our home discipline, namely psychology itself. Without doubt, the advancement of social justice agendas will require, first and foremost, the development and employment of interventions capable of changing the attitudes and behaviors of people in our society. From this perspective, it is clear that professional psychology as a whole has a pivotal role to play. Regardless of whether one considers school, clinical, counseling or organizational psychology, attitudinal and behavioral change is at the heart of our collective expertise and applied practice. As one of the original founding divisions of the American Psychological Association (APA) and one of the original founding specialty practices of contemporary American psychology, it is important to recognize that school psychology has emerged from the "primordial soup" of generic psychology and thus has the best possible foundation upon which to build its social justice work.

However, as noted above, among the many forms of professional psychological practice in our nation, school psychology is particularly well situated to address social justice. And it is important to note that this advantage is not a function of individual contemporary leaders of the field, although many are most certainly deserving of credit for advancing these agendas. Rather, the special position of school psychology in relation to the furtherance of social justice results primarily from foundational elements relating to how our field is structured.

To begin with, the focal point of services provided by school psychologists is, of course, children and youth. We would argue that young people are, in fact, the best possible target population for those hoping to advance social justice. Our logic here is fairly straightforward. As is recognized by virtually (if not literally) every major psychological theory, the "child is the father to the man" (and, obviously, the "mother to the woman" as well). That is, the adult everyone eventually becomes is dramatically and powerfully impacted by experiences during one's youth. Our early years are the foundation of subsequent attitudes and behaviors, including those in the social justice arena. If our society wishes to create meaningful and permanent change regarding social justice, working with children is the ideal place to start. It simply makes more sense to work towards creating prosocial attitudes (e.g., respect for diversity) and behaviors (e.g., treating all people equitably) with youth than to delay our efforts until later developmental periods when people become more set in their ways. As in all areas of socialization, including education and mental health, our society is better served when we intervene as early as possible to prevent problems from emerging rather than passively waiting and then trying to "cure" dysfunction after it is full-blown.

Once one concludes that children and youth are the best target populations for promoting social justice, then it very quickly becomes obvious that schools are the best possible setting in which to work for this purpose. Most importantly, schools give us access to every child in the nation. No other setting provides universal access to this most desirable target population. Just as Willy Sutton was reputed to rob banks because "that's where the money is," those of us who are interested in addressing social justice agendas would be well advised to focus our attention on schools since "that's where the children are." Additional important advantages of working in schools are that they provide access to young people very early in their lives (age five, or often younger when preschool is included), for a long period of time (five to seven hours/day, five days/week, approximately 40 weeks/year, for 12 or more years), and include those portions of life that are considered major developmental periods. And unlike hospitals, clinics, therapists' offices, agencies, etc., all of which are artificial environments, schools are the "real world" for children in that they live out their day-to-day existence in this setting. Attitudinal and behavioral changes made in schools are thus far less likely to suffer from generalization problems, which frequently pose a major threat to the efficacy of psychological interventions (Cooper, Heron, & Heward, 2007; Stokes & Baer, 1977). Finally, schools provide pervasive and near universal access to children's parents, who play such a critical role in socialization and education processes (Buerkle, Whitehouse, & Christenson, 2009).

So, school psychologists have unique access to: (a) the best possible target populations, and (b) the best possible organizational settings in which to access clients. Last but most certainly not least, among the nation's mental health professionals, school psychologists also have unique access to the metaphor and expertise associated with education. Whereas most other professional psychologists work from a medical metaphor, trying to diagnose and cure mental illnesses, school psychologists work in institutions (i.e., schools) where the "prime directive" is education. The difference between educational and medical approaches to human functioning is critical to promoting social justice (Gutkin, 2009, 2012b; Williams & Greenleaf, 2012). Enhancing social justice in our society will require *educational* interventions in which people *learn* about the centrality of equity, fairness, diversity, etc. to the fabric of our society. Expanding social justice is not about curing diseases and pathologies, which is what the traditional medical metaphor would have us focus on. Rather, spreading social justice will require effective *teaching* and *education*, which is at the very core of our expertise as *school* psychologists. Emphasizing this point in one of the most important articles ever written for our field, Bardon (1983) argued that school psychology was not about psychology in the schools *per se* but rather about a psychology of schooling. The core of our field centers on the processes of education, which is also, in our opinion, the epicenter of expertise necessary to facilitate social justice.

## School Psychology: Conceptualizing Our Early History in Relationship to Social Justice

By virtue of the essence of our profession, school psychology has always been a community-based branch of psychology. Schools are an important part of every local community in America, and in a large number of cities and towns across our nation the local school district contributes centrally to the personal identity of local people of all ages. Unlike hospitals, clinics, therapy offices, mental health agencies, etc., what happens in local schools is typically very much a part of the consciousness of local communities. Of course, the relationship flows in the other direction as well. What happens in communities frequently has a crucial impact on local schools. When there is local racial tension, for example, you can often see that drama played out in the classrooms, hallways, and lunchrooms of the neighborhood school district. In light of this unique relationship between schools and communities in American society, it was no coincidence, in our opinion, that one of the most important civil rights cases in our national history, namely Brown v. Board of Education (1954), centered around achieving equity and social justice in school settings. In essence, the dividing line between schools and their local communities is porous in both directions.

All of this was very evident at the time in which school psychology was "born." Although there is no mention of the Brown case's influence in formal documents (Fagan, 2005), it is hard to imagine that it had no influence on the field's first major conference (held at the Thayer Hotel in West Point, NY) during which professional services were identified as being directed toward and for the benefit of "all" children (Cutts, 1955). In other words, from its earliest days, school psychology was always intended to be maximally inclusive and to benefit the entire community served by each school. Collectively, that would mean providing psychological support for all children and youth in our nation. From this perspective, it is easy to understand how school psychology was always in a position to address social justice issues, even if this was not explicitly recognized at the time by the field's leading university trainers, researchers, or field-based practitioners.

Nonetheless, the potential was there. Since the initiation of universal education, injustices that were played out across our nation were always reflected in America's school systems and classrooms. And since the inception of our field, school psychologists have always been in a powerful and strategic position to make an important difference in these social struggles.

## School Psychology: Historical Evolution towards Addressing Social Justice Agendas

As time has progressed and social justice agendas came more to the foreground of America's collective consciousness (e.g., movements related to civil rights, women's equality, the environment, sexual orientation), the field of school psychology has also become increasingly aware of both its potential and its obligations to address these struggles in meaningful ways. The field's growing awareness is symbolized by the content of the various editions of *The Handbook of School Psychology* (Gutkin & Reynolds, 1990, 2009; Reynolds & Gutkin, 1982, 1999) that addressed diversity issues with no chapters in the first and second editions, one in the third edition (Henning-Stout & Brown-Cheatham, 1999) and two in the fourth (Clare, 2009; Frisby, 2009). Likewise, although earlier school psychology textbooks made little or no mention of issues pertaining to the work of school psychologists with culturally and linguistically diverse groups of children (e.g., Bardon & Bennett, 1974; Reynolds, Gutkin, Elliott & Witt 1984), this began to appear as a potentially important issue for the future in similar volumes beginning in the mid-1990s (e.g., Fagan & Wise, 1994) and now is addressed extensively and explicitly in six different chapters of the latest edition of the *Best Practices in School Psychology* series (Thomas & Grimes, 2008).

Of even greater importance, however, has been the steady advancement of the field's body of knowledge and practice, progressing increasingly towards approaches that enhance our collective ability to address social justice. Several of the most important trends in school psychology along these lines are detailed below.

## The Movement toward Consultation Services

Since their inception, with the development of the mental health consultation model (Caplan, 1963), consultation services have become among the most (if not the most) desired job role for school psychologists (Gutkin & Curtis, 2009). The essence of consultation is the provision of indirect services, which means that school psychologists address students' problems by working with their teachers, parents and other caregivers who ultimately provide whatever intervention is developed. This mode of service delivery is intended to address what Gutkin and Conoley (1990) termed the "paradox of school psychology." Specifically, consultation services are an acknowledgment that typically it is not possible to help children unless we focus our professional attention on the adults who control the environments in which children live.

By consulting with the caregivers who interact daily with children (e.g., teachers, parents), school psychologists are able to accomplish multiple goals. Most obviously, it is hoped that consultation will lead to intervention programs that are efficacious for addressing whatever the presenting problem is for a child referred to the school psychologist. Above and beyond that, however, there is an expectation of additional positive outcomes. For one, during the course of school psychologist–caregiver interactions, consultation is designed to "give psychology away," as recommended by Miller (1969) in his APA presidential. That is, the point of consultation is not only to solve problems but also to help teachers, parents, and other consultees *learn* about (a) the intervention being developed, and (b) the problem solving processes via which successful treatments are designed. When successful, consultees will (a) have an intervention for referred students in hand, (b) understand this intervention well enough to apply it to other students in their class this year or in subsequent years, and (c) comprehend the problem solving methodology used to create effective treatments such that they could ultimately apply this process independently with future problems they might encounter. Above and beyond these important outcomes, the consultee might pass on what has been learned to other caregivers (e.g., teachers, parents), leading to the spreading of effective intervention ideas throughout educational systems and local communities. In the consultation process one can clearly see the *education* metaphor at work, with caregivers rather than students being the targets for our *teaching*.

The ability to help teachers solve presenting problems and *learn* how to deal successfully with similar issues in the future, either with or without the support of their school psychologist, has broad implications for advancing social justice agendas. Many of the specifics of this relationship are detailed in a special issue of the *Journal of Educational and Psychological Consultation* (Shriberg & Fenning, 2009). For the purposes of this chapter we will draw upon the example of bullying, which has, in recent years, become more and more problematic, and is often carried out against disenfranchised students from minority groups of one sort or another (e.g., ability, class, race/ethnicity, gender identity/expression). Teachers who become aware of a school bullying incident might call on their school psychologist for assistance with this presenting case. Rather than simply having the school psychologist treat the bully or the bullied student (i.e., direct service), a consultation with the referring teacher could be initiated in which that teacher works with the psychologist (i.e., indirect service) to generate intervention plans. By approaching the problem in this manner, the referring teacher may promote social justice by not only (a) solving the existing problem for a particular bullied student, but also (b) using newly acquired information and insight gained via consultation to create (with or without the school psychologist) a class-wide, school-wide, or even district-wide prevention and intervention program targeted at reducing bullying directed toward minority students across a wide range of school environments (e.g., Espelage & Swearer, 2010). Given that bullying, like most school-based problems (Gutkin, 2012a, 2012b), often has a major environmental component, consulting with those adults who control these environments (e.g., teachers, administrators) opens up a wide array of options for furthering social justice both within schools and more broadly throughout our society.

## Moving towards Ecological Understandings of Human Functioning

Another step forward toward focusing successfully on social justice has been a growing paradigm shift (Kuhn, 1970) in school psychology, moving away from the medical model and towards ecological understandings of human functioning (e.g., Christenson, Abery, & Weinberg, 1986; Gutkin, 2012a, 2012b; Sheridan & Gutkin, 2000). Traditionally, school psychology (and virtually all other professional psychological specializations) has relied almost exclusively on medical model conceptualizations of psychological problems. Human learning, behavioral and emotional dysfunctions were thought to primarily be the result of internal psychic and/or neurophysiological pathologies. When problems arose they were addressed by "curing" the client's diagnosed "mental illnesses." This view of practice, however, has been severely criticized for over 50 years (e.g., Albee & Joffe, 2004; Szasz, 1960) and during that period of time school psychology has been gradually but progressively shifting towards an ecological conceptualization of human psychological and psychoeducational dysfunction. From an ecological perspective, learning, behavioral and emotional problems are the result of interactions between individuals' characteristics and the multilayered (e.g., micro-, meso, exo-, and macro-environments [Bronfenbrenner, 1979]) environmental systems in which they exist on a day-to-day basis.

As recently argued by Williams and Greenleaf (2012) and Greenleaf and Williams (2009), adopting an ecological perspective can have a profound impact on the ability of school-based psychologists and counselors to focus on social justice agendas. Rather than seeing dysfunctional behaviors as emanating solely from within the individual clients with whom we work, an ecological view allows us to see how surrounding school, home, and community environments can lead to serious behavioral, educational, and emotional problems. Instead of "blaming the victim" by reflexively attributing their problems to internal mental illnesses, the ecological model helps us to "environmentalize" the psychological functioning of all human beings and thus opens the door to considering the caustic impact of racism, sexism, homophobia, poverty, religious intolerance, etc. The ecological model allows us to understand the psychological damage caused to children, youth, and adults alike as a result of social injustices such as discrimination, inequity, and powerlessness. Perhaps of even greater importance, the ecological model "greases the skids" for school psychologists to consider making meaningful environmental changes rather than simply determining how to "cure" the disabilities of individual students, many of which may be more accurately attributed to unjust environmental factors.

A simple example can help clarify the obvious importance of ecological thinking. A number of gay adolescents, who live in a homophobic community and attend a high school that is not accepting of homosexuality, are deeply depressed. The traditional medical model leads school psychologists down the road of assessing these students, diagnosing them as depressed, and trying to secure pharmacologic or psychotherapeutic treatments for their depression. The underlying social justice issues are not as obvious as they should be because these mental health professionals are focused on unearthing intrapsychic or neurologic pathologies and thus are not sufficiently focused on surrounding environmental contexts. For school psychologists who think ecologically, however, assessing the environmental context surrounding students' psychological distress is at the forefront of their thinking. Moreover, by considering the interaction between each of these individual students and their surrounding environments, school psychologists with this orientation are in a much better position to "connect the dots" between the individual cases and see a pattern of discrimination and social rejection for gay students at their schools in this community. Intervention under these circumstances would include not only providing psychological support for the depressed students, but also include systemic actions and advocacy directed toward enhancing social justice for gay people in this community.

As long as the assessment, diagnosis, and treatment foci of school psychologists remain almost exclusively on the internal psychological and biological workings of individual students, it is difficult to see how social justice agendas can possibly receive the attention they deserve. "Blaming the victim" serves to take our collective eyes off pivotal environmental and systemic variables that require our professional expertise if our cause is to advance social justice practices. The continuing progress of our field towards ecological conceptualizations of student functioning means that increasingly greater attention can, and most likely will, be given to enhancing social justice in our nation's school systems.

## Understanding School Psychological Services as Public Health

Historically, school psychologists have approached mental health and educational problems one student at a time. Overwhelming statistical evidence suggests, however, that this approach is failing for the general population, children at large, and for children from poor, disenfranchised and minority groups in particular (e.g., Kazdin, 2011; Kazdin & Blase, 2011). Gutkin (2009, 2012b) describes our current situation as a mental health and education pandemic. Sample statistics leading to this conclusion are presented in Table 2.1. What is clear from these data is that we are dealing with a public health crisis for both the general population and children in particular. Trying to address this by focusing our attention on individual students is like trying to put out a forest fire one tree at a time. It simply does not work. As Albee (1999) noted, no disease has ever been prevented by treating those who have it. With this in mind, there have been a number of calls to move the field of school psychology in the direction of public health models (Dawson et al., 2003; Erhardt-Padgett, Hatzichristou, Kitson, & Meyers, 2003; Gutkin, 2009, 2012b; Nastasi, 2004; Strein et al., 2003; Ysseldyke et al., 2006). Doing so would have profound implications for social justice in our schools and communities.

**TABLE 2.1.** Sample data reported in Gutkin (2012b) regarding the nation's mental health and education pandemics

**Statistics pertaining to the general US population**

1. A recent representative national survey ($N$ = 10,000) conducted by the National Institute of Mental Health (NIMH) found that: (a) each year more than a quarter of the American population has a diagnosable mental disorder, with nearly six in 10 of these individuals having difficulties characterized as either "moderate" or "serious" (Kessler, Chiu, Demler & Walters, 2005), and (b) the bulk of these people "remain either untreated or poorly treated" (Wang et al., 2005, p. 629).
2. Approximately 85% of Americans will not receive health care treatment for their diagnosable mental or substance-abuse disorder within a year. In fact, more than 70% of them will never receive specialized mental health care, as reported by Norcross (2006).
3. Data such as these led Thomas Insel, the Director of NIMH, to describe the quality of contemporary mental health services as an "unacceptable failure" (Insel & Fenton, 2005, p. 590).

**Statistics pertaining to America's children and youth populations**

1. "Approximately one in five children and adolescents experiences the signs and symptoms of a DSM-IV disorder during the course of a year" (US Department of Health and Human Services, 1999, p. 193).
2. "One in ten children and adolescents suffers from mental illness severe enough to result in significant functional impairment" (National Advisory Mental Health Council Workgroup on Child and Adolescent Mental Health Intervention Development and Employment, 2001, p. 9).
3. "Approximately 70% of children and adolescents who are in need of mental health treatment do not receive any such services," as reported by Strein, Hoagwood, and Cohn (2003, p. 24).
4. Comparisons of 15-year-olds in 2006 showed that the US ranked 23rd and 16th for mathematics and science literacy, respectively, out of 29 developed nations (National Center for Education Statistics, 2009).
5. (a) Only about 30% of America's fourth and eighth graders are reading at grade level, (b) only about 25% of America's 12th graders are doing math at grade level, (c) a public school student is suspended every second, and (d) a high school student drops out of school every 11 seconds (The Children's Defense Fund, 2009).

The central point is that public health intervention almost always includes elements of *teaching* populations how to (a) cope effectively with extant problems, and/or (b) prevent problems from arising in the future. Public health treatment involves collaborative *educational* processes (Gutkin, 1999) that could be, should be, and are coming to be seen by school psychologists as their "home base." Situated in virtually the only institution (i.e., school) that has long-term and intensive access to the entire population of our nation's children (who will grow up to be the entire population of our nation's adults) *and* having unique expertise in broadly based educational processes, school psychologists reside at the very nexus from which public health actions can emerge.

With schools reflecting all the problems of social injustice that permeate contemporary society, they are among the very best institutional settings in which to intervene, potentially catching problems early and preventing them from becoming serious impediments to healthy development for America's children. Schools are a venue in which systemic advocacy on behalf of social justice could be and has been extremely powerful (e.g., racial desegregation). Again, interested readers are referred to the special issue of the *Journal of Educational and Psychological Consultation* guest-edited by Shriberg and Fenning (2009).

For the purposes of illustration, let's consider public health advocacy for the purposes of enhancing social justice in the area of effective schooling. Currently, there exists an extensive body of knowledge regarding effective teaching (e.g., Doll, LeClair, & Kurien, 2009; Gettinger & Stoiber, 2009). In view of today's technologically oriented, information-based society, garnering an effective education is closely linked to occupational and mental health outcomes. Clearly, those who fail to achieve successful educational outcomes face lifelong challenges pertaining to poverty and psychological stress (e.g., Heflin & Iceland, 2009; Nikulina, Widom, & Czaja, 2011; Sznitman, Reisel, & Romer, 2011; Wamba, 2010). Given statistics showing over-representation of ethnic and racial minorities among those who drop out of school and fail to graduate (e.g., Aloise-Young, & Chavez, 2002; Griffin, 2002), education itself becomes an issue of social justice. In light of this analysis, work done by school psychologists to enhance the teaching effectiveness of educators is, in and of itself, a social justice intervention. Given the disproportionate representation of ethnic and racial minorities among those who experience educational failure, however, advocacy for enhanced education needs to be particularly focused on the schools and educators serving these racial and ethnic minority students. A public health advocacy approach demands a population-based solution rather than attempting to resolve this dilemma one student at a time.

An example of this comes from the first author's personal experience working as a school psychologist in an inner-city middle school. At this school, the principal noticed that nearly 85% of the students were below grade level in reading. His request was that I start testing all of the reading-delayed students to find out which of them were learning disabled so that they could be placed in special education. Rather than proceeding along those lines, my response was to suggest that we sit down with the school district's curriculum consultant and the teachers from the feeder elementary schools to discuss changes that could be made to the reading curriculum so that fewer students would be below grade level in reading when they arrived in middle school. In this suggestion, I was advocating for a public health, population-based, preventive approach (see Doll & Cummings, 2008) to solving the educational problems facing the ethnically diverse students in the middle school I was serving, and was thus promoting crucial social justice outcomes.

## Conclusion

It is the thesis of this chapter that although school psychologists have not historically been fully aware of their potential role in the promotion of social justice, in point of fact no mental health professional is in a better position to accomplish these outcomes. As our field has developed, so has its understanding of this phenomenon. With growing attention being paid to consultation services, ecological conceptualizations of human functioning, and the public health nature of our work, social justice agendas and advocacy are becoming increasingly salient. This book is one of several outstanding examples of the progress that is being made along these lines. In regard to advancing social justice, the field of school psychology is like a "slumbering giant" that has begun to wake up. Surely, given the nature of our mission, the nature of our job roles, and the nature of the pandemics that confront our clients, continued momentum in school psychology towards addressing social justice issues is all but inevitable.

# References

Albee, G. W. (1999). Prevention, not treatment, is the only hope. *Counselling Psychology Quarterly, 12*, 133–146.

Albee, G. W., & Joffe, J. M. (2004). Mental illness is NOT "an illness like any other." *Journal of Primary Prevention, 24*, 419–436.

Aloise-Young, P. A., & Chavez, E. L. (2002). Not all school dropouts are the same: Ethnic differences in the relation between reason for leaving school and adolescent substance use. *Psychology in the Schools, 39*, 539–548.

Bardon, J. I. (1983). Psychology applied to education: A specialty in search of an identity. *American Psychologist, 38*, 185–196.

Bardon, J. I., & Bennett, V. C. (1974). *School psychology*. Englewood Cliffs, NJ: Prentice Hall.

Bronfenbrenner, U. (1979). *The ecology of human development.* Cambridge, MA: Harvard University Press.

Brown v. Board of Educ., 347 U.S. 483 (1954).

Buerkle, K., Whitehouse, E. M., & Christenson, S. L. (2009). Partnering with families for educational success. In T. B. Gutkin & C. R. Reynolds (Eds.), *The handbook of school psychology* (4th ed., pp. 655–680). New York, NY: Wiley.

Caplan, G. (1963). Types of mental health consultation. *American Journal of Orthopsychiatry, 33*, 470–481.

Children's Defense Fund, The (2009). *The state of America's children 2008.* Washington, DC: Children's Defense Fund.

Christenson, S., Abery, B., & Weinberg, R. A. (1986). An alternative model for the delivery of psychological services in the school community. In S. N. Elliott & J. C. Witt (Eds.), *The delivery of psychological services in schools: Concepts, processes, and issues* (pp. 349–391). Hillsdale, NJ: Lawrence Erlbaum Associates.

Clare, M. C. (2009). Thinking diversity: A habit of mind for school psychology. In T. B. Gutkin & C. R. Reynolds (Eds.), *The handbook of school psychology* (4th ed., pp. 840–854). New York, NY: Wiley.

Cooper, J. O., Heron, T. E., & Heward, W. L. (2007). *Applied behavior analysis.* Upper Saddle River, NJ: Pearson Merrill Prentice Hall.

Cutts, N. E. (1955). *School psychologists at mid-century.* Washington, DC: American Psychological Association.

Dawson, M., Cummings, J. A., Harrison, P. L., Short, R. J., Gorin, S., & Palomares, R. (2003). The 2002 multisite conference on the future of school psychology: Next steps. *School Psychology Quarterly, 18*, 497–509.

Doll, B., & Cummings, J. A. (2008). *Transforming school mental health services: Population-based approaches to promoting the competency and wellness of children.* Thousand Oaks, CA: Corwin Press.

Doll, B., LeClair, C., & Kurien, S. (2009). Effective classrooms: Classroom learning environments that foster school success. In T. B. Gutkin & C. R. Reynolds (Eds.), *The handbook of school psychology* (4th ed., pp. 791–807). New York, NY: Wiley.

Erhardt-Padgett, G. N., Hatzichristou, C., Kitson, J., & Meyers, J. (2003). Awakening to a new dawn: Perspectives of the future of school psychology. *School Psychology Quarterly, 18*, 483–496.

Espelage, D. L., & Swearer, S. M. (2010). A social–ecological model for bullying prevention and intervention: Understanding the impact of adults in the social ecology of youngsters. In S. R. Jimerson, S. M. Swearer, & D. L. Espelage (Eds.), *Handbook of bullying in schools: An international perspective* (pp. 61–72). New York, NY: Routledge.

Fagan, T. K. (2005). The 50th anniversary of the Thayer Conference: Historical perspectives and accomplishments. *School Psychology Quarterly, 20,* 224–251.

Fagan, T. K., & Wise, P. S. (1994). *School psychology: Past, present, and future.* New York, NY: Longwood.

Frisby, C. L. (2009). Cultural competence in school psychology: Established or elusive construct? In T. B. Gutkin & C. R. Reynolds (Eds.), *The handbook of school psychology* (4th ed., pp. 855–885). New York, NY: Wiley.

Gettinger, M., & Stoiber, K. (2009). Effective teaching and effective schools. In T. B. Gutkin & C. R. Reynolds (Eds.), *The handbook of school psychology* (4th ed., pp. 769–790). New York, NY: Wiley.

Greenleaf, A. T., & Williams, J. M. (2009). Supporting social justice advocacy: A paradigm shift towards an ecological perspective. *Journal for Social Action in Counseling and Psychology, 2,* 1–14.

Griffin, B. W. (2002). Academic disidentification, race, and high school dropouts. *High School Journal, 85,* 71–81.

Gutkin, T. B. (1999). Collaborative versus directive/prescriptive/expert school-based consultation: Reviewing and resolving a false dichotomy. *Journal of School Psychology, 37,* 161–190.

Gutkin, T. B. (2009). Ecological school psychology: A personal opinion and a plea for change. In T. B. Gutkin & C. R. Reynolds (Eds.), *The handbook of school psychology* (4th ed., pp. 463–496). New York, NY: Wiley.

Gutkin, T. B. (Ed.) (2012a). Ecological approaches to mental health and educational services for children and adolescents. Special double issue of *Journal of Educational and Psychological Consultation, 22* (1–2).

Gutkin, T. B. (2012b). Ecological psychology: Replacing the medical model paradigm for school-based psychological and psychoeducational services. *Journal of Educational and Psychological Consultation, 22,* 1–20.

Gutkin, T. B., & Conoley, J. C. (1990). Reconceptualizing school psychology from a service delivery perspective: Implications for practice, training, and research. *Journal of School Psychology, 28,* 203–223.

Gutkin, T. B., & Curtis, M. (2009). School-based consultation: The science and practice of indirect service delivery. In T. B. Gutkin & C. R. Reynolds (Eds.), *The handbook of school psychology* (4th ed., pp. 463–496). New York, NY: Wiley.

Gutkin, T. B., & Reynolds, C. R. (Eds.). (1990). *The handbook of school psychology* (2nd ed.). New York, NY: Wiley.

Gutkin, T. B., & Reynolds, C. R. (Eds.). (2009). *The handbook of school psychology* (4th ed.) New York, NY: Wiley.

Heflin, C. M., & Iceland, J. (2009). Poverty, material hardship, and depression. *Social Science Quarterly, 90,* 1051–1071.

Henning-Stout, M., & Brown-Cheatham, M. (1999). School psychology in a diverse world: Considerations for practice, research, and training. In C. R. Reynolds & T. B. Gutkin (Eds.), *The handbook of school psychology* (3rd ed.) New York, NY: Wiley.

Insel, T. R., & Fenton, W. S. (2005). Psychiatric epidemiology: It's not just about counting anymore. *Archives of General Psychiatry, 62,* 590–592.

Kazdin, A. E. (2011). Evidence-based treatment research: Advances, limitations, and next steps. *American Psychologist, 66,* 685–698.

Kazdin, A. E., & Blase, S. L. (2011). Rebooting psychotherapy research and practice to reduce the burden of mental illness. *Perspectives on Psychological Science, 6,* 21–37.

Kessler, R. C., Chiu, W. T., Demler, O., & Walters, E. E. (2005). Prevalence, severity, and comorbidity of 12-month DSM-IV disorders in the National Comorbidity Survey Replication. *Archives of General Psychiatry, 62,* 617–627.

Kuhn, T. S. (1970). *The structure of scientific revolutions* (2nd ed.). Chicago, IL: University of Chicago Press.

Miller, G. A. (1969). Psychology as a means of promoting human welfare. *American Psychologist, 24,* 1063–1075.

Nastasi, B. K. (2004). Meeting the challenges of the future: Integrating public health and public education for mental health promotion: *Journal of Educational and Psychological Consultation, 15,* 295–312.

National Advisory Mental Health Council Workgroup on Child and Adolescent Mental Health Intervention Development and Employment. (2001). *Blueprint for change: Research on child and adolescent mental health.* Rockville, MD: National Institute of Mental Health.

National Center for Education Statistics. (2009). *Digest of Education Statistics: 2008.*Washington, DC: National Center for Education Statistics.

Nikulina, V., Widom, C., & Czaja, S. (2011). The role of childhood neglect and childhood poverty in predicting mental health, academic achievement and crime in adulthood. *American Journal of Community Psychology, 48,* 309–321.

Norcross, J. C. (2006). Integrating self-help into psychotherapy: 16 practical suggestions. *Professional Psychology: Research and Practice, 37,* 683–693.

Reynolds, C. R. & Gutkin, T. B. (Eds.). (1982). *The handbook of school psychology* (1st ed.). New York, NY: Wiley.

Reynolds, C. R. & Gutkin, T. B. (Eds.). (1999). *The handbook of school psychology* (3rd ed.). New York, NY: Wiley.

Reynolds, C. R., Gutkin, T. B., Elliott, S. N., & Witt, J. C. (1984). *School Psychology: Essentials of Theory and Practice,* New York, NY: Wiley.

Sheridan, S. M., & Gutkin, T. B. (2000). The ecology of school psychology: Examining and changing our paradigm for the 21st century. *School Psychology Review, 29,* 485–502.

Shriberg, D., & Fenning, P. A. (2009). School consultants as agents of social justice: Implications for practice: Introduction to the special issue. *Journal of Educational & Psychological Consultation, 19* (1), 1–7.

Stokes, T. F., & Baer, D. M. (1977). An implicit technology of generalization. *Journal of Applied Behavior Analysis, 10,* 349–367.

Strein, W., Hoagwood, K., & Cohn, A. (2003). School psychology: A public health perspective I. Prevention, populations, and, systems change. *Journal of School Psychology, 41,* 23–28.

Szasz, T. S. (1960). The myth of mental illness. *American Psychologist, 15,* 113–118.

Sznitman, S. R., Reisel, L., & Romer, D. (2011). The neglected role of adolescent emotional well-being in national educational achievement: Bridging the gap between education and mental health policies. *Journal of Adolescent Health, 48,* 135–142.

Thomas, A. & Grimes, J. (Eds.). (2008). *Best practices in school psychology V.* Bethesda, MD: National Association of School Psychologists.

US Department of Health and Human Services. (1999). *Mental health: A report of the Surgeon General.* Rockville, MD: US Department of Health and Human Services.

Wamba, N. G. (2010). Poverty and literacy: An introduction. *Reading & Writing Quarterly: Overcoming Learning Difficulties, 26* (3), 189–194.

Wang, P. S., Lane, M., Olfson, M., Pincus, H. A., Wells, K. B., & Kessler, R. C. (2005). Twelve-month use of mental health services in the United States: Results from the National Comorbidity Survey Replication. *Archives of General Psychiatry, 62,* 629–640.

Williams, J. M., & Greenleaf, A. T. (2012). Ecological psychology: Potential contributions to social justice and advocacy in school settings. *Journal of Educational and Psychological Consultation.*

Ysseldyke, J., Burns, M., Dawson, P., Kelly, B., Morrison, D., Ortiz, S., et al. (2006). *School psychology: A blueprint for training and practice III.* Bethesda, MD: National Association of School Psychologists.

three

# School Psychology and Social Justice in the Global Community

## Bonnie Kaul Nastasi and Kris Varjas

An international perspective in psychology, and specifically school psychology, has a long history. The American Psychological Association's (APA) Committee on International Relations in Psychology (CIRP) was first established in 1944[1] and the International School Psychology Committee (ISPC), predecessor of International School Psychology Association (ISPA), was established in the 1970s.[2] The focus of international efforts in psychology has changed over the past 70 years. The initial purpose of the CIRP was to assist the European psychological community, following World War II, with the reestablishment of laboratories and libraries. ISPC was established for the purpose of facilitating collaboration among school and educational psychologists worldwide. Currently, the international focus in both organizations encompasses aspects of psychology research, practice, training, global outreach, and policy. Furthermore, the global perspective in American psychology has encompassed school psychology through activities within the School Psychology Division of APA (Division 16) and the National Association of School Psychologists (NASP).

Of particular importance to our discussion is the recognition of the responsibility of American psychology to address global social problems such as poverty, discrimination, violence, oppression, human rights violations, and lack of access to mental health services (Bullock, 2011; Marsella, 1998; Nastasi, 2011). This focus is exemplified in school psychology by the work of Division 16 and NASP to address issues related to globalization, social justice, and child rights.[3] These efforts are consistent with the activities of ISPA's Task Forces on Child Well-being and

Advocacy and Professional Development and Practices related to child rights and social justice at a global level.[4]

The purpose of this chapter is to discuss how an international, or *global*, perspective can help to inform the definition and practice of social justice in school psychology, and present a model for culturally responsive and socially just *"global-community school psychology"* practice. We examine the global nature of school psychology and the global relevance of social justice. The chapter concludes with discussion of future directions in school psychology research, practice, and professional development. We begin with a discussion of "global-community" psychology as a meta-discipline.

## Global-Community School Psychology

To represent the interdependence and holistic nature of psychology in the global (worldwide, international) community, Marsella (1998) proposed *global-community psychology* as a "superordinate or meta-psychology concerned with understanding, assessing, and addressing the individual and collective psychological consequences of global events and forces by encouraging and using multicultural, multidisciplinary, multisectoral, and multinational knowledge, methods, and interventions" (p. 1284). The notion of the global community is particularly relevant to our discussion as we consider the scope of social injustice and the increasingly global focus within school psychology. Moreover, the problems posed by social injustice require complex solutions that go beyond the boundaries of a single discipline and necessitate culturally and contextually relevant solutions directed to systems as well as individuals. Thus, we adopt the concept of *global-community school psychology*.

## School Psychology in the Global Community

Global-community school psychology can be best described as a *developing* specialty. As such, this is an opportune time to consider how best to integrate social justice goals with a global focus in the research, practice, training, and policies that guide the profession. To this end, the School Psychology Division (Division 16) of the APA is engaged in initiatives since 2010 to promote the globalization of the specialty and to address social justice and child rights as critical responsibilities for school psychologists. An example of one of the initiatives is the development of modules for preparing school psychologists in child rights and social justice advocacy in collaboration with ISPA. Furthermore, viewing the practice of school psychology within a global community affords a perspective on social justice issues that can inform domestic and local practices, exemplified by the joint Division 16–ISPA social justice and child rights project. In this section, we examine the status of school psychology at a global level and subsequently explore the integration of social justice goals into this evolving field.

Research conducted under the auspices of ISPA examined the status of professional school psychology across 43 countries (see Jimerson, Oakland, & Farrell, 2007, for a detailed presentation of findings for each country). In recognition of the variations in title (e.g., school/educational psychologist, counselor, psychopeda-gogue, psychologist in schools/education), Jimerson and colleagues (2007) defined the specialty of "school psychology" as embodying the following responsibilities:

> individual assessment of children who may display cognitive, emotional, social, or behavioral difficulties; develop and implement primary and secondary intervention programs; consult with teachers, parents, and other relevant professionals; engage in program development and evaluation; conduct research; and help prepare and supervise others (p. 1.)

Based on a cross-country analysis, Farrell, Jimerson, and Oakland (2007) identified several countries, including Australia, Canada, Israel, most of the Western European countries, New Zealand, and the United States, as reflecting "better established" professional school psychology. Table 3.1 presents a list of external (country/culture-specific) and internal (professional) factors related to the level of

**TABLE 3.1.** Internal and external factors contributing to development of school psychology (Farrell et al., 2007; Oakland & Jimerson, 2007)

| Internal (Professional) Factors | External (Country, Cultural) Factors |
| --- | --- |
| • Established discipline of psychology (of which school/educational psychology is a specialty)<br>• Legal status of psychology and school psychology<br>• Credentialing bodies (e.g., accreditation, certification/licensure)<br>• Professional organizations such as national school psychology organization<br>• Established professional preparation programs with foundational courses in child development, individual differences and disabilities, research and statistics; and applied courses in assessment, intervention, and supervised field experiences (practicum, internship)<br>• Relationship of school psychology to system of education, including special education<br>• Theoretical–empirical foundations (e.g., research and scholarly publications)<br>• Technical advances in the field (e.g., standardized tests) | • Economic status of the country, as measured by gross national product (GNP)<br>• Geographic location, such as proximity to countries with established school psychology<br>• National priorities related to provision of public education and health services<br>• Established system of education at primary, secondary and tertiary (higher education) levels<br>• School-based special education services<br>• Historical and current cultural factors, including language (e.g., fluency in English is critical to accessing professional literature) |

development of school psychology (Farrell et al; 2007; Oakland & Jimerson, 2007). An examination of these variables suggests that developmental status is closely tied to adherence to established models of school psychology and education in the US and Western Europe. For example, the inclusion of standardized tests and special education as critical factors (see Table 3.1) reflects their importance to the role of the school psychology in assessment, diagnosis, and eligibility determination for special education in the US and Western Europe.

Professionals interested in globalizing school psychology must be cautious in exporting established, and possibly outdated, models as the standard for globalization. Instead, the development of school psychology service-delivery models should be guided by cultural construction based on country-specific priorities, needs, and resources (Nastasi & Varjas, 2011). The work of Hatzichristou (1998, 2002; Hatzichristou, Lampropoulou, & Lykitsakou, 2006) in the development of school psychology in Greece, for example, reflects the dynamic process in which grounded theory and research provided the basis for development and adaptation of an "alternative" model of school psychology. Program development followed formative research to identify the "profiles" of average as well as at-risk students, and school and community systemic needs. In addition, Hatzichristou and colleagues (2006) assumed a culturally synthetic approach, described as using a "meta-cultural" perspective, that "focuses on similarities of cultures and individuals (common needs and adversities) and builds on positive potential, competencies and strengths as a means of enhancing resiliency" (pp. 121–122), rather than viewing "minority" cultures as alternatives or "subordinate" (subcultures) to the dominant "majority" culture. Applied at a global level, a meta-cultural approach would be characterized by a mutual valuing of perspectives and would facilitate transfer of knowledge and meaning across cultures. This perspective is consistent with one of the goals of the APA's CIRP, fostering receptivity of American psychologists to learning and knowledge generated outside of the US.[5]

An examination of trends in research and scholarship in global-community school psychology over the past 20 years suggests that the international school psychology community may have different priorities than those countries with "western-centric" concerns, and we may benefit from consideration of global priorities for the field. Little, Akin-Little, and Lloyd (2011) conducted a content analysis of trends in the peer-reviewed journal *School Psychology International* from 1990 to 2011, and compatibility of the content with the current practice model of NASP (2010a). Although the majority of authors were from North America (44.91%) or Europe (31.50%), authors from 57 countries were represented. Moreover, 13.31% of the publications reflected international collaboration. The content reflected in this literature base was not highly consistent with the NASP (2010a) model,[6] with the content of 33% of publications focused outside of the NASP practice categories (i.e., categorized as "other"). Among the 10 NASP categories, the most frequently represented was "legal, ethical, and professional practice," followed by "prevention," which encompassed issues such as truancy, dropout, bullying, and crisis intervention. Furthermore, although standardized testing has played an important role in the development of school psychology in some countries, Farrell et al. (2007) cite examples of countries such as Albania, Hungary, and Italy in which the development of the profession has been associated with promotion of psychological well-being or mental health of children, rather than more traditional "Western" models of assessment, diagnosis, and special education eligibility.

In summary, the field of international, or global, school psychology is best characterized as evolving, with established traditional models of school psychology balanced by opportunities to create new models to meet culture- and context-specific needs. Nastasi and Varjas (2011) proposed a process for cultural construction of global-community school psychology that relies on partnership, capacity building, and the integration of research and practice. In constructing models of global-community school psychology, it behooves professionals to examine the global as well as the local landscape related to social justice and human rights.

## Social Justice in the Global Community

Social justice within school psychology at a global level necessitates consideration of issues that affect children transnationally and transculturally. Although we acknowledge the importance of culturally constructed and context-specific definitions and approaches to social justice, we begin with guiding principles formed at an international level for addressing social justice issues. We give particular attention to those principles that have relevance to children and youth and the practice of school psychology. The United Nation's (UN) Convention on the Rights of the Child (CRC; UN, 1989) and Millennium Development Goals (MDGs; UN, 2000) provide a "universal" set of principles for guiding the actions of school psychologists in promoting social justice on a global as well as a local scale.[7]

The CRC (adopted by the UN General Assembly, November 20, 1989) was the first legally binding international instrument to encompass the full range of human rights for children. Governments that ratify the CRC are accountable for respecting, protecting and realizing child rights in their respective countries; to date, only two countries have *not* ratified the Convention (US[8] and Somalia). The guiding principles of the CRC (non-discrimination, realizing the best interests of the child, right to participation, and right to life, survival and development) are embodied in the categories of rights outlined by UNICEF (2011), as follows.

- *Survival and development* —ensuring life, survival and development to full potential through adequate food, shelter, clean water, formal education, primary health care, leisure and recreation, cultural activities, and information about rights. These rights protect children from minority/indigenous or refugee groups and those with disabilities. They also ensure freedom of thought, religion, and conscience.
- *Protection* —ensuring safety from harm through protection from all forms of abuse, neglect, exploitation, violence, and cruelty. These rights address child abduction, sale and trafficking; child labor; detention, punishment,

and juvenile justice; adoption and separation from family; war and armed conflict.

- *Participation*—ensuring the child's "voice" by protecting and promoting freedom to express opinions and have views respected in matters affecting their social, economic, cultural, and political life; right to information (e.g., through mass media); freedom of association; freedom of thought, conscience, and religion; right to privacy. These rights in particular are focused on ensuring that children can actively participate in realizing their rights and as adults take an active role in society.

The UN Millennium Declaration (adopted by the UN General Assembly, September 18, 2000) was the foundation for a set of eight global partnership goals (MDGs) related to alleviating poverty worldwide by 2015:

1. eradicate extreme poverty and hunger
2. achieve universal primary education
3. promote gender equality and empower women
4. reduce child mortality
5. improve maternal health
6. combat HIV/AIDS, malaria, and other diseases
7. ensure environmental sustainability
8. develop a global partnership for development.

The MDGs are reflected in the statement by UN Secretary-General Ban Ki-moon, which emphasizes the social issues faced by the global community:

> Eradicating extreme poverty continues to be one of the main challenges of our time, and is a major concern of the international community. Ending this scourge will *require the combined efforts of all, governments, civil society organizations and the private sector, in the context of a stronger and more effective global partnership for development.* The Millennium Development Goals set timebound targets, by which progress in reducing *income poverty, hunger, disease, lack of adequate shelter and exclusion*—while promoting *gender equality, health, education and environmental sustainability*—can be measured. They also embody *basic human rights—the rights of each person on the planet to health, education, shelter and security.* The Goals are ambitious but feasible and, together with the comprehensive United Nations development agenda, set the course for the world's efforts to alleviate extreme poverty by 2015. (emphasis added; www.un.org/millenniumgoals/bkgd.shtml; accessed January 2, 2012)

Of particular importance to our discussion of global-community school psychology is the combined emphasis on social justice and child/human rights issues. Moreover, as noted by Ban Ki-moon, resolving these issues requires collaborative actions on both local and global levels.

A recent report from the United Nations (2011) indicates progress toward the MDGs, including reductions in poverty, child mortality, and deaths due to malaria and tuberculosis; and improvements in access to education and clean drinking water, and treatment and prevention of HIV. Despite these gains, the UN calls for continued actions that "target the hardest to reach: the poorest of the poor and those disadvantaged because of their sex, age, ethnicity or disability," and those living in "informal [urban slum] settlements throughout the developing world" (p. 5). Of particular importance are goals related to poverty (MDG1), gender equity and empowerment (MDG3; e.g., women's employment), universal education (MDG2; particularly for those who are poor, female, or living in conflict zones), and health (MDG4 & 6; through improved sanitation and access to clean drinking water).

In the next section, we present a model for global-community school psychology informed by a social-justice orientation. Inherent in this model is a commitment at the local level to culturally and contextually relevant actions that address issues reflected in the UN Convention on the Rights of the Child and the UN's Millennium Development Goals.

## Model for Integrating Social Justice and Global-Community School Psychology Practice

In developing a model of global-community school psychology with foundations in social justice (depicted in Figure 3.1), we considered several key domains and pertinent factors (see Table 3.2 for definitions of each factor).

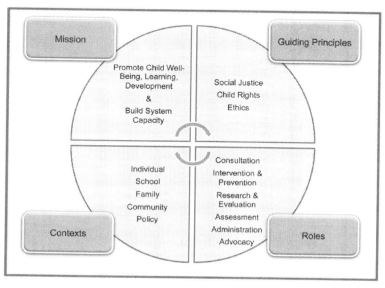

**FIGURE 3.1.** Social justice as guiding principle for global-community school psychology practice.

**TABLE 3.2.** Key terms for culturally responsive global practice model for school psychology: An etic perspective

| Term | Definition | Source |
|------|-----------|--------|
| | Guiding Principles | |
| Child rights | Entitlement of all children to have requisite physical, psychological, spiritual, social and cultural needs met to ensure optimal growth, development, physical health, psychological well-being, and learning.<br>The UN Convention on the Rights of the Child (adopted 1989), an international human rights treaty, delineated the human rights of children as the responsibility of adults and societies (e.g., governments, agencies, policy makers). | ISPA & CRED-PRO (2010); UNICEF, 2011 |
| Social Justice | Promoting social and economic equity (e.g., distribution of power and resources), liberation, and personal, interpersonal and collective well-being; and combating discrimination, oppression, and poverty through personal and collective action. | Eade (1997); Nelson & Prilleltensky (2005); Nastasi (2008a); Shriberg et al. (2008) |
| Ethics | Standards of professional conduct related to all activities of school psychologists (see Roles), as delineated in ethical codes of relevant professional organizations (e.g., NASP, APA, ISPA). Includes principles such as (italicized principles particularly relevant to social justice):<br>APA—Beneficence and nonmaleficence, integrity, justice, fidelity, responsibility, and *respect for people's rights and dignity.*[a]<br>ISPA—Beneficence and nonmaleficence, competence, fidelity and responsibility, integrity, and *social justice.*[b]<br>NASP—Respecting dignity and rights of all persons, professional competence and responsibility, honesty and integrity in professional relationships, and *responsibilities to schools, families, communities, the profession, and society.*[c] | APA (2002, 2010); ISPA (2011); NASP (2010b) |

## Mission

| | | |
|---|---|---|
| Well-being | "Physical, emotional, cognitive, social, spiritual, moral, and behavioral health . . . consistent with the WHO's definition of *health* as 'a state of complete physical, mental and social well-being and not merely the absence of disease or infirmity'." | ISPA & CRED-PRO (2010) |
| Learning | "Acquisition of thinking, reasoning, language, and numerical skills, typically associated with academic achievement resulting from schooling/education, but greatly facilitated by informal education through planned and incidental experiences within and across the social ecology." | ISPA & CRED-PRO (2010) |
| Development | Optimal growth of individual in physical, emotional, cognitive, behavioral, social, spiritual, and moral domains. | ISPA & CRED-PRO (2010) |
| System capacity | The capability (dependent on system's competencies, infrastructure, resources) of a given system (e.g., school, family, community, society) to facilitate the well-being, learning, and development of its members (children and adults); and to ensure social justice and child/human rights (as defined above). | Eade (1997); Nastasi (2010); Nelson & Prilleltensky (2005); Prilleltensky & Nelson (2002); Ysseldyke et al. (2006) |

## Contexts[d]

| | | |
|---|---|---|
| Individual | The *child as an active agent* embedded within a series of interconnected social–cultural contexts or ecosystems. | Bronfenbrenner (1989, 1999); ISPA & CRED-PRO (2010) |
| School | The *ecosystem of formal education*, which includes microsystems such as classroom, in which child interacts directly with other members (students, teacher), embedded within the broader context of the school (exosystem) and the school's culture (norms, beliefs, practices, and policies; i.e., macrosystem). | Bronfenbrenner (1989, 1999); ISPA & CRED-PRO (2010) |

TABLE 3.2. *Continued*

| Term | Definition | Source |
|------|------------|--------|
| Family | The *ecosystem of family members/caregivers*, which includes microsystems such as home, in which child interacts directly with other members (caregivers, siblings, other family members), embedded within the broader context of the family (exosystem) and the family's culture (norms, beliefs, practices, and policies; i.e., macrosystem). | Bronfenbrenner (1989, 1999); ISPA & CRED-PRO (2010) |
| Community | The *ecosystem of local community or neighborhood in which child lives*, which includes microsystems (e.g., peer group, neighbors, immediate vicinity of home, playground) in which child interacts directly with other members, embedded within the broader community (e.g., city, state, region) and the community culture (norms, beliefs, practices, and policies; i.e., macrosystem). | Bronfenbrenner (1989, 1999); ISPA & CRED-PRO (2010) |
| Policy | Refers collectively to formal culture of the key ecosystems (*macrosystems*) affecting the individual, including school, family, community, state, regional, country. | Bronfenbrenner (1989, 1999); ISPA & CRED-PRO (2010) |
| | Roles[e] | |
| Consultation | Using communication and collaboration to facilitate problem solving to address individual or systemic issues and/or facilitate change. | Nastasi (2010); NASP (2010a); Rodolfa et al. (2006); Ysseldyke et al. (2006) |
| Intervention & Prevention | Designing and implementing evidence-based practices to promote well-being and learning; ameliorate learning, behavioral, and mental health problems; and/or build system capacity. | Nastasi (2010); NASP (2010a); Rodolfa et al. (2006); Ysseldyke et al. (2006) |
| Research & Evaluation | Using research methods (quantitative, qualitative, single case designs) to assess incidence and prevalence of problems (e.g., learning, behavioral, physical health, mental health); identify contributing factors (e.g., individual, social– | Nastasi (2010); NASP (2010a); Rodolfa et al. (2006); Ysseldyke et al. |

| | cultural); plan or develop culturally and contextually relevant interventions; and evaluate acceptability, integrity and effectiveness of interventions. | (2006) |
|---|---|---|
| Assessment | Using systematic data collection methods (e.g., observations, interviews, record review, standardized measures) for the purposes of diagnosis, problem solving, treatment or intervention planning, at individual or systemic levels. | Nastasi (2010); NASP (2010a); Rodolfa et al. (2006); Ysseldyke et al. (2006) |
| Administration | Directing, managing, or supervising the delivery of school psychological services. | Nastasi (2010); NASP (2010a); Rodolfa et al. (2006); Ysseldyke et al. (2006) |
| Advocacy | Engaging in actions to promote the development and/or implementation of policies to protect and promote children's well-being, learning, and development at all levels of the social ecology (microsystem, exosystem, macrosystem, mesosytem). | ISPA & CRED-PRO (2010) |

[a] "Psychologists respect the dignity and worth of all people, and the rights of individuals to privacy, confidentiality, and self-determination. Psychologists are aware that special safeguards may be necessary to protect the rights and welfare of persons or communities whose vulnerabilities impair autonomous decision making. Psychologists are aware of and respect cultural, individual, and role differences, including those based on age, gender, gender identity, race, ethnicity, culture, national origin, religion, sexual orientation, disability, language, and socioeconomic status, and consider these factors when working with members of such groups. Psychologists try to eliminate the effect on their work of biases based on those factors, and they do not knowingly participate in or condone activities of others based upon such prejudices" (APA, 2002, p. 1061).

[b] "Consistent with the reciprocal commitment between their profession and society, school psychologists are committed to the principle that all people are entitled access to and benefit from the contributions of school psychology. Thus, they strive to promote free access to educational, social, and psychological services, to promote changes in schools or other educational practice settings that are beneficial to children and youth as well as educational staff, and to minimize biases" (ISPA, 2011, p. 6).

[c] "School psychologists promote healthy school, family, and community environments. They assume a proactive role in identifying social injustices that affect children and schools and strive to reform systems-level patterns of injustice. They maintain the public trust in school psychologists by respecting law and encouraging ethical conduct. School psychologists advance professional excellence by mentoring less experienced practitioners and contributing to the school psychology knowledge base" (NASP, 2010b, pp. 11–12).

**TABLE 3.2** *Continued*

d Contexts or *ecosystems* are conceptualized based on Bronfenbrenner's ecological–developmental theory (1989, 1999). Each ecosystem includes a series of embedded systems: (a) *microsystems*, immediate environment with which the individual interacts directly, embedded in (b) *exosystem* or broader structural context (e.g., school), which indirectly influences the individual, embedded in (c) *macrosystem*, informal culture (system of shared norms, beliefs, values practices) and formal culture (laws, policies), which indirectly influence the individual through the exosystem and microsystems. Connecting the key ecosystems (e.g., school, family, community) are *mesosystems*, interactions or relationships among the systems (e.g., home–school), which indirectly influence the individual.

e Consistent with the Child Rights Curriculum for School Psychologists (ISPA & CRED-PRO, 2010), the school psychologist is conceptualized as a *mesosystem* or connector among the child's ecosystems, and *role* is conceptualized as professional responsibility to facilitate interactions among the ecosystems to promote individual well-being, learning, and development and system's capacity, and to ensure promotion and protection of child rights and social justice.

1. *Mission of global-community school psychology*: To promote child well-being, learning, and development; and to build system capacity.
2. *Guiding principles for practice/action*: Social justice, child rights, professional ethics.
3. *Context for practice/action*: Individual, school, family, community, policy (consistent with an ecological orientation).
4. *Roles of the school psychologist*: Consultation, intervention and prevention, research and evaluation, assessment, administration, and advocacy.

Given the potential diversity of cultures and contexts for conducting school psychology on a global scale, we propose an *etic* model (Figure 3.1) based on existing research, theory, practice, and policy (Table 3.2) as the foundation for articulating practice at the local, or *emic*, level. We recognize the limitations of a model formulated on the basis of American school psychology; however, this etic model reflects the limited research conducted outside of the US and Western Europe and limited access to documents in languages other than English (Farrell et al., 2007; Nastasi & Varjas, 2011). As indicated in Table 3.2, we have included consideration of professional ethics and standards for training set forth by the ISPA. With this caveat in mind, it behooves the global-community school psychology community to persist in efforts to facilitate research and communication across national and regional boundaries and to remain vigilant to the importance of culturally constructing practice at the local level.

We borrow the term *cultural construction* from the work of the medical anthropologist Arthur Kleinman (1986, 1988, 1992), who has made significant contributions to global psychiatry and medicine by calling attention to the dynamic nature of clinical practice (Kleinman, Eisenberg, & Good, 1978). Kleinman and colleagues refer to the interaction between practitioners (e.g., school psychologists) and clients (children, parents, teachers, administrators) as the "cultural construction of clinical reality" (p. 254). Thus, each interaction is viewed as a unique integration, or co-construction, of the cultural experiences and cognitive schemas of the participants (practitioner–clients; see also Nastasi et al., 2011).

Applied at a systemic level, cultural construction refers to the negotiation of local philosophy, mission, goals, policies, and actions relevant to social justice. For example, a school's priorities related to physical and psychological safety of students could help inform prevention programming within a comprehensive mental health model, and address social issues such as discrimination, bullying, and community violence. The negotiation or co-construction requires integration of cultural realities of the practitioner (e.g., personal mission, theoretical orientation, empirical knowledge, and roles of the local school psychologist) with the cultural realities of the local stakeholders (i.e., existing norms, beliefs, values, and practices of the school administrator, teachers, parents, students). The cultural construction process requires (a) building and maintaining partnership with stakeholders; (b) thorough understanding of the local culture and context (ecology), for example, through local ethnographic research; (c) knowledge of relevant theory and research to inform action; and (d) data-based decision making (see Nastasi, Moore, & Varjas, 2004; Nastasi, Schensul et al., 2011; Nastasi & Varjas, 2011). In addition, sustainable action requires building local system capacity through organizational infrastructure, professional development, and systematic evaluation. In the next section, we illustrate the application of the cultural construction process in a local US context with the dual purpose of providing psychological services and ensuring human rights and social justice for all students.

## Constructing an Emic Model for Local Practice

Figure 3.1 provides the foundation for defining global-community school psychology and for guiding the work of international organizations such as ISPA. Application at national, regional, state/provincial, and local (e.g., community, school) levels requires translation based on cultural and contextual factors. In this section, we describe a process for culturally constructing school psychology practice in localized contexts and illustrate for one hypothetical school community. The process of cultural construction is recursive; that is, it involves a continuous interaction between research (data collection) and action (practice). (This process has been described in detail elsewhere; see Nastasi et al., 2004; Nastasi & Varjas, 2011.) For the sake of simplicity, we describe the process in steps, with the understanding that one can recycle through these steps as needed.

### Local Context

The focus of our work is an elementary school serving students, grades K-8, from an urban low-income community. The ethnic composition of the school is reflective of the local community, with 50% African American, 30% Hispanic (including recent immigrants from Central and South America), 10% Asian American (including recent immigrants from South Asia), and 10% European American. The school staff is primarily European American (90%) and female (85%) from local middle class suburban communities. The school is facing challenges related to academic and behavioral functioning of students and is currently seeking consultation to address increases in peer violence that parallel increases in local community violence. An important component of the school's mission is to foster learning and psychological well-being within a physically and psychologically "safe" environment. The school's mission is consistent with universal CRC principles related to survival and development, protection, and participation. In addition, global MDGs related to poverty and universal primary education are relevant in this local context.

## Step 1. Select or Construct an Etic Model, Based on Existing Theory, Research, Practice, Policy

The first step is to examine existing theory, research, practice and policy to construct a model for practice within the local context. Using the framework depicted in Figure 3.1, the school psychologist addresses the following questions: What is my *mission* as school-based mental health professional? What *principles* guide my practice, and how do these principles align with universal principles related to child rights? What *contexts* are relevant to the current concerns? What is my *role* in this setting? Table 3.2 illustrates responses to these questions, drawing from existing literature, and provides a framework for guiding next steps.

## Step 2. Examine and Articulate the Cultures and Contexts Relevant to the Various Partners or Stakeholders

This constitutes the initiation of the "cultural construction" process among the stakeholders (e.g., school psychologists and other mental health professionals, policy makers, administrators, teachers, parents, students, community members). That is, articulating the range of cultural values, norms, beliefs and practices is necessary for integration of cultural perspectives or schemas. Furthermore, gathering data about the needs and resources of the relevant contexts (e.g., classroom, school, community, families) is requisite for goal setting. Cultural construction in this example requires examination of the values, beliefs, norms and practices of students from various ethnic groups, their parents, school staff, and local community, within the context of the school's mission (i.e., promoting learning and psychological well-being in a safe environment) and the current problem (peer violence). Of particular relevance to promoting well-being and ensuring social justice are the cultural variations in terminology (How is "well-being" labeled?), expectations (What are behavioral norms for fifth graders?), definitions (How is "well-being" defined?), social issues (What are the important social justice issues?), and socialization practices (How do we ensure non-violent behavior among children?). Understanding how various partners view the problem, contributing factors, and potential solutions is critical to problem solving. This understanding can be achieved through formal data collection (e.g., interviews, surveys) as well as informal interactions (e.g., meetings, personal communication) and review of artifacts (e.g., newspapers, local media productions). Ensuring that students have opportunities to express their perspectives can help safeguard their rights to participation (consistent with CRC).

## Step 3. On the Basis of Information from Steps 1 and 2, Co-Construct the Components of the Emic Model of Practice, Using Figure 3.1 and Table 3.2 as the Etic Foundation

This involves negotiation among partners to answer the following questions:

a.   *What is the mission of school psychology practice in this context?* Is the primary mission promoting individual health, safety, emotional well-being, and/or learning? To what extent is systemic change necessary to achieve this mission?
b.   *What are the guiding principles for school psychology practice?* What social justice principles are relevant to this population? How do we ensure individual child rights while serving all students? What are the ethical responsibilities for school psychologists?
c.   *What are the critical ecosystems (microsystems, exosystems, macrosystems) and relationships among those systems (mesosystems) that need to be considered?* In order to address psychological well-being and ensure safety of all students, what actions are necessary school-wide? What practices need to be instituted at different grade levels? What are the roles of parents and other stakeholders? How do we ensure safety in the school when there is ongoing violence in the local neighborhood?
d.   *What are the possible roles and responsibilities of the school psychologist?* What can I do as an individual professional? How can I advocate for child well-being and social justice through consultation with parents? With teachers? What prevention programs can I help to initiate? How do I influence school policies? How can I facilitate better communication among the cultural groups represented in the school and community? How do I ensure that principles inherent in universal CRC are brought to bear in this context?

Responding to these questions with reference to global guidelines such as CRC and MDGs can help to bring the global perspective to local practice.

## Step 4. Using the Emic Model (developed in Step 3), Articulate Short- and Long-Term Goals Relevant to Promoting Social Justice at Individual (Student) and Collective (School) Levels

For example, assuming one of the primary social justice issues, and perceived cause of peer violence, is discrimination (e.g., on basis of race, ethnicity, gender, sexual orientation), what changes need to occur in policies and practices to create a just environment for students? To what extent do policies address discrimination? To what extent are policies implemented and monitored? What are reasonable short-term goals (e.g., stopping peer violence)? What goals require long-term efforts (e.g., eliminating discrimination)? How do these local goals reflect global princi-ples and issues related to CRC and MDGs? Thus, how does local context mirror global context? And how do local goals mirror global goals related to social justice and child rights?

## Step 5. Working in Partnership with Stakeholders, Develop a Plan of Action to Effect Change in Policies and Practices

Assume, for example, that the long-term goal is to create a socially just school environment, as defined by the stakeholders. Achieving this goal requires setting short-term priorities and making changes in day-to-day practices as well as school policies. In developing the plan, stakeholders should consider the following: Who will be involved (e.g., students, parents, teachers, community members or organi-zations)? What roles will each play (e.g., in planning and implementation of new school policies)? What resources are needed (Are current human and financial resources adequate? How can resources be reallocated? How can community resources contribute to school efforts?)? What actions are needed to change prac-tice in the classroom, the school, perhaps even the community (What is necessary in terms of education and skill building for students, teachers, parents, commu-nity members?)? What are the policy implications for addressing the problem sys-temically (Are changes in school policies necessary or do existing policies just need to be implemented?)? What advocacy actions are needed to effect policy changes (How do we best create awareness and influence policy makers?)? Who will serve in an advocacy role with administrators and policy makers (What roles can stu-dents, teachers, parents play?)? How will implementation be evaluated, with regard to acceptability, social validity, integrity, effectiveness, and sustainability (What data can be collected to assess changes in school climate, peer violence, attitudes of students and teachers?)? What roles will the school psychologist assume (e.g., coordination, consultation, teacher training)? How can we draw on global initia-tives to inform action at the local level?

## Step 6. Implement and Evaluate Action Plans

Through a continued co-construction process, the school psychologist makes changes to action plans based on ongoing data collection (evaluation). For example, following changes in school policies, monitor changes in actual prac-tice through data collection, and reconvene stakeholders to discuss progress and change plans accordingly (Do we need further parent and teacher education to effect changes in practice? How do we ensure change across contexts, from class-room to playground, lunchroom, the whole school? Who will take leadership in monitoring implementation?).

## Step 7. Plan for Institutionalization and Sustainability of Changes

Maintaining policy and practice changes requires attention to the system infra-structure and human resources. Consider the following questions in planning: What infrastructure needs to be in place (Are additional resources needed to facilitate long-term attention to social justice issues?)? What are the long-term professional development needs of staff, and how will they be addressed over time (How will the school administration ensure that teachers remain current on social justice issues and practices? Who will be responsible for maintaining professional development?)? What are sources of support/resources outside of the system (e.g., in the surrounding community) that can be accessed (Are there community agencies that can become long-term partners in promoting social justice in the school? How can this school partner with other schools in the community? What global resources can be accessed?)? How do we develop long-term relationships with partners within and outside the system (i.e., local school and community stakeholders, and global partners)? How do we monitor and re-evaluate social justice goals over time? What process do we use to address other social justice issues as they arise (Do we need a "social justice" professional or team in the school to assume primary responsibility for monitoring social justice?)?

## Globalizing School Psychology for Social Justice: Future Directions

> If psychology is to advance significantly as a science . . . psychologists around the world must work together to understand human development and mental health and intervene accordingly. (Leong & Ponterotto, 2003, p. 383)

The current professional and political *Zeitgeist* sets the stage for school psychol-ogy to assert its role in promoting social justice and human rights at global and local levels. The current professional practice models (e.g., NASP, 2010a; Rodolfa et al., 2005), ethical standards (APA, 2002, 2010; ISPA, 2011; NASP, 2010b), and organizational priorities (e.g., ISPA & CRED-PRO, 2010; Nastasi, 2011), in con-junction with global priorities (e.g., UN, 1989, 2000; UNICEF, 2011), provide the basis for conceptualizing the future of school psychology as a specialty committed to a socially just global society. As we move forward, it is imperative that school psychology takes an active role in addressing social justice issues such as universal education, migration and immigration, gender equality, poverty, violence, oppres-sion, and discrimination (Marsella, 1998). Realizing such a future has implications for theory, research, practice, professional development, and advocacy at individ-ual and collective levels.

One of the major challenges facing global-community school psychology is the inadequacy of theory and research to inform practice outside of the US and Western

Europe (Farrell et al., 2007; Little et al., 2011; Nastasi & Varjas, 2011). The development of psychological interventions for a diverse global population of children and adolescents requires close attention to cultural and contextual factors (Nastasi & Varjas, 2011; Sue, 1999) and the current body of evidence has questionable relevance to global practice. This is not unique to the specialty of school psychology, but characterizes the general discipline of psychology (Leong & Ponterotto, 2003) and the health sciences (e.g., Gaines, 2011). Gaines' (2011) comments about global health have relevance to global-community school psychology as well:

> I suggest here that we rethink Global Health and come up with another way to function that does not have the culture and trappings of Biomedicine riding in on a white horse to aid the world, a happenstance that can in fact make matters worse for laypeople in many contexts. (Gaines, 2011, p. 87)

Addressing these limitations requires collaboration among professionals to facilitate transcultural research, exemplified by recent ISPA-sponsored projects (Lam & Jimerson, 2008; Nastasi, 2008b). In addition, research to inform cultural construction of school psychology will likely require the use of non-traditional qualitative and mixed methods research designs (Nastasi & Varjas, 2011), which are only beginning to influence mainstream school psychology. Qualitative research methods, for example, are particularly well suited to inductive examination of culture, perspectives on social issues, and representing the views of the minority. Whereas quantitative methods can facilitate representation of an aggregate or normative view, qualitative methods can enable depiction of the range of views. In combination, these methods (i.e., mixed methods research) can help to ensure both breadth and depth of understanding. Furthermore, a social change orientation is inherent in mixed methods research approaches such as Mertens' (2007) *transformative–emancipatory* approach and Denscombe's (2008) *communities of practice* model. Such approaches can help researchers to "address the cultural and political complexities inherent in the social settings in which research is conducted, and engage research participants as partners in creating social change" (Nastasi, Hitchcock, & Brown, 2010, p. 309).

Furthermore, the importance of culture and context, especially given the recognized diversity worldwide, necessitates greater emphasis on translational research and implementation science. A major concern in this era of "evidence-based practice" is the applicability of evidence to the diverse domestic and world population, and to the diversity of settings in which psychological and educational practices occur. Efforts to understand how to translate our current evidence base across diverse populations and settings are critical to global practice. In addition, applying science to understanding the conditions under which evidence-based practices work is important to ensuring effective application of best practices. As we expand the focus of school psychology practice, questions related to what works under what conditions, and for whom, become increasingly important.

Another challenge to globalizing school psychology is the adequacy of existing professional preparation programs, which typically focus on preparing psychologists to function within the local (state, national) context and are guided by provincial credentialing bodies. The development of courses or program emphases in global-community school psychology is at its infancy. Addressing this challenge likely requires transnational collaboration among professional organizations to identify critical program components and facilitate development of educational resources. In addition, a global program focus should address the needs of immigrant, refugee, and undocumented youth within a given country. Inherent in efforts to promote a global perspective is the willingness of school psychologists to learn from knowledge generated outside of the US.

Lastly, the capacity of school psychologists to engage in advocacy related to social justice and human rights is dependent on the requisite knowledge, beliefs, and skills. Professional organizations and university training programs can play critical roles in preparing school psychologists in advocacy. First of all, school psychology as a profession needs to adopt social justice and human rights as central to its mission and philosophy, and then to identify relevant ways to act globally and locally. (We provide a list of resources at the end of this chapter for those interested in developing school psychology programs that encompass a global focus and address social justice issues.)

In summary, global-community school psychology is an emerging focus within the specialty and has implications for school psychology research, training, practice, and policy at international and domestic levels. As we develop models for global-community school psychology, we can be proactive in the integration of social justice and school psychology. The myriad social issues faced by children and youth worldwide and the increasing awareness of cultural diversity in domestic and global communities provide a starting point for reconceptualizing school psychology practice at local and global levels.

## Notes

1  See CIRP website: www.apa.org/international/governance/cirp/index.aspx
2  See ISPA website: http://ispaweb.org/about.aspx
3  APA's Division 16 established a working group on Social Justice and Child Rights in 2010, which is currently working to adopt and expand the ISPA Child Rights curriculum for school psychologists (see www.apadivisions.org/division-16/leadership/working-groups/index.aspx). NASP has an interest group on social justice (see www.nasponline.org/index.aspx) and position statements supporting the role of school psychology in addressing social problems such as discrimination, violence, child rights, access to effective mental health services; see www.nasponline.org/about_nasp/position_paper.aspx.
4  These Tasks Forces, in partnership with the International Institute for Child Rights and Development (IICRD), have developed a curriculum to prepare school psychologists in child rights advocacy, available at www.cred-pro.org/group/internationalschoolpsychologycurriculum; see also http://ispaweb.org/About%20ISPA/committees.aspx.

5  See CIRP website: www.apa.org/international/governance/cirp/strategic-plan.aspx
6  The NASP model for comprehensive service delivery encompasses 10 broad categories: data-based decision making and accountability; consultation and collaboration; interventions and instructional support to develop academic skills; interventions in mental health services to develop social and life skills; school-wide practices to promote learning; preventive and responsive strategies; family–school collaboration services; diversity in development and learning; research and program evaluation; and legal, ethical and professional practice. Little et al. used these 10 categories to examine content of research articles. An additional category, "other," was used to capture content that was not consistent with NASP model.
7  In recent years, ISPA and Division 16 (School Psychology) of the APA have collaborated in the development of professional development modules to prepare school psychologists in advocacy for child rights and social justice. Although professional organizations such as ISPA, APA, and NASP have adopted positions in support of child rights and social justice, the recent efforts are focused on preparation of school psychologists within the US and internationally to incorporate these principles in their practice.
8  For those interested in discussion of the issues relevant to the US opposition to ratification, see http://assets.opencrs.com/rpts/R40484_20091202.pdf

## References

American Psychological Association (APA). (2002). Ethical principles of psychologists and code of conduct. *American Psychologist, 57,* 1060–1073.
American Psychological Association (APA). (2010). 2010 Amendments to the 2002 "Ethical Principles of Psychologists and Code of Conduct". *American Psychologist, 65,* 493.
Bronfenbrenner, U. (1989). Ecological systems theory. In R. Vasta (Ed.), *Annals of child development* (Vol. 6, pp. 187–249). Greenwich, CT: JAI Press.
Bronfenbrenner, U. (1999). Environments in developmental perspective: Theoretical and operational models. In S. L. Friedman & T. D. Wachs (Eds.), *Measuring environment across the life span: Emerging methods and concepts* (pp. 3–28). Washington, DC: American Psychological Association.
Bullock, M. (2011). APA's international responsibility. *Monitor on Psychology, 42* (10), 9.
Denscombe, M. (2008). Communities of practice: A research paradigm for the mixed methods approach. *Journal of Mixed Methods Research, 2,* 270–283.
Eade, D. (1997). *Capacity building: An approach to people-centred development.* Oxford, UK: Oxfam.
Farrell, P. T., Jimerson, S. R., & Oakland, T. D. (2007). School psychology internationally: A synthesis of findings. In S. R. Jimerson, T. D. Oakland, & P. T. Farrell (Eds.), *The handbook of international school psychology* (pp. 501–510). Thousand Oaks, CA: Sage.
Gaines, A. D. (2011) Millennial medical anthropology: From there to here and beyond, or the problem of global health. *Culture, Medicine and Psychiatry, 35,* 83–89.
Hatzichristou, C. (1998). Alternative school psychological services: Development of a data-based model in the Greek schools. *School Psychology Review, 27,* 246–259.
Hatzichristou, C. (2002). A conceptual framework of the evolution of school psychology: Transnational considerations of common phases and future perspectives. *School Psychology International, 23* (2), 1–17.
Hatzichristou, C., Lampropoulou, A., & Lykitsakou, K. (2006). Addressing cultural factors in development of system interventions. *Journal of Applied School Psychology, 22,* 103–126.

International School Psychology Association (ISPA). (2011). Proposed ISPA Code of Ethics. *World Go Round*, 38(2), 5–11. [Adopted by the ISPA General Assembly in July 2011]. ISPA's full ethical code is available at www.ispaweb.org/Documents/ethics_fulldoc.html.

International School Psychology Association (ISPA) & Child Rights Education for Professionals (CRED-PRO). (2010). *Child rights for school psychologists and other school-based mental health professionals curriculum.* New Orleans, LA: School Psychology Program, Tulane University.

Jimerson, S. R., Oakland, T. D., & Farrell, P. T. (Eds.) (2007). *The handbook of international school psychology.* Thousand Oaks, CA: Sage.

Kleinman, A. (1986). *Social origins of distress and disease.* New Haven, CT: Yale University Press.

Kleinman, A. (1988). *The illness narratives: Suffering, healing and the human condition.* New York, NY: Basic Books.

Kleinman, A. (1992). Local worlds of suffering: An interpersonal focus for ethnographies of illness experience. *Qualitative Health Research, 2,* 127–134.

Kleinman, A., Eisenberg, L., & Good, B. (1978). Culture, illness, and care: Critical lessons from anthropological and cross-cultural research. *Annals of Internal Medicine, 88,* 251–258.

Lam, S., & Jimerson, S. R. (2008). Exploring student engagement in schools internationally. *World Go Round, 35* (2), 7–8.

Leong, F. T. L., & Ponterotto, J. G. (2003). A proposal for internationalizing counseling psychology in the United States: Rationale, recommendations, and challenges. *Counseling Psychologist, 31,* 381–395.

Little, S. G., Akin-Little, A., & Lloyd, K. (2011). Content analysis of *School Psychology International,* 1990–2011: An analysis of trends and compatibility with the NASP Practice Model. *School Psychology International, 32,* 569–591.

Marsella, A. J. (1998). Toward a "global-community psychology": Meeting the needs of a changing world. *American Psychologist, 53,* 1282–1291.

Mertens, D. M. (2007).Transformative paradigm: Mixed methods and social justice. *Journal of Mixed Methods Research, 1,* 212–225.

Nastasi, B. K. (2008a). Social justice and school psychology. *School Psychology Review, 37,* 487–492.

Nastasi, B. K. (2008b, July). *Promoting Psychological Well-Being Globally Project: Updates from research partners.* Symposium presented at the 30th annual ISPA Conference, Utrecht, The Netherlands.

Nastasi, B. K. (2010). How much theory do we teach? In E. García-Vázquez, T. Crespi, & C. Riccio (Eds). *Handbook of education, training and supervision of school psychologists in school and community. Volume I: Foundations of professional practice* (pp. 85–108). New York, NY: Routledge.

Nastasi, B. K. (2011). President's message. *School Psychologist, 65* (1), 4–6.

Nastasi, B. K., Hitchcock, J. H., & Brown, L. M. (2010). An inclusive framework for conceptualizing mixed methods design typologies: Moving toward fully integrated synergistic research models. In A. Tashakkori & C. Teddlie (Eds.), *Handbook of mixed methods in social and behavioral research* (2nd ed., pp. 305–338). Thousand Oaks, CA: Sage.

Nastasi, B.K., Moore, R. B., & Varjas, K. M. (2004). *School-based mental health services: Creating comprehensive and culturally specific programs.* Washington, DC: American Psychological Association.

Nastasi, B. K., Schensul, S. L., Mekki-Berrada, A., Pelto, B., Maitra, S., Verma, R. K., et al. (2011). *A model for translating ethnography and theory into culturally constructed clinical practice* (submitted for publication).

Nastasi, B. K., & Varjas, K. (2011). International development of school psychology. In M. A. Bray & T. J. Kehle (Eds.), *Oxford handbook of school psychology* (pp. 810–828). New York, NY: Oxford University Press.

National Association of School Psychologists (NASP). (2010a). *Model for comprehensive and integrated school psychological services.* Bethesda, MD: NASP.

National Association of School Psychologists (NASP). (2010b). *Principles for professional ethics.* Bethesda, MD: NASP.

Nelson, G., & Prilleltensky, I. (2005). *Community psychology: In pursuit of liberation and well-being.* New York, NY: Palgrave Macmillan.

Oakland, T. D., & Jimerson, S. R. (2007). School psychology internationally: A retrospective view and influential conditions. In S. R. Jimerson, T. D. Oakland, & P. T. Farrell (Eds.), *The handbook of international school psychology* (pp. 453–462). Thousand Oaks, CA: Sage.

Prilleltensky, I., & Nelson, G. (2002). *Doing psychology critically: Making a difference in diverse settings.* NewYork, NY: Palgrave Macmillan.

Rodolfa, E., Bent, R., Eisman, E., Nelson, P., Rehm, L., & Ritchie, P. (2005). A cube model for competency development: Implications for psychology educators and regulators. *Professional Psychology: Research and Practice, 36,* 347–354.

Shriberg, D., Bonner, M., Sarr, B. J., Walker, A. M., Hyland, M., & Chester, C. (2008). Social justice through a school psychology lens: Definitions and applications. *School Psychology Review, 37* (4), 453–468.

Sue, S. (1999). Science, ethnicity, and bias: Where have we gone wrong? *American Psychologist, 54* (12), 1070–1077.

UNICEF (2011). *Rights under the Convention on the Rights of the Child.* Available at www.unicef.org/crc/index_30177.html

United Nations (UN). (1989). *Convention on the Rights of the Child.* Available at www2.ohchr.org/english/law/crc.htm

United Nations (UN). (2000). *Millennium Development Goals.* Available at www.un.org/millenniumgoals

United Nations (UN). (2011). *The Millennium Development Goals report, 2011.* Available at www.un.org/millenniumgoals/reports.shtml

Ysseldyke, J., Burns, M., Dawson, P., Kelley, B., Morrison, D., Ortiz, S., et al. (2006). *School psychology: A blueprint for training and practice III.* Bethesda, MD: NASP.

## Resource List

## Organizations

*American Psychological Association (APA) Division 16 School Psychology*
www.apa.org/about/division/div16.aspx

*APA Division 52 International Psychology*
www.apa.org/about/division/div52.aspx

*APA Committee on International Relations in Psychology (CIRP)*
www.apa.org/international/governance/cirp/index.aspx

*Human Trafficking*
www.humantrafficking.org/issues/24

*International School Psychology Association (ISPA)*
www.ispaweb.org

*NAFSA: Association of International Educators*
www.nafsa.org/about/default.aspx

*National Association of School Psychologists (NASP)*
www.nasponline.org

*Network of European Psychologists in the Education System (NEPES)*
www.nepes.eu

*Oxfam Education*
www.oxfam.org.uk/education

*UNESCO International Bureau of Education*
www.ibe.unesco.org/en.html

*UNICEF*
www.unicef.org

*UNICEF Convention on the Rights of the Child*
www.unicef.org/crc

*United Nations*
www.un.org/en/index.shtml

*World Health Organization (WHO)*
www.who.int/en

## Journals

*International Journal of Special Education*
www.internationaljournalofspecialeducation.com

*School Psychology International*
http://spi.sagepub.com

## Other Materials

*APA's Resolution on the Convention on the Rights of the Child*
www.apa.org/about/policy/child-rights.pdf

*Commercial Sexual Exploitation of Children: What Do We Know and What Do We Do About It? (US)*
www.ncjrs.gov/pdffiles1/nij/215733.pdf

*Convention on the Rights of the Child*
www2.ohchr.org/english/law/crc.htm

*Education Resources, for teaching students about child rights, MGDs, and other social justice issues; materials for teaching in classroom (as part of range of content areas (e.g., art, music, drama, literacy, math, social studies), for education in early childhood to adolescence*
www.oxfam.org.uk/education/resources

*Education for Global Citizenship: A Guide for Schools*
www.oxfam.org.uk/education/gc

*Education, Training, Professional Profile and Service of Psychologists in the European Educational System*

*Humanitarian Action for Children: Building Resilience*
www.unicef.org/hac2011

*Immigration Policy in the United States (2006)*
www.cbo.gov/ftpdocs/70xx/doc7051/02-28-Immigration.pdf

*ISPA Code of Ethics*
www.ispaweb.org/Documents/ethics_fulldoc.html

*Millennium Development Goals Annual Report*
http://www.un.org/en/development/desa/publications/mdg-report-2012.html

*Millennium Development Goals: Basic facts and measureable targets*
www.undp.org/mdg/basics.shtml

*NAFSA: Association of International Educators—online guide to educational systems around the world*
www.nafsa.org/resourcelibrary/default.aspx?id=10822

*NASP Position Statements*
www.nasponline.org/about_nasp/position_paper.aspx

*Project CHILD: Children and the International Landscape of Disabilities Project* http://vimeo.com/26835390 (see closed caption version)

*Searching for Best Practices to Counter Human Trafficking in Africa: A Focus on Women and Children*
http://unesdoc.unesco.org/images/0013/001384/138447e.pdf

*State of the World's Children 2012: Children in an Urban World*
www.unicef.org/sowc2012

*Teaching Controversial Issues*
www.oxfam.org.uk/education/teachersupport/cpd/controversial/files/teaching_controversial_issues.pdf

*World Health Statistics Report 2011*
www.who.int/whosis/whostat/2011/en/index.html

four

# What Do We Mean When We Say *Social Justice* in School Psychology?

## Mary M. Clare

Social Justice means for something to be equal. Just like race it should't matter if yr black or white. Its the same thing with gender, females shoulnd't vote just because they're female, they should vote because they have the right to. It's the same thing with animals also. Animals cant speek for them selves, so as a person living in america we should stand up for animals social justice and humans social justice together we can stop animal testing, we can stop slautering animals and we as americans can stop being rasis.

(Public School Student, 11 years of age)

Here's my definition of social justice: Forced redistribution of wealth with a hostility toward individual property rights, under the guise of charity and/or justice.
   (Glenn Beck, March 23, 2010, www.foxnews.com/story/0,2933,589832,00.html)

Social justice is . . . an overarching framework centered around (a) ensuring that all individuals are treated with respect and dignity and (b) protecting the rights and opportunities for all.

(Shriberg & Fenning, 2009, p. 1)

The *raison d'être* for the profession of school psychology is the support of learning. As school psychologists we [do that] provide that support by using tools and techniques grounded in empirical research and validated in practice. We support learners. We support teachers and administrators and organizational systems [such as] school[s] buildings, and districts. We support parents and families and communities, all intimately linked with learners and their educational experiences.

There is not one role in our profession that does not call us to the best service we can provide in support of the dignity and thriving of each learner and all whose lives touch learners. By my observation, that's pretty much everyone. Given that sweep of relevance, the quick application of the phrase, *social justice*, can lead us to believe we're saying something useful when we may lack common theoretical and practical ground for our meaning. For example, the ideas invoked in our profession's use of the language of *best practice* can be conflated with the term *social justice* linking highly regarded (even evidence-based) techniques with the assumption that those practices must be best for everyone. The problem with this logic is in the necessary failure of most approaches to generalize across all people and circumstances. Nonetheless, the term *social justice* and its inspiration have caught on in school psychology and that is why the editors of this volume have taken on the project of pulling together the writing you hold in your hands.

This fact of school psychology's relevance to nearly everyone can be read as lofty inspiration or as demanding in-your-face immediacy. It is both. Everyday learning in and out of schools interacts with the range of human knowledge and action in ways that render our shared future a mystery—as daunting as it is inspiring. Our profession's chosen responsibility to support learning and learners is a significant variable influencing how people come to know and act. Most directly enacting this support is the task of school psychologists in practice. These are the members of our profession who encounter circumstances daily that signify compromises to social justice

This week, for example, I heard a practitioner colleague describe a pattern she was seeing in her school. When children miss school, calls are made immediately to the parents of students from families in stable economic situations but less readily to families that are struggling economically. In addition, home visits to the families who are more economically and culturally marginal go uninitiated. Practitioners watch this sort of dynamic, some of them knowing that while phone calls may work with middle class families, the same technique with other families has no effect. They know this from experience—from being in practice. The research literature bears out what these practitioners know (e.g., Christenson & Sheridan, 2001), but there is no deep or lasting evidence of real change in the cultural responsiveness of general practices of schools. It is the daily practice of school psychology that shows most clearly the many injustices yet to be repaired.

More subtle than many of the injustices in schools are the instances of compromise to fairness and equality in settings where school psychologists are prepared for entry into the profession—in the academic culture that educates, supervises and generates the knowledge base informing practice. That is the realm of school psychology with which I have had the most experience. I have made regular effort to practice in schools because I feel it is necessary to my credibility as an instructor and scholar, but most of my time has been spent in the rarefied air of the academy. Because of the influence academic systems and scholars have on setting the culture of school psychology, I begin this investigation of what *social justice* means to our profession with a story from my own experience.

## Scholarship in Context

Although there were no models in my birth family for what it might mean to pursue an academic career, I experienced enough encouragement through graduate school to give it a try. It also made a huge difference that I had married a man newly out of the Ivy League and into a career as a professor of German literature and language. This was probably the single most insulating and emboldening variable in my early career. My sense of efficacy and confidence inflated with the intoxication of young academics in love. At the same time, I was gaining access to socialization and education in the ways of higher education without any overt awareness of what was happening.

As a result of the privilege and access inhering in my circumstances, I moved through the early years of my own career knowing I would need to write, to publish. I watched my husband, listened to his older colleagues and my own professors, and came to understand that the publishing process involved both practical and emotional skills. I learned I would need to build capacity for enduring rejection and misunderstanding of my writing. At the same time, I learned to modify my writing to be sufficiently complementary with existing scholarly literature and thus acceptable to the editorial reviewers on the boards of professional journals. These faceless authorities read and responded to my articles (usually three readers per submission). Their critiques, based unavoidably in their worldviews and values, determined whether or not my writing made it into print.

On several occasions over the course of my early experience contributing to the literature in school psychology, I was criticized directly for being *journalistic* or *personal*. Once, this was a misunderstanding of ethnographic research and voice. On another occasion the criticism was directed at my use of the first person and at what the reviewer saw as disrespect for the conventions of the genre; i.e., scholarly writing. I was a young woman writing with a voice that, in my considered judgment, had great integrity both scientifically and personally. Science, I figured, was always filtered through human perception, thus, to me and to other women whose models I followed (e.g. Carol Gilligan, 1982; Janet Helms, 1990, Evelyn Fox Keller, 1986), writing in the first person was the most honest way of acknowledging the individual worldview sculpting the knowledge presented in print.

Perhaps the two reviewers I describe here were displeased with the implication of first person voice. Perhaps they hadn't given thought to the way authors may hide behind the authority historically invoked with third-person presentation of research findings or theoretical developments. Likely they were interested in my looking (at least in print) more like them. Most certainly, their feedback could have stopped me cold, except that both criticisms came in the context of blind review and in each instance the other two reviewers were complimentary and encouraging. So I proceeded with my writing style as it was, but I haven't forgotten. At some level, I registered these critical observations as warnings and took them quite seriously. They were assertions of socialization by scholarly authorities. They were direct indications of the rules of the publishing game and the edges I could push, but likely only so far.

I didn't really know it at the time, but I was already good at this kind of game. I was raised as a white woman, the eldest daughter of a service professional—a protestant minister. My father's profession earned meager income but significant respect and he (and by extension, the whole family) behaved in ways that ingratiated us to the most powerful and landed congregants. By my gender and my parents' models I learned to navigate the middle zone between engaging innovation and compliant deference. In essence my childhood offered constant lessons in how to work the dominant system by accommodating, like a chameleon, into its midst.

At the same time, my mother and her mother offered quiet models of defiance under the radar for recognition by the power elite. As a young girl early in the 1900s, my grandmother taught young black women in Georgia how to read. At the time, such a service still had to be secretive. It was so secret, I did not know about it until my grandmother's death in 1989 when I encountered two older African American women outside the funeral home who asked if they could view my grandmother's body. "Miss Mary taught us how to read." No one in the family knew. Following her mother, and across my childhood my own mother consistently took me and my sisters along when she volunteered in community service initiatives during the Civil Rights days. Without knowing that what she was doing could later qualify as social justice work, my mother took action—she quietly put the talk of white allies of the day into full practice.

All of this filtered the meaning I made of the criticisms that came from editorial reviewers in these moments of socialization into academic publication and professionalism. While I continued to assert the legitimacy of first-person reporting in scholarly writing (Henning-Stout, 1999) I know I have reined in my personal voice more than I might have otherwise, and across my career I've carried the nagging doubt that my scholarship might be unworthy. There is something powerful in the subtlety of this story—the way the socialization and gatekeeping inherent in the *culture* of scholarly publication are largely invisible to those who succeed within it and glaringly obvious to those who, time after time, do not.

I've chosen to use this story to structure this chapter since it speaks to social justice in school psychology in three ways. Most directly, it illustrates the socialization of academic school psychologists into access to and use of the privilege of publishing. Published scholarship then provides the canon of our profession that thus serves as a mainstay to pre-service and in-service curricula and practice standards (e.g., designations of *best practice*). It is a powerful part of our profession's culture—how we know who we are and what we do. Second, and more broadly, this is a story of socialization into the profession as a whole, into professionalism in general, and thus into reasoning and behavior that link with the professional ethic of justice and principle. Finally, in the context of these two considerations, this otherwise unremarkable story of encountering the social rules of our discipline provides a narrative pathway into considering the phrase *social justice*, its gradual inclusion in our professional language and the necessary problem of knowing what we are saying when we use the term.

## Socialization into Privilege in School Psychology

Looking back 20-some years later (words I never imagined I'd be "senior" enough to write . . .), I see two angles on the privilege in my story of the editorial critiques. First was my privilege in the situation. In the end, I didn't have to alter my writing voice to fit the reviewers' observations because I was the fortunate recipient of support for my academic self-esteem from established scholars, the white men and women who were my mentors. As a young white woman, I had also experienced success in an educational system (all the way through a doctoral program) with which my culture and language essentially matched. Those circumstances together with the family situations I describe above vastly facilitated my learning how to decode at least some of the prevailing power system filtering school psychology publications. Because of the many benefits of my cultural match with the professoriate, the graduate curriculum and, later, the journal review board members, I was fairly easily socialized. I fit my submissions sufficiently within the accepted paradigm, while I also had a bit of luck with knowing how far to push my writing on the discomforting stuff. In large part, I had been afforded social justice—what Sander et al. (2011) describe as "specific, but not always distinct, ecological system qualities that promote educational success and psychological well-being: *access* to necessary and appropriate resources, experiences of being treated with *respect*, and *fairness*" (emphasis in original).

Of course there were exceptions, particularly in the area of experiencing respect and fairness. I had, after all, been a child in my early school days—an experience all of us share, a circumstance that is still quite vulnerable to unjust disrespect (Nastasi, 2011; Chapter 3, this volume). I had also spent my life moving through the world as female, a classification that continues (yes, still and daily) to equate with discounted ideas, observations, and worth (Burman, 2005; Gilligan, 2011). The very fact that I hesitate to write this because I do not want to lose readers to the "she's whining" attribution is evidence of both the persistence and the internalization of this socio-cultural reality. Poet Lorna Dee Cervantes (1981) describes this as "my excuse me tongue." Like many who deal with similar and multiple microaggressions (Sue et al., 2007), I do not keep count. While unconscious discounts and criticisms take their toll—and I receive far fewer than many of my colleagues of color and/or sexual minority—I am fortunate to have skills for remaining focused on what is most important in my life and work (Ibarra, 2001).

Still, because of the racial and socioeconomic situation into which I was born, I benefited early in my career, and still do, from access. That together with the many experiences of respect and fairness I did encounter supported my confidence as a young scholar. I applied that confidence in using slightly less formal approaches to writing to present content revealing systems of oppression and their potential antidotes. Part budding scholar, part angry young (and self-proclaimed) visionary, and part unconsciously cunning social ingénue, I used my ability as a product of the dominant culture to read the system in order both to succeed and to push it a little. At the time, I could not see my privilege in the situation, but I was playing by the rules. I was standing firm in the principles of justice.

There is a second aspect of privilege in this story of the journal reviewers' comments; in some ways more obvious and in other ways more invisible given its structural justification. That privilege resides in the gate-keeping, and thus the socializing role, played by editorial board members (for graduate students, this socializing agent is the professoriate and for new practitioners, socialization continues via supervisors and officials who set performance evaluation standards). The reviewers had themselves been well socialized in what they came to deem the most appropriate ways of constructing and conducting research or developing theory, drawing conclusions and then using prose to report the scholarship. Although generally not a formal charge to people agreeing to serve on editorial boards, these reviewers were appointed as conveyers of the conventions of scholarship in school psychology; their roles and actions thus based in justice.

This is true of any of us asked to serve as reviewers for refereed journals in our discipline. Membership on an editorial board is a service position and it is also an honor, validating de facto each member's understanding of what connotes scholarly writing and content. Each time any of us reviews a manuscript, we are applying such understandings as mediated by all the things I describe in the preceding paragraphs, plus a few. Although every reviewer's understanding varies slightly, as an elite collective we set the parameters of what is and is not acceptable subject matter and narrative presentation for inclusion in the professional literature. This dynamic is mirrored in student–professor and new practitioner–supervisor relationships as well as in the evaluation standards set by both the graduate school accrediting agencies (e.g., NASP, NCATE) and school district administrators responsible for performance evaluation. Each of the socializing relationships and contexts in the profession of school psychology is a culturally mediated process with implications for what we mean when we say *social justice*.

## Professionalism and the Ethics of Care and Justice

Larger considerations of school psychology within the universe of professionalism also have relevance to our understanding and conveyance of *social justice*. Privilege is an undeniable player both in professionalism and in our thinking and speaking of *social justice* as an action. Alongside privilege a more subtle tug-of-war persists, one I've felt in myself my entire professional career. Most of that time my awareness of this tension remained under wraps because its acknowledgment was too inconsistent with what I understood as "being professional." Other times, through better uses of my access to teaching and publication, the tension found expression with, for example, my use of first-person narrative and my presentation of case-based or ethnographic data. The source of the tension was evident in my consistent experience of having to choose whether to act from a standpoint of objective principle or from a standpoint of relationship. The professional world seemed to pit these two against one another with justice (objective principle) always more reasonable and recognizable as a justification than care (relationship) for any professional act.

However, the default in my personal system of responding to the world had been (and continues) grounded in my understanding almost everything in the context of relationship. This reflex is so deeply a part of my character that even socialization as a successful academic has not removed it. In fact, my judgments of what was finally most just always arise from my sense of what would provide the most support for the relationships involved; for example, a student's relationships with peers, with a teacher and within herself or himself. Perhaps this is an example of proactive inhibition in learning with my acquisition of an early epistemological mainstay causing relational context always to arise first no matter my training and accomplishment with what qualifies as objective reasoning. Far earlier in my learning than illustrated by my initial forays into submitting articles to refereed journals in school psychology, I came to understand that there were rules and ways of knowing that superseded relationship. My reflexive tendency toward thinking in terms of social connection was less valued and less visible than another way of thinking that placed principled justice at the helm.

Even as I awkwardly took on objectivity over relational thinking, at least in academic arenas, scholars like Carol Gilligan (1982) and Nel Noddings (1984) began to describe this relational orientation as an ethic of care. What I see now regarding the ethics of justice and care, particularly as the two have bearing on what we call *social justice*, is threefold. First, when I originally read Gilligan and Nodding's work in the early 1980s I was awash with awareness of the oppressions of women at the hands of patriarchs across time. This inspired important resistance and energy leading to my work on behalf of women and girls in schools, clinics and communities (e.g., Henning-Stout, 1994a, 1997, 1998). It was good work identifying ways for addressing some of the circumstances that perpetuate women and girls being less supported, less valued, less visible and thus less likely to contribute from their talents and passions to the well-being of human society. It was not long before I could see that not only was I as a woman a victim of oppressive systems tied to concentrating power among the patriarchs, all of us were. All of us are. At the same time, however, I joined many other scholars of the day (of all genders) in pitting care against justice by going for a handy gendered attribution. Care was the personal purview of women and subordinate to justice, which was mediated by rational individuality and attributed socially to men.

Turns out, while that description continues widely accurate in function (Burman, 2005), it was never accurate in any absolute way (Gilligan, 2011). Thus, the second observation with implications for the idea of *social justice*; pitting care and justice against one another was and continues a false opposition. In her revisiting and timely elaboration of the ideas she developed in her influential book, *In a Different Voice*, Carol Gilligan (2011) writes:

> This brings me back to a major point: care and caring are not women's issues, they are human concerns . . . The moral injunction—do not oppress, do not exercise power unfairly or take advantage of others—lives side by side with the moral injunction to not abandon, to not act carelessly or neglect people

who need help, meaning everyone including oneself. But they draw on different aspects of ourselves. Fairness and rights are matters of rules and principles. The logic is clear . . . Caring requires paying attention, seeing, listening, responding with respect. Its logic is contextual, psychological. Care is a relational ethic grounded in the premise of interdependence. (p. 23)

Finally, and following Gilligan's observations, there is the third way the ethics of care and justice speak to the idea of *social justice* in school psychology. It may be that what we mean when we say *social justice* points to the reunification of these two entirely complementary, coherent, and interdependent ethical motives. On the way to developing this suggestion further, it is important to investigate more deeply the idea of *social justice* as it has emerged in school psychology.

## School Psychology and Social Justice

One direct requirement of applying the phrase *social justice* to our profession is rigorous attention to the theoretical and empirical traditions underlying the practice of school psychology for the oppressive ways in which they may be applied. We act on issues of unfairness in schools in our daily practice and we discuss these things in our literature. Yet, in general, the oppressions of our own discipline's practices are unseen by their well-intentioned authors and followers; a circumstance that renders them more intractable and thus more problematic. In response to this situation, efforts have grown to address overt injustice and inequalities, to reveal those unseen and to pursue elimination of and restitution for all oppressive practices in school psychology and in society in general. Of late, these efforts have collectively been referred to as *social justice initiatives.*

In this section, I offer a very brief exploration of what these words mean in the current literature, practices and social contexts of school psychology. Of necessity this exploration and its report here are framed and limited by my worldview and experience. That's the way it is with authorship, so as I say to my students, "It is important that you not believe me but check these things out for yourself." Tipping my hand a bit, this statement points toward what enacting social justice means to me. From my observation and experience, true social justice involves every one of us bringing our considered and lived wisdom to bear in inquiry and action that supports the well-being of each and all. That phrase, *every one of us*, is entirely inclusive, acknowledging, for example, every learner we assess as an expert who has significant contributions to make to her or his own and our shared welfare (Henning-Stout, 1994b). But, don't believe me. Check it out.

## Definitional Challenges

Like many of the words we use in our work (e.g., *attention deficit, autistic, learning disabled, behaviorally disturbed, inclusion, diversity, appropriate*), the term *social justice* seems at risk of being too amorphous. What are the larger contexts of this phrase? What do we intend and hope for? What have we signed on for that we may not see, as a profession or even as a subset of a profession?

In all areas of social science and practice, the words *social* and *justice* are used together with increasing frequency. The popularity of the term is reflected in its presence on the worldwide web. Near noon (PDT) today (8–25–2011), a Google search following the entry, *social justice*, draws 357,000,000 results. Wikipedia, the public access and publicly constructed web-based encyclopedia, has a sophisticated entry on the term (http://en.wikipedia.org/wiki/Social_justice). Nonetheless, as the excerpts opening this chapter illustrate, it remains all too easy to think we are saying the same things when what we mean may be very different (cf. *diversity*; Clare, 2002).

The meaning of communication is necessarily mediated by language, worldview, social context and immediate variables such as physical, emotional, and cognitive circumstance. To advance my current investigation of the meaning of *social justice* in school psychology, I employ what may at first seem an esoteric focus, exploring the social context and functions of language as they influence what we can see and what we then do. First are the prevailing definitions and related desires linked with the term as employed in school psychology. Following from those statements, I consider the situation of the idea of *social justice* relative to privilege, in particular the privilege of naming. While the symptoms of injustice and the signs of justice are often identified in our literature, attention to the role of language is rarely applied with eyes toward changing the ways we act in the social structures we sustain. Cultivation of skills, knowledge and perspectives that support wise and just responses for resolving, redressing and preventing injustice is essential to our work. With more clarity on the term and the responsibility it implies, actions and practices in school psychology that carry *social justice* as a banner will be more likely to support our commitment to "walking the talk."

## What School Psychology Means and Wants

The last three words of the last paragraph offer an important place to pause. They provide necessary context for what school psychology says and wants with the term *social justice*. As with many expressions from the margins, the phrase "walk the talk" has been adopted (or, more accurately, co-opted) by people with more access to power and privilege; i.e., people who are part of the dominant socio-political group. The phrase *dominant culture* serves as shorthand for the constantly shifting demographic including people who have most access to resources and influence via a combination of educational, economic, gender, race, language and physical appearance characteristics (all mediated by physical and emotional status). Use of the term *dominant* implies a power differential. While not necessarily actively aware of having and using power, people of a dominant group have privileges at a cost to people not in the group. Privilege is not the problem. Almost all people experience and report privileges—connections with family and friends, love of landscapes or animals (cf. Lourde, 1988). Privilege at someone else's expense, however, is dominance and from a social justice perspective is the concern. As I've already mentioned, the particularly difficult aspect of dominance is that the people it privileges often cannot see the ways their privilege costs others.

Good intentions reside at the intersection of privilege and sincere concern for human well-being. I have good intentions. You have them, too. And we who are most fortunate have the option of walking away. We don't walk away—not always—but we can, and that makes intentions quite distinct from having no option but to be on the receiving end of disrespect and unfairness. Privilege makes it possible not to see the oppressions in our practices (research, teaching, service); and when we do see them, we have the option of acting as if we don't. Those of us who do not walk away have known our own measure of being on the receiving end of injustice. Still, we can walk away and that is our privilege.

It is in this context, specifically as it is lived out daily in schools and their surrounding communities, that the profession of school psychology has taken interest in social justice. We have the option of using our privilege to identify and dismantle unfair privilege systems. Our literature and practice have a consistent history of addressing overt inequalities in the educational experiences of learners (e.g., Alpert & Meyers, 1983, Barona & Garcia, 1990, Barona & Santos de Barona, 2006; Prilleltensky, 1991, 2011; Tractman, 1971). Only recently have we begun to use the term *social justice* to signify this tradition of inquiry and practical action (Shriberg & Fenning, 2009). The term has gained growing adoption and use and, as Shriberg, Wynne, Briggs, Bartucci, and Lombardo (2011) report, recent surveys of school psychologists indicate one shared meaning: *Social justice* is "ensuring the protection of educational rights and opportunities and promoting nondiscriminatory practice" (p. 41).

We as school psychologists are benefactors of the prevailing social system and qualify as privileged by virtue of access to resources and influence. We are entirely able, however, to pursue goals of nondiscrimination and equal rights by using our access to identify, repair, correct and prevent overt inequalities. In this way, we advance aspirations to social justice from across human history—causes heroically forwarded by the Civil Rights Movement, held in the founding documents of the United States and originally articulated in the Constitution of the Iroquois Confederacy. Each of these historic expressions recognized the practicality in the paradox that unity relies on multiplicity (McPhail, 1996). Now with the term *social justice*, we as school psychologists continue to probe and identify behavior that accepts inspiration from this paradox instead of defying it in what history shows is an equally enduring habit of separating and opposing in order to prevail.

The paradox in the interdependence of unity and multiplicity poses a particular challenge for those of us in school psychology who champion the social justice idea. We are aware that too much of the research and technology of education and psychology can be demonstrated to be essentially and/or practically in opposition to this idea. Yet the above definition (Shriberg et al., 2011) requires nondiscriminatory practices such as equal voice. In discussions of actions our profession can take toward social justice, therefore, equal voice means including those who conceive of and advance theory and practice at odds with our idea of *social justice*.

This is where a consideration of language may be helpful.

## Theory and Praxis: The Power of Language

A word is just a word, a phrase is just a phrase—neither has meaning outside of experience. The act of giving the name *social justice* to professional efforts supporting the well-being of all people is based:

- in the experience of observing and/or being subject to injustice
- in the experience of desire for justice for oneself and all others—for respect, fairness and equal access to resources such as education
- in the privilege to be in the position of naming; coming up with the phrase and applying it.

Too often in the low-context linguistic systems characteristic of Western cultures (Hall, 1976; Ibarra, 2001), we stop with the naming, as if putting words on something is taking action. It is a privilege to see an unfair situation, give a name to it, and then employ that name in writing and speaking. It is a shortcoming of privilege to stop there without taking direct and sustained action to redress the original situation. In completely functional terms, redress would eliminate the problem and render the named idea obsolete. Maybe that's finally what we're after with *social justice* work in school psychology—putting ourselves out of business. Nevertheless, it seems vital to note that in the tricky context of privilege, naming can too easily equate with absence of actual corrective action.

At the same time, naming is vital to directing attention so that action may be conceived, developed, and carried through. Theory gets a bad rap in graduate classrooms and political arenas in large part because of the entirely justifiable question, "So what?" What difference does a theory make without action? The question is rarely reversed to consider what action is of use or even of existence without an idea—without theory? Thus, the defining, the naming, and the aspiration to this collection of actions and circumstances held in the phrase *social justice* are both a privilege and a necessity for focusing attention and action.

Given these considerations, it is clear that social justice requires wisdom. Wise practice requires conscious dispositions, knowledge, actions. It requires using access and its privilege to identify and dismantle systems of oppression. This happens in large public actions such as the Civil Rights Movement, and in small common place actions such as those that school psychologists engage daily. Fortunately, there are precedents, even traditions in our profession from which we can learn. Across our history, school psychologists have been allies (Conoley, 1981; Sarason, 1996; Tractman, 1971). With our roots in the consultation initiatives of Caplan and his colleagues in post-World War II Israel (Caplan & Caplan, 1993), followed in the mid-1970s by our close association with Public Law 94–142, the Education for All Handicapped Children Act, later revised in iterations of the Individuals with Disabilities Act (IDEA), we have grounded our profession in advocacy for learning and learners. In keeping with the unavoidable nature of human society and the rule of justice,[1] we participate in contradictions. We commit ourselves to a system that aspires to guarantee access to education for all children (the rule of justice). Within that system we also apply practices that can contribute to perpetuating stigma by continuing to rely on the medical model. At worst, medicalized thinking privileges the diagnostic gaze and language of pathology and, among its other effects, results in over-qualifiying learners from non-dominant groups. The latter effect stems in part from unresolved bias in standardized test instruments (Helms, 2007; Shellenberg, 2004) and over-reliance on tests as truth rather than as tools for seeking the best instructional strategies for a given learner (Henning-Stout, 1994b). Given our decades of focus on ecological (Gutkin, 2009) and systemic considerations (Maher, Illback, & Zins, 1984) for situating behavior, we would like to believe that we are "post" medical model. However, in the wake of our long encounter with "No Child Left Behind" a visit to almost any school multidisciplinary team, a read through of almost any assessment report or a review of district benchmark accounts provides sobering reminder of the entrenched authority of removed diagnostic expertise that persists in placing the problem in the learner.

Over-qualification and the persistence of the medical model come from privileging the characteristics of the dominant group as the standard next to which all thus marginal individuals and groups appear deviant, or at least lacking. The practices arising with popularization of ideas such as curriculum-based measurement (Shinn, 2002) and evidence-based assessment (Fletcher, Francis, Morris & Lyon, 2005) only serve to extend the privileging of dominant culture characteristics and values. This is most often not a calculated move on the part of assessment scholars, but it is the only logical outcome since the culture originating and defining both curricula and assessment technologies is the culture that dominates (Helms, 2007; Henning-Stout, 1994).

One powerful antidote to this tendency comes from direct personal and professional contact with members of marginalized groups. Beyond contact involving presence in the same space, direct experience requires school psychologists to listen closely and for extended periods of time to the interests and concerns from the lives of those individuals. This is an activity requiring the willingness and capacity to place oneself in the position of being a "student" to the people one serves. In this way, listening supports socially just practice—practice that is developed, established and maintained with great attention to the authority, presence and input from marginal voices and perspectives (see "strong objectivity", Harding, 2008; Henning-Stout & Meyers, 2000). The role of allies then remains vital in the pursuit and sustenance of social justice with full and enacted recognition that the deepest understanding of social justice and its solutions will always be found in the people who most directly experience the injustice. These are the realities that define social justice in practice. Here, *social justice* means engaging in the messiness guaranteed with opposing injustice while being true to our commitment to coherence—the interdependence of all of us alongside the dignity of each.

In spirit and tradition, practices guided by the idea of *social justice* can provide linguistic and social circumstances for the exploration and reparation of issues of oppression in school psychology. But the two problems described earlier remain:

1.  our profession's identity with unjust practices and our adherence to policies that can and do lead to inequalities
2.  the requirement of the rule and spirit of justice that all have voice, policy makers and assessment authors included.

Good consultation practice (please see Chapter 13 for further discussion on the potential relationship between social justice and consultation efforts involving school psychologists) offers a structure for this kind of conversation. Before any progress can be made toward solving a socially situated problem, clear and thorough identification of the problem must occur. This maxim has persisted from early research findings of Bergan and Tombari (1975) indicating that clear problem identification predicts consultation success in 95% of cases, while failure to identify the problem all but guarantees consultation failure. And problem clarification is only complete when all parties involved in the "problem" agree on a description. In school psychology we have implied the existence of social injustices, but outside the definitional exercise described by Shriberg et al. (2011), we have yet to identify the problem(s) with all involved.

It is fair to say that individual school-based consultants may have been chipping away at this problem for a long time (e.g., Conoley, 1981; Clare, 2009). Each clear problem-identification with issues of social justice in classrooms, buildings and districts that in turn leads to the development of relevant and successful intervention contributes to the process of seeing and addressing unfairness and disrespect. In this way the conscious practice of each school psychologist can build our profession's understanding and practice of social justice. However, for individual learning to contribute to the understanding of the whole, we must talk with each other and we in the academy with access to synthesizing and publishing must listen. All of that being said, questions remain quite open when it comes to what we mean as a profession and the extent to which we've really begun to clarify problems of social justice in our discipline's research and technologies.

## Social Justice: What We Say and Where We Stand

So, here we are with social justice in school psychology—here we may always be—pointing with our language toward the ideal of fairness, respect and access even as we know that the goals held in the phrase pitch us into necessary paradox. To inquire and act in the ways of social justice requires wisdom and patience of the most radical and functional kinds. Acting in support of social justice requires engaging knowingly in the messy reality that involves both opposition for countering injustice and continuous opening to the practices of inclusion and coherence toward the well-being of each and all. This practice requires justice *and* it requires care.

For school psychologists the phrase *social justice* is a call to reflective practice for ourselves and our profession. We are necessarily privileged in our position of doing the naming and the pointing. We are bound for opposition in staying true to the inclusion.

Social justice, like language itself, is a social strategy and structure that can be used to privilege and divide or to dignify and unify. In the first case, language functions to sustain opposition and related power differential (we/they, good guy/ bad guy). In the second case, language can support the dignity of individuals and the collective. In responding to matters of social justice, our power and access as school psychologists provide us opportunities to see, question and correct injustice, thus using our power to give it up.

One correction comes in using language and social justice initiatives to reveal our inescapable interdependence. As rhetoric scholar Mark L. McPhail suggests, language is "the perfect vehicle for imparting an understanding to the many of the One" (1996, p. 111). In school psychology, our adoption and employment of the phrase *social justice* may be the use of language and action toward that same understanding. We are dedicated to supporting access, fairness and respect, and at the same time we are inescapably affected by being in relationship with each other. In recent decades, even the disciplines of neuroscience (Damasio, 1994, 1999; Rilling et al., 2002) have shown conclusively that we are relational beings born with hardwiring for mutual understanding, cooperation, and empathy. Many suggest the evidence indicates these essential features of our nature are vital to the survival of human community. The findings of neuroscience provide explanations for the impulse to advance social justice. As Gilligan (2011) writes, each of us has an essential orientation to relationship, "leading the healthy psyche to resist an initiation that mandates a loss of voice and a sacrifice of relationship. It fights for freedom from dissociation, from the splits in consciousness that would keep parts of ourselves and our experience outside our awareness" (p. 33). If we truly want social justice we must have both the social part—care—and the justice part. We must have room for first-person voice, for autobiographical narrative of real lives and real experiences. We must bring all of who we are into the work in relational justice with others; and as importantly, in relational justice with ourselves.

In closing, I offer a direct and relational example of the meaning and action of social justice in the profession of school psychology. This example arises from my distinct gratitude to the editors of this book both for conceiving and for pursuing the idea of it, to the publishers for supporting the book's availability and distribution, and for the invitation to contribute. I received and accepted this invitation within an hour of having heard news on complex and competing global interests in the outcomes and thus the storyline of events in Libya. The details in this news report called forth in me great concern for the people of that country and for our shared capacity globally to solve disagreements of such complexity and magnitude.

I remember being struck by how easily we, the public, can be kept off balance with too little and/or inaccurate information. I segued to school psychology's embrace of social justice—to the simple fact that telling the truth without blame or judgment is an early and necessary step toward making real our profession's ambitious ideals. The step just before truth is listening, and the kind of listening that leads to truth-telling arises from care and connection. Telling the truth without blame or judgment guides justice even as it maintains and strengthens relationship. Being champions for social justice demands that we live the listening and truth-telling we value. This book is one way for each of us, authors and readers, to use our privilege to bring both care and justice to bear in addressing and dismantling systems of privilege that depend for their existence on oppression of any kind.

## Note

1 The rule of justice "requires giving identical treatment to beings or situations of the same kind" (Perelman & Tyteca, 1969, p. 218).

## References

Alpert, J. & Meyers, J. (1983). *Training in consultation: Perspective from mental health, behavioral and organizational consultation.* Springfield, IL: Charles C Thomas.

Barona, A., & Garcia, E. E. (Eds.). (1991). *Children at risk: Poverty, minority status, and other issues in educational equity.* Washington, DC: National Association of School Psychologists.

Barona, A., & Santos de Barona, M. (2006). School counselors and school psychologists: Collaborating to ensure minority students receive appropriate consideration for special educational programs. *Reading Rockets.* Available at www.readingrockets.org/article/26362 (accessed August 28, 2012).

Bergan, J. R., & Tombari, M. L. (1975). The analysis of verbal interactions occurring during consultation. *Journal of School Psychology, 13*, 209–226.

Burman, E. (2005). Engendering culture in psychology. *Theory & Psychology, 15*, 527–548.

Caplan, G., & Caplan, R. B. (1993). *Mental health consultation and collaboration.* Long Grove, IL: Waveland Press.

Christenson, S. L., & Sheridan, S. M. (2001). *School and families: Creating essential connections for learning.* New York, NY: Guilford Press.

Clare, M. M. (2002). Diversity as a dependent variable: Considerations for research and practice in consultation. *Journal of Educational and Psychological Consultation, 13*, 251–263.

Clare, M. M. (2009). Thinking diversity: A habit of mind for school psychology. In T. B. Gutkin & C. R. Reynolds (Eds.), *The handbook of school psychology* (4th ed.). New York, NY: Wiley.

Cervantes, L. D. (1981). *Emplumada.* Pittsburgh, PA: University of Pittsburgh Press.

Conoley, J. C. (1981). Advocacy consultation: Promises and problems. In J. C. Conoley (Ed.), *Consultation in schools* (pp. 157–178). New York, NY: Academic Press.

Damasio, A. (1994). *Descartes' error: Emotion, reason, and the human brain.* New York, NY: Putnam.

Damasio, A. (1999). *The feeling of what happens: Body and emotion in the making of consciousness.* San Diego, CA: Harcourt.

Fletcher, J. M.; Francis, D. J.; Morris, R. D., & Lyon, G. R. (2005). Evidence-based assessment of learning disabilities in children and adolescents. *Journal of Clinical Child and Adolescent Psychology, 34* (3), 506–522.

Gilligan, C. (1982). *In a different voice.*Cambridge, MA: Harvard University Press.

Gilligan, C. (2011). *Joining the resistance.* Malden, MA: Polity Press.

Gutkin, T. B. (2009). Ecological school psychology: A personal opinion and a plea for change. In T. B. Gutkin & C. R. Reynolds (Eds.), *The handbook of school psychology* (4th ed., pp. 463–496). New York, NY: Wiley.

Hall, E. T. (1976). *Beyond culture.* New York, NY: Random House.

Harding, S. (2008). *Sciences from below: Feminisms, postcolonialities, and modernities.* Durham, NC: Duke University Press.

Helms, J. E. (Ed.). (1990). *Black and White racial identity attitudes: Theory, research and practice.* Westport, CT: Greenwood Press.

Helms, J. E. (2007). Fairness is not validity or cultural bias in racial-group assessment: A quantitative perspective. *American Psychologist, 61*, 845–859.

Henning-Stout, M. (1994a). Consultation and connected knowing: What we know is determined by the questions we ask. *Journal of Educational and Psychological Consultation, 5*, 5–21.

Henning-Stout, M. (1994b). *Responsive assessment: A new way of thinking about learning.* San Francisco, CA: Jossey-Bass.

Henning-Stout, M. (1997). Must smart equal eminent? Issues for girls and giftedness. *Contemporary Psychology, 42*, 122–124.

Henning-Stout, M. (1998). Assessing the behavior of girls: What we see and what we miss. *Journal of School Psychology, 36*, 433–455.

Henning-Stout, M. (1999). Learning consultation: An ethnographic analysis. *Journal of School Psychology, 37*, 73–98.

Henning-Stout, M. & Meyers, J. (2000). Consultation and human diversity: First things first. *School Psychology Review, 29*, 419–420.

Ibarra, R. A. (2001). *Beyond affirmative action: Reframing the context of higher Education.* Madison, WI: University of Wisconsin Press.

Keller, E. F. (1985). *Reflections on gender and science.* New Haven, CT: Yale University Press.

Lourde, A. (1988). *A burst of light: Essays.* Ithaca, NY: Firebrand Books.

Maher, C. A., Illback, R. A., & Zins, J. E. (1984). *Organizational psychology in the schools: A handbook for professionals.*Springfield, IL: C. C. Thomas.

McPhail, M. L. (1996). *Zen in the art of rhetoric: An inquiry into coherence.* Albany, NY: State University of New York Press.

Nastasi, B. (2011, July). *School psychologist as an advocate of children's rights.* Paper presented at the annual meeting of the International School Psychology Association, Vellore, India.

Noddings, N. (1984). *Caring: A feminine approach to ethics & moral education.* Berkeley, CA: University of California Press.

Perelman, C. & Tyteca, O. (1969) *The new rhetoric: A treatise on argumentation* (J. Wilkinson & P. Weaver, Trans.). Notre Dame, IN: University of Notre Dame Press.

Prilleltensky, I. (1991). The social ethics of school psychology: A priority for the nineties. *School Psychology Quarterly, 6*, 200–222.

Prilleltensky, I (2011). Wellness as fairness. *American Journal of Community Psychology, 49*, 1–21.

Rilling, J. K., Gutman, D. A., Zeh, T. R., Paqgnoni, G., Berns, G. S., & Kilts, C. D. (2002). A neural basis for social cooperation. *Neuron, 35*, 395–405.

Sander, J. B., Sharkey, J. D., Groomes, A. N., Krumholz, L. L., Walker, K., & Hsu, J. Y. (2011). Social justice and juvenile offenders: Examples of fairness, respect and access in educational settings. *Journal of Educational and Psychological Consultation* (in press).

Sarason, S. B. (1996). *Revisiting "The culture of the school and the problem of change"*. New York, NY: Teachers College Press.

Shellenberg, S. J. (2004, April 14). *Test bias or cultural bias: Have we really learned anything?* Paper presented at the annual meeting of the National Council for Measurement in Education, San Diego, CA.

Shinn, M. R. (2002). Best practices in using curriculum-based measurement in a problem-solving model. In A. Thomas & J. Grimes (Eds.), *Best practices in school psychology IV* (pp. 671–693). Bethesda, MD: National Association of School Psychologists.

Shriberg, D., & Fenning, P. (2009). School consultants as agents of social justice: Implications for practice: Introduction to the special topic issue. *Journal of Educational and Psychological Consultation, 19*, 1–7.

Shriberg, D., Wynne, M. E., Briggs, A., Bartucci, G., & Lombardo, A. C. (2011). School psychologists' perspectives on social justice. *School Psychology Forum, 5*, 37–53.

Sue, D. W., Capodilupo, C. M., Torino, G., Bucceri, J. M., Holder, A., Nadal, K., et al. (2007). Racial microaggressions in everyday life: Implications for clinical practice. *American Psychologist, 62*, 271–286.

Tractman, G. (1971). Doing your thing in school psychology. *Professional Psychology, 2*, 377–381.

# Part 2

# Major Issues that Affect Practice

# five

# Understanding and Addressing Inequities in Special Education

## Amanda L. Sullivan

The field of education is plagued with disparities in the treatment and outcomes of culturally and linguistically diverse (CLD) learners and those from low-income households relative to their peers even as these students comprise a growing proportion of the student population. Nationwide, CLD students are subject to inequitable quality of instruction, educational facilities, and materials; and access to rigorous curriculum, effective interventions, and appropriate learning supports (Brayboy, Castagno, & Maughan, 2007). The implications of such disparities for academic and long-term outcomes are startling, underscoring the need for social justice efforts to support equity in educational access, participation, and outcomes.

The disparate identification and placement of diverse students in special education, often referred to as *overrepresentation* or *disproportionality* (i.e., disproportionate identification and/or placement), is one area of persistent inequity, or social disparity, in opportunity and access with particular relevance to the field of school psychology. Inequity in special education represents a social justice concern because it is, at its roots, an issue of equity, or fairness, in the treatment of diverse learners—that is, that CLD students are identified as disabled only when they demonstrate true disabilities not because of cultural differences or bias and that they receive appropriate educational services to address their learning needs. This chapter will provide a context for understanding disproportionality in special education as a social justice issue and describe recommendations for engaging in school psychological practice to ensure that struggling learners are provided with appropriate educational services and supports.

## Background

More than four decades ago, the overrepresentation of children from racial minority, immigrant, and low-income households in classes for children with special needs was brought to light in Dunn's (1968) commentary on the flaws of special education. Dunn (1968) also called attention to pervasive stigmatization, poor-quality services, biased assessment and placement, and unnecessarily restrictive services, all of which continue to trouble special educators and policy makers today. Indeed, in the decades that followed, scholars have consistently documented troubling patterns of differential identification and placement among CLD students. These findings spurred two federally funded studies by the National Research Council (NRC; Donovan & Cross, 2002; Heller, Holtzman, & Messick, 1982) confirming racially based disparities in disability identification, which resulted in recommendations for changes in federal, state and local policy and practice. This disproportionality has also prompted decades of resolutions and actions by professional organizations, including the National Association of School Psychologists (e.g., Klotz, 2007), as well as millions in dedicated advocacy and federally and state-funded technical assistance to struggling school systems (e.g., the National Center for Culturally Responsive Educational Systems).

For policy grounded in the rhetoric of the Civil Rights movement and intended to reduce the exclusion of students with special needs (Blanchett, 2006), ongoing disproportionality is a dilemma that suggests systemic inequities in access and opportunity. The question of whether overrepresentation of certain groups is indeed *problematic* is something that has been heavily debated. Some contend that because special education affords additional services and supports it is a benefit, while others argue that bias present in any stage of the educational processes leading to identification or placement must be considered problematic (Heller et al., 1982). Further, given evidence of the limited effectiveness of special education (e.g., Morgan, Frisco, Farkas, & Hibel, 2010) and the poor long-term outcomes of students who receive services, any overrepresentation of diverse learners in special education programs should be scrutinized.

Many consider special education to be a *double-edged sword* in that it ensures access for students who were historically excluded from public schools while also serving to stigmatize children and marginalize them from general education (Sullivan, Kozleski, & Smith, 2008). This phenomenon has also been dubbed the "paradox of special education," and has been recognized as the crux of disproportionality as an educational *problem*, as noted by Donovan and Cross (2002):

> The same program that can separate disadvantaged students from their peers, distinguish them with a stigmatizing label, and subject them to a curriculum or low expectations can also provide additional resources, supports, and services without which they cannot benefit from education . . . disproportionality is a problem when it stigmatizes or otherwise identifies a student as inferior, results in lowered expectations, and leads to poor educational outcomes. (p. 20)

# Legal and Policy Issues Related to Disproportionality

Disproportionality in special education is a concern not only for educators, but for the courts and policy-makers as well. Local evidence of inequities in special education identification and placement has resulted in several notable legal cases (e.g., *Diana v. California State Board of Education*, 1970; *Guadalupe Organization v. Tempe Elementary School District*, 1972; *Larry P. v. Riles*, 1979; *PASE v. Hannon*, 1980; *Crawford et al. v. Honig*, 1998; *Hobson v. Hansen*, 1967) that have informed state and federal special education statutes. Cases prior to the 1975 passage of P.L. 94–142 often challenged professional practices in assessment and diagnosis, while later cases concerned equity in treatment and outcomes (Artiles & Trent, 1994). Rulings in these cases were mixed, ranging from judicial decrees barring the use of IQ tests in *Larry P.* to those finding that disproportionality is not discriminatory (e.g., *Marshall et al. v. Georgia*, 1985). Overall, cases have both supported and refuted the claim that differential identification and placement is due to bias and discrimination.

The Individuals with Disabilities Education Act (IDEA) mandates multifaceted, nondiscriminatory assessment, and includes ethnic, linguistic, and cultural differences under its exclusionary clauses in order to ensure that only children with true disabilities are identified. Under this statute, assessment practices should be chosen and interpreted with full consideration of the child's background. However, decades of research suggests that this is often not what takes place when CLD students are evaluated for special education (e.g., Figueroa & Newsome, 2006; MacMillan, Gresham & Bocian, 1998; Ochoa, Rivera, & Powell, 1997; Sullivan & Cohen, 2010; Ysseldyke, Algozzine, Richey, & Graden, 1982). Instead, this research indicates that there is little use of data or formal criteria in special education eligibility determinations, with little consistency in determinations from one district to the next.

The 2004 amendments to IDEA required states to monitor racial disproportionality in special education; implement improvement activities aimed at reducing disparities in identification, placement, and student outcomes; and publicly report on progress towards eliminating disproportionality on an annual basis. School districts flagged as having significant disproportionality are also required to engage in systematic review to identify and correct any policies, practices, or procedures that contribute to inappropriate identification, and allot 15% of their special education funding for early intervening efforts aimed at preventing special education needs among students not yet involved in special education.

At the national level, discrimination in special education identification and treatment is also prohibited under the Civil Rights Act of 1974, Section 504 of the Rehabilitation Act of 1973, and the Equal Protection Clause of the 14th Amendment to the US Constitution. The US Department of Education Office for Civil Rights (OCR) also collects district data and investigates discrimination claims regarding minority placement in special education. Through this office, disproportionality in the high incidence categories is monitored for districts nationwide, including those with histories of violations or complaints, and inappropriate identification and placement are considered possible civil rights violations. When such complaints are made, OCR can investigate and order corrective action such as policy changes, professional development, and program reform.

## Recent Trends in Special Education Inequity

Despite decades of professional, legal, and policy efforts to reduce or prevent disproportionality, inequities in special education identification, placement and outcomes persist. Much of the attention to this issue revolves around the categories of learning disabilities (LD), cognitive or intellectual impairments (CI; previously referred to as mental retardation), and emotional disabilities (ED), considered to be both high-incidence because of the large number of students identified, and "soft" or "subjective" because of reliance on clinical judgment in making diagnoses, vague disability definitions, and wide variability in identification rates (MacMillan & Reschly, 1998). Many scholars question the validity of these diagnoses and suggest that the likelihood of misidentification, particularly of CLD learners, is high (Coutinho & Oswald, 1998; Osher, Woodruff, & Sims, 2002). In contrast, disproportionality is rarely observed in the physically or medically based disabilities and these diagnoses are not often challenged.

The empirical literature has largely focused on examinations of race-based patterns in identification and placement. As of 2010, at the national level, Black students were twice as likely as Whites to be identified ED and 2.7 times as likely to be identified CI (US Department of Education, 2010). Meanwhile, Native American students were nearly twice as likely to be identified LD and 60% more likely to be labeled CI, and Asian or Pacific Islander students were grossly underrepresented across categories. This underrepresentation of Asian-American children in special education is largely understudied, but the research from the medical and public health fields suggests that widespread underutilization of certain medical and mental health services and avoidance of the stigma of certain diagnoses, such as mental retardation (Leong & Lau, 2001) may contribute to underservice of special needs. Further, it may be that educational professionals, falling prey to notions of the "model minority," fail to recognize learning and/or social-emotional difficulties among these students.

Identification rates vary considerably across states. For example, Latino students are not overrepresented at the national level, but state- and district-level analyses show that overrepresentation is present in school systems where their enrollment is high (Artiles, Harry, Reschly, & Chinn, 2002; Gaviria-Soto & Castro-Morera, 2005). In fact, one of the most consistent predictors of minority disproportionality is minority enrollment. If identification were due solely to within-child factors, the demographic characteristics of school systems should have no bearing on overall risk. That is, overall prevalence of specific disabilities should be the same across school contexts if those school contexts have no bearing on identification patterns. Instead, research consistently demonstrates that school characteristics do indeed predict patterns of group risk and relative risk for minority groups compared to Whites.

Further, not only are certain racial minority students overrepresented in certain special education categories, but they are more likely to be served in restrictive, segregated placements (Donovan & Cross, 2002; Parrish, 2002; Serwatka, Deering, and Grant, 1995) and are subject to harsher, more frequent disciplinary consequences than their White peers (Skiba, Michael, Nardo, & Peterson, 2002b). What's more, minority students, particularly Black children and youth, make fewer academic gains and are less likely to exit special education than White students (Blanchett, 2006). Gender disparities are also pervasive, with boys nearly 3.5 times as likely to be identified as emotionally disabled and twice as likely to be identified as learning disabled as female students (Coutinho & Oswald, 2005). When race and gender are examined simultaneously, Black males are at the greatest risk of identification of any group (Coutinho, Oswald, & Best, 2002; Oswald, Coutinho, Best, & Nguyen, 2001) and are generally subject to the poorest outcomes (e.g., grades, suspension, graduation). It is also notable that CLD students experience less positive long-term outcomes in terms of enrollment in post-secondary education, employment, independent living, and incarceration relative to their White peers regardless of specific disability (e.g., Affleck, Edgar, Levine, & Kortering, 1990; Osher et al., 2002). Thus, the implications of disproportionality are far-reaching.

Emerging research indicates that language minority students (also known as English language learners [ELLs]) are also overrepresented in the high-incidence disabilities in some contexts—particularly in the Southwest (Artiles, Rueda, Salazar, & Higerada, 2005; Sullivan, 2011). Overrepresentation is particularly pronounced for secondary ELL students lacking proficiency in both their home and second languages (Artiles et al., 2005). It is notable that increasing overrepresentation has been found in California and Arizona following the implementation of English-only educational policy that bars schools from providing native language supports or bilingual education programs (Artiles, Klingner, Sullivan, & Fierros, 2010).

## Explanations of Disproportionality

Research has examined numerous factors thought to contribute to disproportionality, including, but not limited to: differences in academic achievement; test bias; bias in referral, assessment, or placement; interpersonal bias and misinterpretation of behaviors of students who are CLD; inequitable opportunities to learn; system characteristics that limit family and community involvement in education; insufficient professional training to work effectively with diverse students; inequitable resource allocation; and structural inequities and systemic bias. To date, it is clear that no one factor produces disparate identification. Instead, disproportionality appears to be a complex phenomenon influenced by a number of factors, which differ from group to group and may vary from one context to another (Skiba et al., 2008).

Explanations of disproportionality range from deficit perspectives foregrounding supposed deficiencies in intelligence, academic skills, or parenting that contribute to differential risk of disability, to theories of structural or systemic bias that point to bias as the cause of differential identification. Some scholars point to poverty as the cause because of its impact on children's physical, cognitive, and social development (O'Connor & Fernandez, 2006), but when the observed relations of poverty are studied, they vary across racial and disability groups—even showing inverse relations to identification of Black students—leading many to question its role in differential risk (Skiba, Poloni-Staudinger, Simmons, Feggins-Azziz, & Chung, 2005).

Many suggest that bias in the referral, assessment, and placement processes contribute to differential identification and outcomes (e.g., Coutinho & Oswald, 1998). Diverse students may be treated differently by general educators and other services providers, including school psychologists, who often come from very different cultural backgrounds than the students they serve. Indeed, the vast majority of educators and school psychologists come from middle-class, White households, leading scholars to wonder if they are not susceptible to misinterpreting and pathologizing the behaviors of CLD students and families based on ethnocentric norms and expectations coupled with a general lack of awareness and respect for cultural differences (Cartledge, 2005; Chamberlain, 2005). This perspective is bolstered by research showing that teachers are more likely to refer racial minority students (e.g., Gottlieb & Gottlieb, 1991) and that the high presence of minority teachers reduces the likelihood of overrepresentation of Black students (Serwatka, Deering, & Grant, 2005) and Latino students (Sullivan & Artiles, 2011).

Nonetheless, the isolation of disproportionality to the subjective disabilities leads to the supposition that these categories are socially constructed, with diagnoses driven by conceptualizations of normality that disadvantage CLD students because they may not adhere to culturally based expectations of appropriate performance or interaction (Minow, 1985). This notion of social construction is reinforced by empirical research documenting that disability identification is subject to idiosyncrasies across school systems (Singer et al., 1989) and that many students identified as LD fail to meet any criteria (MacMillan & Reschly, 1998). Further, these identifications also rely on normative comparisons that can differ from one context to the next and are often linked to tests in which CLD students are poorly represented among the norming samples. Indeed, arguments of social construction of disability predate special education. See for example, discussions of the "six-hour retarded child"—children classified as CI by virtue of test scores but who demonstrated typical functioning in their home environments (President's Committee on Mental Retardation, 1969). Recently, researchers found that early academic skills were the strongest predictor of special education risk, mediating the effects of both race and socioeconomic status, and that students in high-achieving schools were more likely to be identified than students in lower achieving settings (Hibel, Farkas & Morgan, 2010). These scholars posited that these results supported the notion that identification was contextually driven and may be more due to difference than to actual disability.

Other authors point to the histories of marginalization and oppression that may negatively affect children's development and academic progress, as well as their experiences of discrimination, and by extension their risk of special education identification, as possible contributors to disproportionality (Carter & Goodwin, 1995). These scholars contend that the problem of disproportionality cannot be separated from broader social issues of institutional racism, ethnocentrism, mental health stigma, and the intersections thereof (Blanchett, 2006; Osher et al., 2004) and related disparities in education, health care, and social opportunity (Patton, 1998). This has led to the suggestion that disproportionality is a result of inequities in CLD students' access, relative to White students, to school funding, quality instruction and curriculum, qualified and experienced teachers, research-based behavior management, and school facilities and materials that reduce opportunities to learn, thereby negatively affecting student achievement, and increasing risk of special education identification (Valenzuela, Copeland, Qi, & Park, 2005). In general, disproportionality scholars believe that disproportionality is a complex, multiply determined phenomenon shaped by diverse factors—interpersonal, environmental, and systemic (Artiles, Kozleski, Trent, Osher, & Ortiz, 2010; Skiba et al., 2008). Despite a growing body of research, causal links have yet to be identified. Nonetheless, professional efforts increasingly focus on prevention through improved advocacy, early intervening, family–school collaboration, professional development, and systemic change.

## Addressing Inequities in Special Education through School Psychology Practice

Effectively addressing inequities in special education requires attention to issues of access to and distribution of educational resources. Recommendations for correcting long-standing inequities in special education are grounded in a distributive view of social justice—that is, one concerned with the equitable allocation of resources—that underscores the need to ensure that all students have access to appropriately trained professionals and are provided with high-quality opportunities to learn (e.g., appropriate instruction and evidence-based interventions to remediate learning or behavioral problems before they become severe enough to warrant consideration of special education) (Artiles, Bal, & King Thorius, 2010). For school psychologists specifically, this requires a broad conceptualization of practice that encapsulates prevention, consultation, assessment, advocacy, leadership, and systems change. School psychologists can ensure that they avoid contributing to inappropriate identification by developing culturally responsive professional attitudes, promoting systems change that supports equity, and engaging in strong assessment, intervention, and evaluation practices.

## Developing Professional Attitudes Responsive to Cultural Differences

An important aspect in ensuring students' access to competent professionals is developing the professional attitudes conducive to equitable services. The first step in addressing inequity in special education requires critical reflection on one's own attitudes, values, and beliefs about difference, learning, behavior, and opportunity. One might explore his or her beliefs, values, and/or expectations in a variety of domains (e.g., individual ability, achievement, child rearing, appropriate child–adult interactions, the role of children in families, what makes a family) and ask oneself (a) how such values or beliefs come into play during interactions with students, families, and colleagues; (b) how they shape how one thinks about professional roles and practices; (c) what biases are held toward individuals with similar and different values; and (d) how they influence reactions to and interactions with individuals who are similar to and different from oneself. Two central aspects of this process are (1) being able to identify one's values, beliefs, and expectations and (2) accepting that everyone has biases. The challenge then becomes examining how these shape our behavior and then working to ensure that we minimize or eliminate their effects on our professional behaviors. This process should be facilitated both in formal training and through ongoing self-reflection. Such consciousness raising is a critical element of social justice (Ali, Liu, Mahmood, & Arguello, 2008), because without it school psychologists may inadvertently harm students or support continued marginalization of CLD students (Li & Vazquez-Nuttall, 2009).

This also involves the challenging process of considering one's own privilege, how it relates to the oppression of others, and acknowledging that self-professed neutrality and objectivity in values and attitudes are myths (Ali et al., 2008). Further, it is necessary to consider the power structures affecting one's interactions with others, and the broader power dynamics in one's sites as these might influence the treatment received by diverse learners and their families. Beyond understanding one's own values and beliefs—especially those pertaining to learning, socialization, and communication—school psychologists must be cognizant of the culture of the school and the values held by staff and reflected in educational practices. Where potentially detrimental values, policies, or practices are identified, school psychologists must be prepared to act as advocates for the needs of students and the development of a more equitable school culture.

## Promoting Systems Change

Supporting systemic change requires shifting focus from individual students to structural features of the school environment. Focusing on individual pathology while ignoring discriminatory policies and practices simply perpetuates inequities and prevents school psychologists from acting as effective advocates and change agents. The issues surrounding disproportionality—discrimination, inequality, power, and privilege—are often uncomfortable for educators to address, but it is essential to do so in order to foster policies, procedures, and everyday practices to avoid advantaging some while disadvantaging others. School psychologists should be proactive in exploring those aspects of school culture and policy that may perpetuate the inappropriate special education labeling of CLD students and helping the school community to develop systems that support the development and wellbeing of all.

School psychologists can assist administrators and teachers in beginning to unpackage the problem of disproportionality through careful examination of data on special education referral, identification, placement, and outcomes (Sullivan et al., 2010). School psychologists should assist administrators and other education professionals to ask the question, "Why are some students overrepresented in special education?" Doing so will lead to examination of not only of individual student-level data on academic and behavioral performance, but also data on school and classroom instructional and intervention practices, classroom management, school climate, professional development, and family involvement (National Alliance of Black School Educators (NABSE) & ILIAD Project, 2002). More specific considerations that should be explored at the school or district-level include the following:

- Do all students participate in high-quality curriculum and instructional programs? If no, why not?
- Are all teachers and related services providers trained to provide appropriate services for diverse learners? If no, why not?
- When students experience academic or behavioral difficulties, how are environmental factors ruled out as the cause of their difficulties before internal causes are considered?
- Do struggling learners receive appropriately implemented, research-based intervention before special education is considered? If no, why not?
- Why are students referred for evaluation of special education eligibility and needs?
- How do multidisciplinary teams determine special education eligibility?

These are essentially questions of opportunity and access. Answering these complicated questions requires critical examination of how instruction and intervention are provided to all students. These questions should be considered in all schools, not just those where significant disproportionality is found, and can represent one part of a larger process of assessing equity within school or district settings (for examples of assessment tools, see Kozleski & Zion, 2006; Richards, Artiles, Klingner, & Brown, 2005). This type of exploration is a difficult and complicated process that requires support and commitment from all involved parties. It may be beneficial to link this process to broader data reviews, analyses of system strengths and needs, and efforts to improve system-wide achievement.

Ensuring the appropriateness of special education determinations requires taking a step back to determine the appropriateness of the multidisciplinary evaluation process. This, in turn, is dependent on the appropriateness of the pre-referral intervention system, which, in turn, presupposes that all students are provided with high-quality curriculum and instruction. The provision of quality educational programming is reliant on the preparedness of staff to provide this instruction in ways that support the learning needs of students with diverse backgrounds and experiences. Thus, as the questions above suggest, addressing the issue of disproportionality in special education begins with examination of general education. All school personnel must accept responsibility for supporting the academic and social–emotional well-being of all learners (NABSE & ILIAD, 2002). Doing so may require exploring organizational and interpersonal biases that may advantage some groups over others. It also requires acknowledging the strong influence of teachers' instructional and classroom management practices on children's academic and behavioral outcomes independent of other factors (Donovan & Cross, 2002). Thus, while CLD children come to school with different funds of knowledge and behavioral repertoires, educators have the potential to have a significant impact on students' in-school learning. Unfortunately, teachers and administrators may incorrectly assume that outside experiences inhibit potential for academic growth, and this is not the case.

Where examination of the questions above reveals problematic school functioning, policies, procedures, and/or practices should be revised to ensure that all students are provided with quality curriculum and instructional programs, staff are trained to work with diverse learners, and research-based interventions are provided in general and special education. When students experience learning and behavioral challenges, environmental factors should first be ruled out as the cause and research-based interventions should be implemented before special education is considered. When it is, multidisciplinary teams should determine special education eligibility, guided by legal and professional guidelines, and based on thorough collection and review of data through multidomain (e.g., cognitive, academic, social, adaptive), multisource (e.g., parents, teachers, child), multimethod (e.g., observations, interviews, testing) evaluation procedures. Ensuring these things may occur through a rigorous self-review process of school policies and procedures, a structured problem-solving or pre-referral intervention process, and/or school improvement planning.

## Improving Intervention and Referral Practices

Pre-referral practices should emphasize early screening to identify students for preventative and/or remedial intervention in order to curb the development of more severe academic or behavioral difficulties that may eventually lead to special education identification. When screening is followed by effective intervention, this maximizes students' opportunities to learn and ensures that those students eventually identified for special education are those most in need of specialized services (Donovan & Cross, 2002). As Donovan and Cross (2002) noted, it is necessary to acknowledge that universal screening will predictably lead to high rates of identification of children from disadvantaged backgrounds given documented differences in school readiness and early achievement. Unless such screening is consistently tied to evidence-based interventions that are validated for use with diverse groups, this practice will simply reify notions of inherent group differences and perpetuate inequities in opportunities to learn. Ensuring that screening practices are strong will require that screening processes do not happen in isolation, but are instead tied to broader discussions of school improvement and analysis of outcomes data beyond the screening. As described in the preceding section, decision-making relative to screening outcomes should be tied to considerations of opportunity to learn and access to instruction. Moreover, school teams should discuss the assumptions behind, purposes of, and goals for screening before initiating such a program to ensure that it is consistent with efforts to improve student learning.

There is a consensus among scholars and in state statutes that high-quality intervention (i.e., evidence-based, based on explicitly defined target behaviors and established goals for improvement, properly implemented for sufficient time with progress monitoring) should be provided before consideration of special education needs (Donovan & Cross, 2002). Unfortunately, intervention quality is often poor, signaling the need for targeted efforts to improve teacher readiness to implement interventions with fidelity. School psychologists are well positioned, given their training, to provide support to classroom teachers by providing necessary pre-intervention training, monitoring of treatment integrity, and data analysis. Assuring the quality of general education curriculum and instruction, as well as the interventions provided in these settings, is essential because special education decisions that follow lack of responsiveness to intervention assume that high-quality instruction and intervention were provided. Without this, there is no way to rule out educational disadvantage as the primary cause of students' learning problems.

It is also widely acknowledged that more is known about effective instruction and intervention than is actually implemented in schools. School psychologists possess a wealth of knowledge regarding how intervention agents—commonly the classroom teacher—can foster behavior change and improved learning. Unfortunately, classroom teachers do not always share this knowledge. Therefore, it is imperative that school psychologists bridge this gap to help teachers develop the knowledge and skill necessary to foster productive behavior and learning among struggling students.

## Implementing Effective Evaluation Procedures to Prevent Inappropriate Identification

Skiba, Knesting, and Bush (2002a) defined nonbiased assessment as the "process of assessment that does not contribute to the overrepresentation of minority students in special education" (p. 62). In order to prevent inappropriate identification of diverse learners for special education, school psychologists must ensure that they engage in comprehensive, individualized, culturally appropriate assessment with any student for whom there are special education concerns. Given the sociocultural nature of learning, evaluation practices should take an ecological approach to understanding the multiple levels of factors shaping students' competencies and difficulties (i.e., one that takes account of the nested systems in which the child develops, beginning with consideration of environmental factors that may contribute to the child's difficulties). Cultural considerations should inform test selection, administration, and interpretation. Considerations of the environmental factors that may support or hinder the learning and development of social behavior of CLD students—before ascribing internal causes—are especially important in attempts to minimize inappropriate special education identification. This should include considering possible discrepancies between the norms and expectations of the student's home and school cultures, as disjunctions may contribute to academic or behavioral difficulties that can be corrected through instruction and intervention, as well as careful examination of the educational environment. Considerations of educational opportunity are critical to the evaluation process. It should be intervention, not labeling, that drives the school psychologist's evaluation process. Henning-Stout (1994) endorsed adopting a holistic perspective during the assessment process in order to ensure that all relevant aspects of the learner's environment are accounted for and to involve all relevant stakeholders (e.g., teachers and family members) in the process. This approach emphasizes social context and learner–task interactions in making sense of students' educational difficulties in order to arrive at conclusions that inform instructional changes and support learning.

Formal assessment procedures should be matched to the characteristics of the individual and the specific referral concerns. School psychologists should be knowledgeable of the psychometric properties of any instruments they use and recognize the limitations of standardized assessment, particularly for populations (e.g., ELLs) on which they have not been normed or validated (Rogers et al., 1999). For instance, cognitive assessments are not context-free, nor do cognitive abilities develop independent of one's environment, indicating the cultural nature of problem solving and intellectual performance, and suggesting that CLD students may be disadvantaged in the assessment process because of the sometimes vast differences between the home and school cultures (Donovan & Cross, 2002). Thus, the cultural norm associated with testing can influence both children's performance and professionals' judgments of cognitive ability. What's more, test publishers now acknowledge that cognitive assessments are measures of learning, so it is important to consider a student's cultural and school backgrounds when interpreting test performance (Donovan & Cross, 2002). School psychologists must make similar acknowledgements, and use this knowledge to temper test interpretations.

Children's competencies should be assessed not only using standardized instruments, but also through observation in the classroom setting over multiple occasions, with assessment focusing on those differences that are relevant for instruction and intervention (Donovan & Cross, 2002). In addition, school psychologists should utilize performance-based assessment, dynamic assessment, or functional assessment when appropriate (Rogers et al., 1999). Family members should be fully involved in the process and thoroughly informed of the purposes and implications of special education evaluations. All too often, family members are involved in only the most superficial ways and never truly informed of the complexities of diagnosis or placement (Harry, Allen, & McLaughlin, 1995). School psychologists should strive to ensure that families are fully informed of and integrated into the referral, intervention, and assessment processes.

Through reflective, purposeful professional action school psychologists can contribute to the development of more socially just educational policies, procedures, and practices that prevent continued inequities in special education. Three decades ago, the NRC outlined the duties of school professionals in supporting equity in special education as follows:

1.  It is the responsibility of teachers in the regular classroom to engage in multiple educational interventions and to note the effects of such interventions on a child experiencing academic failure before referring the child for special education assessment.
2.  It is the responsibility of assessment specialists to demonstrate that the measures employed validly assess the functional needs of the individual child for which there are potentially effective interventions.
3.  It is the responsibility of the placement team that labels and places a child in a special program to demonstrate that any differential label used is related to a distinctive prescription for educational practices and that these practices are likely to lead to improved outcomes not achievable in the regular classroom.
4.  It is the responsibility of the special education and evaluation staff to demonstrate systematically that high-quality, effective special instruction is being provided and that the goals of the special education program could not be achieved as effectively within the regular classroom.
5.  It is the responsibility of the special education staff to demonstrate, on at least an annual basis, that a child should remain in [special education] ... only after it has been demonstrated that he or she cannot meet specified educational objectives and that all efforts have been made to achieve these objectives.
6.  It is the responsibility of administrators ... to monitor on a regular basis the pattern of special education placement, the rate for particular groups of children ... and the types of instructional services offered to affirm than appropriate procedures are being followed or to redress inequities found in the system. (Heller et al., 1982, p. 94)

Today, these same basic recommendations hold even though their enactment seems limited. Nonetheless, improvements in policies and practice are possible. School psychologists can contribute to each of these efforts through a social justice orientation that permeates all aspects of practice through an emphasis on supporting equitable access and opportunity for all children. This chapter has discussed disproportionality in special education as a multifaceted challenge for school psychologists, involving many social justice considerations. The following case example describes Lana's experience in a new school site. Discussion questions are provided at the end for classroom or small group use.

## Case Study

Fresh out of her internship, Lana accepted a position at an elementary school in a large school system spanning the urban and suburban areas of the city. Her site was nestled in an area of the city stricken with housing foreclosures and loss of local businesses alongside dilapidated apartment complexes and housing projects. As Lana settled into her site, she committed herself to learning about the school's special education service delivery model since there were several self-contained classrooms on site: three classrooms for students with mild to moderate cognitive impairments (CI), two classrooms for students with learning disabilities, and two classrooms for students with emotional and behavioral disorders.

Touring the school during the first month of the term, Lana was surprised to see that nearly every student in these seven self-contained settings was Black or Latino, and many were English language learners. During the monthly staff meeting for special services, she shared her concerns with the special education director, who noted that the district had been cited for disproportionality but no administrative attention was directed at Lana's site because of the low-income community in which the school was located and the low academic performance of the school overall. Staff at Lana's school expressed similar sentiments, but she was unconvinced. As she reviewed the file of a student due for a re-evaluation, several issues were apparent. Byron was a sixth grader who had been placed in one of the CI classrooms at age six. His performance on state assessment showed that he performed at a first- or second-grade level across all academic subjects and his teachers repeatedly complained that he was overly hyperactive and distractible. Lana was dismayed to see that Byron had not had a comprehensive evaluation since his initial placement, which lacked assessment of functional skills or formal assessment of academic skills despite his categorization as CI. Instead, his placement appeared to have been based solely on an IQ test in which his performance had ranged from moderately delayed to average across domains, causing Lana to hypothesize that his difficulties might be due to the inappropriateness of his placement and low expectations rather than his presumed disability. Lana insisted on a comprehensive evaluation despite the contrary insistence of Bryon's classroom teacher. The evaluation confirmed Lana's suspicions as Bryon performed average across all domains except academics, where he nonetheless demonstrated typical learning potential during dynamic testing. Consequently, Byron's eligibility was changed to learning disabled, though Lana suspected his performance was due to his long-term placement in the CI classroom.

This instance served as an impetus for Lana to undertake a systematic review of the special education files of all the students in the self-contained classes at her school. She consistently noted questionable evaluation practices and eligibility determinations that went against the disability criteria. Lana shared her findings with the special education director and lead psychologist, who agreed that this needed to be addressed. With the help of two practicum students from the local school psychology program, Lana undertook comprehensive re-evaluations of most of the students in the self-contained classrooms during her first year. Many were reclassified or declassified from special education and provided support and intervention within their new general education placements. Over the course of these evaluations, Lana began to wonder how so many children would be incorrectly identified and placed in such segregated placements. Her interactions with the pre-referral team indicated that few research-based interventions were attempted and most efforts were implemented for a few days only. The self-contained placements were also the default for any children with the corresponding diagnoses. Thus, Lana saw numerous aspects of the pre-referral, evaluation, and service planning process that needed to be modified to better serve the students. With the support of the director, Lana enlisted the assistance of a local technical assistance organization to develop and implement a multi-year professional development plan for the general and special education staff, as well as the district's school psychology team. Training began with guided self-reflection on staff's assumption of difference and disability and progressed through embedded training in effective instruction, intervention, and assessment practices.

- What are some social justice considerations in this scenario?
- How might a school psychologist who is not operating from a social justice framework differ from what Lana has done?
- What else might you have done that Lana did not do?

# References

Affleck, J. Q., Edgar, E., Levine, P., & Kortering, L. (1990). Post-school status of students classified as mildly mentally retarded, learning disabled or non-handicapped: Does it get better with time? *Education and Training in Mental Retardation, 25*, 315–324.
Ali, S. R., Liu, W. M., Mahmood, A., & Arguello, J. (2008). Social justice and applied psychology: Practical ideas for training the next generation of psychologists. *Journal for Social Action in Counseling and Psychology, 1* (2), 1–13.
Artiles, A. J., Bal, A., & King Thorius, K. A. (2010). Back to the future: A critique of response to intervention's social justice views. *Theory into Practice, 49*, 250–257.
Artiles, A. J., Harry, B., Reschly, D. J., & Chinn, P. C. (2002). Over-identification of students of color in special education: A critical overview. *Multicultural Perspectives, 4*, 3–10.
Artiles, A. J., Klingner, J., Sullivan, A. L., & Fierros, E. (2010). Shifting landscapes of professional practices: ELL special education placement in English-only states. In P. Gándara & M. Hopkins (Eds.), *Forbidden language: English learners and restrictive language policies* (pp. 102–117). Los Angeles, CA: UCLA Civil Rights Project.
Artiles, A., Kozleski, E., Trent, S., Osher, D., & Ortiz, A. (2010). Justifying and explaining disproportionality, 1968–2008. *Exceptional Children, 76*, 279–299.
Artiles, A. J., Rueda, R., Salazar, J. J., & Higareda, I. (2005). Within-group diversity in

minority disproportionate representation: English language learners in urban school districts. *Exceptional Children, 71*, 283–300.

Artiles, A. J., & Trent, S. C. (1994). Overrepresentation of minority students in special education: A continuing debate. *Journal of Special Education, 27*, 410–437.

Blanchett, W. (2006). Disproportionate representation of African American students in special education: Acknowledging the role of White privilege and racism. *Educational Researcher, 35*, 24–28.

Brayboy, B. M. J., Castagno, A. E., & Maughan, E. (2007). Equality and justice for all? Examining race in education scholarship. *Review of Research in Education, 31*, 159–194.

Carter, R. T., & Goodwin, A. L. (1995). Racial identity and education. *Review of Research in Education, 20*, 290–336.

Cartledge, G. (2005). Restrictiveness and race in special education: The failure to prevent or return. *Learning Disabilities, 3*, 27–32.

Chamberlain, S. P. (2005). Recognizing and responding to cultural differences in the education of culturally and linguistically diverse learners. *Intervention in School and Clinic, 40*, 195–211.

Coutinho, M. J., & Oswald, D. P. (1998). Ethnicity and special education research: Identifying questions and methods. *Behavioral Disorders, 24*, 66–73.

Coutinho, M. J., & Oswald, D. P. (2005). State variation in gender disproportionality in special education: Findings and recommendations. *Remedial and Special Education, 26*, 7–15.

Coutinho, M. J., Oswald, D. P. & Best, A. M. (2002). The influence of sociodemographic and gender on the disproportionate identification of minority students as having learning disabilities. *Remedial and Special Education, 23*, 49–59.

Donovan, M. S. & Cross, C. T. (Eds.). (2002). *Minority students in special and gifted education.* Washington, DC: National Academies Press.

Dunn, L. M. (1968). Special education for the mildly retarded: Is much of it justifiable? *Exceptional Children, 35*, 5–22.

Figueroa, R. A. & Newsome, P. (2006). The diagnosis of LD in English learners: Is it nondiscriminatory? *Journal of Learning Disabilities, 39*, 206–214.

Gaviria-Soto, J. L., & Castro-Morera, M. (2005). Beyond over-representation: The problem of bias in inclusion of minority group students in special education programs. *Quality and Quantity, 39*, 537–558.

Gottlieb, J., & Gottlieb, B. W. (1991). Parent and teacher referrals for a psychoeducational evaluation. *Journal of Special Education, 25*, 155–167.

Harry, B., Allen, N., & McLaughlin, M. (1995). Communication versus compliance: African-American parents' involvement in special education. *Exceptional Children, 61*, 364–377.

Heller, K. A., Holtzman, W. H., & Messick, S. (Eds.). (1982). *Placing children in special education: A strategy for equity.* Washington, DC: National Academy Press.

Henning-Stout, M. (1994). *Responsive assessment: A new way of thinking about learning.* San Francisco, CA: Jossey-Bass.

Hibel, J., Farkas, G., & Morgan, P. L. (2010). Who is placed into special education? *Sociology of Education, 83*, 312–332.

Klotz, M. B. (2007). NASP position statement on identification of students with learning disabilities. *NASP Communiqué, 36* (1). Retrieved September 15, 2007 from www.nasponline.org/publications/cq/mocq361idea.aspx

Kozleski, E., & Zion, S. (2006). *Preventing disproportionality by strengthening district policies and procedures: An assessment and strategic planning process.* Tempe, AZ: National Center for Culturally Responsive Educational Systems.

Leong, F. T. & Lau, A. S. L. (2001). Barriers to providing effective mental health services to Asian Americans. *Mental Health Services Research, 3*, 201–214.

Li, C. & Vazquez-Nuttal, E. (2009). School consultants as agents of social justice for multicultural children and families. *Journal of Educational and Psychological Consultation, 19*, 26–41.

MacMillan, D. L., Gresham, F. M., & Bocian, K. M. (1998). Discrepancy between definitions of learning disabilities and school practices: An empirical investigation. *Journal of Learning Disabilities, 31*, 314–326.

MacMillan, D. L., & Reschly, D. J. (1998). Overrepresentation of minority students: The case for greater specificity or reconsideration of the variables examined. *Journal of Special Education, 32*, 15–24.

Minow, M. (1985). Learning to live with the dilemma of difference: Bilingual and special education. *Law and Contemporary Problems, 48*, 157–211.

Morgan, P. L., Frisco, M. L., Farkas, G., & Hibel, J. (2010). A propensity score matching analysis of the effects of special education services. *Journal of Special Education, 43*, 236–254.

National Alliance of Black School Educators (NABSE), & ILIAD Project. (2002). *Addressing over-representation of African American students in special education.* Arlington, VA: Council for Exceptional Children, and Washington, DC: National Alliance of Black School Educators.

Ochoa, S. H., Rivera, B. D., & Powell, M. P. (1997). Factors used to comply with the exclusionary clause with bilingual and limited-English-proficient pupils: Initial guidelines. *Learning Disabilities Research & Practice, 12*, 161–167.

O'Connor, C., & Fernandez, S. D. (2006). Race, class, and disproportionality: Reevaluating the relationship between poverty and special education placement. *Educational Researcher, 35*, 6–11.

Osher, D., Cartledge, G., Oswald, D., Sutherland, K. S., Artiles, A. J., & Coutinho, M. (2004). Cultural and linguistic competency and disproportionate representation. In R. B. Rutherford, M. M. Quinn, & S. R. Mathur (Eds.), *Handbook of research in emotional and behavioral disorders* (pp. 54–77). New York, NY: Guilford Press.

Osher, D., Woodruff, D., & Sims, A.E. (2002). Schools make a difference: The overrepresentation of African American youth in special education and the juvenile justices system. In D. J. Losen and G. Orfield (Eds.), *Racial inequity in special education* (pp. 93–116). Cambridge, MA: Harvard Education Press.

Oswald, D. P., Coutinho, M. J., Best, A. L., & Nguyen, N. (2001). Impact of sociodemographic characteristics on the identification rates of minority students as having mental retardation. *Mental Retardation, 39*, 351–367.

Parrish, T. (2002). Racial disparities in the identification, funding, and provision of special education. In D. J. Losen and G. Orfield (Eds.), *Racial inequity in special education* (pp. 15–38). Cambridge, MA: Harvard Education Press.

Patton, J. M. (1998). The disproportionate representation of African Americans in special education: Looking behind the curtain for understanding and solutions. *Journal of Special Education, 32*, 25–31.

President's Committee on Mental Retardation. (1969). *The six-hour retarded child.* Washington, DC: Bureau of Education for the Handicapped, Office of Education, US Department of Health, Education, and Welfare.

Richards, H. V., Artiles, A. J., Klingner, J. & Brown, A. (2005). *Equity in special education placement: A school self-assessment guide for culturally responsive practice.* Tempe, AZ: National Center for Culturally Responsive Educational Systems.

Rogers, M. R., Ingraham, C. L., Bursztyn, A., Cajigas-Segredo, N., Esquivel, G., Hess, R., et al. (1999). Best practices in providing psychological services to racially, ethnically, culturally, and linguistically diverse individuals in the schools. *School Psychology International, 20,* 243–264.

Serwatka, T. S., Deering, S., & Grant, P. (1995). Disproportionate representation of African Americans in emotionally handicapped classes. *Journal of Black Studies, 25,* 492–506.

Singer, J. D., Palfrey, J. S., Butler, J. A., & Walker, D. K. (1989). Variation in special education classification across school districts: How does where you live affect what you are labeled? *American Education Research Journal, 26,* 261–281.

Skiba, R. J., Knesting, K., & Bush, L. D. (2002a). Culturally competent assessment: More than nonbiased tests. *Journal of Child and Family Studies, 11,* 61–78.

Skiba, R. J., Michael, R. S., Nardo, A. C., & Peterson, R. L. (2002b). The color of discipline: Sources of racial and gender disproportionality in school punishment. *Urban Review, 34,* 317–342.

Skiba, R. J., Poloni-Staudinger, L., Simmons, A. B., Feggins-Azziz, R., & Chung, C. (2005). Unproven links: Can poverty explain ethnic disproportionality in special education? *Journal of Special Education, 39,* 130–144.

Skiba, R. J., Simmons, A. B., Ritter, S., Gibb, A. C., Rausch, M. K., Cuadrado, J., et al. (2008). Achieving equity in special education: History, status, and current challenges. *Exceptional Children, 74,* 264–288.

Sullivan, A. (2011). Disproportionality in special education identification and placement of English language learners. *Exceptional Children, 77,* 317–334.

Sullivan, A. L., & Artiles, A. J. (2011). Theorizing racial inequity in special education: Applying structural theory to disproportionality. *Urban Education, 46,* 1526–1552.

Sullivan, A. L., A'Vant, E., Baker, J., Chandler, D., Graves, S., McKinney, E., et al. (2009, October). Confronting inequity in special education: Promising practices for addressing disproportionality. *NASP Communiqué, 38* (2), 1.

Sullivan, A. L., & Cohen, S. (2010, February). *Examining psychoeducational reports to understand cultural considerations and eligibility determinations.* Presentation at the annual convention of the National Association of School Psychologists, Chicago, IL.

Sullivan, A., Kozleski, E., & Smith, A. (2008, March). *Understanding the current context of minority disproportionality in special education: Federal response, state activities, and implications for technical assistance.* Paper presentation at the American Educational Research Association Annual Meeting, New York, NY.

US Department of Education. (2010). *The 29th annual report to Congress on the implementation of the Individuals with Disabilities Education Act, 2007, vol. 1.* Washington, DC: Office for Special Programs.

Valenzuela, J. S., Copeland, S. R., Qi, C. H., & Park, M. (2006). Examining educational equity: Revisiting the disproportionate representation of minority students in special education. *Exceptional Children, 72,* 425–441.

Ysseldyke, J. E., Algozzine, B., Richey, L., & Graden, J. (1982). Declaring students eligible for learning disability services: Why bother with the data? *Learning Disabilities Quarterly, 5,* 37–44.

## six

# Systemic School Discipline: Issues of Equity from a Social Justice Perspective

## Amity Noltemeyer and Pamela Fenning

Despite calls for proactive and preventative approaches (e.g., Sugai & Horner, 2002) school discipline in the United States has largely been characterized by control-driven punitive mechanisms intended to maximize student compliance. This type of "get tough" approach has resulted in the widespread use of exclusionary discipline, particularly suspension and expulsion, to address student misbehavior (Fenning et al., 2010). By definition, suspension and expulsion are associated with removal of students from the school setting for a designated period of time. On a national basis, suspension is widely used, as approximately 3.3 million students in the United States received out of school suspensions in 2006 alone (Planty et al., 2009), and some data suggest the practice may be increasing (e.g., Krezmien, Leone, and Achilles, 2006). The use of suspension and expulsion is particularly prevalent in urban schools (e.g., Noltemeyer & Mcloughlin, 2010a). Further, over 40 years of evidence has documented that these exclusionary discipline approaches have been disproportionately used with particular groups, including African American (Children's Defense Fund, 1975; Skiba, Michael, Nardo, & Peterson, 2002; Skiba et al., 2011) and male students (e.g., Raffaele Mendez & Knoff, 2003).

Relying on exclusionary approaches to discipline is concerning for many reasons. Not only do such punitive forms of discipline fail to promote appropriate behavior (Farmer, 1996), but they actually may exacerbate existing behavioral concerns (Greenberg, 1974; Mayer, 1995; Sugai & Horner, 2002). Exclusionary discipline also has been linked to later involvement with the juvenile justice system (e.g., Chobot & Garibaldi, 1982; Florida State Department of Education, 1995) in what is referred to as the "school-to-prison pipeline" (Wald & Losen, 2003). Finally, suspension and expulsion from school have been associated with a variety of negative academic outcomes, including academic failure (Gersch & Nolan, 1994; MacMillan & Reschly, 1998; Rausch & Skiba, 2004a; Safer, Heaton & Parker, 1981), high school drop-out (Costenbader & Markson, 1998; DeRidder, 1990; Ekstrom, Goertz, Pollack, & Rock, 1986; Wehlage & Rutter, 1986), and grade retention (Safer, 1986).

These negative outcomes are particularly salient for those groups of students who are overrepresented as recipients of exclusionary discipline, such as African American males. Using a social justice perspective, the focus of this chapter will be to critically analyze school discipline practices that likely contribute to the further disenfranchisement of these populations. The history and current trends in ethnic discipline disproportionality (aka the "discipline gap") will be reviewed from a social justice perspective. For example, sociocultural and school contextual factors will be explored as systemic social justice issues that contribute to long-standing ethnic disparities in school discipline. We further assert that ecological and system-wide school policies and practices have contributed to the long-standing inequities in discipline among our most disenfranchised students. Using a case study approach, we offer recommendations that school psychologists can facilitate for adopting practices that are conceptualized and delivered from a social justice perspective, including prevention-oriented practices that are intended to meet the needs of all students. An emphasis will be placed on moving away from a traditional focus on punitive discipline consequences provided to individual students to a contextually based model that considers the larger school and societal factors that contribute to inequity in school discipline. We argue throughout this chapter that the "discipline gap"—in which particular disenfranchised groups such as African Americans and males disproportionately receive negative exclusionary consequences—is a social justice issue that school psychologists are poised to prioritize and address. By focusing on school factors and policies that may reinforce discipline inequities rather than viewing discipline as a punitive consequence delivered to an individual student, we can begin to move toward more socially just discipline practices.

By applying a social justice perspective to exclusionary discipline in our schools, particularly among those historically marginalized in education (e.g., African American males), school psychologists can serve as catalysts for system reform. Due to our professional roles, we have a privileged status and can use our voice to question inequitable discipline practices when they occur and to address system-level issues that might be maintaining the "status quo" of exclusionary discipline. We are often in a position to "speak up" when the students and families that we work with on a daily basis cannot due to power imbalances. School psychologists can capitalize on their training and skills in prevention science and data analysis by working collectively with others to advocate for discipline practices that keep students in school rather than excluding them. We are also in a position to share literature findings and relevant federal and state legislation (e.g., Individuals with Disabilities Education Act (IDEA), 2004) related to exclusionary discipline with key stakeholders. By partnering with those most impacted by exclusionary discipline (e.g., families and students), community members, school board members and other educators, we can collectively address the long-standing "status quo" of exclusionary discipline. By enacting a social justice perspective, we can go beyond "best practices" in designing prevention-oriented discipline and using data to evaluate these systems by serving as advocates for those historically marginalized in our schools.

# Historical and Contemporary Issues in School Discipline

## History of School Discipline in the US

Adult frustration over the misbehavior of youth has been documented as early as 2000 BC (Hyman & Wise, 1979 as cited in Hyman, 1997). In the earliest American schools, student misbehavior was minimal, as disruptive students were either expelled or discouraged from attending schools (Hyman, 1997). Following the gradual enactment of compulsory schooling laws around the start of the 20th century, and the consequent influx of students required to attend schools, an increase in the adoption of schoolwide behavior standards emerged (see Fenning et al., 2010). These policies assumed the dual purpose of maintaining order in the classroom and socializing the masses to assimilate to "American" morals and values (Noguera, 1995). Consequently, the behavioral standards articulated in school policies were consistent with middle-class Anglo-Saxon values, as those in power at that time tended to hold to these cultural values (Hyman et al., 2004; Noguera, 1995). Throughout the 19th and early 20th centuries, corporal punishment, humiliation, and other punitive measures were used to bring students in compliance with these policies (Hyman, 1997).

Although corporal punishment has largely fallen out of favor due to its overly harsh and ineffective nature, other reactive responses to misbehavior have supplanted it. Starting in the 1970s, exclusion of students exhibiting misbehavior through suspensions and expulsions from school widely increased (Losen & Skiba, 2010). Some have speculated that the punitive nature of discipline in schools is a reflection of a larger societal tendency in the United States to prefer solutions based on punishment to those based on prevention and rehabilitation (Hyman, 1997). This exclusion-based tendency may be in part a product of the individualistic social ethos characterizing the United States (Cavadino & Dignan, 2006).

The propensity of those in positions of authority to rely on exclusionary practices persisted into the 1990s, when "zero tolerance" frameworks for guiding school discipline policy became even more institutionalized (American Psychological Association (APA) Task Force on Zero Tolerance, 2008). Zero tolerance policies mandate that predetermined, often severe consequences be applied to student behaviors, regardless of the circumstances or context surrounding the behaviors (APA Task Force on Zero Tolerance, 2008). These policies were precipitated by the passage of the Gun Free Schools Act (1994), which mandated automatic school removal for students who brought weapons or drugs to school. Although initially conceptualized to pertain only to serious behaviors that pose significant threats, many schools extend and unilaterally apply zero tolerance policies to less serious behaviors including tardiness, failing to complete homework, or non-compliance (Bear, 2010). Zero tolerance policies have contributed to a disproportionate increase in policing, closed campus policies, uniform policies, and other control-driven tactics in urban schools (Verdugo, 2002). Student expulsions have been documented for such seemingly inconsequential events as bringing over-the-counter medication to school and failing to wear a student uniform when a child's family could not afford one (Reyes, 2006). Despite research that questions the validity and utility of zero tolerance approaches, such policies have become widespread in schools and, many have argued, have been used to an even greater extent with ethnic minority youth (APA Task Force on Zero Tolerance, 2008; Skiba & Rausch, 2006). Rather than serving as deterrents of misbehavior, these policies are often associated with exacerbations in exclusionary discipline rates (Verdugo, 2002)—particularly in the urban settings where they are most frequently applied.

Because of the abovementioned concerns about the application of zero tolerance, a movement toward more positive and preventative forms of discipline has been gaining momentum (APA Task Force on Zero Tolerance, 2008). Ironically, the intention of written discipline policies, which became widespread in schools in the late 1970s, was the rationale that behaviors need to be taught to students on a preset basis rather than punished. The National Institute of Education (NIE, 1978), commissioned by the federal government to study school violence at the time, recommended that schools create written discipline policies as a means of avoiding unclear or haphazard expectations (Fenning et al., 2010). The intent was to establish preset standards for behavior, focusing on what students "should do" to prevent problem behaviors rather than reacting punitively to behavior problems (Fenning et al., 2010). This notion of clearly articulating expectations nearly 40 years ago undergirds current conceptualizations of proactive multi-tiered models of academic, behavioral, and mental health supports, aligned with Response to Intervention (RtI; Brown-Chidsey & Steege, 2005). Within a multi-tiered approach, prevention-oriented practices are used on a universal basis to address social–emotional needs, behavior, and academics, by providing more support in one or more areas at the group or individual level as needed. One example of a multi-tiered approach in the mental health/social emotional arena is population-based school mental health services, which address the psychological and wellness needs of all children within a school (Doll & Cummings, 2008). Information on the mental health status of all children in the school is used to drive decisions regarding whether responses are adequate at the prevention or intervention level, or more intensive supports are needed at the group and/or individual level (Doll & Cummings, 2008).

Schoolwide Positive Behavior Support (SWPBS) is a related behavioral example of multi-tiered models of support (Fenning & Bohanon, 2006; Horner et al., 2009; Sandomierski, Kincaid, & Algozzine, 2007). SWPBS is a prevention-oriented comprehensive approach designed to promote the appropriate behaviors of all students and enhance the capacity of schools and families to design positive environments (OSEP Center on Positive Behavior Interventions and Supports, 2004). SWPBS involves applying positive behavioral interventions to achieve socially important behavior change (Sugai et al., 2000). Similar to the population-based approach of providing mental health services, SWPBS represents a tiered system of prevention and intervention, with the intensity of intervention matched to student needs.

SWPBS typically involves implementing six components at the schoolwide level: (a) identifying a statement of purpose, (b) establishing schoolwide behavioral expectations, (c) teaching schoolwide expectations, (d) encouraging expected behaviors, (e) discouraging problem behaviors, and (f) engaging in data collection and decision making (Lewis & Sugai, 1999). Among other benefits, research indicates that SWPBS implementation reduces the number of office disciplinary referrals (e.g., Barrett, Bradshaw, & Lewis-Palmer, 2008; Bohanon et al., 2006; Horner et al., 2009), suspension rates (e.g., Barrett et al., 2008), and student instructional time missed due to disciplinary referrals (e.g., Scott & Barrett, 2004). While there is preliminary evidence that SWPBS can be implemented with fidelity and is associated with reductions in discipline referrals in urban environments (Bohanon et al., 2006; Lassen, Steele, & Sailor, 2006), this multi-tiered approach has not yet been shown to reduce disproportionality in exclusionary discipline (Skiba et al., 2011). Vincent, Randall, Cartledge, Tobin, and Swain-Bradway (2011) have recently pointed to the potential of SWPBS to be implemented in a culturally responsive manner, yet the outcomes of this approach on one of the most troubling social justice issues of our time—ethnic disproportionality in discipline—is yet to be documented.

## Disciplinary Disproportionality

The Children's Defense Fund (CDF; 1975) first highlighted the gravity of disproportionality in school discipline with a large-scale national investigation revealing that African American students were two to three times more likely to be suspended than White students. African American students were also significantly more likely to receive repeated suspensions, were exposed to harsher discipline strategies, and were less likely to receive milder alternatives when referred for a discipline infraction.

Unfortunately, such indicators have remained markedly unchanged during the years that have elapsed since this seminal investigation. Research across a wide variety of settings and populations has overwhelmingly replicated findings related to ethnic disproportionality in discipline (Costenbader & Markson,

1998; Garibaldi, 1992; Noltemeyer & Mcloughlin, 2010b; Skiba, Michael, Nardo & Peterson, 2002; Skiba, Peterson & Williams, 1997; Thornton & Trent, 1988; Wu, Pink, Crain & Moles, 1982), with the most recent findings continuing to support this trend. For example, using national data obtained for students in grades 6–12, Aud, Fox, and KewalRamani (2010) found that 43% of African American students had been suspended compared to 16% of White students. The findings were even more discrepant when considering expulsions, with 13% of African American students having been expelled compared to only 1% of White students.

Disproportionality is also evident at the classroom level. For example, in another recent large-scale investigation, Skiba et al. (2011) found that African American students are 2 to 3.78 times more likely to be referred to the office for problem behavior as their White peers. The situation for African American *males* is even more disheartening. Aud et al. (2010) found that African American males are over twice as likely to be suspended from school and over 12 times as likely to have been expelled from school compared to White males. Disproportionality has also been documented for Latino students (e.g., Raffaele Mendez & Knoff, 2003), although the findings are less consistent.

The causes of such overrepresentation are complex and multi-faceted. However, it is clear that the discipline gap is not explained by an increased number or severity of problematic behaviors engaged in by African American students (Skiba et al., 2002, 2011). Even when considering the same behavioral offenses, African American students tend to receive harsher consequences for less severe and more subjective offenses (Skiba et al., 2002, 2011). Statistical artifacts also cannot account for the phenomenon, as studies consistently document some degree of disproportionality regardless of the measurement criteria utilized (Skiba et al., 2002). Finally, although poverty does contribute to disproportionality, it does not account for the role of ethnicity in disproportionality, which remains a factor on its own accord (Skiba et al., 2002; Wu et al., 1982).

## Contextual/Systemic Factors Contributing to Discipline Disproportionality

### School policies and practices

More so than individual student and statistical factors, it is likely that systemic factors have a substantial role in explaining disproportionality. It may be that students who are not perceived to fit behavioral norms of the school—together with staff anxieties to control student behavior—result in inappropriate labeling and discipline of students who are not from the same culture as their predominantly Caucasian teachers (Fenning & Rose, 2007; Monroe, 2005). Relatedly, preferences for European mainstream values among educators may contribute to discipline disproportionality (e.g., Tyler, Boykin, & Walton, 2006). For example, Townsend (2000) discussed how African American students, who often prefer activities that allow them to socialize while completing tasks, may come into conflict with European American preferences for focusing on one task at a time. This incongruence may result in African American students being perceived as insubordinate or oppositional. It also has been suggested that a disproportional lack of proactive or alternative disciplinary options in urban school settings may partially account for overuse of suspension and expulsion (see Fenning & Rose, 2007).

Differential behavioral referrals to the office, and subsequent administrative responses that vary based on student ethnicity, contribute to the long-standing disproportionality (Skiba et al., 2011). At the classroom level, ethnographic research in an ethnically diverse high school, primarily comprising Latino(a), Hmong and Lao students, documented how student verbalizations perceived by teachers as contributing to a loss of behavioral control resulted in the disproportionate referral of ethnic minority students out of the classroom setting (Vavrus & Cole, 2002). The teacher perception of lack of classroom control was the driving force that prompted removal of ethnic minority students rather than actual statements made by the students.

In a related study of school discipline in two large high schools serving primarily African American and Latino(a) students, ethnographic data about staff discussions and decisions about student suspension and expulsion were collected (Casella, 2003). In discipline decisions, ethnic minorities were often labeled as "dangerous" for nonviolent offenses because they were perceived as having the propensity to become dangerous, a term described as "preventative detention." Casella chronicled how the exclusionary discipline decisions made by school staff led to significant challenges for school reentry once students were removed for discipline reasons, and subsequently contributed to a higher probability of ethnic minority students entering the juvenile justice system.

In earlier qualitative research about administrative discipline decisions, researchers videotaped and analyzed interchanges in an inner-city high school discipline office with a population of primarily African American students experiencing poverty and having attendance issues (Bowditch, 1993). The findings revealed that despite the vast majority of referrals being for nonviolent offenses, such as tardiness and classroom defiance, suspension was the most common response applied. There were very few alternatives to exclusionary responses offered in administrative discipline policies. In addition, administrative decisions were impacted by whether the student was perceived as a "good student" or a "trouble-maker." Students of color were the most likely to be labeled as "trouble-makers," based on the perception that they did not possess positive student attributes, such as strong attendance or good grades.

## Societal, historical, and cultural issues

We would argue that the school discipline gap that reflects ethnic disproportionality in discipline referrals and administrative decisions does not exist in a vacuum. Rather, we contend that disproportionate discipline practices reflect larger

US societal and historical norms of institutional racism and discrimination that extend far beyond the walls of 21st century schools (Eitle, 2002, as cited in Artiles, Kozleski, Trent, Osher, & Ortiz, 2010b). For example, beginning with their forcible entry into this country, African Americans were treated inequitably, enduring harsh forms of racism and discrimination. They were denied access to education, and when they were educated it was often in an attempt to bring their behavior and morality in conformance with White expectations (Noguera, 1995). Only very gradually, and with the Civil Rights Movement of the late 1960s and early 1970s, did African Americans gain legal and educational rights. At the same time, even with federal legislative changes stemming from cases such as Brown vs. the Board of Education, biases have remained to this day. For example, urban public schools, which serve primarily ethnic minority populations, tend to provide lower quality instruction and offer inferior educational opportunities compared to schools serving primarily White populations (Kozol, 1991).

In terms of the teaching force that educates our students of color, there is a long-standing paucity of school professionals from under-represented groups, and limited training in culturally relevant educational practices for White majority teachers who do not share the cultural understandings of their pupils (Cartledge & Loe, 2001; Evertson & Weinstein, 2006). Historically, African Americans have rarely been represented in school leadership positions, facilitating the establishment of school culture and expectations revolving around White middle-class norms.

Inequities in the educational opportunities afforded to students of color—including substandard educational conditions, lack of access to high-quality instruction, limited professional role models from similar cultures, and a lack of professional development in culturally competent educational practices—have contributed to the disproportionality we see in our schools with respect to discipline. These sorts of inequities—coupled with larger societal stereotypes perpetuated beyond the school house door through the media and other sources—have set the stage for preconceived biases and notions regarding the status and behaviors of African American students in schools. Disproportionality in discipline is but one example of the larger societal context of inequity and discrimination in education. By examining disproportionality in discipline through a social justice lens in which the larger school and societal context is examined as feeding this long-standing issue, we hope to move toward finding solutions to the issue rather than continuing to document its existence. We next provide a rationale for examining disproprortionality from a social justice perspective.

## Intersection of Social Justice and Discipline

Given the unique issues related to the disenfranchisement of certain students—particularly African American males—through institutionalized school discipline policies and practices, it makes sense to consider the issue using a social justice lens. *Social justice* describes the notion that all individuals and groups should be treated with fairness, respect, and dignity and should be entitled to the resources, opportunities, and protections that schools offer (North, 2006; Shriberg & Fenning, 2009). As a construct, social justice is centered on the notion of recognizing inequities and redistributing resources accordingly. One salient issue in terms of redistribution would be the finding that discipline processes often focus on exclusion from school, which has not been effective for anyone, does not serve its intended purpose of preventing future problems from occurring, and has many well-documented deleterious side-effects, such as entry to prison and school dropout (Sugai & Horner, 2002; Wald & Losen, 2003). As suspension and expulsion are not effective and are associated with many damaging effects, their use is particularly problematic for overrepresented groups and raises the questions of why this inequity is occurring and how it can be addressed. In other words, if being African American and male increases the likelihood that one will be on the receiving end of an ineffective and damaging educational practice, then it is our responsibility as school psychologists to explore why and how to assist schools with changing discriminatory practices. The principles of social justice can facilitate the lens through which we advocate for ethnic minority youth who are disproportionately represented in exclusionary discipline. As school psychologists, we have power through our very roles that may be unearned, consistent with the defining features of social justice (Shriberg, Song, Miranda, & Radliff, Chapter 1, this volume). It is critical that we use our position and our unique access to schools to begin addressing the discipline disproportionality epidemic (Shriberg et al., Chapter 1). In essence, a detrimental practice is being distributed inequitably to a group historically marginalized in our schools. As school psychologists, through our role and status, we have an obligation to address this disparity.

From our perspective, addressing disproportionality in discipline from a social justice orientation means taking a *systemic* approach to examining these questions from a macro level rather than focusing on each individual case (Shriberg & Fenning, 2009). It shifts the focus from looking to internal student factors to explain increased suspensions among ethnic minority students to well-entrenched sociocultural issues and historical barriers. We contend that taking a social justice approach to this long-standing problem means looking at how, as a society, we systematically support the use of exclusionary discipline for some groups more than others. Looking within our entrenched roles in schools may mean grappling with difficult issues of institutional racism and pointing out such instances in our own behavior and that of other school personnel. This is a particularly relevant framework for examining disproportionality, given the absence of evidence suggesting that particular racial groups engage in more severe behaviors that warrant disproportional consequences (e.g., Skiba et al., 2002, 2011). Further supporting such an approach, Imich (1994) and Rausch and Skiba (2004b) found that a small number of schools accounted for a large proportion of school exclusions. While not directly the focus of this chapter, related findings that special education placement of minority students is higher in districts that serve primarily White students offer additional support to the argument that the larger sociocultural context matters when discussing disproportionality (Artiles, Harry, Reschly, & Chinn, 2002).

Taken together, the qualitative and quantitative findings described thus far in this chapter provide support for institutional factors—rather than individual child differences—as contributing to the discipline gap. We would additionally assert that school psychologists have an obligation to call attention to institutional factors, including institutional racism when it occurs, as part of a social justice approach to school discipline.

## Potential Actions from a Social Justice Perspective

A social justice perspective is focused on change and action. Rather than remaining mired in continuing to document the long-standing findings with respect to disproportionality (e.g., does it exist?), this approach begins with examining some of the larger social–cultural institutionalized factors that may contribute to the long-standing disproportionality in discipline statistics. However, an examination of sociocultural factors serves merely as a means to an end, with the ultimate goal of designing solutions to begin addressing the discipline gap. As school psychologists, we often consider the function of behaviors and drive interventions accordingly. Interventions are more likely to be effective if they are tied to the function of behavior (McIntosh, Campbell, Carter, & Dickey, 2009a). It is our perspective that the discipline gap is analogous to functional analysis of behavior in that considerations of factors internal to the student have not been sufficiently helpful in explaining the discipline gap, nor in proposing ways to remedy it (Losen & Skiba, 2010; Skiba & Rausch, 2006). Rather, addressing discipline disproportionality through solutions tied to social contextual factors will more likely tackle the underlying systemic factors by which disproportionality in discipline has been maintained for over four decades (Fenning & Rose, 2007; Skiba & Rausch, 2006). We turn next to a fictitious case study example, drawn from experiences in schools where the authors have worked, to begin illustrating ways in which we can take a social justice perspective in addressing ethnic disproportionality in discipline.

---

### Case Study Example

Mitchell High School is located in the fringes of a large urban area. Approximately 2000 students are enrolled, with an even distribution across grades. The high school is organized by departments, each headed by a chair. Counselors and deans are assigned to grade levels. There are 140 teachers and two school psychologists in the building. One of the psychologists is bilingual (fluent Spanish speaker) and spends a great deal of time conducting assessments. The school is diverse, with 30% of the student population classified as African American, 15% classified as Asian, 35% classified as Hispanic, and 20% classified as White. Approximately 60% of the student population qualifies for free and reduced lunch. Roughly 15% of the students in the building are characterized as English

Language Learners. There is also significant mobility. The high school has not made Adequate Yearly Progress (AYP) for the last several years and is undergoing restructuring as part of a district watch.

Mitchell High School is one of two high schools in a unified district. The partner school, Wright High School, is much less diverse, with its feeder middle school being composed of students from primarily White and Asian families. There are also roughly 2000 students at Wright, about 150 staff, and two school psychologists. Mitchell High School and Wright High School are often in competition for resources and are viewed by the larger community as quite different settings, with the perception that Wright is much more academically rigorous than Mitchell. Families at Wright High School, in general, are much more vocal about the need for academic rigor and successfully lobbied last year for an additional counselor, whose job responsibilities focused specifically on college counseling.

At Mitchell High School, there are several infractions for which staff are unclear as to whether they should refer to the discipline office (e.g., being unprepared for class). At Mitchell last year, there were roughly 2500 discipline referrals to the office. Over 80% of the students in the school generated at least one referral to the office, with 15% of the school population generating the most referrals in the building (six referrals or more). The most common types of referrals were tardiness, class disruption, and improper dress code, as Mitchell High School has a school uniform policy. Suspension was the most common administrative response to discipline infractions, regardless of severity. Students may also receive a suspension if they fail to respond to a lesser consequence, such as serving a detention. Consistent with the literature in the area (e.g., Skiba et al., 2011), there is disproportionality in discipline referrals and administrative consequences of suspension for African American students.

At Wright High School, there are fewer referrals and the perception that most behavioral concerns are "relatively minor in nature." Last year, there were 800 total behavioral referrals. There appear to be slightly different policies in each school as to which behaviors constitute discipline infractions. Students at Wright High School are allowed to use cell phones, for example, in specific designated areas. There is no dress code at Wright High School, so this is not an issue in terms of referrals to the office. Student tardiness tends to be handled within the classroom unless it is perceived as "excessive," at which time a referral might be made to the discipline office.

In both schools, discipline records are kept as part of a larger district-based data warehouse that includes additional data, such as attendance, tardiness, grade information, and credits accrued. It is possible to generate reports that display discipline data by infraction type, month, time, student, ethnicity, gender, grade. However, a request needs to be made to district personnel who maintain the database, and the process takes about a month. In addition, the school staff needs to graph the data if they would like to display them in a visual manner. Therefore, it is difficult for school personnel to have consistent access to these data for continuous review and planning of intervention approaches.

Given this portrait of each school, we could imagine a number of ways in which school psychologists might approach school discipline from a socially just perspective. These avenues include: (a) forming a schoolwide team with a major focus on reviewing schoolwide data, such as discipline referrals, numbers of suspensions and expulsions, academic (e.g., grades in core subjects, on-time to graduate) and attendance data, with a focus on examining whether ethnic disproportionality exists within any of these indicators, (b) facilitating team-based planning for system-level approaches to discipline and school climate, (c) advocating for professional development focused on culturally responsive instructional and discipline practices, and (d) reviewing and modifying school- and district-level discipline policies. Each of these priorities will be examined in depth in the subsequent sections. When considering each action from a social justice perspective, it is critical to remember that social justice is a *process*. In Chapter 1, Shriberg and colleagues remind us that although the goal of "achieving social justice" is an important aspiration, we must be prepared to actively work towards that ideal in an effort to improve unjust situations.

## Focus on Schoolwide Data to Make Decisions

As school psychologists, we are trained as data-based decision-makers. We are at a time within our field when review and use of commonly collected schoolwide data is an expected practice as part of multi-tiered models of academic and behavior support, aligned with RtI (Brown-Chidsey & Steege, 2005). Multi-tiered models of support focus on the delivery and evaluation of scientifically based core instruction, on either the academic or the behavioral side of the equation across multiple tiers, beginning with supports on a universal level for all students, then typically followed by supplemental group and/or individual interventions for those whose needs are not being met at the universal level, based on review of data (Jimerson, Burns, & VanDerHeyden, 2007). Due to the goal of providing high-quality services to *all* students that need them, rather than excluding certain student groups, multi-tiered models of support are aligned with a distributive view of social justice that promotes educational equity (Artiles, Bal, & King Thorius, 2010a).

To facilitate the decision-making process for behavior, inclusive of calling attention to ethnic disproportionality, systematic schoolwide databases have been developed over the past several years. As is illustrated in our fictional case study, it is difficult for a team to effectively use data when the data are difficult to access. One system, Schoolwide Information System (SWIS; May et al., 2003) is an electronic database that is used to systematically collect, report and analyze office disciplinary referrals (ODRs) using a standard protocol. Systematic procedures include training staff in how to define mutually exclusive behavior categories, when to write referrals and ways to generate reports and analyze ODR data (Flannery, Fenning, McGrath Kato, & Bohanon, in press). When these standardized processes are followed and adopted on a schoolwide basis, ODRs, which are already in existence in most schools, can function as valid indices for evaluating the outcomes of universal behavioral schoolwide efforts (Irvin et al., 2006). For example, if 80% or more of students in a school are receiving zero to one ODRs, roughly 10–15% of students are receiving two to five, and 5% of students are receiving six or more referrals, then these data, in general, indicate that the universal schoolwide systems of support that are in place in a building are fairly robust (Clonan, McDougal, Clark, & Davison, 2007; McIntosh, Chard, Boland, & Horner, 2006). In the illustrative case study, Mitchell High School appears to be a setting in which behavioral practices that focus on teaching expectations prior to an infraction are not in place because of the high percentage of students who have *at least one referral* to the office. In a situation like this, it is unlikely that schoolwide prevention-oriented practices focused on teaching behaviors before a problem occurs are in place. In addition, a relatively small percentage of students are generating the *highest number of referrals*, which might indicate that a team would focus on how to intervene as early as possible in the year with this population of students, either through group or individual supports (or both) after addressing system-level issues focused on making expectations explicit for all.

Of particular importance for considering whether particular sub-groups are treated equitably are the capabilities of systems such as SWIS to track referrals and consequences by ethnicity in an expedient manner. However, despite the capabilities of the SWIS database to run behavioral referral reports disaggregated by ethnicity, it is estimated that only 14% of users consistently access the report (Vincent, 2008, as cited in Vincent, Randall, Cartledge, Tobin, & Swain-Bradway, 2011). While SWIS is a relatively inexpensive system, if its adoption is cost-prohibitive, school psychologists can help to align the school discipline referral system with SWIS categories/fields (e.g., type of behavior, location, date/time, student, number of referrals; see www.swis.org/index.php?page=getSWISOverview for more information). In the case of Mitchell High School, it would be important to systematically track under what conditions ethnic minority students end up more frequently in the discipline office and the administrative response. This way, schools can more systematically evaluate the ways that consequences are being used, for what type of infraction and for which subgroups in the school. When interventions are put into place, schools can track whether they are successful based on whether disproportionality issues are diminished. We feel that having these data more readily available than what we experience in many schools has the potential to enhance justice and fairness to diverse students since decisions are informed by data rather than other factors (Li & Vazquez-Nuttall, 2009).

In addition to system-wide review of behavioral data, another source of important information would be schoolwide attendance and academic data. Academics, attendance, and discipline are highly interrelated. Schoolwide interventions could focus on improving not only behavior, but attendance and academics as well. Particularly for our marginalized students, school success is facilitated when students are present and not excluded through discipline or other means (Ward & Burke, 2004). Longitudinal work in inner-city schools documents that academic performance is correlated with student attendance; interventions designed to improve schoolwide attendance are associated with improved academic performance markers in schools and vice versa (Madden et al, 1992). Within the discipline realm, most school responses focus on excluding students through suspension and expulsion, which contributes to loss of instructional minutes, which in turn is associated with further academic challenges for students who are likely to have academic problems in the first place (Morrison, & D'Incau, 1997; Skiba & Rausch, 2006). Ironically, schoolwide interventions meant to address attendance issues may be counteracted by school discipline policies that are primarily equated with removal of students from school (Fenning & Bohanon, 2006; Skiba & Rausch, 2006). Therefore, an integrated approach, by which attendance, academics and discipline data are reviewed, would help to paint a complete picture of the efficacy of the schoolwide policies and practices in place to address each of these domains, either separately or in unison. School psychologists are in a unique position to advocate for marginalized students, and having multiple sources of data will allow for those in the school to make better decisions about the whole student with the goal of keeping our children in school rather than controlling them through discipline means or forcing them out through our restrictive policies.

Given the relative ease of access to disaggregated behavioral and academic screening data, along with the long-standing issues of ethnic disproportionality in both special education and discipline (Artiles et al., 2010b; Children's Defense Fund, 1975; National Education Association/National Association of School Psychologists, 2007; Skiba et al., 2011), it is surprising that more widespread use of these disaggregated data has not occurred. This raises the question as to why schools are not prioritizing the issue of culturally competent instruction and discipline practice, given the disenfranchised condition of our most vulnerable students of color who have historically experienced discrimination from within and without our school walls, in part through the policies we have enacted. As school psychologists, we can address this social justice issue by helping schools to begin the difficult process of asking questions about schoolwide and disaggregated academic, behavioral, and attendance/tardy data. When databases are not available, particularly in urban settings, we can use our skills as part of a data team to create and utilize commonly collected data in a purposeful manner. Understanding how students of color are doing within a particular system is paramount to designing responses to meet their needs in an equitable fashion that breaks from our long-standing history of exclusion, either through suspension within discipline policies or through placement in more restrictive educational settings (Skiba & Rausch, 2006; Skiba, Poloni-Staudinger, Gallini, Simmons, & Feggins-Azziz, 2006).

In our example of Mitchell High School, if we found that 80% or more of students are generating zero to one office discipline referrals, with no disproportionality in referrals for students who are White and Hispanic, but that students who are African American are being referred at a much higher rate, and are generating over 80% of all referrals in the school, then we would want to look at these data and respond accordingly with further inquiries. For example, what type of offenses are students who are African American being referred for? Are they being referred for similar or different infractions than their peers? Students who are African American tend to be referred for subjective offenses, such as disrespect (Skiba et al., 2011). If we have information about the type of offenses, and location, we might want to clarify expectations for referrals, as well as teach all students the behavioral expectations in particular settings (Vincent et al., 2011). If we have attendance and tardiness data, our decisions could be facilitated by looking at these data as well in terms of overall base rates for the school, and then such information could be disaggregated by race/ethnicity.

We can ask a multitude of questions by having data at our disposal that are provided in a workable and systemic format for all students and for particular subgroups of students that may be on the receiving end of instruction that is not meeting their needs. We have posed a few questions to potentially ask about universal/schoolwide data, but we can follow a similar process at the group and individual levels in terms of how our school-based interventions are faring overall and how they might be working for specific students who have been identified as needing more intensive interventions. As school psychologists, we have the training to lead this discussion and to help teams with facilitating decisions, asking difficult questions that pertain to our school, and then proceeding to act on these data in productive and informed ways. In many schools, school psychologists are already in a leadership position as team facilitators who routinely use data to evaluate interventions across tiers of support. Prioritizing the use of disaggregated data will hopefully move us toward shining a light on this significant social justice issue and moving forward with solutions.

## System-Level Approaches to Discipline and School Climate

School psychologists can play an integral role in using schoolwide data that is now more accessible than ever in schools as part of procedures to plan, implement, and evaluate universal schoolwide supports to begin meaningfully addressing the discipline gap. Our premise throughout this chapter is that school contextual factors, such as school discipline policies and a mismatch between student and school personnel cultural style, likely contribute to the pervasive issue of ethnic disproportionality in discipline. Our traditional approach of looking toward factors internal to the student, which we are so wont to do in terms of applying an "internal deficit" model, has been consistently disproven for many years, particularly as an example of the discipline gap (Skiba & Rausch, 2006). Therefore, we argue that we will have more success if we put our energy and efforts into supporting prevention-oriented universal (schoolwide) methods of support that meet the needs of all students, and evaluating the impact of such efforts on all students, as well as groups of students who have been historically marginalized. Two such efforts have received attention in recent years: Schoolwide Positive Behavior Support (SWPBS) and Restorative Justice (RJ).

## Schoolwide Positive Behavior Support

SWPBS has been described as a behavioral example of the multi-tiered approaches of RtI (Sandomierski et al., 2007; Sugai & Horner, 2007). While data specifically supporting SWPBS as a way of addressing ethnic disproportionality in discipline are yet to be realized, the tenets of this universal discipline practice share a number of theoretical underpinnings with what might be termed "culturally responsive practice," as both approaches consider the cultural context and the instructional environment as important considerations for intervention (Vincent et al., 2011). For example, SWPBS should be carefully planned by multiple stakeholders in the school and community to ensure that efforts are adapted to local needs, values, and cultural perspectives (Jones, Caravaca, Cizek, Horner, & Vincent, 2006). Despite this potential alignment with SJ and culturally responsive practice, it should also be noted that even with involvement of multiple stakeholders, SWPBS runs the risk of relying on experts to facilitate the process, something that may be incompatible with bottom-up approaches more consistent with the voices of the marginalized. It is, therefore, very important for stakeholders within the school, such as the students themselves, parents, teachers, related service staff and community members, to be the ones to determine, select and adopt expectations that meet the needs of their building and overall school culture. In addition, perceptions about SWPBS procedures may vary widely between teachers (Frey, Lee Park, Browne-Ferrigno, & Korfhage, 2010), which could potentially manifest in differences in the match between the goals of SWPBS and teachers' actual implementation of culturally responsive practices. In other words, it is very important in practice to listen carefully to those who will be in the throes of implementing SWPBS, particularly in high schools similar to those depicted in the case study. Otherwise, we run the risk of failing to achieve buy-in among key stakeholders and have a system that is intended to be proactive and prevention-oriented, but inadvertently becomes a system based on control of student behavior.

While preliminary in nature, case study evaluations of SWPBS in urban settings are associated with positive outcomes when implemented with fidelity. For example, Bohanon and colleagues (2006, cited in Fenning & Sharkey, 2012) found that implementation of the universal components of SWPBS in one urban high school with a student population composed primarily of Latino(a) and European American students was associated with reductions in office disciplinary referrals. In the same year, Lassen, Steele, & Sailor (2006, cited in Fenning & Sharkey, 2012) reported that universal applications of SWPBS in an inner-city middle school was associated with reductions in office discipline referrals, and suspensions as well as increases in standardized math and reading scores.

More recently, researchers have become interested in ways that SWPBS can be merged with culturally responsive practice. For example, Vincent et al. (2011), based on a review of the literature on culturally responsive practice and SWBPS, recommended that schools consider ways to employ SWPBS as a framework for intervention due to its focus on systems, data, practice and outcomes but additionally employ three major components as part of culturally responsive implementation. These components include a focus on examining disproportionality in relation to implementation, evaluating training materials and tools in terms of sensitivity to cultural responsiveness, and prioritizing the voices of students, parents, and staff from culturally and linguistically diverse backgrounds. Support for the third component is found in a related study, in which Jones et al. (2006) involved students, families, and the larger community, primarily those from Native American backgrounds, in the development of schoolwide behavioral expectations and lesson plans when implementing universal SWPBS in a New Mexico elementary school. The history of key figures in the Native American community was integrated into the development of the instructional materials through citing examples of perseverance into the schoolwide expectations.

Consistent findings documenting whether the integration of universal SWPBS and culturally responsive practices works to meet the needs of the students and families served in school, particularly as it relates to the discipline gap, are yet to be realized. We see a concentrated effort on this type of work among school psychology practitioners and researchers as a priority. We must move from admiring the issue of disproportionality to enacting data-based solutions. There is simply not sufficient application of approaches tied to universal behavior support systems, aligned with culturally relevant practices across multiple settings and with students from a range of diverse cultures and backgrounds. Prioritizing the development, implementation, and evaluation of prevention-oriented efforts to address disproportionality is critical, and we believe a step in the direction of acting through a social justice lens. However, such efforts must be sensitive to local factors. For example, Warren et al. (2003) found that "typical" SWPBS initiatives may be insufficient to meet the unique challenges facing urban schools, which may require systemic schoolwide improvement efforts and coordination of efforts across multiple environments as prerequisites to set the stage for effective SWPBS implementation. In addition, case study evaluations of SWPBS in urban settings (e.g, Bohanon et al., 2006; Warren et al., 2003) reported in the literature have been supported by external technical assistance and/or funding, which is not likely to exist in most urban environments and counter to an approach that is bottom-up and grassroots.

Relatedly, just as we have a long way to go in terms of developing culturally relevant instructional practices for behavior and academics, it is also recommended that evaluation of outcomes go beyond what we typically find in the literature related to universal SWPBS applications (Horner et al., 2009). While it is important to evaluate overt measures of behavior, such as office disciplinary referrals and academic benchmarks for schools, we also feel, from a socially just perspective, that it is important to consider the impact of universal schoolwide efforts on other issues that students face in schools, such as their sense of belongingness, if the school is a welcoming and comfortable environment, and if the school climate is one of acceptance for all. These additional issues should be evaluated, from the perspective of students who come from all environments, as part of an evaluation process for prevention-oriented supports to address behavior as we move away from more punitive and exclusionary procedures in schools. Hearing the voice of the students themselves in terms of desired outcomes is an important component of moving towards more socially just practice. Focusing solely on desired outcomes of school personnel may put what are intended to be positive alternatives to traditional suspension, such as SWPBS, at risk of focusing only on external control of student behavior (Bear, 2009). School psychologists can be integral in facilitating a team that considers a broader range of foci when implementing approaches to addressing discipline from a socially just perspective and broadening the evaluation of outcomes beyond externalized behaviors captured in office discipline referrals as a primary method of evaluating SWPBS and other related schoolwide discipline efforts (McIntosh, Campbell, Carter, & Zumbo, 2009b).

## Restorative justice

RJ is another systems-wide approach that holds promise for creating supportive environments that facilitate positive behavior (Sumner, Silverman, & Frampton, 2010). RJ is a theory of justice undergirded by the notions of student responsibility and the sustainability of relationships, rather than retribution for misbehavior (Sumner et al., 2010). RJ seeks to create safe and supportive schools communities that—rather than relying on exclusionary discipline to address misbehavior—encourage students to take responsibility for their actions in an attempt to prevent future similar behaviors. For example, this may involve students repairing the harm caused by their behavior.

RJ is aligned with a social justice perspective in several ways. First, it focuses on protecting the rights, opportunities, and safety of victims of harm. RJ models also attempt to minimize conditions that would result in reoffending and empower the student offender to avoid similar problems in the future (Sumner et al., 2010). RJ promotes individual responsibility in the student who engaged in the problem behavior, but also focuses on viewing problem behaviors within their social context (Marshall, 1999, as cited in Littlechild, 2011) and harnessing the power of the larger community in finding solutions (Wearmouth, Mckinney, and Glynn, 2007). RJ also is congruent with Shriberg, Song, Miranda, and Radliff's (Chapter 1, this volume) notion of doing things *with* and not *for* others, by providing student offenders with opportunities to take responsibility for their actions and remedy them.

The Dignity in Schools Campaign (DSC) is one example of an initiative consistent with RJ practices. In essence, the organization's mission is to challenge the systemic problems related to exclusion from schools, advocate for the rights of all children to be treated with dignity, and promote alternatives to zero-tolerance and school exclusion (Dignity in Schools Campaign, 2011). The Alliance for Educational Justice (AEJ, 2011) is another group that seeks to improve educational justice. These may be organizations that school psychologists can turn to for information as they work towards every child being treated with dignity and reduce the overrepresentation of marginalized groups in suspension and expulsions.

At this time, RJ has strong theoretical appeal; however, empirical data supporting the effectiveness of RJ are limited. We hope that the research base examining the outcomes of these and similar RJ initiatives will continue to expand, so that we can better understand how these practices influence student behavior and school disciplinary practices. Some of the initial findings in this area are promising. For example, Sumner et al. (2010) reported case study results of a single school implementing RJ in California. The researchers concluded that RJ strengthened relationships at the school; helped students and adults deal with community violence; and resulted in positive perceptions from students, parents, and educators (Sumner et al., 2010). In addition, during the implementation of RJ, suspensions decreased by 87%, although the exact contribution of RJ is unknown due to other changes documented during implementation (i.e., a new principal and reduced student enrollment; Sumner et al., 2010). An evaluation of an RJ approach in a youth residential care facility (Littlechild, 2011), and another in Scottish schools (McCluskey et al., 2008) have also yielded positive outcomes.

In the face of this limited but promising research base, practicing school psychologists could conduct program evaluations of RJ that might be in place in their schools (Sharkey & Fenning, 2012). Also, when planning or implementing RJ initiatives, school psychologists should keep in mind several features that research suggests may facilitate effective implementation. For example, McCluskey et al. (2008) found that restorative practices had the most impact when school staff were willing to reflect on their interactions and values as well as when there was visible commitment, enthusiasm, modeling, and professional development provided by building leadership. In addition, Wearmouth et al. (2007) found that implementation of RJ requires substantial planning and deliberation, and that schools must learn to be responsive to families and communities rather than completely controlling the process. Finally, Reimer (2011) revealed that having the necessary structures and cultural systems in place to support RJ is essential, even in schools where there is a personal commitment from teachers.

## Professional Development on Culturally Responsive Practices

Earlier in this chapter, we provided some qualitative data that documented the likely contribution of behavioral interpretations and mismatches among the cultural understandings of students and school personnel (Casella, 2003; Vavrus & Cole, 2002). To move in the direction of more culturally responsive behavioral and academic support of students and to address the issue of discipline disproportionality, professional development is necessary (Vincent et al., 2011). As school psychologists, who largely come from European backgrounds, we also need to participate in our own professional development and exploration of biases that we might bring to the table in terms of cultural understandings. As discussed in Chapter 1, knowing oneself and constantly engaging in self-reflection about one's biases and growth is a critical aspect of being a social justice change agent. In addition, we often are in leadership roles and spend significant time with administrators and others who make discipline decisions. Through the privilege we have within our professional role in schools, we can advocate for professional development in culturally responsive teaching (Ladson-Billings, 1994). For example, as Ladson-Billings (1994) articulates, culturally relevant teaching focuses on adapting one's lessons to reflect the community and culture of the students in the classroom. Student-driven instruction, rather than that directed by the teacher, could entail cooperative learning and collaborative projects that focus on issues important to the culture and community of those in the classroom. Teachers need to gain an understanding of the cultures represented in the classroom in order to do this effectively (Ladson-Billings, 1994).

Applied to discipline, qualitative analysis of classroom interchanges supports the notion that classroom discipline exchanges resulting in the removal of ethnic minority students may be based on cultural misunderstandings of communication styles rather than the behavior of the student (Vavrus & Cole, cited in Fenning & Rose, 2007). School psychologists can advocate for professional development for themselves and other educators to gain a better understanding of culturally based language and communication style. Listening to student and family voices from a range of cultural backgrounds can help us to establish a positive school culture that is inclusive and respectful.

In order to effect powerful change that results in truly understanding children from different backgrounds and treating them fairly and effectively, professional development should be an ongoing exercise rather than a one-time event. Applied to our fictional case study example, the district could support initiatives in which both Mitchell High School and Wright High School receive professional development that is aligned with understanding the larger community that is served. Helping each school to clearly delineate its priorities for the education of its youth and then supporting interventions to meet these needs would be important. District and building support of systematic databases would allow for an evaluation of the efforts associated with professional development. In addition, professional development should allow multiple opportunities and avenues for learning, self-reflecting, modeling, and application to promote self-awareness, cultural awareness, and socially just instructional practices.

## Reviewing and Modifying School- and District-Level Discipline Policies

Finally, we see the role of a school psychologist as having a hand in advocating for prevention-oriented discipline policies for all students. As has been described elsewhere, suspension remains the most widely used consequence for any behavioral infraction, including nonviolent ones (Fenning et al., 2008; Skiba & Rausch, 2006). We have also documented early the ill effects of using suspension and its lack of efficacy. It is quite a defensible conclusion that suspension does not work and because ethnic disproportionality in disciplinary consequences has existed for over four decades, our students of color are more likely to be on the receiving end of an unjust school practice that is simply ineffective. We certainly advocate for more prevention-oriented procedures that are aligned with examining the broader school environmental context in which behavioral issues emerge. This includes our focus on universal schoolwide behavioral applications and professional development for all school professionals, including school psychologists, to gain cultural awareness and understanding of culturally relevant instructional practices.

However, while in practice we are hopefully moving toward more prevention-oriented approaches, what remains in formal written discipline policies is punitive procedures that focus on suspension, even for minor behaviors such as tardiness (Fenning et al., 2008). We would argue that a role for school psychologists in developing and enacting just discipline practices for all students, but most notably students of color who find their way disproportionately in the web of exclusionary discipline, is to advocate for written policies that contain the prevention-oriented schoolwide approaches to which we aspire (Fenning & Rose, 2007; Skiba & Rausch, 2006). It makes no sense to plan and implement prevention-oriented schoolwide approaches, yet maintain written discipline policies that have none of these procedures, and are focused exclusively on punishment. As an example extrapolated from our case study, tardies are handled differently across buildings—whereas in Mitchell High School tardies are behavioral infractions treated as referrals and likely suspension, in Wright High School tardies seem to be interpreted on a case-by-case basis and more likely to be handled in the classroom. It is possible that ethnic minority students who are more likely to attend Mitchell High School end up with referrals and suspensions because of the policies in the particular school they attend.

An approach in which school building and district discipline policy reflects prevention-oriented practices will involve advocacy and consultation. For example, school board members and attorneys are typically the ones to set discipline policy and school psychologists will need to collaborate and collectively examine what the literature says about the futile role of suspension, the disproportionality issue and the lack of efficacy for suspension in general. While we might dialogue in our writings on this topic, we are implored to explore the issue of discipline disproportionality with those who are in positions of authority to make such decisions. Often, we collaborate with teachers and administrators; however, in the case of discipline, we need to think more broadly in terms of key decision-makers, which expand to the larger community context in which schools are situated, operate, and receive funding.

## Conclusion

Our concluding comments focus on the need to recognize that ethnic disproportionality in discipline is a long-standing and well-documented discipline issue (Children's Defense Fund, 1975; Skiba et al., 2011). Conceptualizing disproportionality from a focus on the internal child has not got us very far in designing ways to remedy the situation. We argue in this chapter that the larger historical context and school contextual context through which disproportionality has been allowed to exist is evidence that we need to take another approach: one that is enacted through a social justice lens. This is an ideal time to turn away from an individually focused approach to one that is contextually based, given the shift in education to multi-tiered models of support that focus on systems, contextual factors, data and outcomes (Horner et al., 2009; Jimerson et al., 2007). Using an illustrative case study, we highlighted some ways in which school psychologists can begin to engage in action through a social justice lens: collecting and reviewing of schoolwide data, planning and implementing system level approaches to school discipline and school climate, promoting professional development in culturally competent practices within our profession and for our education colleagues, and integrating prevention-oriented approaches into formal building and district policy. Taking a social justice perspective and examining difficult issues of long-standing racism and bias when having an honest discussion about the discipline gap will hopefully move us further to a plan of action rather than continuing to document the existence of the problem (Skiba et al., 2011).

## References

Alliance for Educational Justice (2011). Retrieved from www.allianceforeducationaljustice.org

American Psychological Association Task Force on Zero Tolerance Policies (2008). Are zero tolerance policies effective in the schools? An evidentiary review and recommendations. *American Psychologist, 63* (9), 852–862.

Artiles, A.J., Bal. A., & King Thorius, K. (2010a). Back to the future: A critique of Response to Intervention's social justice views. *Theory into Practice, 49,* 250–257.

Artiles, A. J., Harry, B., Reschly, D. J., & Chinn, R C. (2002). Over-identification of students of color in special education: A critical overview. *Multicultural Perspectives, 4* (1), 3–10.

Artiles, A.J., Kozleski, E.B., Trent, S.C., Osher, D., & Ortiz, A. (2010b). Justifying and explaining disproportionality, 1968–2008: A critique of underlying views of culture. *Exceptional Children, 76* (3), 279–299.

Aud, S., Fox, M., and KewalRamani, A. (2010). *Status and trends in the education of racial and ethnic groups* (NCES 2010–015). US Department of Education, National Center for Education Statistics. Washington, DC: US Government Printing Office.

Barrett, S. P., Bradshaw, C. P., & Lewis-Palmer, T. (2008). Maryland statewide PBIS initiative: Systems, evaluation, and next steps. *Journal of Positive Behavior Interventions, 10* (2), 105–114.

Bear, G. G. (2009). The positive in positive models of discipline. In R. Gilman, E. S. Huebner, & M. Furlong (Eds.), *Handbook of positive psychology* (pp. 305–321). New York, NY: Routledge.

Bear, G. (2010). *School discipline and self-discipline : A practical guide to promoting prosocial student behavior.* New York, NY: Guilford Press.

Bohanon, H., Fenning, P., Carney, K. L., Minnis-Kim, M.J., Anderson-Harriss, S., Moroz, K., et al. (2006). School-wide application of positive behavior support in an urban high school: A case study. *Journal of Positive Behavior Interventions, 8,* 127–140.

Bowditch, C. (1993). Getting rid of troublemakers: High school disciplinary procedures and the production of dropouts. *Social Problems, 40,* 493–509.

Brown-Chidsey, R. & Steege, M. W. (2005). *Response to intervention: Principles and strategies for effective practice.* New York, NY: Guilford Press.

Brown v. Board of Education of Topeka (1954) *347 U.S. 483.*

Cartledge, G., & Loe, S. A. (2001). Cultural diversity and social skill instruction. *Exceptionality, 9,* 33–46.

Casella, R. (2003). Punishing dangerousness through preventive detention: Illustrating the institutional link between school and prison. In J. Wald and D. J. Losen (Eds.), *New directions for youth development: Deconstructing the school-to-prison pipeline* (pp. 55–89). San Francisco, CA: Jossey-Bass.

Cavadino, M., & Dignan, J. (2006). Penal policy and political economy. *Criminology & Criminal Justice, 6,* 435–456.

Children's Defense Fund. (1975). *School suspensions: Are they helping children?* Cambridge, MA: Washington Research Project.

Chobot, R. B., & Garibaldi, A. (1982). In-school alternatives to suspension: A description of ten school district programs. *Urban Review, 14* (4), 317–336.

Clonan, S. M., McDougal, J. L., Clark, K., & Davison, S. (2007). Use of office discipline referrals in school-wide decision making: A practical example. *Psychology in the Schools, 44* (1), 19–27.

Costenbader, V., & Markson, S. (1998). School suspension: A study with secondary school students. *Journal of School Psychology, 36* (1), 59–82.

DeRidder, L. M. (1990). The impact of school suspensions and expulsions on dropping out. *Educational Horizons, 68,* 153–157.

Dignity in Schools Campaign. (2011). Retrieved from www.dignityinschools.org

Doll, B., & Cummings, J.A. (2008). *Transforming school mental health services: Population-based approaches to promoting the competency and wellness of all children.* Thousand Oaks, CA: Corwin Press and the National Association of School Psychologists.

Eitle, T. M. (2002). Special education or racial segregation: Understanding variation in the representation of black students in educable mentally handicapped programs. *Sociological Quarterly, 43,* 575–605.

Ekstrom, R. B., Goertz, M. E., Pollack, J. M., & Rock, D. A. (1986). Who drops out of high school and why? Findings from a national study. *Teachers College Record, 87,* 357–373.

Evertson, C.M. & Weinstein, C.S. (Eds.) (2006). *Handbook of classroom management: Research, practice and contemporary issues.* Mahwah, NJ: Lawrence Erlbaum Associates.

Farmer, C. D. (1996). Proactive alternatives to school suspension: Reclaiming children and youth. *Journal of Emotional and Behavioral Problems, 5* (1), 47–51.

Fenning, P., & Bohanon, H. (2006). Schoolwide discipline polices: An analysis of the discipline code of conduct. In C. M. Evertson & C. S. Weinstein (Eds.), *Handbook of classroom management: Research, practice and contemporary issues.* Mahwah, NJ: Lawrence Erlbaum Associates.

Fenning, P., Golomb, S., Gordon, V., Kelly, M., Scheinfield, R., Morello, T., et al. (2008). Written discipline policies used by administrators: Do we have sufficient tools of the trade? *Journal of School Violence, 7* (2), 123–146.

Fenning, P. McArdle, L., Wilson, R., Horwitz, A., Morello, T., Golomb, S., et al. (2010). Schoolwide discipline policies: An analysis of the past, present and future. in J. E. Warnick, K. Warnick, & A. Laffoon (Eds.), *Educational policy and practice: The good, the bad, and the pseudoscience. Volume 1: Educational Theory and Policy* (pp. 67–82). New York, NY: Nova Science Publishers.

Fenning, P., & Rose, J. (2007). Overrepresentation of African American students in exclusionary discipline: The role of policy. *Urban Education, 42*, 536–559.

Fenning, P. & Sharkey, J. D. (2012). Addressing discipline disproportionality with positive behavior support. In A. L. Noltemeyer & C. S. Mcloughlin (Eds.) *Disproportionality in education and special education*. Springfield, IL: Charles C. Thomas.

Flannery, K. B., Fenning, P., McGrath Kato, M., & Bohanon, H. (in press). A descriptive study of office disciplinary referrals in high schools. *Journal of Emotional and Behavioral Disorders*. doi: 10.1177/1063426611419512

Florida State Department of Education. (1995). *Florida School Discipline Study: 1994 Juvenile Justice Reform Act*. Tallahassee, FL: Florida State Department of Education.

Frey, A. J., Lee Park, K., Browne-Ferrigno, T., & Korfhage, T.L. (2010). The social validity of program-wide positive behavior support. *Journal of Positive Behavior Interventions, 12*, 222–235.

Garibaldi, A. M. (1992). Educating and motivating African American males to succeed. *Journal of Negro Education, 61*, 4–11.

Gersch, I., & Nolan, A. (1994). Exclusions: What the children think. *Educational Psychology in Practice, 10*, 35–45.

Greenberg, B. (1974). School vandalism: Its effects and paradoxical solutions. *Crime Prevention Review, 1*, 105.

Gun Free Schools Act (1994).*20 U.S.C. Chapter 70 Sec 8921.*

Horner, R., Sugai, G., Smolkowski, K., Eber, L., Nakasato, J., Todd, A., et al. (2009). A randomized, wait-list controlled effectiveness trial assessing school-wide positive behavior support in elementary schools. *Journal of Positive Behavior Interventions, 11*, 133–145.

Hyman, I. A. (1997). *School discipline and school violence: The teacher variance approach*. Boston, MA: Allyn and Bacon.

Hyman, I., Mahon, M., Cohen, I., Snook, P., Britton, G., & Lurkis, L, (2004). Student alienation syndrome: The other side of school violence. In J. C. Conoley & A. P. Goldstein (Eds.) *School violence and intervention: A practical handbook* (2nd ed., pp. 483–506). New York, NY: Guilford Press.

Imich, A. J. (1994). Exclusions from school: Current trends and issues. *Educational Research, 36* (1), 3–11.

Individuals with Disabilities Education Act (IDEA) of 2004. (2004). *Public Law*, 108–446.

Irvin, L. K., Horner, R. H., Ingram, K., Todd, A.W., Sugai, G., Sampson, N. K, et al. (2006). Using office discipline referral data for decision-making about student behavior in elementary and middle schools: An empirical investigation of validity. *Journal of Positive Behavior Interventions, 8* (1), 10–23.

Jimerson, S., Burns, M. K., & VanDerHeyden, A. (Eds.). (2007). *Handbook of response to intervention: The science and practice of assessment and intervention*. New York, NY: Springer.

Jones, C., Caravaca, L., Cizek, S., Horner, R. H., & Vincent, C. G. (2006). Culturally responsive schoolwide positive behavior support. *Multiple Voices for Ethnically Diverse Exceptional Learners, 9*, 108–119.

Kozol, J. (1991). *Savage inequalities: Children in America's schools*. New York, NY: Crown Publishers.

Krezmien, M. P., Leone, P. E., & Achilles, G. M. (2006). Suspension, race, and disability: Analysis of statewide practices and reporting. *Journal of Emotional and Behavioral Disorders, 14* (4), 217–226.

Ladson-Billings, G. (1994). *The dreamkeepers: Successful teachers of African American children*. San Francisco, CA: Jossey-Bass Publishers.

Lassen, S. R., Steele, M. M., & Sailor, W. (2006). The relationship of schoolwide positive behavior support to academic achievement in an urban middle school. *Psychology in the Schools, 43*, 701–712.

Lewis, T. J., & Sugai, S. (1999). Effective behavior support: A systems approach to proactive schoolwide management. *Focus on Exceptional Children, 31* (6), 1–24.

Li, C., & Vazquez-Nuttall, E. (2009). School consultants as agents of social justice for multicultural children and families. *Journal of Educational and Psychological Consultation, 19*, 26–44.

Littlechild, B. (2011). Conflict resolution, restorative justice approaches and bullying in young people's residential units. *Children & Society, 25*, 47–58.

Losen, D. J., & Skiba, R. J. (2010). *Suspended education: Urban middle schools in crisis.* Retrieved May 30, 2011 from http://civilrightsproject.ucla.edu/research/k-12-education/school-discipline/suspended-education-urban-middle-schools-in-crisis/Suspended-Education_FINAL-2.pdf

MacMillan, D. L., & Reschly, D. J. (1998). Overrepresentation of minority students: The case for greater specificity or reconsideration of the variables examined. *Journal of Special Education, 32*, 15–24.

Madden, N. A., Slavin, R. E., Karweit, N. L., Dolan, L., & Wasik, B. A. (1992). *Success for all: Longitudinal effects of a restructuring program for inner city elementary schools.* Center for Research on Effective Schooling for Disadvantaged Students. Baltimore, MD: Abell Foundation and Washington, DC: Office of Educational Research and Improvement.

May, S., Ard, W., III, Todd, A. W., Horner, R. H., Glasgow, A., & Sugai, G. (2003). *School-wide Information System* [Computer software]. Eugene, OR: Educational and Community Supports. Retrieved from www.swis.org

Mayer, G. R. (1995). Preventing antisocial behavior in the schools. *Journal of Applied Behavior Analysis, 28*, 467–478.

McCluskey, G., Lloyd, G., Kane, J., Riddell, S., Stead, J., & Weedon, E. (2008). Can restorative practices in schools make a difference? *Educational Review, 60*, 405–417.

McIntosh, K., Campbell, A. L., Carter, D. R., & Dickey, C. R. (2009). Differential effects of a tier two behavior intervention based on function of problem behavior. *Journal of Positive Behavior Interventions, 11* (2), 82–93.

McIntosh, K., Campbell, A. L., Carter, D. R., & Zumbo, B. D. (2009). Concurrent validity of office discipline referrals and cut points used in school-wide positive behavior support. *Behavior Disorders, 34* (2), 100–113.

McIntosh, K., Chard, D. J., Boland, J. B., & Horner, R. H. (2006). Demonstration of combined efforts in school-wide academic and behavioral systems and incidence of reading and behavior challenges in early elementary grades. *Journal of Positive Behavior Interventions, 8*, 146–154.

Monroe, C. R. (2005). Understanding the discipline gap through a cultural lens: Implications for the education of African American children. *Intercultural Education, 16*, 317–330.

Morrison, G. M. & D'Incau, B. (1997). The web of zero tolerance: Characteristics of students who are recommended for expulsion from school. *Education and Treatment of Children, 20*, 316–335.

National Education Association/National Association of School Psychologists. (2007). *Truth in labeling: Disproportionality in special education.* Washington, DC: NEA/NASP.

National Institute of Education. (1978). *Violent schools—safe schools: The safe school study report to the congress.* Washington, DC: Superintendent of Documents.

Noguera, P. A. (1995). Preventing and producing violence: A critical analysis of responses to school violence. *Harvard Educational Review, 65*, 189–212.

Noltemeyer, A., & Mcloughlin, C. S. (2010a). Patterns of exclusionary discipline by school typology, ethnicity, and their interaction. *Perspectives on Urban Education, 7,* 27–40.

Noltemeyer, A. L. & Mcloughlin, C. S. (2010b). Exclusionary discipline: Changes in disproportionality over time. *International Journal of Special Education, 25* (1), 59–70.

North, C. E. (2006). More than words? Delving into the substantive meaning(s) of "social justice" in education. *Review of Educational Research, 76,* 507–536.

OSEP Center on Positive Behavior Interventions and Supports. (2004). *Schoolwide positive behavior support implementers' blueprint and self-assessment* (H326S980003). Eugene, OR: OSEP.

Planty, M., Hussar, W., Snyder, T., Kena, G., KewalRamani, A., Kemp, J., et al. (2009). *The condition of education 2009* (NCES 2009–081). National Center for Education Statistics, Institute of Education Sciences. Washington, DC: US Department of Education.

Raffaele Mendez, L. M., & Knoff, H. M. (2003). Who gets suspended from school and why: A demographic analysis of schools and disciplinary infractions in a large school district. *Education and Treatment of Children, 26* (1), 30–51.

Rausch, M. K., & Skiba, R. (2004a). *Disproportionality in school discipline among minority students in Indiana: Description and analysis.* Children Left Behind Policy Briefs. Supplementary Analysis 2-A. Bloomington, IN: Center for Evaluation and Education Policy (ERIC Document Reproduction Service No. ED488897).

Rausch, M. K., & Skiba, R. (2004b). *Unplanned outcomes: Suspensions and expulsions in Indiana.* Bloomington, IN: Center for Evaluation and Education Policy.

Reimer, K. (2011). An exploration of the implementation of restorative justice in an Ontario public school. *Canadian Journal of Educational Administration and Policy, 119,* 1–42.

Reyes, A. H. (2006). *Discipline, Achievement, & Race: Is Zero Tolerance the Answer?* Lanham, MD: Rowman & Littlefield Education.

Safer, D. J. (1986). Nonpromotion correlates and outcomes at different grade levels. *Journal of Learning Disabilities, 19,* 500–503.

Safer, D., Heaton, R., & Parker, F. (1981). A behavioral program for disruptive junior high students: Results and follow-up. *Journal of Abnormal Child Psychology, 9,* 483–494.

Sandomierski, T., Kincaid, D., & Algozzine, B. (2007). Response to intervention and positive behavior support: Brothers from different mothers or sisters from different misters? *Positive Behavioral Interventions and Support Newsletter, 4* (2), retrieved from Office of Special Education Program Technical Assistance Center on Positive Behavioral Interventions and Support at www.pbis.org/pbis_newsletter/volume_4/issue2.aspx

Scott, T. M., & Barrett, S. B. (2004). Using staff and student time engaged in disciplinary procedures to evaluate the impact of school-wide SWPBS. *Journal of Positive Behavior Interventions, 6* (1), 21–27.

Sharkey, J. D., & Fenning, P. (2012). Rationale for designing school contexts in support of proactive discipline. *Journal of School Violence, 11* (2), 95–104.

Shriberg, D., & Fenning, P.A. (2009). School consultants as agents of social justice: Implications for practice: Introduction to the special issue. *Journal of Educational and Psychological Consultation, 19,* 1–7.

Skiba, R. J., Michael, R. S., Nardo, A., & Peterson, R. L. (2002). The color of discipline: Sources of racial and gender disproportionality in school punishment. *Urban Review, 34* (4), 317–342.

Skiba, R. J., Horner, R. H., Chung, C., Rausch, M. K., May, S. L. & Tobin, T. (2011). Race is not neutral: A national investigation of African American and Latino disproportionality in school discipline. *School Psychology Review, 40,* 85–107.

Skiba, R. J., Peterson, R.L., & Williams, T. (1997). Office referrals and suspension: Disciplinary intervention in middle schools. *Education and Treatment of Children, 20,* 295–315.

Skiba, R. J., Poloni-Staudinger, L., Gallini, S., Simmons, A. B., & Feggins-Azziz, R. (2006). Disparate access: The disproportionality of African-American students with disabilities across educational environments. *Exceptional Children, 72* (4), 411–424.

Skiba, R. J. & Rausch, M. K. (2006). Zero tolerance, suspension, and expulsion: Questions of equity and effectiveness. In C. M. Evertson & C. S. Weinstein (Eds.), *Handbook of classroom management: Research, practice, and contemporary issues* (pp. 1063–1092). Mahwah, NJ: Lawrence Erlbaum Associates.

Sugai, G. & Horner, R. (2002). The evolution of discipline practices: School-wide positive behavior supports. *Behavior Psychology in the Schools, 24,* 23–50.

Sugai, G., & Horner, R. (2007). *Evidence base for schoolwide positive behavior support.* Retrieved from Office of Special Education Program Technical Assistance Center on Positive Behavioral Interventions and Support at www.pbis.org

Sugai, G., Horner, R. H., Dunlap, G., Hieneman, M., Lewis, T. J., Nelson, C. M., et al. (2000). Applying positive behavior support and functional behavioral assessment in schools. *Journal of Positive Behavior Interventions, 2,* 131–143.

Sumner, M. D., Silverman, C. J., & Frampton, M. L. (2010). *School-based restorative justice as an alternative to zero-tolerance policies: Lessons from West Oakland.* Berkeley, CA: Thelton E. Henderson Center for Social Justice, University of California, Berkeley, School of Law.

Thornton, C. H., & Trent, W. (1988). School desegregation and suspension in East Baton Rouge Parish: A preliminary report. *Journal of Negro Education, 57,* 482–501.

Townsend, B. L. (2000). The disproportionate discipline of African American learners: Reducing school suspensions and expulsions. *Exceptional Children, 66,* 381–391.

Tyler, K. M., Boykin, A. W., & Walton, T. R. (2006). Cultural considerations in teachers' perceptions of student classroom behavior and achievement. *Teaching and Teacher Education 22,* 998–1005.

Vavrus, F. & Cole, K. (2002). "I didn't do nothing": The discursive construction of suspension. *Urban Review, 34,* 87–111.

Verdugo, R. R. (2002). Race–ethnicity, social class, and zero-tolerance policies: The cultural and structural wars. *Education and Urban Society, 35,* 50–75.

Vincent, G. G. (2008). *Do schools using SWIS take advantage of the "school ethnicity report"? Evaluation brief.* Retrieved from http://pbis.org/evaluation/evaluation_briefs/default.aspx

Vincent, C. G., Randall, C., Cartledge, G., Tobin, T. J., & Swain-Bradway, J. (2011). Toward a conceptual integration of cultural responsiveness and schoolwide positive behavior support. *Journal of Positive Behavior Interventions, 13* (4), 219–229.

Wald, J., & Losen, D. J. (2003). Editors' notes. In J. Wald & D. J. Losen (Eds.), *New directions for youth development: Deconstructing the school-to-prison pipeline* (pp. 1–2). San Francisco, CA: Jossey-Bass.

Ward, R. E., & Burke, M. A. (2004). *Improving achievement in low-performing schools: Key results for school leaders.* Thousand Oaks, CA: Corwin Press.

Warren, J. S., Edmonson, H. M., Griggs, P., Lassen, S. R., McCart, A., Turnbull, A., et al. (2003). Urban applications of school-wide positive behavior support: Critical issues and lessons learned. *Journal of Positive Behavior Interventions, 5,* 80–91.

Wearmouth, J., Mckinney, R., & Glynn, T. (2007). Restorative justice in schools: A New Zealand example. *Educational Research, 49,* 37–49.

Wehlage, G. G., & Rutter, R. A. (1986). Dropping out: How much do schools contribute to the problem? *Teachers College Record, 87,* 374–392.

Wu, S., Pink, W., Crain, R. L., & Moles, O. (1982). Student suspension: A critical reappraisal. *Urban Review, 14,* 245–303.

seven

# Paving the Way for Cosmopolitan Resilient Schools: Promoting Resilience and Social Justice in Urban, Suburban, and Rural Schools

Geraldine V. Oades-Sese, Mark Kitzie, and Wai-Ling Rubic

Schools serve as "islands of hope" for all children, especially for those whose environments and experiences have placed them at risk (Schorr, 1997). Schools are central and a highly influential part of children's lives that can provide protective influences that cultivate personal, social, and academic competence as well as the future economic value of children, despite differences in socioeconomic, ethnic, and cultural backgrounds. This chapter examines resilience in the schools through the lens of a social justice framework rooted in social capital theory. A worldview perspective of resilience is proposed, which transcends culture, language, socioeconomic status, gender, and ethnicity—the *Cosmopolitan Resilience* perspective—humanity at its best.

In this chapter, we will introduce the concept of resilience by defining the construct, providing related research in the area, and connecting it with social justice and social capital theory. We will then present a new concept of Cosmopolitan Resilience and argue how this concept is consistent with a social justice framework and timely with respects to our changing world. In order to move towards this new perspective, we survey the strengths and weaknesses of urban, suburban, and rural schools in order to provide recommendations that will lay the foundations necessary to accomplish this vision.

## What is Resilience?

Resilience is the capacity for successful developmental outcomes despite adversity or threatening circumstances and challenges (Masten, Best, & Garmezy, 1990). Factors that promote resilience, or protective factors, originate from multiple sources found within the child, family, and the community (i.e., schools). These protective factors are essential ingredients for building relationships (i.e., social capital) and academic achievement (i.e., human capital).

Protective factors found within a child include average or better intelligence, social competence, emotion regulation (Oades-Sese, Esquivel, Kaliski, & Maniatis, 2011; Oades-Sese et al., 2012), an internal locus of control, and a sense of self-worth (Masten et al., 1990; Rutter, 1987). In poor environments, resilient African American children that possess these protective factors demonstrate social and academic competence despite significant barriers of peer pressure, racial identity, discrimination, and negative relationships with educators (Ford, 1994). Similarly, talented children within ethnically diverse urban schools additionally exhibit determination, motivation, inner will, independence, realistic aspirations, and a heightened sensitivity to others and the world around them (Reis, Colbert, & Herbert, 2005).

In families, resilience is evidenced by close nurturing relationships, respectful communication between family members, emotional support, marital satisfaction (McCubbin & McCubbin, 1996), having high expectations for children, and setting routines and core values (Seccombe, 2002). Cohesive and supportive relationships within these families are essential for children's development (Orthner, Jones-Sanpei, & Williamson, 2004; Werner & Smith, 1989). Many such low-income families have the capacity to avoid involvement in crime and violence, and school dropout, and to engage in developmentally appropriate activities (Furstenberg, Cook, Eccles, Elder, & Sameroff, 1999). However, within-group differences among low-income families indicate that minority families demonstrate lower levels of these protective factors (Orthner et al., 2004).

Finally, schools have the potential to foster resilience in children early on, especially by building trusting relationships with students (a philosophy of caring) and by developing a curriculum that reflects children's experience with respect to their culture, values, experience and language (Wang, Haertel, & Walberg, 1997). This culturally relevant instructional approach has the capacity to empower marginalized students (Ladson-Bilings, 1994), particularly when a school's climate, policy, and structure promote equity, resilience, and social justice within the school–community environment. Transforming schools and communities into environments that foster resilience is a major, but attainable, challenge.

## Social Justice, Social Capital Theory, and Resilience Connection

Social justice provides equality for all children with respect to education. In order to achieve this, a paradigm shift is required of the current beliefs, attitudes, and behaviors of school psychologists and educators—they must view differences in students' experiences, cultural backgrounds, prior knowledge, and language as sources of strengths rather than deficits (Winfield, 1994). Essentially, school attitudes and belief systems have a significant impact on relationships and interactions among students, educators, school psychologists, and other professionals (social capital), which affect academic achievement (human capital). Changing a narrow mindset toward a more resilience-building one will be challenging for school psychologists working in schools that inadvertently espouse a philosophy that maintains the status quo (Shriberg, Bonner, Sarr, Walker, Hyland, & Chester, 2008).

Social justice issues in urban, suburban, and rural school environments can be understood according to Social Capital Theory and the theoretical framework of resilience. A person is said to possess social capital if he or she has a network of people with shared norms and values that facilitate cooperation and trust, enabling the community to pursue common goals (Cote & Healy, 2001). Social capital gains its value in its ability to create human capital such as skills, competence, and relevant talents related to future economic activity (Coleman, 1988; Zhang, De Blois, Deniger, & Kamanzi, 2008). This is related to becoming a competent and productive adult in society, as well as contributing to overall health, mental health, and quality of living.

Social capital theory can be viewed as synergic with resilience because it provides added value to resilience in the following ways. When we think about resilience, we equate it with close, personal, and nurturing relationships such as in children's relationships with their parents, teachers, mentors, and peers. As researchers, we examine the quality of these relationships as they relate to resilience and social capital theory. Social capital, however, identifies the types and qualities of relationships that contribute to both current and future well-being including the potential and economic contribution of children. Most importantly, social capital theory brings social justice to the forefront more directly than resilience theory. The unequal access to social capital is an indicator of social injustice because of its potential to exclude individuals and divide communities. It can also reduce achievement and contribute to health disparities. Therefore, social capital theory opens one's eyes to viewing resilience from another vantage point or from a larger global point of view.

Resilience is synergistic with the construct of social capital, particularly in terms of the concept of connectedness within social relationships and interactions (Zhang et al., 2008). Family social capital is gauged by parent–child discussions, intergenerational closure (i.e., social ties among parents whose children are friends or peers), taking part in religious activities, parent involvement, parent expectations, and family structure (Zhang et al., 2008). Educational indicators of social capital encompass teacher expectations, school climate, teacher–student ratio, and teacher–child and peer relationships. Higher levels of social capital are associated with academic achievement, better health, lower rates of school dropout, and lower crime rates.

The tenets of resilience and social capital theory underlie the *Theory of Success for Disadvantaged Children* (Zhang et al., 2008), which posits that social and school human capital can act as protective factors for disadvantaged children, becoming powerful contributors to their level of resilience. Social capital plays an important role in equity and social justice in that the more social relationships children have, the greater the availability of support and resources for developing abilities and skills (i.e., human capital) to compensate for their disadvantaged backgrounds (Zhang et al., 2008). Through high quality and caring relationships (social capital) and related protective factors, children develop social and academic competence. This highlights, in our view, the potential roles that schools, educators, and school psychologists can play in fostering resilience in children by creating conditions to build these types of capital. These individuals are the key players in nurturing these relationships that have the power to overcome what Shriberg et al. (2008) describe as institutionalized or systemic inequity placed on minority children and their families.

## Toward a Cosmopolitan Resilient Perspective

Culture and language have often been neglected as important sources of resilience for children and adolescents (Oades-Sese et al., 2012). Ethnic identity, in particular, is found to have a significant impact on how adolescents cope with adverse situations such as discrimination (Yasui & Dishion, 2007). Ethnic identity defines how one views the world—attitudes, values, opinions, concepts, and emotions—and how we think, define events, make decisions, and behave (Sue & Sue, 2003). For African Americans, ethnic identity serves as a "suit of armor" to deflect adverse situations (Arroyo & Zigler, 1995), while for Euro-Americans, ethnic identity helps one get through difficult times (Grossman & Charmaraman, 2009), or, for Hispanic Americans, guards against antisocial behaviors and substance abuse (Brook, Whiteman, Balka, Thet Win, & Gursen, 1998).

For indigenous people (i.e., Inuit, Métis, Mi'kmaq, and Mohawk communities), resilience is defined by distinct cultural concepts of identity, the importance of collective history, the richness of language and traditions, individual and collective agency, political activism, empowerment, and reconciliation (Kirmayer, Dandeneau, Marshall, Phillips, & Williamson, 2011). For indigenous people, learning their language, culture, and traditions strengthened their sense of identity and helped them overcome the adversities brought about by colonialism and its aftermath. Therefore, culture, identity, and language are crucial protective factors in promoting social justice for students. Given the importance of ethnic or cultural identity to the development of children and adolescents, how do the current structure and belief systems of schools in the US foster these protective factors?

Expanding on one's cultural or ethnic identity, we go further to introduce a higher-level form of social consciousness, a cultural integrative perspective that builds resilience beyond the self/person (via individual protective factors), family (family protective factors), or community (community protective factors). In order to develop resilient children in a society fraught with inequalities, it is vital to equip children with the capacity to develop an identity by which they can adapt and act upon the challenges and threats of today's world. Taken separately, the definition of a cosmopolitan person is someone who has been exposed to many different cultures and languages and is free of prejudices or bias; resilience is the capacity to adapt to challenging circumstances. A *cosmopolitan resilient individual* has the capacity to understand and respect different worldviews and integrate them with his or her own; thereby, expanding his/her cognitive, social–emotional, linguistic, and behavioral repertoire (Oades-Sese & Rubic, 2013). This individual does not surrender or sacrifice any part of his/her cultural identity; rather, it is enhanced by other cultural perspectives. This flexibility in thinking and acting (thought and action) is key in his/her ability to become resilient in the face of discrimination and inequity in society. Therefore, a cosmopolitan resilient person has the ability to adapt to the changing social landscape of the US and compete in the global economy. This process occurs through awareness and understanding of other cultures in the context of his or her own environmental and historical background, cultural mores, and traditions. As a result, a cosmopolitan resilient person comes to a realization that each person is an essential part of a greater whole—our connectedness.

## Cosmopolitan Resilient Schools

The concept of a cosmopolitan resilience can be applied to creating cosmopolitan resilient schools. In order to do this, it is important to examine the issues that schools face in terms of their strengths, weaknesses, and barriers within the current *Zeitgeist* of social justice. The following paragraphs briefly survey these issues in the context of urban, suburban, and rural schools. Since social capital is inherently embedded in the community, we briefly discuss resilience and social justice within the unique environment of rural schools where diversity is a major challenge compared to the other school settings. Knowing the strengths of each of these types of school will allow us to ameliorate weaknesses and develop recommendations that will lay the initial groundwork for fostering cosmopolitan resilience in students and in schools.

### Urban Schools

#### *Strengths and resources*

The word *urban* is also often used as a euphemism to refer to people of color living in urban areas (Esposito & Swain, 2009). However, urban communities are rich in diversity, where schools are in close proximity to multicultural and multilingual resources such as businesses, cultural centers, libraries, museums, galleries, community centers, shopping malls, restaurants, and sport centers. These places are priceless sources of social and human capital for children and their families. Compared to rural and suburban schools, urban schools allow for easier access to jobs due to close proximity to institutions, public transportation, and a variety of extracurricular activities.

Ideally urban schools can foster a cosmopolitan worldview affording children a natural environment in which to expand their understanding of and respect for different beliefs, customs, traditions, and philosophies. Children have an opportunity to build multicultural relationships, develop conflict resolution and social problem-solving skills, and acquire bilingualism or multilingualism. A cosmopolitan resilience perspective prepares children to become "global citizens" and promote a healthy respect and tolerance for others within the midst of fast-paced, technological advancements that lead us to be globally interconnected. These positive qualities of urban schools (social, human, and financial capital) are often overlooked and underutilized in the daily practice of education and the promotion of physical and mental health.

## Stressors and risk factors

Despite these given assets, urban schools are also fraught with a multitude of problems. Employees of urban schools rarely reside in the community and many do not share the cultural and racial backgrounds of their students (Keyes & Gregg, 2001). Graduates of these communities seldom return to become contributing citizens, further reinforcing the disconnection between schools and the community (Schutz, 2006). Also, poverty is prevalent in most urban areas where resources are scarce and basic needs such as access to clean water, affordable housing, good medical care, and living in safe neighborhoods are limited. Crime rates are greater in urban settings in terms of gangs, drugs, and other criminal activities that impact school failure and delinquent behaviors. Institutionalized oppression is also a cause of psychosocial problems of marginalized populations, resulting in a blaming game where schools blame family structure and cultural values for poor student performance, while families attribute their children's failure to discrimination and insensitivity of schools (Atkinson & Juntunen, 1994).

Children from low-income families are faced with many challenges and are at risk for negative outcomes (Garcia Coll et al., 1996). Children from poor urban communities, especially African American and Latino children, may not have the fundamental social–emotional, cognitive, and linguistic skills as they enter school. Despite poverty, hardships, and negative expectations, many children have developed into successful, well-respected, and resilient adults for reasons mentioned above from research of low-income families. Within urban schools, class sizes are large, making it difficult for teachers to provide individual attention to the various academic, social–emotional, and behavioral needs of students. Small class sizes along with other factors have enduring effects on the academic and economic success of students (Reynolds, Temple, Ou, Arteaga, & White, 2011). Diversity within these large classrooms equates to the diversity of communication styles, worldviews, and learning styles that challenge one-size-fits-all curriculum and instructional models. These challenges result in the disproportional number of African American and Latino students suspended, held back, referred and placed in special education, and underrepresented in programs for the gifted and talented (National Research Council, 2002).

The employment and retention of highly qualified teachers and school psychologists, who are culturally competent and aptly represent the students they serve, are major issues. Awareness, understanding, and integrating multicultural and second language acquisition principles in daily practice are still much needed, despite higher education efforts to ameliorate this gap through training and professional development. The lack of access to computers and technology in poor urban schools also limits the academic achievement of urban students (Berg, Ridenour-Benz, Lasley, & Raisch, 1998), and stymies the forging of national and international relationships and understanding among students that is normally afforded by direct access and proximity granted by cyberspace.

The recent influx of immigrants in urban schools is rapidly changing their landscape. One of the major challenges of schools is benchmarking student achievement with a fair comparison to ensure that students reach attainable goals and that teachers hold high levels of expectation (Bainbridge, Lasley, & Sundre, 2003). Assessment procedures, process, and intervention models also need to move away from a one-size-fits-all model to reflect culturally relevant methods that support multiple ways of learning, knowing, and communicating. The lack of culturally and linguistically diverse school psychologists is a significant barrier to student achievement as well as social justice. Although attempts have been made to ameliorate this problem by promoting cultural competence and multicultural education, there are certain unrecognized, subconscious, and unsaid cultural nuances in communication styles, linguistic competence, values, and ways of viewing the world that have not been explored, researched, or documented because these nuances are automatically embedded in an individual's thinking, attention, and cognitive processes.

## Suburban Schools

### Strengths and resources

Suburban schools have higher levels of social/educational and financial capital compared to urban or rural schools. These include better qualified teachers, newer facilities, more challenging courses and higher academic expectations, positive school climate, a lower teacher–student ratio, and a greater variety of sports, clubs, and extracurricular opportunities. Advantages in social capital include a higher percentage of two-parent households, a greater likelihood of one parent being available, higher parental support and expectations, greater opportunity for travel and exposure to enriching activities and strong social and community supports. In addition, affluent parents tend to be better educated and are better able to advocate for their children in order to facilitate their access to educational, cultural, and vocational opportunities.

## Stressors and risk factors

Despite a trend of increasing minority population in suburban schools, segregation between more and less affluent districts has increased. Konstantopoulos (2006) reported that the gap between high and low achieving schools from the 1970s to the 1990s increased, and that this increase was associated with differences in race and socioeconomic status (SES).

Two-thirds of the increase in school enrollment between 1993 and 2007 was in suburban schools and minority enrollment accounted for virtually all of this increase (Fry, 2009). Despite these demographic changes, the percentage of White students exposed to minority students only increased from 17% to 25%, which is about half of the level expected. As a result, the racial/ethnic diversification of suburban school districts has not led to a commensurate increase in exposing suburban White students to culturally and ethnically diverse students (Fry, 2009). This is particularly true for suburban Hispanic students, who are more highly segregated than other minority groups in suburban schools.

Several Supreme Court decisions have been central to the goal of desegregating schools. The landmark *Brown v. Board of Education* decision in 1954 found separate, but equal laws to be "inherently unequal" and unconstitutional. This was followed by the 1973 ruling in *Keyes v. Denver School District No. 1* which held that techniques such as placing schools in racially isolated neighborhoods or drawing attendance zones that increased isolation were illegal. However, in 1974, in *Milliken v. Bradley,* the Supreme Court decided that it was not necessary for suburban schools to be integrated unless it could be shown that suburban districts contributed to the segregation of urban schools. This ruling had a chilling effect on interdistrict attempts at integration. Recent (2007) Supreme Court decisions in *Parents Involved in Community Schools v. Seattle School District* and *Meredith v. Jefferson County Board of Education* cited the equal protection clause of the constitution in placing limits on the ability of school districts to consider race in desegregation schemes. However, a majority of the Supreme Court justices held that promoting diversity and avoiding racial isolation in schools are "compelling national interests that school districts can and should pursue" (Tefera, Frankenberg, Siegel-Hawley, & Chirichigno, 2011, p. 61). As a result, current strategies to increase diversity in schools need to demonstrate a compelling reason to use race as a factor in integration decisions. The door was left open for districts to consider other race-neutral factors such as SES, culture or ethnicity, parent education level, and the type of neighborhood in which a child lives, e.g., drawing school attendance zones that allow school choice.

Integrated schools have been found to have academic, social and psychological benefits for all students. Minority students attending racially diverse schools have higher academic expectations and achievement. Higher graduation rates and access to social networks make it more likely for them to attend higher status colleges and obtain higher status jobs. Increased cross-racial understanding and a reduction of racial stereotypes have been found for children in integrated schools, particularly when they attend these schools at a younger age. Children who experience racial and ethnic diversity while in school tend to live and work in diverse settings and have an increased sense of civic engagement as adults (Tefera et al., 2011). As our society becomes more diverse, it is a moral imperative, as well as of practical benefit, to pursue greater social justice by creating more equal access to human and social capital and therefore contribute toward cosmopolitan resilient schools and students.

## Rural Schools

### Strengths and resources

About 25% of school psychologists work in rural schools (Curtis, Hunley, & Chesno Grier, 2004). One of the unique qualities of rural schools is that they are social and cultural centers for the community and a symbol of community pride (Dewees, 1999). By their nature, rural schools are smaller schools, which is an advantage that affords teachers more time to individualize the curriculum according to student needs, monitor student learning, and increase student achievement (Greenwald, Hedges, & Laine, 1996). Smaller schools with smaller class sizes outperform larger schools as measured by higher scores on standardized tests.

Social capital and cohesion in rural communities serve as a protective factor for children, which enables them to develop resilience to cope with challenges and to "bounce back" when faced with adversity (Hegney et al., 2008). Core values of children in rural farming communities include hard work, a sense of responsibility, and commitment to family (Larson & Dearmont, 2002). Rural families also tend to value church activities highly and encourage their children to develop religiosity and spirituality (Brody, Stoneman, & Flor, 1996). These values support the development of protective factors (social capital) that can help children succeed academically (human capital). The development of school–family–community partnerships fosters resilience in children and helps to dissolve barriers inherent to rural schools. School psychologists in rural communities are in a position to facilitate or lead the development and maintenance of these partnerships—bridging the three environmental contexts (school, home and community) that support children's development.

### Stressors and risk factors

According to Johnson and Strange's (2009) *Why Rural Matters*, more than nine million (19%) children in the United States are enrolled in rural schools. About 40% of rural students live in poverty and 35.5% of rural female-headed households with pre-school-age children live below the federal poverty line. Rural schools face a number of other barriers such as shortage of health care resources, limited school funding, low teacher pay, lack of professional development for teachers, limited access to technology and enrichment programs, as well as a lack of community resources to support children's physical, creative, and intellectual growth. Rural schools are faced with extreme financial obstacles, relying on taxation of local property, which is a major determinant of the quality of education students receive. Insufficient funding gives rise to a limited range of curricular options and advanced placement course offerings; a diminished number of enrichment programs, remedial classes, and available computers; and limited access to online resources and social networks. Access to health care providers, which is also a predictor for children's school success, is at a shortage in rural communities (Larson & Dearmont, 2002).

## Resilience and social justice

Because of the high percentage of Whites in many rural communities, oppression and racism may be present, which motivates children of immigrant families toward assimilation of the dominant culture rather than developing a bicultural identity (Rubic, 2003). The ability to maintain a bicultural identity among immigrant and second-generation immigrant children becomes a challenge in rural schools. Incidences of bullying and teasing in schools are present, especially if a child has an accent or differs in appearance from mainstream children.

Addressing social justice in rural schools begins with student–teacher relationships. Caring, supportive teachers who have high student expectations and provide opportunities for children to participate in meaningful and challenging educational activities are sources of social/human capital, and therefore resilience, in children (Benard, 1995). Teachers typically reside in the rural community in which they are employed and are therefore invested in their community and knowledgeable about its needs and resources. As a result, they can provide a certain degree of social and personal trust that contributes to the resilience of rural children (Larson & Dearmont, 2002). According to Nodding (1984), the philosophy of caring as a pedagogical choice is reflective of a social justice pedagogy. Teachers, who are strong opponents of discrimination and racism, use education to liberate and empower their students (Esposito & Swain, 2009). Culturally relevant pedagogy integrates values, experiences and perspectives of students' cultures into the curriculum—bridging home and school cultures—by drawing on students' home culture to help them achieve academic success, and enabling students to think critically about the injustices inherent in schools and in the broader society (Esposito & Swain, 2009). Validating students' primary culture and language is one of the first steps in building cosmopolitan resilience in the schools.

Rural schools are in a position to develop successful and cosmopolitan resilient children by virtue of being strongly and visibly connected with their communities. In these smaller, tight-knit communities families can get involved in sharing family/cultural information and history, which can provide resources for teachers to develop culturally appropriate (Au & Jordan, 1981), culturally congruent (Mohatt & Erickson, 1981), culturally responsive (Cazden & Leggett, 1981), and culturally relevant (Ladson-Billings, 1994) curriculum. Developing culturally relevant curriculum opens the door to implement social justice pedagogy, which involves teaching critical thinking skills and empowering students to see themselves in relation to others (Esposito & Swain, 2009).

## Implications for School Psychologists

There are a number of ways school psychologists can begin to promote resilience and social justice across school settings to empower all. The following is not an exhaustive list of recommendations (due to limited space), but are highlighted as approaches that will *initiate* change and pave the way toward cosmopolitan resilience in schools.

- Awareness: First, it is important that school psychologists be aware of and examine their own attitudes and behaviors about diversity (for further details see Chapter 1). School psychologists can then advocate equity for marginalized students by raising their conscious awareness about the oppressive forces and injustices in their lives, which empowers them to reject societal stereotypes and transform them (Diemer, 2009). Adapting Shin et al.'s (2010) approach for counselors, school psychologists can (a) educate school personnel about their own attitudes and behaviors related to diversity and about possible deficit-oriented perceptions of marginalized students, (b) address systemic oppression by challenging groups' internalized racism and confronting institutional barriers that may inhibit students' academic goals, and (c) increase their critical consciousness while working with marginalized students to decrease the possibility of perpetuating larger systemic forms of cultural domination.
- Within-school variability in student achievement is about five times greater than variability found in student achievement between schools, indicating that individual teachers may be more influential than the school that students attend (Konstantopoulos, 2006). School psychologists can promote school environments that guard against the deficit model of thinking by which the student's cultural or language differences are seen as a justification for poor academic achievement. As a result, an important role of the school psychologist is to educate key stakeholders about approaches associated with more positive outcomes and to help develop positive expectations for marginalized students.
- School climate: Creating a diversity-friendly school climate (a type of social capital) and having a profound respect for all individuals regardless of race, culture, and language are steps for building cosmopolitan resilience. School psychologists can facilitate discussions of these issues via an in-service

consultation, or workshops. Schools psychologists can also support teachers' efforts in developing a culturally relevant curriculum that validates students' prior knowledge, experiences, and values. This allows the school psychologist to make connections more explicitly between students' identity and culture and their academic achievement and psychological well-being. Because teachers have a significant influence on student achievement, schools should promote high student expectations, especially for marginalized children. Other ways to improve school climate are to highlight the experiences and contributions of individuals from different racial and ethnic groups in curricula and to engage parents in ways that are sensitive to racial and ethnic diversity. Promoting communication among diverse students within the classroom, across communities, and nationwide will also facilitate multicultural friendships and working relationships. Finally, well-designed use of online social networks in the classroom can increase international and cross-cultural relationships, and foster deeper understanding and respect (Tefera et al., 2011).

- Home–school–community connections: School psychologists can engage parents and members of the community as valued partners. Such partnerships can be major sources of social capital from which families can draw to succeed (Epstein & Sanders, 2000) and effectively combat systemic barriers in schools. Partnerships have a powerful role in improving school programs and school climate, increasing parental skills and leadership, connecting families with school and community resources, and improving students' academic achievement. Often, parents of marginalized students may be hesitant to voice their ideas and opinions for fear of school personnel reactions. School psychologists can use group process skills to ensure that the voices of minority or low-SES parents are heard in the collaboration and decision-making process. They can model open dialogue to have partners listen to each other with respect, value others' opinions, and respect the views of diverse partners with different experiences. School psychologists can also ensure that school committees are representative of the children they serve in terms of racial composition, which is found to be effective in increasing the participation of marginalized families in school activities. School personnel, as a result, will begin to understand, construct, seek, and value participation from families in ways other than the traditional parent–teacher organizations, conferences, field trips, open houses, and fundraisers. School psychologists can also create multilingual forums, family communication, and culturally relevant school events.

- Community maps: School psychologists must be familiar with the community where the school is located in order to develop a community asset map to indicate key influential people in the local community, and learn where resources are located (service agencies, libraries, mentoring programs, clubs, organizations). Community mapping is one way to engage school–family–community partnerships in collaborative efforts to help all members (Witten, Exeter, & Field, 2003).

■    Educational workshops and programs: School psychologists can assist in developing committees, parent educational workshops, and family outreach programs that promote interracial and cultural friendships, strengthen school involvement, and reduce alienation of isolated minority students and negative peer pressure (Winfield, 1994). School psychologists can first conduct a needs assessment to identify the needs of minority families. For example, a workshop that educates parents about school policies, rules, and expectations in their native language via a translator or family liaison is important in ensuring parent involvement and student success. Parent workshops and programs can be held in schools, community centers or place of employment to accommodate parents who are difficult to reach due to work or other situational circumstances. Church or other places of worship are potential places to hold workshops and outreach programs, especially for African American, Hispanic, African, and Caribbean families (Day-Vines, Patton, & Baytops, 2003). School psychologists can also develop workshops to increase teachers' knowledge and skills in developing supportive relationships with diverse students, thereby building social capital and increasing the likelihood of student success. Lastly, school psychologists can contribute to teacher training of high-quality, culturally relevant, evidence-based instructional models and evaluate their effectiveness on student outcomes.

## Conclusion

This chapter discussed the important contribution that social justice and social capital theory play in promoting resilience in disadvantaged children. When children, regardless of their socioeconomic, cultural, and ethnic backgrounds, are treated with equity and fairness, schools become islands of hope for children. Schools can provide the necessary support systems to help all children reach their fullest potential. By understanding the common and unique strengths and weaknesses of schools within urban, suburban, and rural communities, we are in a position to capitalize on strengths and ameliorate weaknesses. Recommendations that may curtail social injustices within the school setting were provided, but this is just the tip of the iceberg. In order to achieve the ideals of social justice and a cosmopolitan resilient perspective, a major overhaul in thinking and a change in attitude about people from culturally and linguistically diverse populations are much needed—a difference that would also significantly contribute to the reduction of poverty by equalizing the allocation of resources and opportunities. Although not discussed in detail, a major source of inequality among urban, suburban, and rural school systems throughout the nation is the disparity between the wealthy and the poor. Rectifying this "savage inequality" will help perpetuate a domino effect of reducing inequities and providing the basic human needs of healthy food, shelter, safety, health care and education.

Equity in per student expenditure and school funding will result in increased student resources, opportunities, fair teacher salaries, and the retention of educators and school psychologists. In addition, improvements in student–teacher ratios and professional development driven by social justice pedagogy (developing a socio-political consciousness or awareness, a sense of agency, and a positive social and cultural identity), and in developing culturally sensitive teaching styles will enhance a school's ability to help *all* children to develop into morally and globally connected citizens. When school psychologists, educators, children, and community members are socialized in this manner, understanding, respect, and acceptance of all people will result in social and human capital far beyond that of segregated communities embedded with passive ignorance. Cultivating this new mindset, however, must ideally start during early childhood to have a profound effect.

School psychologists and educators are in the position to exert social change so that all students (minority and majority) have the opportunity to reach their fullest potential without the obstruction of discrimination, prejudice, inequity, and poor educational and assessment practices. As a result, each student can come to a realization that they *are* an essential and worthy part of the greater whole, which is our connection with each other. Together as global citizens, we can profit from the wealth that multiculturalism, linguistic diversity, and international relations offer, leading toward a peaceful, cosmopolitan resilient society.

Jeffrey Sachs (2005) reminds us of Robert Kennedy's words on the power of the individual in shaping society:

> Each time a man stands up for an ideal, or acts to improve the lot of others, or strikes out against injustice, he sends a tiny ripple of hope, and crossing each other from a million different centers of energy and daring, those ripples build a current which can sweep down the mightiest walls of oppression and resistance. (pp. 367–368)

This chapter has discussed resilience from a social justice lens. Apply your knowledge gained from this chapter to discuss the following case study describing Robert's experience in his school district.

## Case Study

Robert is a school psychologist in an affluent district which has a "pocket" of low-income, culturally diverse families, most of whom live in the same housing development. These families are characterized by a high proportion of single parent households and parents that tend to work long hours with inflexible schedules. Many of the children of these families struggle with academic and/or behavioral issues. A disproportionately higher percentage of these students are being referred for an evaluation to qualify for special education. Upon observing these students in their classrooms, Robert noticed that they seem to be disconnected from their teachers and peers, and disengaged from classroom instruction. When discussing these students, school personnel often refer to them by the name of the housing development in which they live. Robert also noticed that these families hardly ever attend social functions and parent meetings in the school.

Keeping a cosmopolitan resilient perspective in mind:

- What can Robert do to address the lack of sensitivity or respect for diversity in his school?
- How can Robert establish positive relationships between the school and these parents and how can he encourage these parents to become involved with school activities and meetings?
- What can Robert do to reduce the isolation felt by these students and better engage them in learning?

## Answer Key (Answers May Vary)

Robert could meet with the director of special education and building principal to voice his concerns about the differential treatment of parents. At the meeting, he can offer to identify training opportunities and to lead guided discussion groups as part of in-house professional development that addresses how to better accept and incorporate diversity. Robert can provide an in-service to raise awareness about possible deficit-oriented perceptions held by school personnel about diverse students and families, and to address systemic oppression of internalized and institutional racism that may contribute to inhibiting students' academic achievement. He can recruit school personnel with similar cultural backgrounds of target families to assist in the presentation, which would enhance the relevance and "buy-in" for teachers. In the presentation, they can address important core values, beliefs, and traditions that many of these families hold and show brief movie clips that present these families in a positive light. The goal of the in-service would be to increase school personnel's level of critical consciousness when working with these students and their families.

Robert can nurture the relationships between parents and the school by forming a committee which requires members to work collaboratively in promoting a welcoming school climate and discussing shared goals for their children's academic success. He also can invite key players in the community, who would be nominated by these families, to participate. He can identify staff members who can serve as interpreters for parents for whom English is not their primary language. He can also make an effort to learn key phrases in the families' language to establish rapport. During meetings, he can take the opportunity to model active listening, respect and empathy with parents. He can take care to solicit and understand parental questions and concerns and use group process skills to ensure that their voices are heard in the collaboration and decision-making process. Given the work demands of these families, he can hold committee meetings during breakfast at the school cafeteria, while their children can eat breakfast with the principal in a separate room. Through this committee, Robert can advocate for the initial foundations to develop awareness, understanding, and respect for different cultural perspectives for all committee members. This endeavor will likely deepen relationships between these families and school, and prompt active participation by parents.

The foundation of effective teaching and academic success for all students is respectful, responsive, reciprocal relationships between students and teachers. Robert can help develop the skills of school personnel to connect with their students to build trustworthy relationships and develop the skills to engage students through a culturally responsive curriculum that utilizes students' prior knowledge and experiences. This has the potential for bridging home and school cultures that will help students feel welcomed, respected, and validated. Developing a culturally relevant curriculum also opens the door to implement social justice pedagogy, which teaches critical thinking skills and empowers students to see themselves in relation to others by caring and supportive school personnel. Moreover, Robert can advocate for a strength-based approach in teaching, by helping school personnel view and validate the richness of students' cultural and linguistic experiences and by promoting high student expectations.

# References

Arroyo, C. G., & Zigler, E. (1995). Racial identity, academic achievement, and the psychological well-being of economically disadvantaged adolescents. *Journal of Personality and Social Psychology, 69* (5), 903–914.

Atkinson, D. A., & Juntunen, C. L. (1994). School counselors and school psychologists as school–home–community liaisons in ethnically diverse schools. In. P. Pederson & J. C. Carey (Eds.), *Multicultural counseling in schools: A practical handbook* (pp. 103–119). Needham Heights: MA: Allyn & Bacon.

Au, K., & Jordan, C. (1981). Teaching reading to Hawaiian children: Finding a culturally appropriate solution. In H. T. Trueba, G. P. Guthrie, & K. Au (Eds.), *Culture and the bilingual classroom: Studies in classroom ethnography* (pp. 139–152). Rowley, MA: Newbury House.

Bainbridge, W. L., Lasley, T. J., II, & Sundre, S. M. (2003). Policy initiatives to improve urban schools: An agenda. *Education and Urban Society, 35,* 292–299.

Benard, B. (1995). Fostering resilience in children. Urbana, IL: ERIC Clearinghouse on Elementary and Early Childhood Education (ERIC Document Reproduction Service No. ED386327).

Berg, S., Ridenour-Benz, C., Lasley, T. J., & Raisch, C. D. (1998). Exemplary technology use in elementary classrooms. *Journal of Research on Technology in Education, 31,* 111–122.

Brody, G. H., Stoneman, Z., & Flor, D. (1996). Parental religiosity, family processes, and youth competence in rural, two-parent African American families. *Developmental Psychology, 32* (4), 696–706.

Brook, J. S., Whiteman, M., Balka, E., Thet Win, P., & Gursen, M. (1998). Drug use among Puerto Ricans: Ethnic identity as a protective factor. *Hispanic Journal of Behavioral Sciences, 20* (2), 241–254.

Cazden, C., & Leggett, E. (1981). Culturally responsive education: Recommendations for achieving Lau remedies II. In H. T. Trueba, G. P. Guthrie, & K. Au (Eds.), *Culture and the bilingual classroom: Studies in classroom ethnography* (pp. 69–86). Rowley, MA: Newbury House.

Coleman, J. S. (1988). Social capital in the creation of human capital. *American Journal of Sociology, 94* (Supplement), S95–S120.

Cote, S., & Healy, T. (2001). *The well-being of nations: The role of human and social capital.* Paris, France: Organization for Economic Cooperation and Development.

Curtis, M. J., Hunley, S. A., & Chesno Grier, E. (2004). The status of school psychology: Implications of a major personnel shortage. *Psychology in the Schools, 41* (4), 431–442.

Day-Vines, N., Patton, J., & Baytops, J. (2003). African American adolescents: The impact of race and middle class status on the counseling process. *Professional School Counseling, 7,* 40–51.

Dewees, S. (1999, December). The school-within-a-school model. ERIC Digest. Charleston, WV: ERIC Clearinghouse on Rural Education and Small Schools. (ERIC Document Reproduction Service No. EDO-RC-99-2.)

Diemer, M. (2009). Pathways to occupational attainment among poor youth of color: The role of sociopolitical development. *Counseling Psychologist, 37,* 6–35.

Epstein, J. L, & Sanders, M. G. (2000). Connecting home, school, and community: New directions for social research. In M. Hallinan (Ed.), *Handbook of sociology and education* (pp. 285–306). New York, NY: Plenum.

Esposito, J., & Swain, A. N. (2009). Pathways to social justice: Urban teachers' uses of culturally relevant pedagogy as a conduit for teaching for social justice. *Perspectives on Urban Education, 1,* 38–48.

Ford, D. (1994). Nurturing resilience in gifted Black youth. *Roeper Review, 17,* 80–85.

Fry, R. (2009). *The rapid growth and changing complexion of suburban public schools.* Washington, DC: Pew Hispanic Center.

Furstenberg, F., Jr., Cook, T., Eccles, J., Elder, G., Jr., & Sameroff, A. (1999). *Managing to make it: Urban families and adolescent success.* Chicago, IL: University of Chicago Press.

Garcia Coll, C., Lamberty, G., Jenkins, R., McAdoo, H., Crnic, K., Wasik, B., et al. (1996). An integrative model for the study of developmental competencies in minority children. *Child Development, 67,* 1891–1914.

Greenwald, R., Hedges, L. V., & Laine, R. D. (1996). The effect of school resources on student achievement. *Review of Educational Research, 66* (3), 361–396.

Grossman, J. M., & Charmaraman, L. (2009). Race, context, and privilege: White adolescents' explanations of racial–ethnic centrality. *Journal of Youth Adolescence, 38,* 139–152.

Hegney, D., Ross, H., Baker, P., Rogers-Clark, C., King, C., Buikstra, E., et al. (2008). *Identification of personal and community resilience that enhances psychological wellness: A Stanthorpe study.* Toowoomba, Australia: Centre for Rural and Remote Health, University of Southern Queensland.

Johnson, J., & Strange, M., (2009). *Why rural matters 2009: The facts about rural education in the 50 states.* Washington, DC: Rural School and Community Trust.

Keyes, M. C., & Gregg, S. (2001). *School–community connections: A literature review.*Washington, DC: AEL.

Kirmayer, L. J., Dandeneau, S., Marshall, E., Phillips, M. K., & Williamson, K. J. (2011). Rethinking resilience from indigenous perspectives. *Canadian Journal of Psychiatry, 56* (2), 84–91.

Konstantopoulos, S. (2006). Trends of school effects on student achievement: Evidence from NLS: 72, HSB: 82, and NELS: 92. *Teachers College Record, 108* (12), 2550–2581.

Ladson-Billings, G. (1994). *The dreamkeepers: Successful teachers of African American children.* San Francisco, CA: Jossey-Bass.

Larson, N. C., & Dearmont, M. (2002). Strengths of farming communities in fostering resilience in children. *Child Welfare, 81* (5), 821–836.

Masten, A. S., Best, K. M., & Garmezy, N. (1990). Resilience and development: Contributions from the study of children who overcome adversity. *Development and Psychopathology, 2*, 425–444.

McCubbin, H. T. A., & McCubbin, M. (1996). *Family assessment: Resiliency, coping and adaptation—Inventories for research and practice.* Madison, WI: University of Wisconsin.

Mohatt, G., & Erickson, F. (1981). Cultural differences in teaching styles in an Odawa school: A sociolinguistic approach. In H. T. Trueba, G. P. Guthrie, & K. Au (Eds.), *Culture and the bilingual classroom: Studies in classroom ethnography* (pp. 105–119). Rowley, MA: Newbury House.

National Research Council. (2002). *Minority students in special and gifted education.* Committee on Minority Representation in Special Education. Washington, DC: National Academy Press.

Nodding, N. (1984). *Caring: A feminine approach to ethics and moral education.* Berkeley, CA: University of California Press.

Oades-Sese, G. V., Esquivel, G. B., Kaliski, P. K., & Maniatis, L. (2011). A longitudinal study of the social and academic competence of economically disadvantaged bilingual preschool children. *Developmental Psychology, 47* (3), 747–764.

Oades-Sese, G. V., Kitzie, M., Velderman, C., Rubic, W., Rutstein, S., & Waltuck, M. (2012). Cultural considerations for building social-emotional and academic resilience in Hispanic preschool children. In S. Prince-Embury & D. H. Saklofske (Eds.), *Resilience in children, adolescents, and adults: Transtlating research into practice.* New York, NY: Springer.

Oades-Sese, G. V., & Rubic, W. (2013). *Cosmopolitan resilient schools.* Manuscript in preparation.

Orthner, D. K., Jones-Sanpei, H., & Williamson, S. (2004). The resilience and strengths of low-income families. *Family Relations, 53*, 159–167.

Reis, S. M., Colbert, R. D., & Herbert, T. P. (2005). Understanding resilience in diverse, talented students in an urban high school. *Roeper Review, 27* (2), 110–120.

Reynolds, A. J., Temple, J. A., Ou, S. R., Arteaga, I. A., & White, B. A. (2011). School-based early childhood education and Age-28 well-being: Effects by timing, dosage, and subgroups. *Science, 333* (6040) 360–364.

Rubic, W. (2003). *Tightrope: The bicultural identity formation of second generation Filipino-Americans.* Unpublished Master's Thesis.

Rutter, M. (1987). Psychological resilience and protective mechanism. *American Journal of Orthopsychiatry, 57*, 316–331.

Sachs, J. (2005). *The end of poverty: Economic possibilities for our time.* New York, NY: Penguin.

Schorr, L. (1997). *Common purpose: Strengthening families and neighborhoods to rebuild American.* New York, NY: Doubleday.

Schutz, A. (2006). Home is a prison in the global city: The tragic failure of school-based community engagement strategies. *Review of Educational Research, 76* (4), 691–743.

Seccombe, K. (2002). "Beating the odds" versus "changing the odds": Poverty, resilience, and family policy. *Journal of Marriage and Family, 64* (2), 384–394.

Shin, R. Q., Rogers, J., Stanciu, A., Silas, M., Brown-Smythe, C., & Austin, B. (2010). Advancing social justice in urban schools through implementation of transformative groups for youth of color. *Journal for Specialists in Group Work, 35* (3), 230–235.

Shriberg, D., Bonner, M., Sarr, B., Walker, A., Hyland, M., & Chester, C. (2008). Social justice through a school psychology lens: Definitions and applications. *School Psychology Review, 37*, 453–468.

Sue, D. W., & Sue, D. (2003). *Counseling the culturally diverse: Theory and practice* (4th ed.). New York, NY: Wiley.

Tefera, A., Frankenberg, E., Siegel-Hawley, G., & Chirichigno, G. (2011). *Integrating suburban schools: How to benefit from growing diversity and avoid segregation.* University of California, Los Angeles: The Civil Rights Project/Proyecto Derechos Civiles.

Wang, M. C., Haertel, G. D., & Walberg, H. H. (1997). Fostering educational resilience in inner-city schools. *Children and Youth, 7*, 119–140.

Werner, E., & Smith, R. (1989). *Vulnerable but invincible: A longitudinal study of resilient children and youth.* New York, NY: Adams, Bannister, & Cox.

Winfield, L. F. (1994). *Developing resilience in urban youth.* Urban Monograph Series. Oak Brook, IL: North Central Regional Educational Laboratory.

Witten, K., Exeter, D., & Field, A. (2003). The quality of urban environments: Mapping variation in access to community resources. *Urban Studies, 40*, 161–177.

Yasui, M., & Dishion, T. J. (2007). The ethnic context of child and adolescent problem behavior: Implications for child and family interventions. *Clinical Child and Family Psychology, 10*(2), 137–179.

Zhang, X. Y., DeBlois, L., Deniger, M., & Kamanzi, C. (2008). A theory of success for disadvantaged children: Reconceptualization of social capital in the light of resilience. *Alberta Journal of Education Research, 54*(1), 97–111.

# eight
# Institutional Barriers: Poverty and Education

## Stacy A. S. Williams and Deborah Peek Crockett

Although the discussion of social justice in school psychology is a novel concept, the premise of the model is aligned with what we do as practitioners and scholars. For years, scholars have discussed social justice issues indirectly via research in diversity, multiculturalism, and culturally responsive practices (Crockett and Brown, 2009; Miranda, 2009; Shriberg et al., 2008). Although indirectly researched and discussed in our field, social justice issues were being articulated in other scholarly areas. Shriberg et al. (2008) were the first to attempt to conceptualize social justice through the lens of school psychology. Using a Delphi method of analysis, they interviewed 44 school psychology cultural diversity experts regarding: (a) their definition of social justice, (b) important social justice topics, (c) advocacy strategies, and (d) facilitators and barriers to social justice work in school psychology. In their attempts to define social justice, Shriberg et al. (2008) found that many of the experts in their study defined social justice as "ensuring the protection of rights and opportunities for all, nondiscriminatory/inclusive practices, advocacy for others, ecological/systemic view, and personal responsibility" (pp. 459–460). Germane to the ensuing discussion is the ecological and systemic view of social justice. Shriberg et al. (2008) further describe this view as "working beyond the immediate context and thinking beyond the school to the larger impact educational decisions have" (p. 461). One of the sample responses coded in this area was "I'd say the practice of social justice in school psychology would work to correct the injustices of our society—poverty, lack of access to mental health and health care services" (p. 461). Hence, a discussion about the development of a social justice perspective in school psychology would be remiss if it excluded the ecological perspective.

In an attempt to understand the educational and psychological needs of the child, it is necessary to move beyond the traditional medical model, which places the brunt of the child's difficulties on the child and fails to take into consideration the environmental influences on the child's development. Gutkin (2012) argues that an individual operates among four "interlocking levels of the environment, each of which continuously affects and is impacted by all the others" (p. 9). Doll, Spies, and Champion (2012) effectively argue that academic achievement is either facilitated or impeded by "multiple tiers of influence including the microsystem (immediate settings for children's behavior), the mesosystem (the developmental niche formed by multiple settings that children move among), the exosystem (people and places that the child does not interact with but which affect the child's experience indirectly) and the macrosystem (involves culture, institutions, and polices)" (p. 45). Gutkin (2012) further articulates that the relationships between the systems are bidirectional and reciprocal.

Understanding the child through a social justice lens is a function of exploring the reciprocal relationships between the macrosystem (i.e., institutional barriers to academic achievement), microsystem (i.e, community), mesosystem (i.e., home–school relationships, curriculum, instruction), and exosystems (i.e., educational policies that continue to perpetuate inequalities). In this vein, the following chapter will focus on the environmental variable of poverty and its relationship with the interlocking levels of the environment. The objective is to assess the barrier of poverty and issues of educational equity for children living in low-income communities. The issue of poverty cuts across each of the interlocking environmental levels because it not only influences the community in which the child lives (i.e., access to educational resources), but affects the quality of education the child receives (i.e., effective teachers, effective curriculum, high-achieving role models). Additionally, we'll explore the lack of diverse educators and school psychology practitioners and its impact on meeting the needs of students living in these communities.

## Poverty Trends

The ongoing economic crisis has negatively affected the livelihoods of millions of Americans. According to the US Census Bureau, the unemployment rate was 8.3% in January 2012. Despite the data showing a decline of 0.2% from December 2011, the unemployment rate is still high by all accounts, having doubled since the beginning of the recession in December 2007. As unemployment rates have risen, so have poverty rates. The US Census Bureau data shows that the US poverty rate rose to 15.1% (46.2 million) in 2010, an increase from 14.3% (approximately 43.6 million) in 2009 and the highest level since 1993. In 2008, 13.2% (39.8 million) of Americans lived in relative poverty. In 2000, the poverty rate for individuals was 12.2% and for families was 9.3%. In 2010, the poverty threshold, or poverty line, was $22,314 for a family of four and $18,310 for a family of three (Addy & Wight, 2012). The official poverty definition counts income before taxes and excludes capital gains and noncash benefits such as public housing, medicaid, and food stamps (Addy & Wight, 2012). Over 15% of the population fell below this threshold in 2010. The percentage of people in deep poverty was 13.5% of all Blacks and 10.9% of all Hispanics, compared to 5.8% of Asians and 4.3% of Whites. While non-Hispanic Whites still constitute the largest single group of Americans living in poverty, ethnic minority groups are overrepresented (27.4 % African American; 28.4% American Indian and Alaskan Native; 26.6% Hispanic, and 12.1% Asian and Pacific Islander compared with 9.9% non-Hispanic White). These disparities are associated with the historical marginalization of ethnic minority groups and entrenched barriers to good education and jobs (Darling-Hammond, 2010; Gorski, 2007).

Millions of children and families are reported to be in poverty in 2012. According to the National Center for Children in Poverty (Addy & Wight, 2012), children represent 34% of people in poverty but are only 24% of the population. US Census data reveals that from 2009 to 2010, the total number of children under age 18 living in poverty increased to 16.4 million from 15.5 million. Child poverty rose from 20.7% in 2009 to 22% in 2010, and this is the highest it has been since 1993. Racial and ethnic disparities in poverty rates persist among children. The poverty rate for Black children was 38.2%, 32.3% for Hispanic children, 17% for non-Hispanic White children, and 13% for Asian children. The National Center for Children in Poverty (Addy & Wight, 2012) reports that 17.2 million children living in the US have a foreign-born parent, and 4.2 million children of immigrant parents are poor. It is reported that child poverty in immigrant families is more closely related to low-wage work and barriers to valuable work supports.

Many of the children in poverty live in single-parent households. The US Census Bureau (2012) reports that 24% of the 75 million children under age 18 in the US live in a single-mother household. The poverty rate for children living in female-householder families (no spouse present) was 42.2% in 2010. Seven in 10 children living with a single mother are poor or low-income, compared to less than a third (32%) of children living in other types of families. A staggering 50.9% of female-headed Hispanic households with children below 18 years of age live in poverty (48.8% for Blacks; 31.6% Asian, and 32.1% non-Hispanic White) (Addy & Wight, 2012). Single-mother headed households are more prevalent among African American and Hispanic families, contributing to racial/ethnic disparities in poverty (Hummer & Hamilton, 2010). Hummer and Hamilton (2010) note that financial status more than race, ethnicity, or education influences family stability.

Addy and Wight (2012) reported that only 9% of children living in poverty live in two-parent homes. At the time of the report, at least one family member was employed in two-thirds of the population of poor children. The majority of children living in poverty resided in eight states (California, Texas, New York, Florida, Illinois, Ohio, Georgia, and Michigan). Hispanic children made up the largest number of poor children (5.6 million); White children were the next largest group with 4.9 million children, while Black children in poverty were 4.0 million. However, Black children had the largest increase of all groups in 2009.

Twenty-four percent or greater of children aged five or under live in poverty. Of this group, 41% are Black and 35% are Hispanic. Seventy percent of the parents of children five and younger are employed in the workforce. It is not uncommon for members of these families to hold several jobs to support the basic needs of their family (Jensen, 2009). Fourteen percent of three year olds are in special education, Head Start or other state-funded preschool programs. The cost of center-based childcare for a four-year-old is prohibitive for families living in poverty. The cost is more than the annual in-state tuition for four-year colleges in 33 states and the District of Columbia (Addy & Wight, 2012).

Understanding the environmental constraints that impact children's learning and development is a precondition to providing effective and appropriate services against a social justice backdrop. In order for school policies to be responsive to the needs of families and students, environmental conditions need to be integrated in any analyses and solution of the problem. Hence, it is essential to understand the effects of poverty on child development, health, psychosocial behaviors, and academic achievement.

## Poverty and child development

Research has demonstrated that living in poverty has a wide range of negative effects on the physical and mental well-being of children (Artiles, Bal, & Thorius, 2010; Fram, Miller-Cribbs, & Horn, 2007; Gorski, 2007; Hilferty, Redmond, & Katz, 2010; Jensen, 2009). Poverty impacts children within their various contexts at home, in school, and in their neighborhoods and communities. Poverty is linked with negative conditions such as substandard housing, homelessness, inadequate nutrition and food insecurity, inadequate child care, lack of access to health care, unsafe neighborhoods, and under-resourced schools (Darling-Hammond, 2010; Jensen, 2009), which adversely impact our nation's children. In their study on poverty, race, and context of achievement in children living in the south, Fram et al. (2007) found that children of single parents overwhelmingly attended schools with a high ethnic student population. These students also had mothers who had lower levels of education and tended to live in homes with limited financial resources. High ethnic minority schools tended to have teachers with fewer years of teaching experience at that school, lower levels of certification, and there was disproportionately less diversity in the teaching staff. Additionally classrooms were less adequately equipped with educational resources, students exhibited low levels of reading, students were grouped by achievement levels, instruction centered on child-directed activities, and schools used universal evaluation standards. Hence, children living in low-income communities tended to attend schools with limited funding and high teacher attrition rates, which in turn impacted their access to educational resources.

Poorer children and teens are also at greater risk for several negative outcomes such as poor academic achievement, school dropout, abuse and neglect, behavioral and socioemotional problems, physical health problems, and developmental delays. These effects are compounded by the barriers children and their families encounter when trying to access physical and mental health care. Economists estimate that child poverty costs $500 billion a year to the US economy, reduces productivity and economic output by 1.3% of GDP, raises crime and increases health expenditure (Holzer, Schanzenbach, Duncan, & Ludwig, 2008).

Persistent rather than transient poverty has been demonstrated to have negative effects on all levels of functioning in children (D'Aoust, 2008). Persistent poverty is defined as poverty that is present through time intervals while transient poverty is not present at all times. For some families, poverty persists throughout the family's life (e.g., low or no employment, lack of employable skill, recurrent homelessness); for other families, poverty is transitory, with episodes occurring through the life events of the family (Betti & Verma, 1998).

Child development research has long indicated that the foundation for children's development of cognitive, social, behavioral, and emotional skills occurs within the first five years of life. Children born in poverty, which often includes poor health care and nutrition, are at risk for experiencing barriers to their maximum development. The outcome for them is often beginning school with lower achievement and a continuation of this gap throughout their school career (Artiles et al., 2010).

## Poverty and health

Children and teens living in poorer communities are at increased risk for a wide range of physical health problems (e.g., low birth weight, poor nutrition). Poor nutrition and inadequate access to food may lead to food insecurity and hunger. Additionally, lack of access to healthy foods can lead to childhood overweight or obesity. Maternal undernutrition during pregnancy increases the risk of negative birth outcomes, including premature birth, low birth weight, smaller head size, and lower brain weight (Federal Interagency Forum on Child and Family Statistics, 2011). Babies born prematurely are vulnerable to health problems and also to academic problems when they reach school age.

The first three years of a child's life marks the period of rapid brain development. Too little energy, protein, and nutrients during this sensitive period can lead to lasting deficits in cognitive, social, and emotional development. Protein-energy malnutrition, iron deficiency anemia, iodine, zinc, and other vitamin deficiencies in early childhood can cause brain impairment. Failure to reach major developmental milestones due to undernutrition affects 5–10% of American children under the age of three. Hunger reduces a child's motor skills, activity level, and motivation to explore the environment. Movement and exploration are important to cognitive development, and more active children elicit more stimulation and attention from their caregivers, which promotes social and emotional development (Jensen, 2009).

During childhood, families often work to keep their food insecurity hidden, and some parents may feel shame or embarrassment that they are not able to feed their children adequately. Children may also feel stigmatized, isolated, ashamed, or embarrassed by their lack of food. A community sample that classified low-income children ages six to 12 as hungry, at risk for hunger, or not hungry found that hungry children were significantly more likely to receive special education services, to have repeated a grade in school, and to have received mental health counseling than at risk for hunger or not hungry children (Jensen, 2009). In the same study, hungry children exhibited seven to 12 times as many symptoms of conduct disorder (such as fighting, blaming others for problems, having trouble with a teacher, not listening to rules, stealing) than their at risk or not hungry peers. Among low-income children, those classified as "hungry" showed increased anxious, irritable, aggressive, and oppositional behavior in comparison to peers (Jensen, 2009).

School-age children who experience severe hunger are at increased risk for the following negative outcomes: homelessness, chronic health conditions, stressful life conditions, psychiatric distress, behavioral problems, internalizing behaviors, including depression, anxiety, withdrawal, and poor self-esteem (Jensen, 2009). The effects of undernutrition depend on the length and severity of the period of hunger and may be mediated by other factors (i.e., improved nutrition, increased environmental stimulation, emotional support, and secure attachment to parents/caregivers). These factors can compensate for early undernutrition. Babies who receive adequate nutrition while in the womb appear to show higher cognitive performance in later childhood. The human brain is flexible and can recover from early deficits, but this also means that brain structures remain vulnerable to further negative experiences throughout childhood. Breastfeeding, attentive caretaking, and attention to environmental factors, such as sleep cycles and noise, can also promote healthy development (Jensen, 2009).

Furthermore, children living in poverty tend to exhibit chronic conditions such as asthma, anemia, or pneumonia. They also tend to engage in risky behaviors such as smoking or sexual activity. Fram et al. (2007) noted that many of the children living in poverty in high ethnic schools were born to mothers who became pregnant as teenagers. Additionally, exposure to environmental contaminants—for example, lead paint and toxic waste dumps—can lead to disability and mortality (Fram et al., 2007). The multiple stressors associated with poverty result in significantly increased risk for developing psychiatric and adaptive problems.

## Poverty and psychosocial behaviors

Children living in poverty are at greater risk for behavioral and emotional problems. Behavioral problems may include impulsiveness, difficulty getting along with peers, aggression, attention-deficit/hyperactivity disorder (ADHD) and conduct disorder. Emotional problems may include feelings of anxiety, depression, and low self-esteem. Poverty and economic hardship is particularly difficult for parents, who may experience chronic stress, depression, marital distress and exhibit harsher and/or inconsistent parenting behaviors (Jensen, 2009). These are all linked to poor social and emotional outcomes for children. Unsafe neighborhoods may expose low-income children to violence, which can cause a number of psychosocial difficulties. Violence exposure tends to predict future violent behavior in youth, which places them at greater risk of injury and mortality and entry into the juvenile justice system (Addy & Wight, 2011).

Poor behavioral functioning by children can lead to problems in school and society. According to the research, children from poor homes exhibit high degrees of social/behavioral problems. Some researchers have attributed this to lack of parental responsive interaction with children and more punitive forms of discipline (Jensen, 2009). According to Eamon (2000), as the number of years in poverty increases, the severity of problems with depression, anxiety, and dependence rises. Additionally it was determined that there is an association between persistent poverty and a child's internalizing of behaviors.

Currently the justice system competes with the educational system for funding (Darling-Hammond, 2010). Data from the juvenile justice system shows that the number of young girls has increased by 50% since 1980. Black and Native American girls are three to four times respectively more likely to be incarcerated than White girls. Two thirds of youth in the juvenile justice system are minority youth. Additionally, Black youth are three times more likely to be arrested for a violent offense. Although Black youth only make up 17% for the total youth population, they account for 62% of the youths prosecuted in adult courts. Black youth are four times more likely and Hispanic youth are three times more likely to be placed in residential treatment than their White counterparts (Addy & Wight, 2011). Hence, there appears to be a correlation between the development of psychosocial issues, placement in the juvenile justice system, and living in poverty.

## Poverty and education

President Obama reiterated the value of education in his letter preceding the reauthorization of the Elementary and Secondary Education Act (ESEA) with the following comment: "A world-class education is also a moral imperative—the key to securing a more equal, fair, and just society. We will not remain true to our highest ideals unless we do a far better job of educating each one of our sons and daughters. We will not be able to keep the American promise of equal opportunity if we fail to provide a world-class education to every child" (US Department of Education, 2010, p. 1). However, the realities continue to be in contrast with these ideals.

If student progress is an outcome of the reciprocal relationships between the school and home, then schools servicing students from low-income communities should provide resources to stem the effects of poverty on achievement. However, disparities in educational achievement are well documented for students living in poverty as well as for ethnic minorities (Darling-Hammond, 2010; Hilferty et al., 2010; Kozol, 1991, 1995, 2007). Poverty has a particularly adverse effect on the academic outcomes of children, especially during early childhood. Chronic stress associated with living in poverty has been shown to adversely affect children's concentration and memory, which may impact their ability to learn. The National Center for Education Statistics reports that in 2008, the dropout rate of students living in low-income families was about 4.5 times greater than the rate of children from higher-income families (8.7% versus 2.0%). Remaining in and completing school is essential for productive adulthood (Doll et al., 2012) and is a major deterrent to contact with the juvenile justice system. However, some students living in poverty are never able to access this opportunity to complete school. Thus, failure to complete school results in lowered wages over a person's lifetime and contributes to the cycle of poverty for the individual and the community (US Department of Education, National Center for Education Statistics, Institute of Education Sciences, 2010).

The academic achievement gap for poorer youth is particularly pronounced for low-income Black and Hispanic children compared with their more affluent White peers. Under-resourced schools in poorer communities struggle to meet the learning needs of their students and aid them in fulfilling their potential. Inadequate education contributes to the cycle of poverty by making it more difficult for low-income children to lift themselves and future generations out of poverty (Darling-Hammond, 2010; Kozol, 1991, 1995). Lifting oneself out of poverty by the bootstrap is a popular part of cultural American folklore. This folklore is predicated on the cultural notion of independence and individual achievement (Singleton & Linton, 2006). This premise connotes that all individuals are given access to the same resources and are able to compete on an equal playing field. However, inequality in educational resources denies low-income children the "means of competition" (Kozol, 1991) in a global market. Darling-Hammond (2010) argues that instead of talking about the achievement gap, educators and policy makers need to be privy to the "opportunity gap." She defines this as "the accumulated differences in access to key educational resources: expert teachers, personalized attention, high-quality curriculum opportunities, good educational materials, and plentiful information resources—that support learning at home and at school" (p. 28). Limited access to these resources over the course of time manifests itself as educational deficiencies and competing at the national and global levels is unattainable for those with limited access to these resources.

Some blame children and families living in poverty for their condition. For example, Lawrence Mead, a professor of political science at New York University, states "if poor people behaved rationally, they would seldom be poor for long in the first place" (Kozol, 1995, p. 21). Darling-Hammond (2010) notes that limited access to educational resources is a byproduct of institutionally sanctioned discrimination that is based in part on America's ideology of race inferiority. Thus, allocation of resources based on race and/or class is an exosytemic variable that continues to influence the achievement of children living in poverty by denying them access to capital they need for success.

Throughout the 19th and 20th centuries, children of color were excluded from access to competitive educational resources. This denial created generations of individuals who did not have the much-needed cultural capital. Students of color were able to access educational resources in the 1960s and 1970s by gaining entrance to better schools with better curriculums and qualified teachers. Nevertheless, current enrollment and achievement figures suggest that inequality of funds and/or resources continue to impact the achievement of low-income students attending US schools today.

The Children's Defense Fund (2011) presents some startling statistics on the state of education. Schools in the US are becoming resegregated, with 78% of Hispanic and 73% of Black students attending predominantly minority schools. Black, Hispanic, and American Indian students continue to be underrepresented in gifted and talented programs. While underrepresented in gifted classes, Black students are overrepresented in special education classes for mental retardation and emotional disturbances. Black students are three times more likely to be suspended than White and/or Asian Pacific Islander students and twice as likely to be suspended from school as Hispanic students. Black students have the lowest high school graduation rate (61.5%) of the groups represented. Hispanics have a slightly higher rate, with Asian–Pacific Islander students having the highest graduation rate (91.4%). The Black/White gap and Hispanic/White gap for college completion remain wide.

Darling-Hammond (2010) identifies several major stumbling blocks that contribute to the unequal and inadequate educational outcomes for children living in poverty:

> the high level of poverty and the low levels of social supports for low income children's health and welfare, including their early learning opportunities; the unequal allocation of school resources, which is made politically easier by increasing resegregation of schools; inadequate systems for providing high quality teachers and teaching to all children in all communities; rationing of high quality curriculum through tracking and interschool disparities; and factory model school designs that have created dysfunctional learning environments for students and unsupportive settings for strong teaching. (p. 30)

Many of the facilitators of failure are outside the realm of both parents' and children's control, yet they exert the greatest influence on students' academic productivity.

## Poverty, Education, and Academic Skills

There is a growing body of research that implies that early intervention services for children living in poverty are key to stemming the tide of continued failure (Jensen, 2009). However, many children living in low-income communities do not have access to the resources at home or in the community that would enable them to develop "the communication and interaction skills, motor development, cognitive skills, and social–emotional skills" (Darling-Hammond, 2010, p. 33). Hart and Risley (1995) found that what parents did with their children in the first three years of language learning had an enormous impact on how much language the children used and learned. Generalizing from their results, they found that working-class children had 125,000 words of language experience per week, while children of welfare families had 62,000 words of language experience. They further noted that at the end of a year, children of working-class families would have more than 6 million words of language experience, while children of welfare families would have more than 3 million words. In addition, they found that the interactive language experiences of families accounted for 61% of the variance in the rates of vocabulary growth and use.

It has been documented that 30–40% of children enter kindergarten without the prerequisite language and/or social emotional skills necessary for success. By first grade, "only half as many first graders from poor families are proficient at understanding words in context and engaging in basic mathematics as first graders from non-poor families" (Darling-Hammond, 2010, p. 33). Many school curriculums fail to take into consideration the beginning skill level of students from poor families and treat these students as already equipped with the basic skills necessary for educational survival. Lisa Delpit (2006) challenges educators to teach children with limited skills the code to access the curriculum. Immersing limited language proficient students in literature-rich environments will not increase literacy unless these students are taught the skills to access it. Rather than viewing a child's difficulty in the classroom as a mismatch between the demands of the assignment and the skill level of the child, current instructional pacing guidelines blames the child for not keeping pace with the curriculum. Williams and Greenleaf (2012) argue that an "intrapsychic perspective dominates the professional discourse" (p. 141). This discourse ignores the reciprocal relationship between the child and his or her environment.

Although pre-kindergarten and early intervention enrollments are growing, lower-income students continue to participate at a lower rate (Darling-Hammond, 2010). Given this trend, schools need to have supports in place to facilitate learning. Hence, waiting until a child fails would be committing educational malpractice. Having a social justice perspective is looking beyond the individual needs of the child and recognizing the demands of the community and thus creating programs to meet the needs of students who attend schools with limited literacy skills. Consequentially, a social justice perspective in school psychology encourages a preventative approach rather than a reactive approach to problem solving (Williams & Greenleaf, 2012).

In addition to starting school with limited skills, students in these communities are also faced with inadequate curricula. Darling-Hammond (2010) notes that schools educating these children tend to offer more remedial and vocational course work instead of college prep work. In integrated schools, students are further denied access due to honors courses being primarily reserved for Whites and Asians. Many will argue that minority students from low-income communities do not have the skills to access this curriculum and would fail if placed in these courses. While this may be true given the early educational experiences of these children, it is not fair to assume that, given the same early opportunities as many of their peers in non high-ethnic and high-income areas, these students would not be able to achieve (Noguera, 2008).

The notion that parents of low-income children do not care about education needs to be further examined given the environmental constraints of the child's home, community, and school. Although many of these children attend under-resourced schools, this is not initially a deterrent to attendance. However, at some later date, they become disenfranchised and drop out or underperform. A social justice perspective encourages us to move beyond blaming the students who continue to be disenfranchised and instead to understand, identify, and advocate for resources at the school, district, and community levels that are necessary for success.

## Poverty, Education, and Resegregation

As indicated earlier, American schools are currently engaged in resegregation. Although the concept of "separate but equal" was challenged in *Brown v. Board of Education*, American schools appear to be returning to the vestiges of the past. Darling-Hammond (2010) argues that resegregation is a byproduct of the inequalities in resource allocations. It is important to note that segregation occurs not only between schools but within schools, with class-based segregation increasing as a function of tracking. Tracking is a system whereby segregated experiences are created for students in integrated schools. Traditionally, the systems of tracking have prevented minority students from accessing college preparatory courses and instead they are educated in lower level and vocational classes (Broussard & Joseph, 1998). As is evident, students relegated to these courses are in no way prepared to participate in the local and global markets. Broussard and Joseph (1998) classify this form of practice as educational neglect. In many ways, this can also be understood as educational negligence against children living in low-income communities.

Schools high in ethnic minority students often lack resources. For example, these schools are often staffed by uncertified educators, have rapid turnover of uncertified and untrained teachers, have fewer educational resources, and offer limited exposure to high-achieving peers (Darling-Hammond, 2010; Kozol, 1991, 1995; Perry, 2011). Students attending these schools may not see a core-subject teacher and may instead be taught by substitutes all year (Kozol, 1991, 1995). Despite such conditions, these students are expected to excel on state assessments and, if unable to perform, they are penalized with the removal of resources from their schools. Perry (2011) argues that being a teacher in an under-resourced school is depressing for the adult. One then can only imagine what message this sends to the students attending such schools. Hence, the resegregation of American schools can be characterized as "apartheid schools," that is "schools serving exclusively students of color in low-income communities" (Darling-Hammond, 2010, p. 38). Separate but equal did not raise educational standards prior to *Brown v. Board of Education*, nor will it do so now if American schools revert to past failures.

## Poverty, Education, and Teachers

Qualified teachers motivate students to learn regardless of their backgrounds. Teacher education background, certification, preparation for teaching, and years of teaching significantly shape student achievement. The effect of having a qualified teacher was larger than the effects of race and parent education combined (Darling-Hammond, 2010; Kozol, 2007; Perry, 2011). The reality is that students from these communities are routinely assigned the teachers with the least qualifications. The main reason schools hire unqualified teachers is finance. Many public schools in low-income areas are unable to attract qualified teachers with the salaries provided (Kozol, 1995). Research documents the negative effects on student achievement when unqualified teachers are hired (Darling-Hammond, 2010).

Schools in low-income communities also tend to lack a teaching force that is representative of the student body. In November 2001, a National Summit examining diversity in the teaching force concluded, "although teacher quality has been accepted and internalized as a mantra for school reform, the imperative for diversity is often marginalized rather than accepted as central to the quality equation in teaching" (National Collaborative on Diversity in the Teaching Force, 2004, p. 3). There is general agreement among policymakers, teacher educators, school leaders, and ethnic community leaders that the education profession needs more ethnic diversity. Increasing these professionals would provide opportunities for all students to learn ethnic, racial, and cultural diversity; increase the number of role models available for students; and learning would be enriched because of shared racial, ethnic, and cultural identities (National Collaborative on Diversity in the Teaching Force, 2011). Bosser (2011) reported that at a national level, students of color are 40% of the public school population. However, teachers of color are only 17% of the teaching force. It was also noted that students of color do better on a variety of academic outcomes if teachers of color teach them (Bosser, 2011).

Sanchez, Thornton, and Usinger (2009) reported that principals are expected to be instructional leaders who create conditions that significantly improve student achievement. Given the diversity of students in schools, principals who are from minorities make unique contributions to this student population in several ways. These school leaders often increase student comfort levels in school, motivate them, and help to increase student achievement in minorities. Given the positive behaviors a minority school leader can engender, their demographics continue to be out of sync with the student population. In the 2007–2008 school year, 17.6% of principals in the US schools were from minority backgrounds (Sanchez et. al, 2009). Minorities constituted 6.3% of school leaders in rural areas and in small towns only 6.2%.

These data strongly suggest the need for more ethnic minority teachers and school leaders. It should be noted that teachers and leaders from all backgrounds can be effective with minority students. However, many minority teachers/leaders have an understanding of the culture, language, and practices such that they can connect more effectively with people who have some common experiences. Sanchez et al. (2009) noted that minority leaders are able to empathize with certain students in ways that positively influence academic behaviors. Unfortunately, recruiting and retaining educators of color continues to plague the profession.

## Implications for School Psychology Practice

### Poverty, education, and the school psychologist

Dwyer (nd) reported that school psychologists are aware that how the poor are educated is a national crisis. School psychologists strive to be experts in learning and behavior, resiliency leaders in schools, prevention specialists, and systems change advocates. Training and practice make school psychologists prepared to support learning for children in general. For example, current educational policies (i.e., RtI) encourage school psychologists to utilize an ecological perspective when determining the cause of students' academic and behavioral difficulties. However, the specifics related to poverty and an ecological model are not always adequately included/considered when working with children in poverty. In addition to utilizing an ecological perspective, the profession as a whole needs to reflect the diversity of the population it serves. The issues and opportunities provided by having diverse teachers and administrators are also applicable for school psychologists.

However, there is a dearth of minority school psychologists in the profession. Research by Curtis, Castillo, and Gelley (in press) showed that more than 90% of school psychologists identified themselves as Caucasian in 2010. In this period, representation in the field has increased very little for school psychologists who identify themselves as African American (+1.5 percentage points) or Hispanic (+1.9 percentage points). Additionally, the representation of other minority groups seems to have remained relatively unchanged or may have declined. According to Curtis et al. (in press), the majority of all school psychologists participating in the study (97.4%) reported serving students who are members of racial/ethnic minority groups. One half (52.6%) serve a student population that includes 25% or more minority students, and greater than one-third (36%) serve a student population that is 50% or more minority students. It was noted that only 9.3% of school psychologists overall are identified as minorities. In 30 years, the minority representation in the field has changed little, if at all. This trajectory is problematic given the increasingly diverse needs of the public school student body. Students, poor and non-poor, need the opportunity to be exposed to professionals who share similar cultural experiences. As schools become more diverse we must recognize the contributions diverse leaders (e.g., school psychologists) in schools can make to help students succeed (Sanchez et al., 2009). As a field, it is imperative that we highlight barriers to recruitment and retention of professionals from minority communities.

The National Association of School Psychologists (NASP) as well as other professional psychological associations at national and state levels has attempted to increase the number of school psychologists of color. However, the numbers of ethnic minorities in the profession remain at static levels. The issues of cultural competence related to teachers of color are also relevant for school psychologists. Students of color require professional role models that are school psychologists. This is important since school psychologists interact with students, teachers, parents, administrators, and the community in myriad ways. Students of color and their families and community partners need the opportunity to be a part of solutions that often allow a personal connection where they can feel less controlled and more empowered to participate in the educational process. Nevertheless, practitioners, irrespective of color, need to increase their knowledge of working with families and children living in low-income communities.

## Social Justice and the School Psychologist

If you are like us, after having read the bulk of this chapter, you may be feeling overwhelmed by the amount of information presented on children living in poverty. It is probably easier to believe that the trajectory for students living in these conditions cannot be changed. It is more common for the schools we work in to blame the parents for not valuing education and the children for not performing. However, reexamining the system we chose to work in is what is imperative. The NASP 2011 conference motto was "being an advocate for the emotional well-being of our nation's youths." Additionally, two of the three task forces appointed by the 2011 president of the American Psychological Association focused on issues of diversity and poverty with an overlay of social justice. As suggested earlier, incorporating a social justice perspective in the practice of school psychology will mandate advocacy and/or action on our part at the school, district, and community levels. What does it mean to be an advocate? It is necessary to note that advocacy for our students would fail if based on limited and/or faulty information.

How then does one build advocacy? To answer this question, we borrow from Carroll's (2009) discussion on how to build multicultural competence. Carroll identifies four flashpoints for action: awareness, acknowledgement and knowledge, advocacy, and action.

Awareness is the first step in evaluating our personal values and beliefs as it pertains to families living in poverty. Additionally, we need to be aware of systemic issues such as educational, class, and ethnic privilege as they relate to children living in poverty. As we unpack the invisible knapsack (McIntosh, 1990) of privileges we enjoy as educated middle-class professionals, we can begin to understand the journey children living in poverty experience. Awareness promotes acknowledgement and knowledge. Carroll (2009) notes that this is the growth stage that involves two processes: a cognitive process and a reorganization of knowledge.

The cognitive process recognizes and evaluates the systemic institutionalized barriers to equitable education. In the reorganization of knowledge, the student is no longer perceived to be a victim, the parents are no longer seen as not supporting education, and the child's educational difficulties are evaluated from an ecological perspective. One's acknowledgement about the systemic inequalities and burgeoning knowledge energizes advocacy skills. Carroll (2009) defines this as a process by which our awareness, beliefs, knowledge are transformed into a plan for effecting change. As school psychologists, this may affect the types of assessments we complete, when and how we conduct our assessments, or the development and implementation of interventions for the classroom and home. The final stage of this process is action. Advocacy empowers action which leads to renewed awareness. According to Carroll (2009), action is doing something in a proactive and/or preventative way to promote social justice. As school psychologists, this may look different in our school communities depending on our resources, but more importantly this is action both at the systems and individual levels.

A hallmark of our profession is our ability to collaborate successfully with teachers. We need to use our collaborative skills to also work closely with other support staff in and outside the school to support students living in poverty. The schools that succeed in low-income communities also tend to serve as community centers, offering a multitude of services in addition to education.

Finally, for those school psychologists who prefer a prescribed approach to social justice activism, Gorski (nd) provides a five-step process. The first step is food, festivals, and fun. While this step does not have the potential to directly address issues of poverty, racism, etc., it does tend to focus on surface-level cultural awareness, which allows the individual to interact at beginning levels of social contact with others. The second level is charitable giving. This level is one way to contribute to social justice movements by donating money or goods to human rights organizations such as local food banks or United for a Fair Economy. A third step is individual advocacy, which allows for personal relationships with those less privileged than you. Activism at this level is for people who are acutely aware of how injustice has affected the individual but are not ready to advocate at the systems level. The fourth step is service and volunteerism. Organizing fundraisers, helping to build homes for the economically disadvantaged, and/or working at a shelter are examples. Gorski (nd) points out that at this level the individual is doing the work of social justice, not simply supporting the work of social justice. The fifth and final level is systemic reform for social justice. These activities focus on organizing and acting on a larger scale. For example, they are more interested in eliminating overall poverty and in transforming institutions for equity and justice. School psychologists are encouraged to find their "tier" on the social justice activism scale and move into a new arena of advocacy for the children, families, schools, and communities we serve.

In order to effectively work with families and children living in poverty, we need to be cognizant of the inequities in education. We must further recognize that these families and children do not have the same access to resources as high-income communities. As a result, we need to be proactive in implementing programs that reduce the inequities such as early reading interventions, establishing home–school collaborations/partnerships that focus on families' needs rather than the system, and/or parenting classes. We need to learn creative ways of supporting teachers who articulate difficulties working with students from low-income communities. In many ways, we need to learn to work effectively with other support staff to appropriately support students and families. Finally, we must conduct assessments and develop interventions that "counter class inequalities and injustices, that put the onus of responsibility for change on us and the system and not on the students and parents historically underserved by US schools" (Gorski, 2007, pp. 32–33).

## Conclusion

The discourse of social justice in school psychology is relatively new and has been mainly addressed in the literature from a multicultural, diversity, or cultural competence perspective. Nevertheless, traditional discourse can be easily integrated within a social justice purview. Traditional discourse on diversity centers primarily on an individual's development (i.e., school psychologist) of a multicultural/cultural perspective/competence. Carroll's (2009) flashpoints for developing multicultural competence are an example of an introspective journey. Additionally, Gorski (nd) provides a roadmap for developing a social justice action process. However, a social justice lens requires both introspection and systemically understanding the ecological environments in which children living in low-income communities interact. Williams and Greenleaf (2012) argue that the "strength of the ecological perspective is its recognition that a person's mental health is intimately linked with the quality of interactions he or she experiences with the environment" (p. 145). An ecologically infused social justice lens encourages practitioners to evaluate the effects and impacts of systemic injustices that continue to perpetuate the opportunity gap. As such, it provides the practitioner with an opportunity to think about services at a more global than child-specific level (Gutkin, 2012). Williams and Greenleaf (2012) note that school-based professionals can "negotiate systems and services on behalf of students, help students gain access to needed resources, identify potential allies, build a platform of support, and design and implement action plans for confronting environmental barriers" (p. 150). We can positively impact the educational trajectory of children living in poverty by advocating for the equitable allocation of resources at the community, district and school levels.

Finally, the multicultural perspective is an individual perspective while social justice incorporates the multicultural and cultural competence perspectives at a larger, global level. School psychologists have the opportunity to challenge and depart from policies and practices that continue to result in student failure. They can use their skills to become advocates who challenge ineffective paradigms and promote those that enable student learning and success.

# References

Addy, S. & Wight, V. (2012). *Basic facts about low-income children, 2010. Children under age 18.* New York, NY: National Center for Children in Poverty.

Artiles, A. J., Bal, A., & Thorius, K. A. K. (2010). Back to the future: A critique of response to intervention's social justice views. *Theory into Practice, 49*, 250–257.

Betti, G., & Verma, K. (1999). *Measuring the degree of poverty in a dynamic and comparative context: A multi-dimensional approach using fuzzy set theory.* Paper presented at the Sixth Islamic Countries Conference on Statistical Sciences, Lahore, Pakistan.

Bosser, U. (2011). *Teacher diversity matters.* Washington, DC: Center for American Progress.

Broussard, C. A., & Joseph, A. L. (1998). Tracking: A form of educational neglect? *Social Work in Education, 20* (2), 110–120.

Carroll, D. W. (2009). Toward multiculturalism competence: A practical model for implementation in the schools. In J. Jones (Ed.), *The psychology of multiculturalism in the schools: A primer for practice, training, and research* (pp. 1–15). Bethesda, MD: National Association of School Psychologists.

Children's Defense Fund. (2011). *The state of America's children.* Washington, DC: Children's Defense Fund.

Crockett, D., & Brown, J. (2009). Multicultural practices and response to intervention. In J. Jones (Ed.), *The psychology of multiculturalism in the schools: A primer for practice, training, and research* (pp. 117–137). Bethesda, MD: National Association of School Psychologists.

Curtis, M., Castillo, J., & Gelley, C. (in press). School psychology 2010: Demographic characteristics of school psychologists and the context for their professional practice. *Communiqué.*

D'Aoust, R. (2008). *The impact of early childhood poverty on academic achievement and the influence of supportive parenting,* Doctoral dissertation, University of Rochester.

Darling-Hammond, L. (2010). *The flat world and education: How America's commitment to equity will determine our future.* New York, NY: Teachers College Press.

Delpit, L. (2006). *Other people's children: Cultural conflict in the classroom.* New York, NY: New Press.

Doll, B., Spies, R., & Champion, A. (2012). Contribution of ecological school mental health services to students' academic success. *Journal of Educational and Psychological Consultation, 22*, 44–61.

Dwyer, K. (nd). Prioritize educating children living in poverty. *Communiqué Online.* Retrieved from www.nasponline.org/publications/cq/index.aspx?vol=39&issue=6

Eamon, K. (2000). Structure model of the effects of poverty on externalizing and internalizing behaviors of four-to-five year old children. *Social Work Research, 24* (3), 143–155.

Federal Interagency Forum on Child and Family Statistics. (2011). *America's children: Key national indicators of well-being.* Washington, DC: Government Printing Office.

Fram, M. S., Miller-Cribbs, M., & Horn, L.V. (2007). Poverty, race, and the contexts of achievement: Examining educational experiences of children in the U.S. south. *Social Work, 52* (4), 309–319.

Gorski, P. C. (nd). Five approaches to social activism. Retrieved August 29, 2012 from www.EdChange.org

Gorski, P. C. (2007). The question of class. *Teaching Tolerance, 31*, 30–37.

Gutkin, T. B. (2012). Ecological psychology: Replacing the medical model paradigm for school-based psychological and psychoeducational services. *Journal of Educational and Psychological Consultation, 22*, 1–20.

Hart, B. & Risley, T. R. (1995). Meaningful differences in the everyday experiences of young American children. Baltimore, MD: Paul H. Brookes.

Hilferty, F., Redmond, G., & Katz, I. (2010). The implications of poverty on children's readiness to learn. *Australian Journal of Early Childhood, 35* (4), 63–71.

Holzer, H., Schanzenbach, D., Duncan, G., & Ludwig, J. (2008). The economic costs of childhood poverty in the United States. *Journal of Children and Poverty, 14,* 41–61.

Hummer, R. A., & Hamilton, E. R. (2010). Race and ethnicity in fragile families. *Future of Children, 20* (2), 113–117.

Jensen, E. (2009). *Teaching with poverty in mind: What being poor does to kids' brains and what schools can do about it.* Alexandra, VA: ASCD Publications.

Kozol, J. (1991). *Savage inequalities: Children in America's schools.* New York, NY: Harper Perennial.

Kozol, J. (1995). *Amazing grace: The lives of children and the conscience of a nation.* New York, NY: Crown.

Kozol, J. (2007). *Letters to a young teacher.* New York, NY: Random House.

McIntosh, P. (1990). White privilege: Unpacking the invisible knapsack. *Independent School, 49* (2), 31–36.

Miranda, A. (2009). Understanding privilege in America. In J. Jones (Ed.), *The psychology of multiculturalism in the schools: A primer for practice, training, and research* (pp. 67–82). Bethesda, MD: National Association of School Psychologists.

National Collaborative on Diversity in the Teaching Force. (2004). *Assessment of diversity in America's teaching force: A call to action.* Washington, DC: National Collaborative on Diversity in the Teaching Force.

Noguera, P. A. (2008). *The trouble with black boys . . . and other reflections on race, equity, and the future of public education.* San Francisco, CA: Jossey-Bass.

Perry, S. (2011). *Push has come to shove: Getting our kids the education they deserve—Even if it means picking a fight.* New York, NY: Crown.

Sanchez, J., Thornton, B., & Usinger, J. (2009). Increasing the ranks of minority leadership. *Educational Leadership, 67* (2).

Shriberg, D., Bonner, M., Sarr, B. J., Walker, A. M., Hyland, M., & Chester, C. (2008). Social justice through a school psychology lens: Definition and applications. *School Psychology Review, 37* (4), 453–468.

Singleton, G. E., & Linton, C. (2006). *A field guide for achieving equity in schools: Courageous conversations about race.* Thousand Oaks, CA: Corwin Press.

US Census Bureau. (2012). Washington, DC. Retrieved August 29, 2012 from www.census.gov/cps

US Department of Education. (2010). Office of Planning, Evaluation and Policy Development, ESEA. A *blueprint for reform.* Washington, DC: US Department of Education.

US Department of Education, National Center for Education Statistics, Institute of Education Sciences (2010). *Trends in high school dropout and completion rates in the United States: 1972–2008 (NCES 2011–012).* Washington, DC: US Department of Education.

Williams, J. M., & Greenleaf, A. T. (2012). Ecological psychology: Potential contribution to social justice and advocacy in school settings. *Journal of Educational and Psychological Consultation, 22,* 141–157.

nine
# Social Justice in the Air: School Culture and Climate

## Samuel Y. Song and Kelly Marth

The idea that society exerts a force upon individuals has a rich history. Early philosophical views of human nature such as John Locke's *tabula rasa*, stressing the importance of context on child development, and the classic nature/nurture debates within developmental psychology are two important examples of thinking about environmental influence in psychology. The fields of organizational psychology and social psychology have also supported the idea that organizations have a powerful influence on the individuals that constitute them (e.g., Robbins, 2002). Because schools are organizations, it is not surprising to find that the categories of school culture and school climate have been examined across several fields including school psychology. This chapter seeks to review the school culture and climate constructs within a social justice framework for school psychological practice. Specifically, the chapter has three sections and (a) discusses the current state of school culture and climate literature ("The Status Quo of School Culture and Climate"), (b) articulates a vision of social justice practice ("Social Justice Transformation of School Culture and Climate"), and (c) describes what social justice practice might look like ("Social Justice Practice of School Culture and Climate").

## The Status Quo of School Culture and Climate

Before considering how social justice might transform school culture and climate, it is important to examine the existing literature on the topics. This section discusses definitions of school culture and climate, factors that maintain them, and current best practices.

## What Is It?

School culture and climate are important facets of the environment, or context, in schools, which have been shown to influence teachers and students (Anderson, 1982; Kasen, Johnson, Chen, Crawford, & Cohen, 2011; Kasen, Johnson, & Cohen, 1990; Johnson, 2009). Searching the literature on these topics will reveal a rich history, albeit a confusing one, as the numerous definitions for school culture and school climate sometimes overlap with one another, supplement one another, and even contradict one another. Indeed, after reviewing the school climate literature, Anderson noted that school climate is an elusive concept (1982). Now, more than 30 years later, the elusiveness of school climate still appears valid (Johnson, 2009, reviewed school climate effects on violence, showing the variety in the literature). Nevertheless, a definition of each is offered here based on themes from the literature (see Figure 9.1).

School culture refers to the norms and values found in a school (Aleman, 2012; Anderson, 1982; Martin, 2002). *Norms* include common practices in schools that are both formal (e.g., meetings) and informal (e.g., hallway discussions), and commonly held ideas and beliefs that are both explicit (e.g., school rules of behavior) and implicit (e.g., unspoken teacher expectations for behavior). *Values* are largely tacit and implied, preferred goals and standards that underlie norms (e.g., fairness), but also include explicit values such as ones that are expressed in a school mission statement. A subset of school culture is school climate: the collective "feel for a place" that one gets from visiting a school for the first time based on the interactions among school adults and students within a school (Anderson, 1982; Ervin & Schaughency, 2008). Researchers frequently consider school climate as shared perceptions about the school as a whole or facets of the school's environment. For example, school bullying is often conceived as integral to school climate and

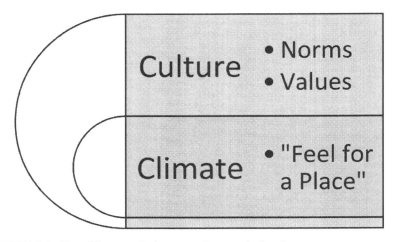

FIGURE 9.1. The difference between culture and climate.

related to perceptions of school safety (Swearer & Espelage, 2011). School climate has also included other factors such as openness and competitiveness among faculty and students (Anderson, 1982). Measurement issues for both school culture and climate are complex, as researchers must decide between multiple methods (i.e., observations, interviews, case studies, surveys) and multiple informants (i.e., administrators, teachers, staff, community, students), which contribute to the varying definitions of these constructs.

To illustrate the concepts of school culture and climate, the following case example entitled *Pink Power* will be used throughout the chapter:

> Sol is a ninth-grade teenager in high school. One day he wears a pink polo to school for the first time. In the hallways, a group of 10 teenage boys bully him by teasing that he is "gay." His friends watch and want to help, but do not help. Other classmates who see the bullying have mixed reactions, some watch and ignore the bullying, some laugh, and some join in by bullying Sol themselves. Sol tells the teacher, Ms Jack, how he feels. She giggles, saying that they are just joking. When Sol disagrees with Ms Jack, she then tells him to "man up," and that it's not a big deal; she had been bullied herself growing up, but she got through it and is a better person now. Ms Jack then tells Sol to stick up for himself by telling the boys to stop it the next time it happens. Sol leaves with his head down.

The case example of Sol's bullying is helpful in identifying school culture and climate and their complex interaction. The first question to ask is why does the color pink elicit such a strong behavioral response in others? It is likely that if Sol had worn a blue polo, he would not have been bullied that day. It is also likely that girls do not get teased for wearing pink at this school. It is as if the other boys were enforcing the unwritten rule that "men don't wear pink" and "if you do, then you are gay." The unwritten rule is an example of a *norm* of the school culture, i.e., heterosexuality is the standard or heteronormativity (Nadal, Rivera, & Corpus, 2010; Schmidt, 2010). Cultural norms are by definition valued more and therefore considered "right" by the dominant group, which is why heteronormativity produced enforcement of the norm within the school culture in the form of bullying, which is part of school climate (McCabe & Rubinson, 2008; Swearer & Espelage, 2011).

Second, going deeper into Sol's case example, we should ask why no one helped Sol as he was being bullied. While the answer here is more complex, it is illustrative to highlight several factors that are most relevant. Clearly heteronormativity also influenced the behavior of Sol's friends, the peer witnesses, and Ms Jack. In addition, the American value of rugged individualism also seems to be at play here (Carter, 2000; Smith, Bond, & Kagitcibasi, 2006). The overvaluing of individualism and autonomy appears to underlie beliefs that only the strong survive and that we are responsible for pulling ourselves up by the bootstraps, which may be related to why no one helped Sol, and especially evident in Ms Jack's response that he should stick up for himself and deal with it because she did as a youth. Finally, because helping others during bullying situations does not appear to be normative in this school culture, Sol's friends and peers who seemed to want to help may have been experiencing that it was unsafe to help Sol, which is part of the school climate.

## How It Is Maintained

Understanding how culture and climate are maintained in a school is foundational to comprehending current best practices in improving them. While there are conceptual differences between school culture and climate, which have been articulated previously, reviewing the literature has revealed that the broad factors that promote and maintain them are the same in schools (see Figure 9.2). This is not surprising given that both constructs are general environmental descriptions of schools with much overlap in the literature. The *Pink Power* case example will be used to illustrate these seven broad factors: structural, community, school leadership, culture of school adults, informal practices, family influence, and student influence.

The *structural* area includes factors that give the school its shape or order, such as laws and policies and the physical building. Laws and policies affect school order by providing guidelines and consequences for schools, which contributes to school culture and climate (see Chapter 6 for discussion of school discipline policy). There are several Federal Civil Rights laws that protect students from harassment and discrimination based on race, color, national origin, sex, or disability (Title VI of the Civil Rights act of 1964, Title IX of the Education Amendments of 1972, Section 504 of the Rehabilitation Act of 1973, and Title II of the Americans with Disabilities Act of 1990). Moreover, most schools across the country have passed

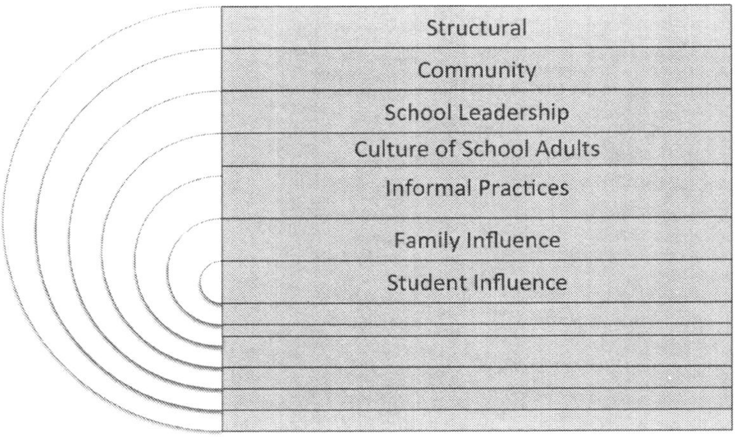

FIGURE 9.2. The various factors that shape the development of culture and climate.

or are in the process of passing state anti-bullying laws and policies (Limber, 2011) that also influence school culture and climate. Unfortunately, however, as laws and policies are being passed throughout the country at higher rates, the explicit inclusion of GLBTQ language is lagging (Gay, Lesbian, and Straight Education Network [GLSEN], 2010). In the case example, while Sol's school may not be in violation of federal and state laws, it is obligated to act in compliance with them and protect Sol from bullying in general. It would be important to also assess whether Sol's school policy includes GLBTQ language. If it did not, then this would be the impetus for advocacy (discussed later in the chapter). Finally, the physical school building literally gives shape to the school and influences school interactions and how school might be perceived (Johnson, 2009). For example, bullying is most likely to occur in physical locations that naturally make it difficult for adults to supervise, such as the back corner of a hallway (Olweus, 1991). More recently, schools that only provide gender-specific restrooms compared to the preferred gender-neutral ones are seen to create an unsafe and uncaring school climate for students with varying gender identities and gender expressions, as opportunities for bullying may increase in gender-specific restrooms (GLSEN, n.d.).

*Community* consists of the neighborhood (i.e., neighborhood issues and demographic factors) as well as the local school board. Collectively, the community directly and indirectly influences the school culture and climate (Felner et al., 1995; Haynes, 1996; Johnson, 2009). For example, a high rate of neighborhood violence and whether the local school board actively addresses bullying has an effect on Sol's school environment. The school board's sensitivity to GLBTQ issues is also likely to have an influence on the school environment.

*School leadership* is the third factor influencing the culture and climate in a school. The best way to understand the importance of leadership is to highlight that the anti-bullying laws and policies are most effective when enforced in a school, which falls primarily under the role of the school principal and other leaders. Moreover, the leadership sets the agenda for a school to embrace certain values over others that are embodied by the teachers and staff, supporting the primary importance of the leadership in directing school culture (Aleman, 2012; Chang & Le, 2010).

Fourth, *school adults* have a profound influence in schools because of their powerful and authoritative roles over students as teachers and staff. It is crucial to understand that the school adults are mediators of their own culture, which typically is mainstream American culture, as the majority of teachers are still from European American backgrounds (Goodwin, 2000). A realistic concern is that teachers may impose their own cultural values onto the students who do not share the same cultural values and beliefs, which is detrimental to diverse students (Chang & Le, 2010; Sue, 2010). In Sol's case, Ms Jack imposed her cultural values and beliefs on Sol by acting in a way that was consistent with valuing individualism—that being bullied is beneficial for children to experience in life. Next, *informal practices* refer to the naturally occurring behavioral patterns that school adults tend to engage in collectively. For example, teachers may develop the informal routine of consulting with one another regarding student concerns including bullying, thereby contributing to a collaborative and trusting climate.

*Family influence* is the sixth broad factor (see Chapter 15 for extended discussion). Families whose children attend the school are an important influence on the school culture and climate (Haynes, 1996). Clearly, whether parents and guardians get involved in the school and its bullying intervention activities will influence culture and climate. Alternatively, how well the school promotes family collaboration is also important. Finally, *students* also contribute to the school environment, as illustrated by the varied peer reactions to Sol's bullying.

## Best practice

Given the seven broad factors that maintain school culture and climate, intervention efforts can theoretically address any and all of them. Still, best practices rely on systems change methods that include following a problem-solving model (Ervin & Schaughency, 2008; Swearer, Espelage, & Napolitano, 2009). Specifically, these steps are followed: (a) develop a collaborative team of relevant stakeholders from school and the community to lead the school; (b) assess important factors of school culture and climate using a survey and/or qualitative procedure; (c) prioritize areas for improvement and select an area for intervention; (d) determine a suitable intervention or strategy to improve the areas of concern and implement it; and (e) evaluate the intervention and repeat the process. For example, a school climate team might consist of an administrator, teachers, bus driver, school resource officer, parents or guardians, and students. The team might focus on reducing school bullying and decide to assess the bullying climate using a survey. Then the team will analyze the findings and decide on strategies to address areas for improvement.

## Social justice transformation of school culture and climate

Now that school culture and climate have been introduced, it is important to critique them from a social justice perspective and offer an alternative. This section begins with a critical discussion of current best practices in school culture and climate and discusses how a social justice framework addresses the concerns.

## Best Practice Is Not Enough

The best practices described previously are essential for improving school culture and climate. However, they are not enough because they do not adequately address a major drawback of school culture and climate. The major drawback is that the function of school culture and climate is to maintain the status quo instead of change via school norms (Martin, 2002; Smith, Bond, & Kagitcibasi, 2006). As we saw in Sol's example of wearing pink, the environment (culture and climate) presses upon and shapes the development of individuals (Moos, 1973). While this tendency of school culture and climate has benefits such as encouraging all children to perform academically, the limitation is that the "environmental press tends to *oppress*" individuals who do not share or match the school norm that is dominant in a particular school, as we saw with Sol. The discrimination against individuals who do not share aspects of the same "culture" (e.g., disability, gender, race, ethnicity, religion, class, language, culture, sexual orientation, or gender expression) as the dominant norm has been well documented throughout US history and psychology (e.g., Sue's work on microaggressions, 2010). The groups who are part of the dominant norm, then, possess *cultural power* at school because they happen to be consistent with the norm. In contrast, the "cultural minorities" suffer in schools. In Sol's case, at church and home, he does not get bullied because he has the cultural power in those settings (e.g., shares the same race and language); however, once he steps in school and wears pink, he loses his cultural power, which highlights the relative nature of his situation, but also heightens the unfairness of it all. A better approach is needed that is informed by these insights.

## Social Justice Vision—Loving Justice

A social justice vision for practice is transformative. It should lead to change in the status quo of school culture and climate practice. If a social justice vision does not transform current best practices, then it suggests that the current practice produces equitable outcomes. In this section, therefore, a social justice vision of practice is outlined.

### Ecological

A social justice vision of practice should be rooted in the ecological model (Bronfrennbrener, 1979; Prilletensky, 2011) with all of its complexity. Multiple systems interact with one another to effect change in the individual. Thus, the ecological model provides numerous factors on which to intervene; said another way, its complexity is its strength. Paradoxically, the problem with the ecological model, however, is its complexity. There are too many factors on which to intervene effectively and efficiently in practice. For this reason, the *Loving Justice* framework of school psychological practice has been developed. Loving Justice comprises two value orientations, outwardness and transformation, giving direction to a way of school psychological practice that is firmly rooted in social justice (Song & Marth, 2012).

### Outwardness

Social justice is really about focusing outward in two ways. Social justice focuses away from those with cultural power (i.e., status quo) and on the needs of disempowered others to ensure equity; and, second, social justice focuses on external environmental factors before individual factors, which is consistent with ecological and systems views of social justice practice (Prilleltensky, 2011). To understand what is meant by outwardness, the Golden Rule of treating others the way that you want to be treated and its variant the Platinum Rule—treating others the way that *they* want to be treated—can be considered together. The Golden Rule's basic assertion centers on empathy and reciprocity toward others in society, i.e., not being self-centered, but other-centered. The importance of this teaching for society is seen throughout human history as variants of the Golden Rule have been taught in virtually all religious and philosophical schools of thought. However, what happens if the other person does not want to be treated the way that you like to be treated? The Platinum Rule then is a second layer of thinking that helps those in power to be culturally sensitive to another person's needs by stating that we should treat others the way that *they* want to be treated. Although this important variant can be addressed in principle by the Golden Rule, it is better to be explicit about this intention to stress the importance of cultural sensitivity. Putting the two rules together, a loving justice vision looks away from those in power to see who is in need, considering their unique needs, and prefers to focus intervention on changeable environmental factors. While everyone likely will need some form of help in schools, special attention is given to those individuals or groups who are in need of cultural power, i.e., cultural minorities, or those who are marginalized and oppressed because of a power imbalance. Thus, Loving Justice is directed outward toward others who are disempowered, and focuses first on external factors on which to intervene, such as improving student–teacher relationships, rather than internal factors.

## Transformation

Secondly, social justice is truly about transformation. Social change and action through advocacy and interventions must be the end result of social justice efforts (Clare, 2009; Prilleltensky, 2005; Shriberg, 2009). But change should also be the *first*, though not the primary, result of social justice efforts. Meeting the immediate needs of a target group is underemphasized in the social justice literature, which appears to favor the larger systemic change that will lead to enduring positive outcomes for the group. While the long-term change should be the primary goal of social justice efforts, it is important to make changes simultaneously when possible, i.e., develop interventions or provide support, to address the pressing needs of students and families who are suffering. In other words, sometimes we can focus so much on teaching hungry people to fish, that we forget to feed them first! Thus, Loving Justice is transformative by focusing on immediate and long-term change and action plans.

## Skills needed

A social justice framework for practice requires reconceptualizing the skills needed to accomplish the goal of social justice. Social justice has been described as an aspirational goal for which to strive in practice (Clare, 2009; Shriberg, 2009), with advocacy skills and an understanding of human diversity identified as important skill areas. While the emphasis placed on each of these components varies by scholar, we suggest the structure illustrated in Figure 9.3. First, knowledge and self-awareness of human diversity is foundational. Human diversity is essential for social justice practice because it provides the practitioner with the lens of multiculturalism, discrimination, and oppression. Without this lens, the practitioner is unable to see the injustices that are occurring (Chang & Le, 2010; see Chapter 1 for discussion on the importance of building self-awareness in human diversity). Still, awareness of the injustices is insufficient without the professional skills to do the job. Best practice then is important to fill this gap. The current best practices in a particular area of practice are essential for a place to begin (see Part 3 for chapters on major school psychology skill sets). Advocacy is the final skill that is needed to practice with a social justice vision, which is a separate set of skills that go beyond best practices (see Chapter 16 for discussion of advocacy). When practitioners have all three skill sets (human diversity, best practices, and advocacy), then work towards social justice begins.

## Social Justice Practice of School Culture and Climate

Given the discussion thus far, what does the vision of social justice practice look like in schools? As the social justice literature in school psychology practice is in its infancy (Shriberg, 2009; Shriberg et al., 2008), we propose the following framework based on the relevant literature (e.g., multiculturalism, social justice theory). This section describes what a social justice vision looks like in practice by discussing how the Loving Justice framework can be applied to the *Pink Power* case example. There are two main steps in this process.

FIGURE 9.3. The skills needed for a social justice framework to practice, starting with an awareness of human diversity and knowledge of best practices, and turning towards advocacy for social justice.

## Step 1: Focus on Outwardness

At first, we need to allow the Loving Justice framework to transform what we currently know and do to address school culture and climate. This is accomplished by considering all the factors that maintain school culture and climate in light of the Loving Justice value orientation of outwardness. Which of the seven areas of school culture and climate described previously are most consistent with outwardness (i.e., lack cultural power and focus on environmental factors)?

The areas that are consistent with those who lack cultural power are family and student influence, with student influence being the most disempowered because they are children. Thus, the work of school culture and climate improvement should focus most of its energy in these areas. Still, a deeper examination is needed within these areas in light of the outwardness value to determine which subgroups of families and students lack cultural power for a particular school setting. Although there are a number of ways to accomplish this task of deeper assessment, they all need to be focused on hearing the stories of those who are disempowered. If a survey is used, then it would be important to analyze them across all subgroups of students and families rather than examining aggregated data alone, which would hide the variability among subgroups. In addition, qualitative methods are most appropriate in the form of class meetings/discussions, focus group interviews with subgroups, and individual interviews with students, teachers, and families.

## Applying Outwardness

Applying outwardness to best practice does not mean to disregard best practice, but to tailor it to make it better. Therefore, following best practices, it is crucial to develop a multi-stakeholder team and have a conversation about what name to call the team. While it would be important to keep the primary emphasis of the team clear (e.g., Anti-Bullying, Racial Equity, or Social Justice Team), there may be school and district politics that make it challenging to do so. For these reasons, it is recommended to have a dialogue about the name as one of the first agenda items for the team and to identify core values or outcomes that the team is wanting to address as possible candidates for a team name. Next, applying the value of outwardness to the case example more directly, while families were not mentioned, collaborating with families on the issue of bullying would be helpful to promote understanding and support; and, within the student area, it appears that boys who do not fit the traditional male gender role lack cultural power. Thus, the targets for assessment have been identified.

The social justice team could consider a survey on bullying that includes choices for students and families to self-identify with multiple subgroups that are traditionally disempowered (e.g., disability, gender, race, ethnicity, religion, class, language, culture, sexual orientation, or gender expression; Swearer et al., 2009). It is also recommended to use an open-ended question on the survey to allow students and families the opportunity to express any other concerns regarding the school culture or climate. In addition, the social justice team should consider qualitative methods as a primary source, not secondary. For example, the work of Beth Doll provides a great model of using class meetings to engage students in problem solving discussions, thereby empowering them to have their voices heard about problems and solutions (Doll & Brehm, 2010), which has also been used to address bullying (Doll, Song, Jones, & Wescott, 2011; Doll, Song, & Siemers, 2004). Because all of these areas of school culture and climate are external factors, it is fine to proceed to Step 2.

## Step 2: Focus on Transformation

Next, the value of transformation is applied. Change and intervention need to occur immediately as well as in the long term. First, in terms of immediate change and intervention, any needs of the families and students, who have been identified in the assessment step above (outwardness), should be met as soon as possible. For example, qualitative interviews and focus groups might reveal that parents and guardians who speak a language other than English may feel unwelcome; or students who cannot afford school supplies do not feel ready to succeed. Interventions that address these issues immediately may include a follow-up "fun gathering" or phone call to these families to listen; or, for the students, interventions may include providing free school supplies. Second, change should also be directed at broader systems change goals that may sustain certain programs and resources for the families and students through changing policies, implementing broad preventive services, and/or securing grant funding.

## *Applying transformation*

Transformation can be applied to the case example to better illustrate this value. School adults need to listen to Sol empathically and provide support and protection from bullying. At the same time, school adults need to look for long-term improvement in bullying by initiating prevention and intervention strategies through the problem-solving model described earlier. Turning to the case example, while Sol's gender identity, gender expression, and sexual orientation are unclear, it may be appropriate to establish a GLBTQ support group or connect it with Sol (see Chapter 16 for more discussion of this topic). In addition, the school psychologist could lead the efforts of school adults (administrators, teachers, staff) to change the heteronormativity in the school by increasing awareness of GLBTQ needs and challenges through continuing education, modeling support and advocacy for GLBTQ students in everyday interactions, adding GLBTQ language into the school's antibullying policy through advocacy efforts with families and the community (McCabe & Rubinson, 2008), and advocating for more gender-neutral restrooms (GLSEN, n.d.). Additionally, using the assessment data to write grants to support antibullying programs at school might also be useful.

Finally, a bullying prevention and intervention program at the school level is clearly needed and should be implemented with fidelity. While there are several programs from which to select with empirical support (Swearer & Espelage, 2011; Swearer et al., 2009), most (if not all) of these were not developed with an explicit social justice orientation and framework, which is unfortunate. Therefore, it is useful to consider how an explicit social justice framework as described here (Loving Justice) might be useful in further transforming an already existing bullying prevention program at the school level.

The value of outwardness would focus our attention to the needs of the disempowered students being bullied and let this group's needs drive a bullying program. Bullied students inherently lack the power (physical, social, cultural) to make the bullying stop (Olweus, 1991). While a large-scale school intervention program is important to change the school culture and climate, often overlooked in these multicomponent programs is the peer ecology (Song & Stoiber, 2008). Indeed, Swearer and colleagues (2009, p. 102) concluded that "very little progress has been made" in interventions that targeted the peer ecology. This is unfortunate because the peer ecology has been suggested as a key factor in combating bullying from a social justice perspective, because peers are powerful enough to correct the power imbalance inherent in bullying, able to observe bullying better than adults, more effective at intervening in bullying episodes than adults, and a naturally existing resource for schools cutting down on implementation costs of multicomponent programs (Song & Sogo, 2010). Therefore, based on the consideration of outwardness, the existing school bullying program should be supplemented with a component that taps into the peer ecology more directly with the goal of developing a *protective peer ecology* (Song & Stoiber, 2008): a peer system that values outwardness (empathic responding for disempowered others) and transformation (protection and advocacy).

Again examining the case example, three strategies may be integrated in Sol's school. First, to develop empathy and respond to bullying incidents, the integration of restorative circles, an adult- and peer-led mediation time focusing on developing mutual understanding, appears promising (Sumner, Silverman, & Frampton, 2010). This strategy may be implemented by any adult with training in the restorative circle, and therefore holds promise for mature students to be co-leaders and leaders. In the case example, Sol and those who bullied him would be brought together in a circle to respectfully share their feelings with one another with the goal of fostering empathy, mutual agreement about repairing damage, and building community (see Chapter 6 for more on restorative circles at a systems level). Second, to empower the peer ecology and build peer advocacy, peers may actually deliver bullying intervention components to one another by leading the dissemination of bullying awareness campaigns and peer support groups (Menesini, Codecasa, Benelli, & Cowie, 2003; Salmivalli, Kaukiainen, & Voeten, 2005). Song integrates empathy development and peer advocacy strategies through the use of class meetings (Song, 2006; Song, Doll, & Marth, in press; Song & Sogo, 2010). Finally, while the continued development of strategies that promote a protective peer ecology in schools is an important goal, it is more important to provide opportunities for students to empower and advocate for themselves by having the adults step back and give students room to embrace outwardness and transformation. While this is hard for schools to do because of the status quo nature of school culture and climate, when a school does this great things can happen.

In the Pink Power case example, what actually happened was that a few seniors in the high school witnessed the bullying and were fed up with the constant bullying that was going on in their school. They decided that they should do something themselves for Sol and for the improvement of their school. These seniors went to local businesses to tell them about their plan and got several businesses to donate pink shirts. Three days after Sol's bullying incident, 400 students in the high school wore pink shirts to school. The school leaders and teachers had no idea about the plan and were pleasantly surprised that the students took it upon themselves to stand up against bullying, as school adults alone cannot stop bullying. The school adults however did their part by passing a school policy for a Stand Up Against Bullying Day, which eventually spread to the district and became a news story. While no one can really say whether this story had a larger impact beyond this particular school, it is interesting that many schools across North America. and even some around the world, practice a day in which bullying is explicitly spoken out against. In this case example, the color pink possessed much power—in the beginning its power provoked a bullying reaction, and in the end the power of pink brought loving justice.

To facilitate deeper learning, here are several discussion questions about the Pink Power case example.

1. Do you think there are additional cultural norms and climate issues that are influencing the bullying dynamics at Sol's school?
2. Have you experienced a school culture and climate that has oppressed who you are in any way, or someone else you know?
3. What are additional intervention strategies that might be helpful to try in Sol's case?
4. How might you promote peer advocacy in school?
5. Is it easy to live out the loving justice values of outwardness and transformation in a school? What obstacles might get in the way of living out loving justice in schools, or your own life?

## Conclusion

In this chapter, school culture and climate were reviewed within a social justice framework for school psychological practice. The current state of the school culture and climate literature was reviewed, including best practices to improve them. It was argued that best practices are not enough, however, for social justice practice to occur. More intentional work needs to be done. To help guide the intentional work of social justice, a Loving Justice vision of practice was discussed and applied to a case of school bullying. The two basic premises of loving justice are outwardness and transformation, or as grandma used to say, "See others who are in need and help them." Some lessons are easy to learn yet hard to live out. Whether we are school psychologists in practice or the academy may we all choose to live out our visions for a more just school experience.

## References

Aleman, E. (2012). Leveraging conflict for social justice: How "leadable" moments can transform school culture. *Journal of Cases in Educational Leadership, 12,* 1–16.

Anderson, C. S. (1982). The search for school climate: A review of the research. *Review of Educational Research, 52,* 368–420.

Bronfenbrenner, U. (1979). *The ecology of human development: Experiments by nature and design.* Cambridge, MA: Harvard University Press.

Carter, R. (2000). Perspectives on addressing cultural issues in organizations (pp. 3–18). In R. Carter (Ed.), *Addressing cultural issues in organizations: Beyond the corporate context.* Thousand Oaks, CA: Sage.

Chang, J., & Le, T. N. (2010). Multiculturalism as a dimension of school climate: The impact on the academic achievement of Asian American and Hispanic youth. *Cultural Diversity & Ethnic Minority Psychology, 16* (4), 485–492.

Clare, M. M. (2009). Decolonizing consultation: Advocacy as the strategy, diversity as the context. *Journal of Educational and Psychological Consultation, 19* (1), 8–25.

Doll, B. & Brehm, K. (2010). *Resilient playgrounds.* New York, NY: Routledge.

Doll, B., Song, S.Y., Jones, K., & Wescott, A. (2011). Classroom ecologies that support or discourage bullying (pp.147–158). In D. Espelage & S.M. Swearer (Eds.), *Bullying in the schools: A social and ecological perspective on intervention and prevention* (2nd ed.). Mahwah, NJ: Lawrence Erlbaum Associates.

Doll, B., Song, S. Y., & Siemers, E. (2004). Classroom ecologies that support or discourage bullying (pp. 161–183). In S. M. Swearer & D. Espelage (Eds.), *Bullying in the schools: A social and ecological perspective on intervention and prevention.* Mahwah, NJ: Lawrence Erlbaum Associates.

Ervin, R. A. & Schaughency, E. (2008). Best practices in accessing the systems change literature (pp. 853–873). In A. Thomas and J. Grimes (Eds.), *Best practices in school psychology.* Bethesda, MD: National Association of School Psychologists.

Felner, R. D., Brand, S., Dubois, D. L., Adan, A. M., Mulhall, P. F., & Evans, E. G. (1995). Socioeconomic disadvantage, proximal environmental experiences, and socioemotional and academic adjustment in early adolescence: Investigation of a mediated effects model. *Child Development, 66,* 774–792.

Gay, Lesbian, and Straight Education Network. (2010). *2009 National school climate survey: Nearly 9 out of 10 LGBT students experience harassment in school.* Retrieved August 30, 2012 from www.glsen.org/cgi-bin/iowa/all/library/record/2624. html?state=research&type=antibullying

Gay, Lesbian, and Straight Education Network. (n.d.). *Model district policy on transgender and gender nonconforming students.* Retrieved November 8, 2011 from www.glsen.org/ cgi-bin/iowa/all/library/record/2049.html?state=policy&type=policy

Goodwin, A. L. (2000). Teachers as (multi)cultural agents in schools. In R. Carter (Ed.), *Addressing cultural issues in organizations: Beyond the corporate context* (pp. 101–114). Thousand Oaks, CA: Sage.

Haynes, N. M. (1996). Creating safe and caring school communities: Comer school development program schools. *Journal of Negro Education, 65*, 308–314.

Johnson, S. L. (2009). Improving the school environment to reduce school violence: A review of the literature. *Journal of School Health, 79* (10), 451–465.

Kasen, S., Johnson, J. G., Chen, H., Crawford, T. N., & Cohen, P. (2011). School climate and change in personality disorder symptom trajectories related to bullying: A prospective study (161–179). In D. Espelage & S. Swearer (Eds.), *Bullying in North American Schools*. New York, NY: Routledge.

Kasen, S., Johnson, J. G., & Cohen, P. (1990). The impact of school emotional climate on student psychopathology. *Journal of Abnormal Child Psychology, 18*, 165–177.

Limber, S. (2011). Implementation of the Olweus Bullying Prevention Program in American schools: Lessons learned from the field (pp. 291–306). In D. Espelage & S. Swearer (Eds.), *Bullying in North American Schools*. New York, NY: Routledge.

Martin, J. (2002). *Organizational culture: Mapping the terrain* (pp. 55–92). Thousand Oaks, CA: Sage.

McCabe, P. C., & Rubinson, F. (2008). Committing to social justice: The behavioral intention of school psychology and education trainees to advocate for lesbian, gay, bisexual, and transgendered youth. *School Psychology Review, 37*, 469–486.

Menesini, E., Codecasa, E., Benelli, B., & Cowie, H. (2003). Enhancing children's responsibility to take action against bullying: Evaluation of a befriending intervention in Italian middle schools. *Aggressive Behavior, 29*, 1–14.

Moos, R. H. (1973). Conceptualizations of human environments. *American Psychologist, 28*, 652–665.

Nadal, K., Rivera, D., & Corpus, M. (2010). Sexual orientation and transgender microaggressions: Implications for mental health and counseling (pp. 217–240). In D.W. Sue (Ed.), *Microaggressions and marginality: Manifestation, dynamics, and impact*. Hoboken, NJ: Wiley.

Olweus, D. (1991). Bully/victim problems among school children: Basic facts and effects of a school based intervention program. In K. H. Rubin & D. J. Pepler (Eds.), *The development and treatment of childhood aggression* (pp. 441–448). Hillsdale, NJ: Lawrence Erlbaum Associates.

Prilleltensky, I. (2005). Promoting well-being: Time for a paradigm shift in health and human services. *Scandinavian Journal of Public Health, 33*, 53–60.

Prilleltensky, I. (2011). Wellness as fairness. *American Journal of Community Psychology, 49*, 1–21.

Robbins, S. (2002). *Organizational behavior*. Upper Saddle River, NJ: Prentice Hall.

Salmivalli, C., Kaukianen, A., & Voeten, M. (2005). Anti-bullying intervention: Implementation and outcome. *British Journal of Educational Psychology, 75*, 465–487.

Schmidt, S. J. (2010). Queering social studies: The role of social studies in normalizing citizens and sexuality in the common good. *Theory and Research in Social Education, 38* (3), 314–335.

Shriberg, D. (2009). Social justice and school mental health: Implications for practice. In J.M. Jones (Ed), *The psychology of multiculturalism in schools: A primer for practice, training, and research* (pp. 49–66). Bethesda MD: National Association of School Psychologists.

Shriberg, D., Bonner, M., Sarr, B. J., Walker, A. M., Hyland, M., & Chester, C. (2008). Social justice through a school psychology lens. *School Psychology Review, 37* (4), 453–468.

Smith, P., Bond, M., & Kagitcibasi, C. (2006). *Understanding Social Psychology across Cultures: Living and Working in a Changing World* (pp. 79–101). Thousand Oaks, CA: Sage.

Song, S. Y. (2006). *The Protective Peer Ecology Program (PPEco): Intervention manual for schools (version 3)*. Unpublished manual.

Song, S. Y., Doll, B., & Marth, K. (2012). Classroom and peer ecological resilience: Practical assessment for intervention. In S. Prince-Embury & D. H. Saklofske (Eds.), *Resilience in children, adolescents and adults*. New York, NY: Springer.

Song, S. Y. & Marth, K. (2012). *Social justice in the air: School culture and climate*. Paper presented in D. Shriberg and A. Sullivan's (Chairs) Symposium, Major Issues of Social Justice in School Psychology, at the Annual Convention of the National Association of School Psychologists, Philadelphia, PA.

Song, S. Y. & Sogo, W. (2010). A hybrid framework for intervention development:
Social justice for bullying in low resource schools. In B. Doll, W. Pfohl, & J. Yoon (Eds.), *Handbook of youth prevention science*. New York: NY, Routledge.

Song, S. Y., & Stoiber, K. (2008). Children exposed to violence at school: Understanding bullying and evidence-based interventions. *Journal of Emotional Abuse, 8* (1/2), 235–253 [Special issue on children exposed to violence].

Sue, D. W. (Ed.). (2010). *Microaggressions and marginality: Manifestation, dynamics, and impact*. Hoboken, NJ: John Wiley.

Sumner, M. D., Silverman, C. J., & Frampton, M. L. (2010). *School-based restorative justice as an alternative to zero-tolerance policies: Lessons from West Oakland*. Berkeley, CA: Thelton E. Henderson Center for Social Justice, University of California, Berkeley, School of Law.

Swearer, S. M. & Espelage, D. L., (2011). Expanding the social–ecological framework of bullying among youth: Lessons learned from the past and directions for the future. In D. Espelage and S. Swearer (Eds.), *Bullying in North American schools* (pp. 1–10). New York, NY: Routledge.

Swearer, S. M., Espelage, D. L., & Napolitano, S. A. (2009). *Bullying prevention and intervention: Realistic strategies for schools*. New York, NY: Guilford Press.

# Part 3

# Roles and Functions of School Psychologists

ten
# A Social Justice Approach to Assessment

Markeda L. Newell and
Gina Coffee

The field of school psychology is rooted in the practice of assessing children to understand their academic, social, emotional, behavioral, and psychological characteristics and needs. Although school psychologists are no longer simply Binet testers (Fagan, 1985), psychological assessment (e.g., IQ, social/emotional functioning, and academic performance) continues to dominate school psychological service delivery. Currently, school psychologists spend about 47% of their time conducting evaluations for special education (Castillo, Curtis, Chappel, & Cunningham, 2011), which does not include other types of assessments that school psychologists conduct for other services (e.g., assessment for developing and evaluating individual interventions as well as school-wide assessments such as program evaluations). While the predominance of assessment in service delivery has been criticized (e.g., too much focus on diagnosing the problem), there is widespread agreement that traditional psychological assessment is integral to effective service delivery (NASP, 2010). School psychologists need to conduct appropriate assessments in order to make valid decisions that can improve outcomes for children, which is part of data-based decision-making (Batsche, Castillo, Dixon, & Forde, 2008; NASP 2010). While requiring school psychologists to engage in data-based decision-making is important, there are significant concerns about the fairness of assessment tools and procedures, particularly for diverse populations (Valencia & Suzuki, 2001).

Concerns about the psychometric quality of assessment tools and procedures have been a longstanding issue in school psychology (Kohn, Scorcia, & Esquivel, 2007; Rhodes, Ochoa, & Ortiz, 2005; Vasquez-Nuttall et al., 2007). Much of the concern about assessment has been whether the tools and procedures fairly gauge the academic, social, emotional, behavioral, and psychological well-being of minority students. The basis of this concern was born out of the sociocultural history of minorities in the United States (Valencia & Suzuki, 2001) and the fact that many assessment tools were developed without consideration of diverse beliefs, views, and experiences of various groups that are represented in the United States (Padilla & Borsato, 2008). As a result, standardized assessment tools were considered potentially biased against minority students. Reynolds and Carson (2005) defined test bias as "a constant or systematic error (as opposed to random error), presumed to be due to group membership or some nominal variable, occurring in the estimation of a score on a psychological or educational test or performance criterion" (p. 796). When psychometric test bias occurs, the student's actual performance (e.g., IQ, academic) is distorted. The issue of psychometric test bias has received significant attention in school psychology and related fields, and significant advancements have been made to reduce this form of test bias. Specifically, test developers are now developing measures using more diverse norming samples that reflect the diversity of the United States. However, obtaining more diverse norming samples is a very limited approach to addressing test bias because the items on the measure must be appropriate across those diverse groups. Reynolds and Carson (2005) identified several methods that test developers are using to reduce the likelihood that items on measures are biased. For example, developers are using item response theory to determine the degree to which items function differentially across groups, selecting better distractors for multiple choice items, and using factor analysis to improve content validity (see Reynolds & Carson, 2005 for a review of these methods).

While these advancements in improving the technical adequacy of many norm-referenced assessment tools are significant and have served to reduce test bias, there is still much work to be done to improve the fairness of measures and the assessment process, more broadly, for diverse populations. As Mpofu and Ortiz (2009) explained:

> Technical adequacy is an important and necessary component of achieving equity in assessment but it is not sufficient. Fairness will be established only when practitioners also consider the structure of conditions of equity in assessment, their sociocultural basis, and engage in nondiscriminatory practices that enhance social justice in assessment. (p. 54)

Therefore, as Padilla and Borsato (2008) explained, while measures can be technically sound, their content may privilege the knowledge of one group over another because all knowledge is culturally embedded and therefore the content of assessment tools reflect the cultural dimensions of the test developers. For this reason, Stobart (2005) argued that fairness or equity in assessment is fundamentally a sociocultural issue and therefore, equitable assessment is also a social justice issue (Gipps, 1999).

Hence, the purpose of this chapter is to explain how a social justice approach to assessment can improve the equity in assessment for all students above and beyond improving psychometric test bias. Specifically, readers will understand how social justice applies to assessment, why a social justice approach to assessment can improve equity, and how a social justice approach can be applied to systems and individual-level assessment in schools. The goal of this chapter is to provide a foundational social justice assessment framework that can be used to create robust, high-quality assessment processes that are appropriate for the diverse beliefs, perspectives, and experiences of the students who attend schools in the United States.

## Integrating the Theory of Social Justice and Assessment

Researchers and scholars have struggled to clearly define and operationalize social justice, particularly as it applies to different fields of study. Nevertheless, there has been one core principle underlying all conceptualizations of social justice: social justice is fundamentally about equitable distribution of resources (see Miller, 1999; Barry, 2005; Rawls, 1971). The notion of equitable distribution of resources is premised upon the idea that "no one chooses to be born into a disadvantaged social group or with natural disabilities ... no one should have to pay for the costs imposed by those disadvantaged circumstances" (Kymlicka, 1989, p. 186 as cited in North, 2006). Therefore, social justice advocates are concerned about the social, economic, and cultural contexts into which individuals are born. More importantly, social justice advocates are invested in understanding how systems interact with individuals, particularly in ways that may be oppressive, so that they can redress unfair policies and practices. For this reason, social justice advocates attempt to answer the following question: "How can we contribute to the creation of a more equitable, respectful, and just society for everyone?" (Zajda, Majhanovich, & Rust, 2006, p. 13). Therefore, it is important to address this question as it applies to assessment. So, the question for school psychologists is "How can we contribute to the creation of a more equitable, respectful, and just society for everyone through assessment?"

## Equitable Assessment: A Social Justice Practice for School Psychologists

It is important for school psychologists as well as students and parents to understand the power of assessment to bring justice to an oftentimes unjust educational system. Equitable assessment is a form of social justice because a fair, appropriate assessment can prevent social problems and/or ensure access to resources (Mpofu & Ortiz, 2009). According to the *Standards for Educational and Psychological Testing* (AERA, APA, & NCME, 1999), "equitable assessment provides examinees an equal opportunity to display the requisite assessment processes, skills, and expectancies, as well as a fair chance to achieve the same level as others with equal ability on a given construct under measurement" (as cited in Mpofu & Ortiz, 2009). Hence, for school psychologists to engage in equitable assessment practices, there must also be equity in opportunities to learn (see Stobart, 2005).

In order for assessments to be fair, all students must have access to the same quality of schools, teachers, curriculum, and resources; otherwise, these children may miss important opportunities for learning that may be reflected during an assessment process. Performing poorly during an assessment can have significant long-term consequences because assessment data is often used to make high-stakes decisions about placement in special education, assignment to educational tracks, admission to college, and decisions for employment (Padilla & Borsato, 2008). When these high-stakes decisions are made based on data that is flawed because there was not equity in opportunities to learn, especially for specific groups of students, then systemic cycles of poverty, unemployment, mental health issues, etc. can arise and disproportionately impact those groups who never had an equal opportunity to learn and demonstrate their knowledge and skills.

Researchers and educators have long been aware of the inequity in educational resources; however, there have been continued disagreements about whether or how much schools themselves versus larger social inequity contribute to educational disparities (Machtinger, 2007). Despite which position you take, "schools should, at least, not reinforce social inequalities and hopefully play a significant role in alleviating them and promoting equality of opportunity (Machtinger, 2007, p. 1). Therefore, school psychologists need to understand how a lack of resources can impact the performance and functioning of students. A social justice approach to assessment would help school psychologists understand the disparities, evaluate the impact of the limited resources on functioning, and take steps to remedy the gap created by limited resources so that they do not further disenfranchise students through inappropriate and inaccurate assessments. In order for school psychologists to take a social justice approach to assessment they do not need to throw out all they know about assessment; rather they need to enhance their assessment practices by infusing the following principles into their assessment practices.

## Principles of Social Justice Assessment

### Principle I: Social Justice Assessment is Strengths-Based

Assessment has traditionally been deficit-focused in that school psychologists were often conducting assessment to find out what was internally wrong with a child. However, from a social justice perspective, assessment should instead focus on understanding current resources and assets that can be maximized to improve well-being. Seligman and Csikszentmihalyi first introduced the concept of positive psychology in 2000. They argued that the field of psychology, in general, has been too focused on deficits and pathology. Hence, "the aim of positive psychology is to begin to catalyze a change in the focus of psychology from preoccupation only with repairing the worst things in life to also building positive qualities" (Seligman & Csikszentmihalyi, 2000, p. 5). While they assert that understanding pathology is important, they also argue that psychology needs to balance that focus with equal or more attention on well-being and identifying what makes life good. Consequently, instead of just reducing pathology, the goal of psychology would be to improve a person's quality of life. Therefore, positive psychology has the goal of identifying and cultivating the positives and strengths of different groups instead of identifying problems (see Hoskins, 2003). Therefore, in taking a social justice approach to assessment, school psychologists first and foremost must focus on identifying students' strengths, skills, and resources.

By infusing a positive psychology approach, assessment begins with understanding what resources (internal as well as external) the student has available to draw upon. In understanding the resources available to the student, school psychologists can better assess not only strengths but also disparities that are contributing to the student's performance. Therefore, the focus of intervention may start with bringing balance to resources, which is ideal from a social justice perspective. So, the first principle is assessing strengths by means of understanding the internal and external resources available to draw upon and maximize.

## Principle 2: Social Justice Assessment Occurs on a Continuum

School psychologists should conceptualize assessment as a continuum from the system to the individual. First, school psychologists should begin with an assessment of the school as a system. Then, the assessment should progress to the classroom level and then the individual level. Therefore, school psychologists should proactively assess how the school as a system is working for all students in the building. Moreover, when an individual student is referred, school psychologists should examine how school-wide and class-wide policies are impacting that student's performance. A continual, systems-level assessment is therefore a required principle of social justice assessment.

Ortiz (2008) explained that school psychologists should assess factors external to the child before conducting individual-level assessment of internal functioning and traits. In order for school psychologists to conduct continual, systems-level assessments, they must collect and examine data on school-wide policies (e.g., attendance, discipline, curriculum, special education referral and placement) and classwide practices (e.g., classroom management, instructional style/format, and teacher–student interactions). In examining these data, school psychologists can determine whether system-level policies and practices are unfairly or disproportionately affecting certain groups, which would be creating inequity in the distribution of resources. Analyzing these data could reveal disparities in suspensions, expulsions, special education referrals, special education placements, etc. In addition to identifying disparities in discipline and placements, examining this systems-level data can also reveal whether school policies are placing an undue burden on families who have limited educational resources: for example, schools that require families to buy expensive school supplies (especially when the family has multiple children), pay for trips or transportation, to attend several school events that occur in the evening that parents cannot attend because of work commitments. So, examining school policies in relation to the resources and needs of families can be another proactive way for school personnel to bring balance to disparities in resources.

In summary, the purpose of social justice assessment principle 2 is to conceptualize assessment on a continuum that begins at the system level. System-level assessment can be proactive and ongoing to ensure that the policies are working for all students. However, system-level assessment should also be part of an assessment with an individual student to ensure that the system is not unduly punishing the student because there is an imbalance in educational resources at the system level that is contributing to the problem.

## Principle 3: Social Justice Assessment is Nondiscriminatory

As assessment moves from the systems-level analysis, school psychologists must also assess functioning at the individual level. Herein lies much of the controversy about fairness in assessment; that is, are the tools and procedures appropriate at the individual level? From a social justice perspective, assessment does not begin with the individual although an individual has been referred. Assessment begins with assessing the balance of internal and external resources and then moves to the impact of systems-level policies and practices on the individual. By following these first two social justice assessment principles, school psychologists can begin addressing some of the criticisms of individual assessment (e.g., focus on pathology, focus on within-child deficits). However, to continue progressing in this vein of social justice, the school psychologist must follow through with nondiscriminatory assessment at the individual level.

Ortiz (2002, 2008) developed a nondiscriminatory assessment framework that incorporates several important elements that reflect a social justice approach to assessment. As described by Ortiz, nondiscriminatory assessment is a process, rather than specific procedures or tests, by which an individual's functioning may be assessed in a way that promotes equity and justice and minimizes discrimination. Although the framework has been more commonly applied in the assessment of individuals who are culturally, racially, and linguistically diverse, it is actually intended for use with all individuals, as diversity also encompasses often overlooked characteristics such as age, gender, sexual orientation, and socioeconomic status (Ortiz, 2008).

The basic components of the model are comprehensive and include the following steps: assess for the purpose of intervention; assess initially with authentic and alternative procedures; assess and evaluate the learning ecology; assess and evaluate language proficiency; assess and evaluate opportunity for learning; assess and evaluate educationally relevant cultural and linguistic factors; evaluate, revise, and retest hypotheses; determine the need for and language(s) of formal assessment; reduce bias in traditional testing practices; and support conclusions via data convergence and multiple indicators. Depending on the nature of the individual's needs, the nondiscriminatory assessment model may be implemented in a linear or reiterative manner and by an individual or a team.

To date, the nondiscriminatory assessment model developed by Ortiz (2008) is one of the most comprehensive approaches to assessment for diverse learners. Although the nondiscriminatory assessment framework is very comprehensive, there are some additional components needed to fully embrace a social justice approach to assessment.

As part of nondiscriminatory assessment, school psychologists should understand how the social world is affecting clients (e.g., racism, discrimination, classism, etc.). Specifically, school psychologists can evaluate how social, economic, and educational injustices are impacting children and families. These data can most easily be obtained by interviewing students and parents. For example, school psychologists can ask how income level is impacting their ability to engage in school activities or provide school supplies. Beyond asking about the impact on material resources, school psychologists can also evaluate how limited resources are impacting their mental health and well-being; therefore interventions can be designed with this information in mind.

In addition to assessing the impact of social/economic/educational disparities, school psychologists should also be more proactive about understanding the perspective of the client (i.e., the student) in nondiscriminatory assessment. School psychologists can use assessment as an opportunity to hear from their clients, which teaches clients how to speak to their own concerns. Consequently, school psychologists can be better informed about clients' needs and clients can learn how to advocate for themselves, which is also integral to social justice. Ultimately, social justice advocates want to empower clients to be able to advocate for themselves. School psychologists can be integral to advancing this skill through assessment.

## Using A Social Justice Assessment Approach

Three core principles of social justice assessment have been presented: (1) social justice assessment is strengths-based, (2) social justice assessment occurs on a continuum, and (3) social justice assessment is nondiscriminatory. With these principles, school psychologists can begin to address many of the concerns about fairness in assessment that have plagued the field of school psychology since the early 1900s. To begin implementing a social justice approach to assessment, school psychologists must start with infusing these social justice principles of assessment at the systems level.

### Systems-Level Assessment

As explained earlier, systems-level assessment is about collecting and analyzing data on a school-wide and class-wide level to understand how the system is working for all students in the school. Schools have a lot of existing data (e.g., discipline, special education placements, attendance, and academic performance). Therefore, school psychologists should first analyze that data to identify any disparities or disproportionate negative impacts, then take steps to redress those disparities. In addition to reviewing existing data, school psychologists may need to collect school-wide or class-wide data to understand the population and begin to make system-level changes.

The establishment of a universal screening system is a first step in the creation of a socially just framework for assessment at the school level. Currently, universal screening of academic skills, especially reading, takes place in most schools approximately three times per year and functions to identify children who may be in need of additional academic supports (Jenkins, Hudson, & Johnson, 2007). This type of screening system is consistent with the core principles of social justice assessment as it is proactive and positive in identifying the academic skills children do possess. In addition, when used within an RtI framework, it promotes an ecological approach to school psychological service delivery, as it prompts stakeholders to examine the sufficiency of external factors such as the core curriculum. Although not as fully developed at this time, universal screening also holds promise for identifying the social, emotional, and behavioral skills of children (Cheney, Flower, & Templeton, 2008; Hawken, Vincent, & Schumann, 2008). Furthermore, some researchers have specifically begun to explore how the traditional response to intervention model that incorporates universal screening practices could be made more culturally responsive to reduce disproportionate minority representation in special education programs for students with emotional disturbances (Harris-Murri, King, & Rostenberg, 2006).

When screening for academic functioning, schools use various instruments. For example, in a study of 41 schools' practices in reading assessment, Mellard, McKnight, and Woods (2009) found schools used published reading assessments (36%), DIBELS (13%; Good & Kaminski, 2002), district or state assessments (11%), or a combination of screeners. Using the data collected from the schools, Mellard and colleagues (2009) then described the screening practices of a school they believed to be a good example of school-wide screening for reading. The school they identified screened kindergarten through third-grade students three times per year with DIBELS either to determine their risk for developing future reading difficulties (kindergarten and first grade) or to assess fluency and accuracy (second and third grades). Second- and third-grade students also took the ITBS (Hoover et al., 2001) in November and the Gates-MacGinitie assessment (MacGinitie, MacGinitie, Maria, Dreyer, & Hughes, 2002) in October (second grade only) and April. Following the district screening three times per year, the school held a "Literacy Day" to give the literacy team an opportunity to study the data, evaluate current interventions, and plan for future interventions. Within a social justice model of assessment, the abovementioned practices (extended to additional academic content areas such as mathematics) would ensure that each child's strengths, skills, and areas of need are identified in an objective and systematic fashion.

As noted previously, systems for screening children's social, emotional, and behavioral functioning at a universal level in schools are less developed (e.g., Cheney et al., 2008; Hawken et al., 2008) but are as crucial as academic skills screening. In particular, universal screening in these domains can promote equity and justice in the identification of children whose social–emotional and behavioral needs are often overlooked, as well as groups of children who are often over-identified.

Given that this area of universal screening is still emerging, instrument development is also in its early stages. Nevertheless, two available instruments seem consistent with a social justice model of assessment in schools: the BASC-2 Behavioral and Emotional Screening System (BESS; Kamphaus & Reynolds, 2007) and the Behavior Intervention Monitoring Assessment System (BIMAS; McDougal, Bardos, & Meier, 2011). The BESS is a universal screener used to assess behavioral and emotional competencies and needs (internalizing problems, externalizing problems, school problems, adaptive skills/personal adjustment, and inattention/hyperactivity) in children in grades pre-kindergarten to 12th grade. The screener is available in teacher, student, and parent forms, and each form consists of between 25 and 30 items, with administration time between five and 10 minutes. Parent and student forms are also available in Spanish. Preliminary data regarding the instrument's psychometric properties is promising (e.g., Dowdy, Chin, Twyford, & Dever, 2011a; Dowdy et al., 2011b).

The BIMAS (McDougal et al., 2011) is also a universal screener used to assess social, emotional, and behavioral functioning in children five to 18 years of age. In addition to its use as a universal screener, it was also developed for use in progress monitoring, outcome assessment, and program evaluation. Although various forms exist, the BIMAS Standard form is used for universal screening. The BIMAS Standard consists of 34 change-sensitive items with five subscales (conduct, negative affect, cognitive/attention, social, academic functioning). Parent and teacher forms are available for children five to 18 years of age, and a student form is available for children 12–18 years of age. Norms were developed via a sample that closely matches the United States census.

As noted, analyzing system-wide and class-wide data in relation to group and individual performance as well as conducting universal screening are two assessment processes school psychologists can use in implementing a social justice model of assessment at the school-wide level. To date, ample resources and support for universal screening of academic functioning exist. In addition, although tools and support for implementing universal screening of social, emotional, and behavioral functioning are still in the early stages of development, some instruments (e.g., BESS and BIMAS) are available and may prove useful to schools interested in screening children in these areas.

## Individual Assessment

In addition to the systems-level assessments that must be done, school psychologists must also evaluate students on the individual level in relation to the data they have analyzed at the systems level. Consider the case of Christina, a sixth-grade girl who lives with her mother and older brother. Her mother moved to the United States from Mexico before Christina's brother was born, and Christina's first language was English. At home, Christina, her brother, and her mother speak both English and Spanish. Christina and her brother have attended school in the same school district since kindergarten and have performed very well academically and behaviorally. This school year, Christina's teachers noticed she was not completing homework assignments consistently, and her academic performance in her morning core classes, Math and English, was below average. Given Christina's history of academic excellence, teachers attributed this change to her transition to middle school. However, shortly after the second grading period began, Christina had not turned in any homework assignments in Math or English and had failed the first two tests in those classes during this grading period. Her teachers also reported that Christina is withdrawn, often lays her head on her desk, and may be depressed. In addition, the school psychologist received reports from other students that Christina has been offering to complete her classmates' homework assignments in exchange for their lunch money. With this information, the school's problem-solving team works together to meet Christina's needs and those of her classmates.

As first steps in nondiscriminatory assessment, the team approaches this case first by generating a null hypothesis reflecting the belief that Christina's difficulties are the result of external, rather than internal, factors. This is one way the team can minimize confirmatory bias. The team also conceptualizes the case around the intention of developing and implementing an individualized intervention plan for Christina, rather than seeking identification of a disability. This is another method of decreasing the chance for confirmatory bias to influence data collection and interpretation.

Following these initial steps, the team begins the assessment process by assessing with authentic and alternative assessment procedures. Consistent with RIOT procedures, the team reviews Christina's school records, interviews Christina, makes several attempts to contact Christina's mother for an interview, interviews her Math and English teachers, observes Christina in Math and English and across the school day in other classes and in unstructured settings, administers math and reading comprehension curriculum-based assessment (CBA) probes, and reviews work samples (e.g., Howell & Nolet, 2000). During the interview, Christina shares that she has been feeling "lazy" and has a hard time concentrating in the mornings at school. She reported adequate sleep as indicated by her bedtime and the time she wakes up in the morning but stated she is starving until lunch, at which time she is able to buy lunch with the money her classmates give her for completing their homework assignments. Observations are consistent with the information provided by Christina and her teachers, as are work samples. However, CBA probes indicate above average performance in math and slightly below average performance in reading comprehension.

The team continues by assessing and evaluating the learning ecology to determine the influence of external factors, or interactions of external factors, on Christina's difficulties. Examples of external factors include cultural or linguistic differences, health, family situations, socioeconomic issues, teacher biases, or ineffective instruction (Ortiz, 2008). At this point, the team builds upon the data already collected and further explores the aforementioned factors among others. During this process, they conduct observations in Christina's English and Math classes, gather additional work samples, and talk with Christina about her performance in English and Math. The team is also able to talk with Christina's mother and learns she recently lost her job, so the family is struggling financially. As the team shares with her Christina's behavior at school, she explains she has had to leave the home early in the morning to catch the bus to the city as she searches for a job. Although there is food for breakfast and for Christina to make her lunch, it appears Christina has not been doing either, as she was used to her mom preparing breakfast and giving her money for lunch.

Together, the team and Christina's mother develop a plan to ensure she eats breakfast and lunch, and the team continues by assessing and evaluating Christina's language proficiency. Given that Christina speaks English and Spanish, her linguistic proficiencies could influence data gathered in other areas such as academic achievement and appropriateness of the curriculum. Although English was Christina's first language, the mere presence of a second language can be influential (Saenz & Huer, 2003). As Christina's language proficiency has never been assessed, the team decides to administer a standardized language test, paying particular attention to Basic Interpersonal Communicative Skills (BICS) and Cognitive Academic Language Proficiency (CALP) (Ochoa & Ortiz, 2005), and finds no areas of difficulty in either language.

With regard to assessing and evaluating opportunity for learning, as well as relevant cultural and linguistic factors, the team examines factors related to the school environment such as curriculum and instructional setting via methods such as direct observations in the classrooms; review of the curriculum; review of Christina's school records; and interviews with Christina, her mother, and current and previous teachers. The team pays particular attention to the cultural relevance of the curriculum, as Christina's mother indicated Christina has recently been talking with her more about her racial–ethnic identity and her identity as a young girl growing up in a single parent home. Given Christina's particular struggle in English, the team meets with Christina's English teacher to brainstorm ways to enhance the cultural relevance for all students in the class and continues to monitor Christina's identity growth.

At this point, the team regroups to evaluate, revise, and retest hypotheses. Since Christina's mother has been preparing her breakfast and lunch, Christina has been completing her homework assignments and has stopped offering to complete her classmates' homework assignments in exchange for their lunch money. In addition, she earned an A on the most recent math test. In English, she seems to have responded positively to her teacher's efforts to make the readings more culturally relevant, as she participates in class discussions and completes homework assignments. However, she earned a C on the most recent test, which is inconsistent with her achievement levels in previous years. She also continues to appear withdrawn across the day and still reports feeling "down."

Although the team sees noteworthy progress, they decide to gather additional data regarding Christina's feelings and competencies in reading comprehension via interviewing and a norm-referenced test of achievement in reading comprehension. The team discussed the possibility of administering a broad-band self-report measure of feelings, thoughts, and behaviors, but decided to use interview data to inform follow-up assessment. Given the results of the language assessment, the team decides to assess in English, rather than English and Spanish. The team also decides to reduce bias by administering the measures in a standardized fashion and using nondiscriminatory assessment guidelines to interpret the results. Another option would have been to modify the measures beforehand, but the team determined this was not necessary given the data they had collected thus far. Data from the interview suggests Christina is struggling with the transition to middle school, along with the family's changed financial situation. She is also preoccupied with questions of identity. The team decides to make a counseling service available to Christina as needed and will continue to monitor her progress. Data from the reading comprehension assessment falls in the low average range, so the team works with the English teacher to enhance instruction in reading comprehension strategies and implement peer interventions in the classroom. Satisfied that data gathered from multiple sources has converged, the team agrees to continue monitoring Christina's progress and revisit any steps of the nondiscriminatory assessment model as needed.

The basic components of a nondiscriminatory assessment model (Ortiz, 2008) align closely with the second core principle of social justice assessment: social justice is an ecological approach to school psychological service delivery. As demonstrated in the case example, nondiscriminatory assessment rests on the foundation of adopting a null hypothesis that the individual's presenting difficulties are caused by factors external to the individual. As such, assessment activities involve the evaluation of systems external to the individual, prior to, or in conjunction with, the assessment of individual variables. This is evident in multiple steps of the nondiscriminatory assessment model from assessing and evaluating the learning ecology to assessing and evaluating the opportunity for learning to assessing and evaluating educationally relevant cultural and linguistic factors. In the case of Christina, the team did not frame the assessment around the presumption that Christina has a disability such as a learning disability. Rather, they assessed Christina with the intention of developing and implementing an intervention (or interventions) to improve functioning. In addition, the team assessed variables outside of Christina, such as the cultural relevance of the curriculum, daily living behaviors such as sleep and eating, and family changes, which could be contributing to her difficulties. The team also conducted classroom observations including an evaluation of instructional methods and materials. Finally, the team reserved formal assessment of individual characteristics for later in the assessment process after they had exhausted other methods of gathering data measuring extrinsic and intrinsic factors.

Although the nondiscriminatory assessment model is comprehensively aligned with one principle of a social justice approach to assessment, it could be enhanced by a more direct focus on the other two principles: social justice is a positive, proactive approach to school psychological services and social justice is an equitable approach to school psychological service delivery. This is not to say that the current nondiscriminatory assessment model does not promote a positive, proactive, and equitable approach to assessment. However, specific focus on the abovementioned principles could strengthen the model's ability to promote equity and justice in assessment. First, the model may be enhanced by infusing it with tenets of positive psychology (Seligman & Csikszentmihalyi, 2000). As is, the model comes into use when concerns are raised about an individual's deficits, and strengths of the individual and the individual's environment are not specifically emphasized in the steps of the model. Instead, perhaps inserting an initial step to specifically identify the individual's strengths, skills, and resources would frame the rest of the assessment process in a positive psychology context. For Christina, an initial assessment of her strengths would have revealed a close relationship with a supportive family, sensitivity to family struggles, a history of educational success, superior achievement in math, interest in issues of identity, and expressive communication skills.

## Conclusions

The purpose of this chapter was to explain how assessment is a form of social justice that school psychologists should embrace to more effectively serve all clients. Assessment has been tarnished (oftentimes justly); however, it is important for school psychologists to turn the tide and demonstrate how assessment can be not only good for diverse populations but also an essential tool for identifying inequity and developing more effective, client-centered solutions. Assessment should be used as a tool to diagnose and place if that is the resource that students need; however, this cannot be the only function of assessment and school psychologists should certainly not diagnose and place students who do not need that resource. Assessment is an opportunity for school psychologists to obtain clients' perspectives, identify patterns in systems-level inequity and needs, and better design interventions that are guided by clients' contexts and needs. Although implementing these principles may seem straightforward, school psychologists not only will need significant training to understand how to reconceptualize assessment from a social justice perspective; they will also need more intensive training to understand how groups are impacted by disparities in educational resources. Newell and colleagues (2010) explained the current status of multicultural training in school psychology, and this review indicated that school psychologists need much more robust training in order to effectively advocate for their clients, particularly from a social justice perspective.

# References

American Educational Research Association, American Psychological Association, and National Council on Measurement in Education (1999). *Standards for Educational and Psychological Testing.* Retrieved August 30, 2012 from www.apa.org/science/programs/testing/standards.aspx

Barry, B. (2005). *Why social justice matters.* Malden, MA: Polity Press.

Batsche, G. M., Castillo, J. M., Dixon, D. N., & Forde, S. (2008). Best practices in linking assessment to intervention. In A. Thomas & J. Grimes (Eds.), *Best practices in school psychology V* (pp. 177–194). Bethesda, MD: National Association of School Psychologists.

Castillo, J. M., Curtis, M. J., Chappel, A., & Cunningham, J. (2011, February). *School psychology 2010: Results of the national membership study.* Paper presented at the annual meeting of the National Association of School Psychologists, San Francisco, CA.

Cheney, D., Flower, A., & Templeton, T. (2008). Applying response to intervention metrics in the social domain for students at risk of developing emotional or behavioral disorders. *Journal of Special Education, 42* (2), 108–126.

Dowdy, E., Chin, J. K., Twyford, J. M., & Dever, B. V. (2011a). A factor analytic investigation of the BASC-2 Behavioral and Emotional Screening System Parent Form: Psychometric properties, practical implications, and future directions. *Journal of School Psychology, 49* (3), 265–280.

Dowdy, E., Twyford, J. M., Chin, J. K., DiStefano, C. A., Kamphaus, R. W., & Mays, K. L. (2011b). Factor structure of the BASC-2 Behavioral and Emotional Screening System Student Form. *Psychological Assessment, 23* (2), 379–387.

Fagan, T. K. (1985). Sources for the delivery of school psychological services during 1890–1930. *School Psychology Review, 14* (3), 378–382.

Gipps, C. (1999). Socio-cultural aspects of assessment. *Review of Research in Education, 24,* 355–392.

Good, R., & Kaminski, R. (2002). *Dynamic indicators of basic early literacy skills* (6th ed.). Eugene, OR: Institute for the Development of Educational Achievement. Retrieved August 30, 2012 from http://dibels.uoregon.edu/measures/orf.php

Harris-Murri, N., King, K., & Rostenberg, D. (2006). Reducing disproportionate minority representation in special education programs for students with emotional disturbances: Toward a culturally responsive response to intervention model. *Education and Treatment of Children, 29* (4), 779–799.

Hawken, L. S., Vincent, C. G., & Schumann, J. (2008). Response to intervention for social behavior: Challenges and opportunities. *Journal of Emotional and Behavioral Disorders, 16* (4), 213–225.

Hoover, H., Dunbar, S., Frisbie, D., Oberley, K., Ordman, V., Naylor, R., et al. (2001). *The Iowa tests of basic skills.* Itasca, IL: Riverside.

Hoskins, M. L. (2003). What unites us, what divides us? A multicultural agenda within child and youth care. *Child & Youth Care Forum, 32* (6), 319–336.

Howell, K. W., & Nolet, V. (2000). *Curriculum-based evaluation: Teaching and decision making* (3rd ed.). Belmont, CA: Wadsworth/Thomson Learning.

Jenkins, J. R., Hudson, R. F., & Johnson, E. S. (2007). Screening for at-risk readers in a response to intervention framework. *School Psychology Review, 36,* 582–600.

Kamphaus, R. W., & Reynolds, C. R. (2007). *Behavior Assessment System for Children–Second Edition (BASC-2): Behavioral and Emotional Screening System (BESS).* Bloomington, MN: Pearson.

Kohn, S. W., Scorcia, D., Esquivel, G. B. (2007). Personality and behavioral assessment: Considerations for culturally and linguistically diverse individuals. In G. B. Esquivel., E.

C. Lopez and S. Nahari (Eds.), *Handbook of multicultural school psychology: An interdisciplinary perspective* (pp. 265–288). Mahwah, NJ: Lawrence Erlbaum Associates.

MacGinitie, W., MacGinitie, R., Maria, K., Dreyer, L., & Hughes, K. (2002). *Gates–MacGinitie reading tests* (4th ed.). Rolling Meadows, IL: Riverside.

Machtinger, H. (2007). What do we know about high poverty schools? Summary of the High Poverty Schools Conference at UNC–Chapel Hill. *High School Journal, 90* (3), 1–8.

McDougal, J. L., Bardos, A. N., & Meier, S. T. (2011). *Behavior Intervention Monitoring Assessment System (BIMAS)*.Cheektowaga, NY: MHS.

Mellard, D., McKnight, M., & Woods, K. (2009). Response to intervention screening and progress-monitoring practices in 41 local schools. *Learning Disabilities Research & Practice, 24* (4), 186–195.

Miller, D. (1999). *Principles of social justice.* Cambridge, MA: Harvard University Press.

Mpofu, E., & Ortiz, S. (2009). Equitable assessment practices in diverse contexts. In E. L. Grogorenko (Ed.), *Multicultural psychoeducational assessment* (pp. 41–76). New York, NY: Springer.

National Association of School Psychologists. (2010). *Model for comprehensive and integrated school psychological services.* Retrieved August 27, 2012 from www.nasponline.org/standards/2010standards/2_practicemodel.pdf

Newell, M. L., Nastasi, B., Hatzichristou, C., Jones, J., Schanding, G. T., & Yetter, G. (2010). Evidence on multicultural training in school psychology: Recommendations for future directions. *School Psychology Quarterly, 25* (4), 249–278.

North, C. E. (2006). More than words? Delving into the substantive meaning(s) of 'social justice' in education. *Review of Educational Research, 76* (4), 507–535.

Ochoa, S. H., & Ortiz, S. O. (2005). Language proficiency assessment: The foundation for psycheducational assessment of second-language learners. In R. Rhodes, S. H. Ochoa, & S. O. Ortiz (Eds.), *Assessing culturally and linguistically diverse students: A practical guide.* New York, NY: Guilford Press.

Ortiz, S. O. (2002). Best practices in nondiscriminatory assessment. In A. Thomas & J. Grimes (Eds.), *Best practices in school psychology IV* (pp. 1321–1336). Washington, DC: National Association of School Psychologists.

Ortiz, S. O. (2008). Best practices in nondiscriminatory assessment. In A. Thomas & J. Grimes (Eds.), *Best practices in school psychology V* (pp. 661–678). Washington, DC: National Association of School Psychologists.

Padilla, A. M., & Borsato, G. (2008). Issues in culturally appropriate psychoeducational assessment. In L. A. Suzuki & J. Ponterotto (Eds.), *Handbook of multicultural assessment* (pp. 5–21). New York, NY: Wiley.

Rawls, J. (1971). *A theory of justice.* Cambridge, MA: Belknap Press/Harvard University Press.

Reynolds, C. R., & Carson, A. D. (2005). Methods for assessing cultural bias in tests. In C. L. Frisby, & C. R. Reynolds (Eds.), *Comprehensive handbook of multicultural school psychology* (pp.795–823). New York, NY: Wiley.

Rhodes, R., Ochoa, S. H., & Ortiz, S. O. (2005). *Assessment of culturally and linguistically diverse students: A practical guide.* New York, NY: Guilford Press.

Saenz, T. I., & Huer, M. B. (2003). Testing strategies involving least biased language assessment of bilingual children. *Communications Disorders Quarterly, 24*, 184–193.

Seligman, M. E., & Csikszentmihalyi, M. (2000). Positive psychology: An introduction. *American Psychologist, 55*, 5–14.

Stobart, G. (2005). Fairness in multicultural assessment systems. *Assessment in Education, 12* (3), 275–287.

188 Newell and Coffee

Valencia, R. & Suzuki, L. (2001). *Intelligence testing and minority students: Foundations, performance factors, and assessment issues.* Thousand Oaks, CA: Sage.
Vasquez-Nuttall, E., Li, C., Dynda, A. M., Ortiz, S.O., Armengol, C., Walton, J., et al. (2007). Cognitive assessment of culturally and linguistically diverse students. In G. B. Esquivel, E. C. Lopez, & S. Nahari (Eds.), *Handbook of multicultural school psychology.* New York, NY: Taylor & Francis.
Zajda, J., Majhanovich, S., & Rust, V. (2006). Introduction: Education and social justice. *International Review of Education, 52* (1/2), 9–22.

# eleven
# Promoting Social Justice by Addressing Barriers to Academic Success

Jennifer I. Durham

## Case Study

It is early afternoon and a school psychologist rushes from an IEP meeting at an elementary school to Overlooked Middle school where she also is assigned. She has come to Overlooked to participate in a Behavioral Support Team meeting. Overlooked is one of three grade six through eight schools in a district that includes upper middle, middle, and lower income neighborhoods. Overlooked is the smallest and most diverse school with 16% of its students Latino, 35% African American and 49% White. The Latino population has been increasing steadily each year and there is growing resentment among teachers and some administrators about the need to become more language-sensitive. Although Overlooked has the lowest standardized test scores within the district the White students perform well and are mostly enrolled in accelerated programs. The school has a dedicated principal who has been at the school for two years and is extremely troubled by the performance of his students of color on state mandated tests. His concern is not shared by the Board of Education or Superintendent who have expressed that the lower scores should be expected due to the racial and economic diversity of the school. This sentiment is shared by many of the teachers in the building. On the agenda for the Behavioral Support Team is the significant increase of discipline referrals from the seventh grade. Most of the repeat referrals are either special education students or a group of Latino boys the school psychologist has come to know quite well. Passing through the main hall of the school she notices her latest re-evaluation student, Enrique, sitting outside of the vice principal's office. She pokes her head in and asks if everything is all right. He sullenly shakes his head and requests to come see her after school. Interestingly enough, the IEP meeting at the elementary school she just left was for his youngest sister, Daria. Similar to her three older siblings, Daria was referred in the fourth grade for having difficulty completing assignments and reading. Her assessment profile was unremarkable except for some perceptual weaknesses and slightly below average achievement. She could "fit" into a learning disability classification. The girl's principal and teacher used the same argument to push for classification that had been used with her siblings. A smaller environment and more individualized instruction would help her to succeed. Unfortunately this had not worked with her sisters or Enrique. The older girls dropped out of school in the 10th grade and Enrique is currently further below average in achievement than he was when he entered special education.

The school psychologist in this case is confronted by a common challenge within the profession of school psychology. Working to ensure that students have a productive and positive experience within school is at the heart of our work, and the reason many school psychologists enter the profession. It is this deep concern for the growth and development of children within positive school environments that drives many of our practices. Unfortunately this work often takes place at a complex intersection between educational, social, political and cultural phenomena, all of which impact the environments in which the work is done. The interaction between these phenomena can create an environment that breeds academic issues related to the underperformance of groups of students that is evidenced by racial and economic gaps in the allocation of resources, academic achievement, and school discipline (Aspen Institute, 2005; Gregory, Skiba & Noguera, 2010; Kruger & Shriberg, 2007; Shriberg et al., 2008). A child's ability to grasp new concepts and thrive in school is affected by the environment in which he or she is learning. If such an environment presents disparate allocations of resources, and discipline practices, which in turn result in African American and Latino children not performing to their potential, it is toxic and unjust. Although the issues of disparate resource allocation (see Chapter 8 for more detailed coverage), academic achievement, and school discipline (see Chapter 6 for more detailed coverage) have been examined in isolation, they have rarely been explored as related symptoms of social injustice. Social injustice can be manifested in school settings and create academic issues that impede student performance. Exploring all of the school-based symptoms of social injustice is beyond the scope of one chapter. For the purposes of this discussion the term "academic issues" will refer to educational issues that reflect and perpetuate the impediments that result in African American and Latino children not achieving their full academic potential. These issues are defined by the outcome of underachievement rather than their etiology or form of expression. As long as the result is underachievement, academic issues can be expressed through educational, emotional, or behavioral means.

Ensuring that schools are socially just places is a noble aspiration for school psychologists. Organizations within the field have made a clear commitment to social justice within the profession. Both the American Psychological Association (APA) and the National Association of School Psychologists (NASP) (APA, 2003, NASP 2010a, 2010b) include social justice as an aspiration in their governing documents. As noted in Chapter 1, the evolution of social justice as a concept within the field of school psychology has resulted in a dynamic definition that incorporates advocacy, equal access to resources, fairness, and respect. Although it is important for school psychologists to help create and maintain a climate of advocacy and equity within their schools, this chapter will provide a framework for school psychologists to promote social justice by addressing social injustices manifested by academic issues. Exploring strategies to confront the social injustice manifested by academic issues will enhance the profession's ability to service children and their families. The purpose of this chapter is to present a process to address social injustice within our work that includes individual and systemic interventions. This will be done in three sections. The first portion of the chapter will explore academic issues within the context of school psychology and social justice. The second section will describe a process for school psychologists to address these issues within schools. The third and final section will explore this process further by demonstrating its application on both individual and systemic levels.

## Academic Issues

The case study illustrates how school psychologists are at the forefront of many of the challenging academic issues facing the education system. There are many debates about the utility of high stakes testing, school reform models, dropout rates, discipline practices, and the achievement gap (Aspen Institute, 2005; Gregory et al., 2010; Kruger & Shriberg, 2007). All of these issues are rooted in the inability of schools to educate many of our students to proficiency. Although the emphasis, breakdown, and labeling of any one of these issues may shift with the social, political, and cultural milieu, they all reflect a failure to educate a population of American students who are children of color or economically disadvantaged. In critiquing this ongoing gap, some place the emphasis on schools focusing on "school failure." Others focus on what Alpert and Dunham (1986) refer to as "academically marginal" students who have poor attendance, standardized test scores and grades.

The nation's scrutiny of the achievement gap, dropout rates, and discipline practices is the result of efforts to boost the performance of a population of students who have not done well historically or who are currently struggling. High stakes testing for all students emerged to create benchmarks to evaluate progress for the purpose of improving academic performance. Similarly, models of school reform such as charter schools, changes in teacher compensation, and adjusting the tenure system introduced market principles of competition into education to improve student performance. There seems to be an overwhelming and justifiable concern about the underperformance of many children within schools (Aspen Institute, 2005; Darling-Hammond, 2010; Ladson-Billings, 2006; New Teacher Project, 2009). It is this underperformance of a specific group of children that molds the academic issues that are the symptoms of social injustice. What is often missing from the discourse about how to address these issues is recognition of their relationship to injustice and an exploration of how social, political, and cultural phenomena cultivate and perpetuate their existence.

When one takes a closer look at this population of children impacted by underperformance, it becomes clear that there is an over-representation of poor children and students of color within the group (Aspen Institute, 2005; Darling-Hammond, 2010; Ladson-Billings 2006). Unequal access to a constructive educational experience for low-income students and children of color is the social injustice root of a tree that bears fruit such as racial and socioeconomic gaps in achievement and discipline practices. Inequity with respect to access due to race and economic status is unjust. School psychologists who have experience with issues related to access can play a crucial role in removing some of the related inequities.

## Academic Issues as Manifestations of Social Injustice

Considerable time and attention has been given to the achievement gap, and the over-representation of poor children and students of color in disciplinary referrals as separate phenomena. As the case example that started this chapter illustrates, Enrique's academic performance was below his White and Asian peers and represents an achievement gap that may have contributed to a classification that isolated him from high-performance peers and possibly promoted feelings of disenfranchisement that could result in poor behavioral choices. Repeated disciplinary action coupled with poor academic growth often fuels dropping out of school.

While these issues may be related and have unique dimensions that are beyond the scope of this chapter, it is what they have in common rather than their differences that provides insight into how to address social injustice within schools on behalf of students and their families. All of these academic issues can be viewed as manifestations of barriers to equal access to resources that disproportionately affect poor children and students of color. This unequal access reveals social injustice. The presence of disparities between groups is often an indicator of inequity with respect to access to services or resources. A closer examination of the underperformance of African American and Latino students reveals disparate access to resources and fair discipline practices which exposes social injustice as a common thread within the tapestry of underperformance.

As mental health professionals working in schools to ensure optimal academic and social growth, school psychologists often encounter issues that have been created and maintained by unequal access to resources and advocacy. Unequal access is often exposed by significant disparities between low-income students and children of color and their White and Asian peers with respect to resources impacting achievement, and in turn discipline (Aspen Institute, 2005). This is not to suggest that all White and Asian students are superior performers, but to highlight that a gap in the aggregate exists between these students and their African American and Latino peers.

Although school districts vary in size, structure, and management models, districts with the highest concentration of low income and children of color on average spend $902 less per pupil. The cumulative effect of this is $22,550 for a class of 25 children. For example in New York City, arguably a very wealthy city where 15% of the students are White, the annual spending per pupil in 2002 was $10,469.00. Within the same state in the district of Manhasset, Long Island, where 80% of the student body is white, $20,981.00 was spent per pupil during the same time period (Aspen Institute, 2005).

Disparities persist when it comes to instructional resources (Aspen Institute, 2005; Gregory et al., 2010). Even when there is parity in test scores and academic performance for African American, Latino, Asian, and White students, there are gross disparities in instructional supports. In schools where White students are in the majority there is double the chance of having access to advanced topics classes compared to students who attend a school where African American and/or Latino students are in the majority. While some argue that this may be due to resources in African American and Latino concentrated schools having to be dedicated to remediation and not acceleration, that argument breaks down if the situation is examined more closely. Research reveals that African American and Latino students with the same test scores as their White and Asian peers are much less likely to be placed in accelerated courses and much more likely to be placed in low-track courses (Aspen Institute, 2005; Elhoweris, Kagendo, Negmeldin, & Holloway, 2005; Ford, 1998).

As discussed in Chapter 6, a lack of equity can also be found in school discipline. This issue has not gone unnoticed by policy makers. The United States Secretary of Education highlighted racial disparities in school discipline and called for more civil rights action to address the issue during a speech to educators (Duncan, 2010). Although studies have shown that when subjective criteria for infractions are in place such as a teacher or administrator interpretation of a behavior, African American and Latino students are over-represented with respect to suspension and expulsion, the focus of most empirical research has been on highlighting the disparities rather than determining causation (Fenning & Rose, 2007; Skiba, Michael, Nardo, & Peterson, 2002). Authors such as Losen suggest that these disparities are related to cultural incompetence and the misinterpretation of behavior by teachers and administrators, in addition to a paucity of academic and social supports in schools where African American and Latino students are in the majority (Bollin & Finkel 1995; Losen 2011).

Whether it involves the allocation of resources for achievement or disciplinary practices, significant racial and economic disparities exist within many schools. These academic issues not only are created by unequal access to resources, they fuel a cycle that perpetuates injustice by strengthening the barriers that facilitated their creation. The cycle can be explained as having dynamic components that interact with one another to reinforce barriers and maintain injustice. Disparities in funding allocation and discipline practices can be viewed as components of the cycle that result in the underperformance of African American and Latino students which in turn result in barriers to higher education and economic upward mobility, which in turn perpetuates disparities in funding allocation and perhaps discipline practices. The fact that this cycle refuels itself to maintain significant racial disparities indicates an absence of advocacy, equity, and fairness. When systemic disparities between groups persist over time it reveals barriers to equal access and fairness, which is socially unjust.

To work most effectively, school psychologists should recognize that such disparities reflect social injustice. In order to address these issues comprehensively a social justice conceptualization should be embraced. Although it may seem daunting, there is a role for school psychologists in unraveling this tapestry of underperformance. By working case by case or school by school, collectively school psychologists have important contributions to make in eradicating disparities, which in turn will combat social injustice. A purpose of this chapter is to present a process to weaken or remove barriers to equal access, and demonstrate how this process can be executed with respect to individual and systemic strategies.

## Ecological Theory and Social Injustice

Interpreting academic issues as manifestations of social injustice demands the use of a lens that can capture barriers to equal access and advocacy. Ecological theory provides such a lens and has been used by school psychologists to add depth to analysis and the development of intervention (Burns, 2011; Gutkin, 2009; Li &Vazquez-Nuttall, 2009). The ecological approach within school psychology facilitates the comprehensive assessment of all systems that have an impact on psychological functioning. It is particularly helpful when examining the multiple systems that can produce barriers to resources related to academic success. Ecological theory is an essential component of any process that seeks to address the barriers to equity that create underperformance and gaps in achievement (Gutkin, 1993). The theory calls for the examination of the various systems present in a child's life and how the interaction between various systems influence the child's development (Brofenbrenner, 1979).

## Microsystems

The first grouping, often referred to as microsystems, refers to entities that interact directly with the child. This includes but is not limited to family and school. If a child were an active member of a church, his or her religious community would also be considered a microsystem. As students progress in age their peer group can also emerge as a microsystem. In the case example, the peer group of Latino boys, the school, and family could all be considered Enrique's microsystems.

## Mesosystems

Mesosystems describe the interaction between the microsystems and can provide a useful point of analysis for school psychologists. Valuable information can be obtained by examining the relationship between different microsystems such as the relationship between school and home and the effects this relationship have on the child's academic and social progress. When there is misalignment between microsystems there is a strong possibility that academic and social performance will be impaired. An example of this might be the microsystems of school and peer group. If a student's peer group does not value or give support for behaviors that support academic progress, there is misalignment between these two microsystems. An increase in chances to make poor choices may result from having to choose between social standing with friends and productivity in school.

## Exosystems

Exosystems refer to systems that do not interact directly with the child, but have an impact on his or her life. The school board would be an example of an exosystem, in that it sets policies that directly impact students, but most children have no contact with board members.

## Macrosystems

The macrosystems represent societal values and perspectives that are influential in a child's life. These values are not static and can change over time. They represent the social and cultural milieux previously discussed. There was a time in American history when it was illegal to teach a person of African descent to read. Although there were laws in several southern states such as the Comprehensive Negro Act as early as 1740 that made it illegal to teach an enslaved African to read, such laws gained in intensity over time and persisted (Foner & Pacheco, 1984). After an organized slave rebellion in Virginia in 1831 many slave owners became concerned about the ability of Africans to obtain and disseminate information about freedom. Harsh laws were enacted throughout the south that prohibited teaching free Blacks, enslaved Blacks, or people of mixed races to read. This was often punishable by hanging (Cornelius, 1991; Foner & Pacheco, 1984). During that time there was a strong value for the illiteracy of a certain population that existed on a macro level that had a significant impact on a large group of people. Although this investment in the illiteracy of African Americans continued in the early twentieth century with unequal resources and access to schooling, by the mid-twentieth century legal action such as Brown versus the Board of Education began eliminating these efforts within national and state law. Some efforts to be more supportive of literacy among previously targeted groups began to emerge on a macro level (Darling-Hammond, 2010). No Child Left Behind and its ensuing regulations and mandates represents a value of quality education for all students and an effort to end inequities that has resulted in significant changes to student experiences with respect to funding and testing for most public school students.

Although individuals can deny or impede access to resources based on personal bias or philosophy, large-scale disparities between distinct populations suggest a more systemic phenomenon. Ecological theory facilitates looking systemically at issues from multiple perspectives, which provides more opportunities to identify barriers to resource access. The effectiveness of taking a broader systemic perspective can be illustrated by the case example. The school psychologists who were under pressure to classify Enrique's siblings may not have agreed to classification based on a bias against Latino students, but acquiesced due to a lack of resources within the various ecological systems. Barriers are often created by policies and procedures that often should not be attributed to any one individual. By exploring these issues using ecological theory the systemic aspects of the barriers can be identified and addressed on multiple levels.

## Process to Address Social Injustice within Schools

Ecological theory is a useful tool for identifying social injustices manifested by academic issues within schools. Ecological theory provides the parameters of a road map for school psychologists, instead of being overwhelmed by a multitude of social, political, and cultural dynamics, to navigate the system using a three-component process. This process is described as having components rather than steps or stages because there may be instances when it is not sequential in nature. Although the most thorough course of action would be to begin with the first component, contextual factors may eliminate that option.

The starting point on the map is the identification of any barriers to equal access to resources at any of level of the ecosystems. Although it may not be practical or feasible for a school psychologist to address all the barriers identified in a case, they all should be examined. This identification will provide valuable information for future work with this child and his or her family.

## Component 1: Identification of Barriers

Identification of such barriers would require the school psychologist to determine the important microsystems within the child or adolescent's life. As indicated earlier in the chapter, this may vary from student to student, and can even differ for siblings within the same family. In the case example Enrique's peers may be considered an important microsystem for him if he spends significant time with them, mirrors their values and/or seeks validation and support from the association. Peers might not be considered a microsystem for his younger sister Daria as she may not have established such influential relationships at this stage of her development. Once the crucial miscrosystems have been determined, identification of any barriers to resources and/or misalignment between microsystems should be conducted. A barrier related to the home could be the lack of a computer and/

or internet services access that impedes a child's ability to complete assignments. This could be viewed as a barrier if the assignments given by the teacher are based on the assumption that all students have computers and internet services in their homes. Misalignment between microsystems may also create barriers. Looking again at the case, it may be determined that the discord between family and school is impeding his family's ability to advocate for their children properly and gain needed resources. Identification of any barriers to resource access and advocacy prepares the school psychologist for the second component of the process.

## Component 2: Selection of Barriers to Address

The second component involves selecting the barriers to resources that the school psychologist would like to address. The criteria for selection should be based on the feasibility of implementing strategies that will successfully remove or weaken the barrier's influence. The contextual issues within the environment and scope required to address them should also be considered. Context refers to the malleable nature of the environment in which the barrier exists. The identified barrier of a lack of technology could be considered embedded within a malleable context, through collaboration with the school social worker, the school psychologist could refer the family to a program that provides internet services and computers to low-income families. If the lack of access to technology is based on a deeply held parental belief that internet access is inappropriate for children, this might not be such a malleable context. Exploring contextual malleability will inform the selection of the barrier to guide the development of strategies to address it.

## Component 3: Strategy Development/Implementation

The third component of the process involves developing strategies to address the selected barrier. The most important aspect of this third and final component is choosing a level for strategy implementation. Prior to developing a strategy, school psychologists should decide whether they want to address the barrier to access on a systems level, which usually involves programming, policies, and institutional practices, or on an individual case level. Similar to the selection process this decision will also be shaped by unique contextual factors related to the student and his or her ecology.

# Process to Address Social Injustice and the Role of the School Psychologist

A process to address the social injustices that are manifested by the underperformance of children of color and those that are economically disadvantaged should be incorporated into daily roles and functions of school psychologists who work in settings where such issues exist. Indentifying the roles and functions of school psychologists has been a popular endeavor that has evolved over time.

As discussed extensively in Chapter 2, the profession of school psychology has been shaped by political, social, and cultural dynamics that required the categorization of children for the purposes of education. During its formative years school psychology grew into a profession that reacted to differences in learning styles and behavior by developing categories of difference, assessing for membership in such categories, and then placing children in educational settings ostensibly designed to meet the unique needs presented by the category. This is referred to as the refer, test, place approach.

This initial model is based on what Cronbach (1957) referred to as the correlational approach. It explains the variance in student performance as emanating from innate individual differences. Within this model the work of the school psychologist focuses on measuring these innate abilities through testing, and matching abilities with a corresponding placement. Since individual differences are experienced within this model as permanent states, significant time and attention is given to matching the right environment to the measured ability level of the student. School psychologists have been moving away from this model to a problem solving approach.

Also referred to as an experimental approach, the problem solving approach strives to improve student performance. Rather than emphasizing labeling and related placement, this approach focuses on identifying what works best under a given set of circumstances to improve a student's functioning. In 2008 Reschly called for a shift from work that centers on a process of referral, testing, and placement to work that utilizes a problem solving approach and broadens the work of school psychologists. He and many others (e.g., Bradley-Johnson & Dean, 2000; Tilly, 2008) argue that the test placement model does not adequately address the needs of students.

This notion of expanding the role of school psychologists beyond individual student diagnostic needs has been promoted by the profession's leading organization. The National Association of School Psychologists presented *Blueprint for Training and Practice III* in 2006, which is the standard for the profession. This document expands the role of school psychologists. It emphasizes that school psychology is a unique blend between best practices in education and mental health, and provides parameters for the work that include three tiers (Ysseldyke et al., 2006). The first tier encompasses the entire student body of a school, which is a firm step away from traditional approaches that often limit the work of a school psychologist to addressing the needs of students who present significant academic and behavioral difficulties. The second tier focuses attention on students who may be struggling or at risk for future difficulties. The third tier delineated in the document addresses the group of students who have been traditionally associated with special education and school psychology. Embracing the mental health aspect of the work while creating parameters that significantly expand beyond the refer, test, place approach is evidence of a strong commitment by the profession to broaden its scope.

This commitment is also demonstrated within the field. Doll uses the term "population-based school psychology" to describe practices that have school psychologists interacting more with the regular education students and working from a preventive framework (Doll & Haack, 2005; Short, 2003; Shriberg, 2009). Gutkin (2012) calls for an ecological approach to school psychology. He argues that school psychologists need to move away from a medical model paradigm and that assessing a student without looking thoroughly at the interaction between his or her home, school, and community environment lessens the impact of intervention and potential scope of work.

Broadening the role of school psychologists is in alignment with addressing social injustices manifested by academic issues within schools. By moving the school psychologist beyond the testing and IEP meeting rooms into more of the mainstream practices of the school building, he or she will have more opportunities to use their expertise to implement the process to address social injustice. In keeping with the tiered approach, this process can be implemented on either the individual or systemic level.

The case of Enrique and Daria allows for further exploration of the application of this process from the perspectives of an individual case and a systemic intervention. The three components of the process will be applied to both levels of intervention to illustrate implementation within the context of an individual case and a systemic approach.

## Component 1: Identification of Barriers to Equal Access to Resources

By examining the ecological systems, a school psychologist can gain insight into the presence of advocacy, equity, fairness, and respect. The process to eliminate social injustice within Daria's school experience should begin with the first component of the process, identification of existing barriers to equity and advocacy. A school psychologist may begin this process by asking the following questions.

- Are there race-based and/or economically based disparities with the school or classroom?
- Is there alignment between the child's microsystems that diminishes her access to resources and advocacy?
- If there is misalignment, has it had an impact on the child's academic and social performance in school?
- Will the effects of this impact be reflected in the child's performance or results of an assessment for special education eligibility?

Asking these questions may yield valuable data that highlights barriers that may result in disparities, which are often correlates of injustice. In Daria's case there is an overrepresentation of students of color within special education at her school. She is also the youngest sibling in a family that has had negative experiences with the local school district that have resulted in intense distrust. By asking such questions the school psychologist may learn that Daria's mother has aggressively been avoiding both contact and engagement with her daughter's school since the child entered kindergarten. This misalignment of home and school has created a barrier to resources for Daria.

The misalignment has resulted in Daria's absence from supplemental reading afterschool programs, and various other parent/child reading interventions suggested by the school since first grade. Further probing may reveal that other students who were performing similarly to Daria in the first grade have made significant improvement and are now demonstrating grade level skills. The misalignment between home and school has impacted Daria's academic performance and probably her perception of herself as a student and member of the school community. There is a strong possibility that this will be reflected in her evaluation. The question now is what should the school psychologist operating with a social justice lens do with this information? The answer depends on the school and district where he or she works, and is related to the second component of the process.

## Component 2: Selection of Barrier to Address

It is now important to examine the context and culture of the school to determine which barrier to address and whether to focus on the development of individual or systemic strategies. The case indicates that there is growing resentment within the district among teachers regarding the need to become more language- and culture-sensitive with respect to Latino students. Therefore the teachers may not be ready for a building-wide effort to improve home/school relations with Latino parents. Therefore an individual intervention may be more feasible at this time, within this context. After the level of intervention has been selected, it is time to move into the third component of the process.

## Component 3: Strategy Development and Advocacy

In this instance the principal who is concerned about the performance of his students of color may be an ally and may support efforts to get Daria engaged in regular education supports before classification. This may involve different approaches from the guidance department, school social worker, teacher, and even the school psychologist herself.

There is evidence of perceptual weakness and below average academic performance, but when this information is examined within the context of a misalignment between home and school that has resulted in minimal access to remediation, classification and special education may not be the optimal intervention. The school psychologist now needs to determine the most feasible course of action within the current context. Perhaps she finds an ally within the community who will help rebuild the relationship between Daria's family and the school to get her enrolled in as many regular education supplemental programs as possible. If the school psychologist determines that her time and attention would be better utilized working with Daria directly to get her more engaged in the school community and supplemental academic supports, the school psychologist may focus on setting up in school supports and culturally relevant interventions such as a peer mentoring, group and in school incentive programs.

Consultation may also be used as an individual intervention with Daria (Brown, Pryzwansky, & Schulte, 2006). Consultation within school psychology refers to working with another person to help improve the functioning of a student. Although (as described in Chapter 13) the consultation triad is usually constructed of the school psychologist, teacher, and student, other configurations are also possible. The school psychologist may successfully work with parents on behalf of the child and even peers of the student needing assistance. The key element of consultation is that the school psychologist is not working directly with the child, but is assisting someone else who has direct contact with the student (Ingraham, 2000). If the school psychologist can increase the capacity of the teacher or parent to remove barriers to resources, this skill can be transferred to other instances where the school psychologist is not involved. For example, if the school psychologist consults with the teacher to rebuild the relationship with Daria's family and is successful, this is a skill the teacher can apply in future situations with similar students.

Another individual strategy could consist of counseling Daria in a group or individualized setting to help her become more engaged with her academics and the school community. Improvements in these areas would increase her ability to take advantage of access to academic and social supports and remove barriers to resources that have resulted in her underperformance.

It is at this point that the advocacy component of the process should emerge. It is not enough just to pursue enrolling Daria in as many regular education reading support programs as possible or connecting some from the community with the family. It is aggressive follow-up and support with all parties involved in repairing the home/school relationship and supporting Daria's consistent participation in these programs. Whether it is connecting Daria with more supports, repairing the relationship between home and school, or counseling, all of these strategies are on an individual level and can be incorporated into the daily practices of the school psychologist. Since these strategies were developed based on an ecological assessment that helps to identify barriers to equity and access to resources and advocacy, they all can work to promote social justice.

## Systemic Interventions

School psychologists are becoming more involved in school- and district-wide interventions. Initiatives such as positive behavioral supports and response to intervention involve universal screenings, which means assessing the academic or behavioral needs of every student within a school, and then addressing the identified need in a manner that touches every student within the school (Doll &

Haack, 2005). School psychologists often work collaboratively with colleagues on such efforts and have the expertise to make valuable contributions. The process to address social injustice can be implemented at a systemic level. Differences between application of the process at the individual and systemic levels are reflected in the ecological systems that come under scrutiny for the barrier identification. Let us go back to Daria's brother Enrique to illustrate the implementation of the process on a systemic level.

## Component 1: Identification of Barriers

The "exosystem" or board of education of the district removed an important and popular incentive from a group of boys who are now struggling behaviorally, which in turn is impacting their academic performance. This has resulted in disparities with respect to discipline within the school. The presence of such a disparity, as stated previously, often correlates with the presence of inequitable access to resources. In this case the restricted access may be related to opportunities to positively engage with the school community. The identification of this policy-based issue that has resulted in disparities and inequity provides valuable information. The school psychologist is now in a position to choose a level of intervention to develop and apply strategies.

## Component 2: Selection of Barrier to Address

Due to the many demands on her time, it may not be practical for the school psychologist to try to develop individual behavioral intervention plans for all the boys involved. Although these plans could include replacing the afterschool sports teams with other activities to improve school engagement on a case-by-case basis, she may not have the time to monitor these plans or provide the resources. It may be more feasible to approach the issue systemically. Once this has been determined, systemic strategies should be developed.

## Component 3: Strategy Development

If the positive behavioral support team is sympathetic to the unique needs of the Latino boys, this may be a time for the school psychologist to advocate for a re-examination of the incentives provided through the positive behavioral support team and reallocate resources to make them more relevant to this population. In addition, the school psychologist could advocate for the physical education department to introduce more soccer into other activities as an incentive. She also may be working in a situation where school-based colleagues are less sympathetic or even resentful of an increase of the Latino population within the school.

In this case building on current district-based resources may be useful. It involves strategies using resources outside of the school but within the district. The psychologist could approach the high school soccer coach and ask if this group of middle school boys can work out and travel with the JV squad. Another example of a systemic or organizational strategy might be designing a mentoring program that utilizes Latino males from the high school to mentor Enrique and the boys who have been exhibiting behavioral infractions. As each one of these mentors gets trained, it increases their ability to mentor students outside of the group.

Using strategies outside of the school district may also be feasible. This would call for engaging community-based organizations that could replicate some of the incentive experiences the students seem to be missing. This might include creating a club that links the boys to afterschool soccer or a sports league and liaising with the personnel from such organizations. The important factor here is that the development of systemic strategies involves intervening at the systems level by creating programs, institutional structures, and/or practices.

## Chapter Summation

Social injustice manifested by academic underperformance of children of color and low-income students can be addressed by school psychologists through the application of a process that involves the identification of barriers to equal access to resources, selection of a barrier or barriers to address, and the development of strategies to intervene at either the individual or systemic level. As the case example that was presented at the beginning of this chapter and then discussed throughout illustrates, school psychologists are confronted with a variety of the complex issues affecting the American education system on a daily basis. Not only must we work within the context of the lives and schools of our students, we must do so in a manner that considers the academic challenges facing their communities and society at large. Issues such as the achievement gap and disparate disciplinary action that result in the underperformance of economically disadvantaged and children of color are like cumbersome, out-of-control vehicles careening between many of our students and their academic success. These vehicles are manifestations of social injustice and are impediments to academic achievement. If school psychologists are able to recognize that social injustice is fueling these vehicles, using an ecological approach will enable them to use their expertise to help students safely cross over into academic success. Through the application of a process to address social injustice as it relates to the underperformance of low-income children and children of color, school psychologists can promote social justice.

## References

Alpert, G., & Dunham, R. (1986). Keeping academically marginal youths in school. *Youth & Society, 17* (4), 346–361.

American Psychological Association. (2003). Guidelines on multicultural education, training, research, practice, and organizational change for psychologists. *American Psychologist, 58,* 377–402.

Aspen Institute, Roundtable on Community Change. (2005). *Structural racism and youth development: Issues, challenges and implications.* Washington, DC: Aspen Institute.

Bollin, G. G., & Finkel, J. (1995). White racial identity as a barrier to understanding diversity. *Equity and Excellence in Education, 28* (1), 25–30.

Bradley-Johnson, S. & Dean,V. J. (2000). Role change for school psychology: The challenge continues in the new millennium. *Psychology in the School, 37* (1), 1–5.

Brown, D., Pryzwansky, W. B., & Schulte, A. C. (2006). *Psychological consultation and collaboration: Introduction to theory and practice* (6th ed.). Boston, MA: Allyn & Bacon.

Brofenbrenner, U. (1979). *The ecology of human development: Experiments by nature and design.* Cambridge, MA: Harvard University Press.

Burns, M. K. (2011). School psychology research: Combining ecological theory and prevention science. *School Psychology Review, 40,* 132–139.

Cornelius, J. D. (1991). *"When I can read my title clear": Literacy, slavery, and religion in the antebellum South.* Columbia, SC: University of South Carolina Press.

Cronbach, L. J. (1957). The two disciplines of scientific psychology. *American Psychologist, 12,* 671–684.

Darling-Hammond, L. (2010). *The flat world and education: How America's commitment to diversity will determine our future.* New York, NY: Teacher's College Press.

Doll, B., & Haack, M. K.(2005). Population based strategies for identifying schoolwide problems. In R. Bowen-Chidsey (Ed.), *Assessment for intervention: A problem solving approach* (pp. 82–102). New York, NY: Guilford Press.

Duncan, A. (2010, March 8). *Crossing the next bridge,* Remarks of the US Secretary of Education, Selma, Alabama: US Department of Education. Retrieved November 5, 2010 from www2.ed.gov/news/speeches/2010/03/03082010.html

Elhoweris, H., Kagendo, M., Negmeldin, A., & Holloway, P. C. (2005). Effects of children's ethnicity on teacher referral and recommendation decisions in gifted and talented programs. *Remedial and Special Education, 26,* 25–34.

Fenning, P., & Rose, J. (2007). Overrepresentation of African American students in exclusionary discipline: The role of school policy. *Urban Education, 42* (6), 536–559.

Foner, P. S., and Pacheco, J. F. (1984). *Three who dared: Prudence Crandall, Margaret Douglass, Myrtilla Miner—Champions of antebellum black education.* Westport, CT: Greenwood.

Ford, D. Y. (1998). The underrepresentation of minority students in gifted education: Problems and promises in recruitment and retention. *Journal of Special Education, 31,* 4–14.

Gregory, A., Skiba, R. J. & Noguera, P. A. (2010). The achievement gap and the discipline gap: Two sides of the same coin? *Education Researcher, 39,* 59–60.

Gutkin, T. B. (1993). Moving from behavioral to ecobehavioral consultation: What's in a name? *Journal of Educational and Psychological Consultation, 4,* 95–99.

Gutkin, T. B. (2009). Ecological school psychology: A personal opinion and a plea for change. In T. B. Gutkin & C. R. Reynolds (Eds.), *The handbook of school psychology* (4th ed., pp. 463–496). New York, NY: Wiley.

Gutkin, T. B. (2012). Ecological psychology: Replacing the medical model paradigm for school-based psychological and psychoeducational systems. *Journal of Educational & Psychological Consultation, 22,* 1–20.

Ingraham, C. L. (2000). Consultation through a multicultural lens: Multicultural and cross-cultural consulation in schools. *School Psychology Review, 29* (3), 320–343.

Kruger, L. J., & Shriberg, D. (Eds.). (2007). High stakes testing: New challenges and opportunities for school psychologists. *Journal of Applied School Psychology, 23* (1).

Ladson-Billings, G. (2006). From the achievement gap to the education debt: Understanding achievement in U.S. schools. *Educational Researcher, 35* (10), 3–12.

Li, C., & Vazquez-Nuttall, E. (2009). School consultants as agents of social justice for multicultural children and families. *Journal of Educational and Psychological Consultation* [special issue], *19* (1), 26–44.

Losen, D. J. (2011). *Discipline policies, successful schools, and racial justice.* Boulder, CO: National Education Policy Center.

National Association of School Psychologists. (2010a). *Model for comprehensive and integrated school psychological services.* Retrieved August 30, 2012 from www.nasponline.org/standards/2010standards/2_practicemodel.pdf

National Association of School Psychologists. (2010b). *Principles for professional ethics.* Retrieved August 30, 2012 from www.nasponline.org/standards/2010standards/1_%20ethical%20principles.pdf

New Teacher Project. (2009). *The widget effect: Our national failure to acknowledge and act on differences in teacher effectiveness.* New York, NY: New Teacher Project.

Reschly, D. J. (2008). School psychology paradigm shift and beyond. In A. Thomas & J. Grimes (Eds.), *Best practices in school psychology V* (pp. 3–16). Bethesda, MD: National Association of School Psychologists.

Short, R. J. (2003). School psychology, context and population-based practice. *School Psychology Review, 32,* 181–184.

Shriberg, D. (2009). Social justice and school mental health: Implications for practice. In J. M. Jones (Ed.), *The psychology of multiculturalism in schools: A primer for practice, training, and research* (pp. 49–66). Bethesda MD: National Association of School Psychologists.

Shriberg, D., Bonner, M., Sarr, B., Walker, A., Hyland, M., & Chester, C. (2008) Social justice through a school psychology lens: Definitions and applications. *School Psychology Review, 37,* 453–468.

Skiba, R. J., Michael, R. S., Nardo, A. C., & Peterson, R. L. (2002). The color of discipline: Source of racial and gender disproportionality in school punishment. *Urban Review, 34,* 317–342.

Tilly, W. D. (2008). The evolution of school psychology to science based practice problem solving and the three tiered model. In A. Thomas & J. Grimes(Eds.), *Best practices in school psychology V* (pp. 3–16). Bethesda, MD: National Association of School Psychologists.

Ysseldyke, J., Burns, M., Dawson, P., Kelley, B., Morrison, D., Ortiz, S., et al. (2006). *School psychology: A blueprint for training and practice III.* Bethesda, MD: National Association of School Psychologists.

# twelve
# Behavioral Issues in the Classroom

## Antoinette Halsell Miranda and Charlotte Risby Eschenbrenner

Developing and sustaining positive interaction between teachers and students in the classroom helps facilitate a positive classroom community and reduces problem behaviors that may occur (Goldstein & Brooks, 2007). Unfortunately, problematic student behavior is often cited as one of the major reasons that teachers leave the teaching profession within the first five years of employment (McCoy, 2003). In addition, discipline in schools has been consistently viewed as a top concern in the public's mind with respect to public schools (Gallup, 2005). The belief by the general public is that schools are rife with discipline problems, especially in urban schools; the reality is far from that. Since 1994, acts of violence in schools have declined (Dinkes, Kemp, & Baum, 2009). Incidents such as the 1999 shooting at Columbine High School have provided a distorted view of violence in schools to the general public. In fact, targeted school violence is extremely rare and according to the School Violence Resource Center violent deaths in schools have declined annually since 1997–1998 (Paine & Cowan, 2009). However, there remain genuine concerns with student behavior and the discipline of those students. Most notably, increasing attention has been given to how classroom management contributes to behavior problems, which ultimately lead to the disruption of learning. In addition, there has been growing concern regarding students of color and their discipline disproportionality. The racial discipline gap, whereby students of color receive the majority of school suspensions and expulsions despite engaging in similar offenses to white students, is a social justice issue.

This chapter will focus on behavioral issues that occur in the classroom, with special attention to how marginalized students are disproportionately affected by the administration of discipline and punishment. Chapter 6 provided an excellent review of the long-term deleterious effects of discipline issues in schools with the most marginalized students when they are not addressed in a proactive, culturally responsive fashion. That chapter viewed discipline from a macro level. This chapter will look at behavior and behavioral issues from a micro level: in the classroom, where school-based discipline problems often initially surface. The chapter will provide an overview of behavioral problems, especially in urban classrooms; review the literature on teachers and classroom management; discuss issues of diversity in classroom management; and finally determine ways to rethink classroom management utilizing socially just practices with diverse students.

## Problem Behaviors and Socially Unjust Practices

Students with problem behaviors have been a concern in education almost since the beginning of compulsory schooling (Goldstein & Brooks, 2007). The most common way of dealing with problem behaviors in the past was to implement a specific model of punishment: corporal punishment. Over the years, corporal punishment has diminished in favor of behavioral principles (Goldstein & Brooks, 2007). However, there continue to be instances of inappropriate discipline and harsh punishment occurring in schools as they attempt to deal with behavior problems exhibited by students.

Many researchers have studied this vexing problem of how to reduce student misbehavior in the classroom (Monroe, 2009; Wheldall & Merrett, 1988). In the 1990s, zero tolerance policies were implemented and viewed as the best approach to reducing violence and behavior problems in school (see Chapter 6: School Discipline). Unfortunately, this policy has had the opposite effect, with discipline rates increasing (APA, 2008). Despite the overwhelming evidence against zero tolerance, schools continue to apply it, with an estimated 110,000 expulsions and three million suspensions each year (US Department of Education, 2002). Most disturbing is the fact that research has convincingly demonstrated that marginalized students, minorities, and low-income students are the most impacted by this policy (APA, 2008). This body of research has led to the often cited phrase of the "school to prison pipeline" which refers to children funneled out of public schools and into the juvenile and criminal justice systems (Wald & Losen, 2003). The notion that the approach to addressing problem behaviors is to punish, and punish harshly, has been shown to be ineffective and has only succeeded in increasing the student drop-out rate (Losen, 2011). Without fail, the most marginalized students are disproportionately represented at all phases of the discipline pipeline; from office referral to suspension and expulsion, to the prison population. Thus, it has become a social justice issue in that these students, despite hard evidence that their infractions are no more severe than those of their white counterparts, received much harsher punishment, which is often a push-out solution (e.g., suspension or expulsion). Even more critical is the fact that those students who are "pushed out" are also more likely to have lower academic achievement (Losen, 2011). At a time when we are desperately trying to close the achievement gap, a commitment to equal educational opportunity for all students needs to be reinforced.

The cause of student behaviors has prompted a wide variety of explanations, from psychiatric diagnosis to a breakdown in the home environment (Goldstein & Brooks, 2007). However, the reality is that student behavior is affected by many different factors. Areas that have received increasing attention are: student, teacher, and classroom variables and their interaction with each other, and how that interaction contributes to what happens in a classroom (Goldstein & Brooks, 2007). Teachers generally attribute students' problem behaviors to internal characteristics of the child (Soodak & Podell, 1994). Thus, there is a desire to have interventions geared towards directly changing the child and encouraging the child to take ownership for their problems, with little attention given to common contributing factors such as the teacher or the environment. While there are a variety of variables that may contribute to students' problem behaviors, it has been found that the teacher–child relationship can have an extraordinary impact on managing student behavior (Goldstein & Brooks, 2007; Gregory & Ripski, 2008; Rimm-Kaufman, n.d.). It has been shown that the vast majority of discipline referrals originate in the classroom (Skiba, Michael, Nardo, & Peterson, 2002). Thus, the classroom seems like a logical place to have a closer examination of the dynamics of the problem.

In considering the role of the classroom, it is important to distinguish between classroom management and discipline since the terms are often used interchangeably. While they are indeed related, they are also very different concepts. As described by Marshall (2007), classroom management generally consists of procedures, routines, and structures. When good classroom management exists, students know what to do and when to do it. Discipline, however, is the negative consequences that a student receives when disobeying the rules. Discipline deals with how people behave and encompasses impulse management and self-control (Marshall, 2007). The general perspective is that classrooms in which teachers employ good classroom management will have reduced discipline problems as students know the expectations of how and when to behave.

## The Conundrum of Classroom Management

In urban school districts, which tend to have large numbers of students of color, classroom management is often portrayed as punitive, with the students needing prison-like policies and an abundance of structure (Ullucci, 2009). In fact, the general public believes that urban schools are rampant with disorderly students who are unaware of how to behave, and popular media does little to dispel the myth (i.e. *Dangerous Minds, The Substitute, Freedom Writers*). Ultimately, teachers, administrators, and other school personnel often operate from a deficit perspective when dealing with urban students (Ullucci, 2009). In other words, they see the problem as residing solely within the child, with little attention given to the dynamics of the teacher and the school. Surprisingly, given that classroom management has been such a conundrum for urban schools, there is little research that has looked at issues of cultural diversity with respect to classroom management (Weinstein, Tomlinson-Clarke, & Curran, 2004). As stated by Weinstein et al. (2004), "conventional classroom management is presented as if it were culturally neutral, rather than a White, middle-class construction" (p. 26). Most of the literature in education that has focused on cultural responsiveness has focused on the curriculum and teaching strategies (Weinstein et al., 2004). Yet classroom management, which can have a powerful influence on student achievement, has been virtually ignored (Weinstein et al., 2004). The reality is that disruptive classrooms diminish the opportunity to learn, which ultimately contributes to academic failure. Thus, closer examination of what occurs in classrooms and asking the hard questions about the contributing factors is necessary to finding solutions. While students are often viewed as the problem, more recently attention has been directed at looking at how teachers manage or do not manage the classrooms and the contributing factors that make it so challenging.

## Teachers

As noted above, the vast majority of disciplinary referrals originate in the classroom (Skiba et al., 2002). Is this because the child is so unruly that they are disrupting the class? Or is it because the teacher lacks the skills to have good classroom management? It is fairly well known that teachers typically enter the classroom with little to no experience in managing student behavior and thus are the least prepared to deal with the behavioral issues students bring to the classroom (Gonzalez, Brown, & Slate, 2008). More specifically, disproportionate discipline of students of color may be due to lack of teacher preparation in classroom management (Vavrus & Cole, 2002). While it is clearly important to have a grasp of the curriculum material, without a sound understanding of classroom management principles, teachers often struggle to teach materials to students effectively due to the distractions that may be present when students are disruptive. In the past, academic success and behavioral issues were seen as separate issues; however, more recently there has been a recognition that they go hand in hand (Goldstein & Brooks, 2007; Weinstein et al, 2004). Students who exhibit behavioral difficulty generally have lower academic achievement and often are the most likely recipients of school suspension, which carries with it serious negative consequences such as the increased likelihood of involvement in the juvenile justice system (APA, 2008).

Teachers consistently share that the one thing they wished they had was classroom management skills (Coalition for Psychology in Schools and Education, 2006; McCoy, 2003). The Coalition for Psychology in Schools and Education (2006) conducted a survey of pre-K through 12th-grade teachers and found that teachers identified help with classroom management as one of their top needs. Teacher responses indicated that they wanted assistance with classroom management because of concerns they had about student safety and their need for effective strategies to deal with students' negative and disruptive behaviors (APA, 2008).

The reality is that teachers generally are not exposed to classroom management techniques until their student teaching practica, which is an experience limited to the particular classrooms in which they participate (Gonzalez et al., 2008). In addition, there is no guarantee that the cooperating teacher will employ sound classroom management techniques for the student teacher to emulate. For teachers whose student teaching is primarily in the suburban or rural setting, they are often surprised that the techniques they have learned for successful classroom management are ineffective in the urban setting (Higgins & Moule, 2009; Weiner, 2003).

Although classroom management may not immediately come to mind when discussing social justice, the apparent lack of pre-service education in urban classroom management leaves those children at a major disadvantage in the classroom. Teachers in urban schools may have a perception, as does much of society, that urban schools are rife with discipline problems, and that the approach to effective classroom management must include behavior-based rewards and punishment systems (Lake, 2004; Ullucci, 2009). Teachers are also at a disadvantage as they often have to recreate models of classroom management that vastly differ from the theory they have studied during their university coursework (Higgins & Moule, 2009). This often leads to misinterpretations of behavior which can then lead to discipline referrals. When teachers lack familiarity with the culture of their students, which is often the case in an urban school, the formation of a trusting relationship is more difficult (Lake, 2004).

While a lack of classroom management techniques is one oft-cited reason for discipline problems, another reason that has gained attention is the lack of multicultural competence of both novice and experienced teachers, which can exacerbate the difficulties they have in their classroom (Weinstein et al., 2004). The teaching workforce is overwhelmingly white, middle class, and female, from suburban and rural communities (Hodgkinson, 2002) and is in classrooms with increasingly diverse student populations. Behaviors are often culturally influenced and conflicts may occur when there are cultural differences (Weinstein et al., 2004) due to a misreading, misinterpretation, and/or miscommunication with respect to behaviors displayed in the classroom. While there has been extensive writing in the area of multicultural education, unfortunately issues of classroom management in multicultural classrooms have been excluded. However, recent attention has been focused on discipline issues and how they disproportionately affect students of color, particularly African American males. There is a growing recognition that educators need to seriously grapple with this issue to determine the root causes and develop solutions that will effectively meet the needs of students (Gregory & Ripski, 2008; Monroe, 2009; Ullucci, 2009).

The teacher is in a unique position to be a great support to children in their classroom, whether in an urban, suburban, or rural setting. As the primary unrelated adult figure in a child's life, teachers can be influential in children's behavior, academic performance and self-esteem in and out of school. However, particularly in the urban setting, this prominent role can be amplified by the fact that often children do not have another adult able to provide that type of support in their lives. Management of the classroom affects not only children's behavior, but their self-esteem, and ultimately their academic performance (Matus, 2001). In such a position, it is important for the teacher to foster an environment of cooperation and trust to aid in management of the classroom (Higgins & Moule, 2009; Weiner, 2003). If the link between behavior and academic success is accepted, teachers are responsible for modeling social skills and modifying behavior in order to support academic performance (Goldstein & Brooks, 2007; Lake, 2004; Weiner, 2003).

## Classroom management practices

As a topic of research, classroom management in urban schools is not well represented (Monroe, 2009; Weiner, 2003). Given the pervasive perception of urban classrooms as unruly and out-of-control places, one would think that this would be an area of research with a focus on solutions to improve the perceived problem. Recent research has exposed the disproportionality of discipline with marginalized students, especially African American males, and has urged the education community to target solutions to reduce this disparity. This is important as the most marginalized students, most often in urban schools, receive the brunt of negative portrayals with respect to disruptive students. Research has shown that disciplinary referrals of African American students are disproportionate when compared to their enrollment (APA, 2008). More than other racial groups, African Americans tend to be perceived as defiant (Ferguson, 2001) and punished for it. It has often been suggested that African American students engage in more severe disruptive behaviors which warranted more severe punishment (Losen, 2011). Empirically sound research has demonstrated that the truth is quite different (Bradshaw, Mitchell, O'Brennan, & Leaf, 2010). In fact, in comparison to white students, African American students are disproportionately referred for offenses that are described as subjective and non-violent, such as defiance, and often involve judgment calls by teachers and administrators (Bradshaw et al., 2010). There is no evidence that students of color engage in more misbehavior than white students (Losen, 2011). The teacher's perception or interpretation of the student's behavior is one major factor that initiates the referral, and it only seems reasonable that attention should be given to how to help teachers improve their classroom management and make good choices when it comes to referral of students.

A number of researchers believe that in order to do this, teachers who are overwhelmingly white and female need to understand cultural clashes that may occur in the classroom that may lead to inappropriate referrals (Gregory & Ripski, 2008; Weinstein et al., 2004). Weinstein et al. (2004) propose that it may be a lack of multicultural competence that influences how teachers approach classroom management. More specifically, the authors suggest that what is defined as appropriate and expected behavior is culturally influenced. For example, urban African American high school students who move to suburban school districts often encounter norms that are quite different than their high school in the urban setting (Eggelston & Miranda, 2009). Unfortunately, these students are unaware of those norms and how they are violating them. The first author, who has conducted many diversity trainings in suburban schools, almost without fail has heard high school suburban teachers question why African American students congregate together in the hallway and speak in very loud voices. Many teachers feel intimidated by this behavior and are reluctant to approach the group of students. Interestingly, when asked if they are concerned about white students forming a group in the hallway, they will admit they do not see it as a problem. When teachers are asked what they think is wrong or inappropriate about the African American students' behavior, they are at a loss for an explanation. Teachers will just say that, "they are intimidating." In this case, teachers are expecting hallway-behavior that is quiet and subdued, especially when a group assembles, and teachers often assume that loud, boisterous behavior signals potential disruption. Thus, there is a need to find a way to divert a problem before it happens, at least in their mind. This is an excellent example of subjective offenses that involve judgment calls by teachers. Unfortunately, these students are often perceived as potential behavior problems and are treated as such, despite the fact they have not engaged in any type of disruptive behavior. Researchers have begun to examine and explore methods that teachers and other educators can effectively use to manage classrooms in ways that understand and respect the diversity that exists in their classrooms. The ultimate goal is to reduce the disproportionality of students of color when it comes to discipline referrals.

## Classroom Management From a Social Justice Perspective

While there is a scarcity of empirical research articles on classroom management in urban or diverse classrooms, there has been considerable research over the years that details what is necessary, in general, for classroom management to work (Goldstein & Brooks, 2007). Kazdin (1975) explored how teachers can manage their own behavior in an effort to produce positive outcomes in the classroom. He described five areas that teachers could utilize to effectively manage their behavior, as follows.

- Knowledge of how various stimuli can trigger certain good or negative behaviors increases the likelihood of successful student behavior.
- Teachers' ability to monitor their own behavior and then make changes accordingly.
- Recognition that teachers may reinforce or punish themselves contingent on their own behavior.
- Teachers can learn to guide and instruct themselves more efficiently through self-monitoring.
- Teachers can learn alternative responses or new ways of responding to problem behaviors exhibited by students.

Engaging in this reflective practice acknowledges the impact teachers have in shaping behavior in the classroom.

In managing student behaviors effectively in the classroom, Goldstein and Brooks (2007) have found that teachers' assumptions about themselves and others can play a significant role in determining their expectations for behaviors. They believe that effective educators approach classroom management and their students with a "mindset" that produces success in managing student behavior in the classroom. Some key characteristics of the mindset of effective educators are an understanding of their lifelong impact on students, a belief in attending to the social–emotional life of students, and a recognition that they must be empathic and able to see the world through their students' eyes, to name a few. Larrivee (1985) found that 15 basic teacher behaviors had a positive correlation with improved behavior and performance in students who exhibited problem behaviors in the classroom:

1.  providing positive feedback to students
2.  offering sustained feedback to students
3.  responding supportively to students in general
4.  responding even more supportively to low-ability students
5.  responding supportively to students with behavioral problems
6.  asking questions that students are able to answer correctly
7.  presenting learning tasks for which students have a high probability of success
8.  using time efficiently
9.  intervening in misbehavior at a low rate
10. maintaining a low ratio of punitive to positive interventions
11. being punitive at a low rate
12. using criticism at a low rate
13. keeping the need for disciplinary interventions low through positive classroom interventions
14. wasting little time on student transitions
15. keeping off-task time to a minimum.

What most research has found is that teachers need to have a basic system to identify and deal with problems and effective interventions at their fingertips that they are able to implement (Goldstein & Brooks, 2007). These principles and strategies are necessary for sound classroom management regardless of whether it is an urban, suburban, or rural school. Unfortunately, many teachers lack these tools (Goldstein & Brooks, 2007), most often because they did not receive them in their teacher education training. In addition, emerging research, in an attempt to understand the discipline disproportionality, indicates that other factors may play a role in exacerbating the gap. The following research addresses other factors to consider when working with culturally different students. They would not necessarily replace the abovementioned strategies that have been shown to be effective, but would be in addition to those strategies and principles previously identified.

## Factors to consider when working with culturally different students

Ullucci (2009) in her research on six teachers who were identified as the "best of the best" in urban schools had several findings. Ullucci found that management was less about rewards and punishment and more about the establishment of norms. She described teachers as warm demanders, defined as "communicating both warmth and a nonnegotiable demand for student effort and mutual respect. This stance . . . is central to sustaining academic engagement in high-poverty schools" (Bondy & Ross, 2008). In addition, teachers relied on community-building, which included a focus on relationships, honest conversations, and affirmation of the student's culture. The most striking finding, according to the author, was the lack of structured behavioral systems (Ullucci, 2009). To be clear, she believes that behaviorist approaches have merit, but that in her observations of these six teachers, their focus was on "establishing limits, creating family-like relations and motivating students to do the right thing" (Ullucci, 2009, p. 24). For these teachers, relationships became the cornerstone of effective classroom management.

Weinstein et al. (2004) have proposed Culturally Responsive Classroom Management (CRCM), which is viewed as a frame of mind that guides the management decisions that teachers make. They state that teachers that employ this frame of reference understand that "CRCM is classroom management in the service of social justice" (Weinstein et al., 2004, p. 27). Ideally, the authors believe that multicultural issues should be infused throughout the pre-service curriculum, especially in courses on classroom management. Weinstein et al.'s conception of CRCM favors an approach that focuses on self-regulation, community-building, and social decision-making. Their goal for classroom management "is to create an environment in which students behave appropriately, not out of fear of punishment or desire for reward, but out of a sense of personal responsibility" (p. 28).

There are five essential components of CRCM:

1.  recognition of one's own ethnocentrism and biases
2.  knowledge of students' cultural backgrounds
3.  awareness of the broader social, economic, and political context
4.  ability and willingness to use culturally appropriate management strategies
5.  commitment to building caring classroom communities (Weinstein et al., 2004).

The authors' preference is that these components be infused in a training program before students enter the field as professionals. However, practitioners can still take these components and apply them to themselves as well as examine how utilizing the components can change their practice.

The first component, recognition of one's own ethnocentrism and biases, is directly related to the awareness stage of developing cross-cultural competence. It is this component in which the individual examines her/his own beliefs, biases and assumptions about human behavior and brings these to a conscious level. For white teachers, it involves examining the pervasiveness of whiteness and having an understanding that white in America is often equated with "normal" and "right." It involves an examination of the concept of privilege and how privilege is bestowed on a chosen few, which often does not include ethnic minorities, especially if they are low income. Peggy McIntosh's (1988) *White Privilege: Unpacking the Invisible Knapsack* is an excellent resource to examine various facets of life through different cultural lenses. Going through this process allows one to look at the issues of culture in a deeper fashion, with particular emphasis on how one's behavior, actions, and/or beliefs might perpetuate inequitable treatment of marginalized students.

Another area to consider under this component is the concept of racial microaggression. "Racial microaggressions are brief and commonplace daily verbal, behavioral, or environmental indignities, whether intentional or unintentional, that communicate hostile, derogatory, or negative racial slights and insults toward people of color" (Sue et al., 2007, p. 271). Sue et al. (2007) identify three forms of microaggressions: microassault, microinsult, and microinvalidation. People who engage in microaggressions are often unaware that they are doing so. For example: an African American male shared the story of being in an AP English class in which the students were required to finish an assigned book. When the teacher (who was white) asked who completed it, he was one of only four students who raised their hand. All of the students were white except him. The teacher looked at him and said, "Did you really finish the book?" The student responded "yes" and left it at that, but he expressed that he really wanted to say "You didn't think I finished it because I am black?" No other student was asked this question. That comment alone damaged the relationship between the student and the teacher because he felt the teacher didn't see him as belonging or deserving to be in the class. Thus, being aware of potential bias will help teachers to avoid engaging in microaggression.

The second component is knowledge of students' cultural backgrounds. This component goes hand in hand with one's awareness of ethnocentrism. In this component, one must strike a balance between defining cultural groups by a set of cultural characteristics and understanding that culture is on a continuum. By focusing exclusively on cultural characteristics there is danger of stereotyping groups. So there needs to be an understanding that "descriptions of culture are merely approximations of reality" (Gay, 2000, p. 12). Having general knowledge about a student's culture can provide information and insight about a student's behavior. It allows you to view the behavior through a different lens, taking into consideration the cultural context, communication styles, values, beliefs, and norms of the group that may have an impact on how they engage in the school environment. It is important to remember that cultural characteristics are influenced by a number of different factors including gender and social class.

The third component is awareness of the broader social, economic, and political context. This recognizes that schools do not exist in a vacuum but are reflective of the larger society, which includes discriminatory practices that may exist. It is in this component that teachers and education personnel become aware of how norms of the dominant group become institutionalized, which has led to researchers saying that schools are reflective of middle class values. In the past, this was considered a cultural mismatch. An example would be the norm in schools to raise your hand when you want to respond to a question posed by the teacher. The African American culture typically uses call-and-response, in which students may blurt out answers, which would be viewed as not following the rules. Gorski (2007) challenges us to think about the existence of classism in our classrooms and schools in terms of policies and procedures that are in place. This component also challenges us to examine how some practices privilege certain groups while marginalizing other groups (Weinstein et al., 2004). Understanding the disproportionality in suspensions and expulsions in schools and how it connects to the larger society in the school-to-prison pipeline is one example.

The fourth component is the ability and willingness to use culturally appropriate management strategies. As educators engage in the abovementioned components they are then able to begin to "reflect on the ways that classroom management practices promote or obstruct equal access to learning" (Weinstein et al., 2004, p. 32). The authors suggest we need to consider three particular challenges as we go through this process. First, we need to examine our own behavior in the classroom and how it promotes equitable treatment. Do we have different standards for different students? And are these standards apparent to the students? Second, there needs to be an examination of our traditional assumptions regarding "what works" in classroom management (Weinstein et al., 2004). Included in this is consideration of the potential mismatch between traditional classroom management techniques (what is typically taught in teacher education that works in suburban classrooms) and culturally diverse classrooms. That is not to say that some classroom management techniques will not work in culturally diverse classrooms, but we do need to consider techniques in the context of where they are being implemented. For example, in urban classrooms, there may need to be more of an intentionality of teaching students the teacher's expectations, helping them understand classroom norms, modeling the behavior desired, and establishing positive relationships with all students. Many urban students need structure and predictability in the classroom. Third, there needs to be a consideration of when to accommodate students' cultural backgrounds and when to expect students to abide by the norms set forth in the classroom and school (Weinstein et al., 2004). While it is important to consider cultural variables, we also have to realize that we have to assist students in understanding that there are values, beliefs, and skills that are necessary for students to succeed in the school culture and to be successful academically. Thus, we need to empower students rather than enable students, which can be a fine line. Teachers and other educators can have a powerful impact and influence on students. As a protective factor, teachers can potentially mitigate at-risk factors that students bring to the school environment which contribute to both academic and behavior problems. Thus, it is necessary for teachers to be aware of the dynamics that play out in classrooms when there is diversity. They must examine their actions and how they might contribute to the inequitable delivery of punishment and discipline.

Finally, the fifth component is the commitment to building caring classroom communities. It is no surprise that students who feel connected to their school, classroom, and teachers, are more likely to be successful academically and behaviorally (Davidson, 1999; Ullucci, 2009; Wentzel, 1997, 1998). The building of relationships is critically important, and is a cornerstone to successful classroom management. Caring classroom communities move us away from classrooms that are highly controlled, punitive places to ones in which there is a focus on communication, relationships, and creating a sense of belonging in the classroom environment (Ullucci, 2009).

While CRCM has promise as a way of helping teachers think differently and in more critical ways about classroom management with diverse populations, it should be noted that research is still needed to verify all components as viable and necessary. Monroe (2009) conducted case studies that examined teachers' approaches to classroom management using the CRCM model, and found that not all teachers engaged in all components of the model, and suggested that elements of the model may operate unevenly. For example, in her research she found that teachers did not engage as much in the component on awareness of the broader social, economic, and political context in which the school existed (Monroe, 2009). However, CRCM can be used as a framework to guide teachers and other educators to think critically about how classroom management can be effective, reducing unnecessary discipline referrals, and ultimately building a classroom community.

Other approaches proposed have been to change the culture of the school to move from suspension as the primary method of discipline to one in which inclusion of all students in the learning process is the goal. Unfortunately, the traditional school of thought has been that suspending the bad students will improve the learning environment and deter future misbehavior by students (APA, 2008). Nothing could be further from the truth. In fact, longitudinal studies demonstrate that suspension seems to act more as a reinforcer for suspended students, as they are more likely to be suspended again later in their school career (Tobin, Sugai, & Colvin, 1998). With respect to the learning environment, research demonstrates that higher rates of out-of-school suspension correlate with lower academic achievement (Skiba & Rausch, 2006). Thus, school-wide Positive Behavior Intervention Support (PBIS) is often suggested as an approach to improve a school's learning environment and create a more positive school climate (APA, 2008). Other suggestions for moving away from a suspension/punishment model are to develop a planned continuum of effective alternatives for those students who are the most challenging, and could include options such as restorative justice, alternative programs, or community service (APA, 2008). To create these alternatives it is suggested that schools engage in system coordination with other agencies (e.g. mental health, juvenile justice, community agencies) to increase the resources to deal with the most challenging behaviors (APA, 2008). Programs that teach Social and Emotional Learning (SEL) are also gaining recognition, especially since these programs have been rigorously evaluated and shown to have positive impact (Collaborative for Academic, Social, and Emotional Learning (CASEL) (n.d.). A large-scale study found that teaching social and emotional skills has numerous benefits including the reduction of students' disruptive behavior in the classroom (Durlak,Weissberg, Dymnicki, Taylor, & Schellinger, 2011). The programs were also found to be effective across ethnic groups, age ranges, and urban, suburban, and rural areas (Durlak et al., 2011). Particularly for many students of color who have life circumstances that may put them at a disadvantage for healthy social and emotional learning, such programs can assist in developing self-management and self-control and also provide teachers with the tools to improve their classroom management. The proposed benefits of SEL programs in schools are the creation of socially and emotionally sound learning and working environments (CASEL, n.d.). It is truly a systems-level change in which not only students improve but teachers and education personnel develop and engage in more positive and proactive ways to ensure long-term academic and personal outcomes for students. The Collaborative for Academic, Social, and Emotional Learning (CASEL) is an excellent resource for educators that may want to establish social and emotional learning as part of their school wide practices to reduce discipline problems in their students.

Gregory and Ripski (2008) interviewed and surveyed 32 teachers and 32 discipline-referred students to examine teachers' relational approach to discipline as a predictor of high school students' behavior and the trust they have in teacher authority. The results of their study demonstrated that teachers who reported using a relational approach were more likely to have students who exhibited lower defiant behavior than those teachers who did not use this type of approach (Gregory & Ripski, 2008). The authors also believe that a relational approach may facilitate culturally relevant discipline in that teachers are able to use an ecological lens to understand why students react against classroom rules and norms (Gregory & Mosley, 2004).

## Promoting Socially Just Practice: The School Psychologist's Role

School psychologists are in a unique position to help teachers and administrators promote socially just practice to fairly and equitably address problem behaviors that occur in the classroom and in-school buildings. Given that teachers and administrators are on the front line of implementing classroom management strategies, intervention strategies, and school policies and procedures, school psychologists can serve as a consultant to assist school personnel in moving towards the goal of incorporating socially just practice when addressing issues of discipline in a school. The following recommendations are suggested to assist school psychologists and other school personnel to engage in culturally appropriate practices that seek to be inclusionary, not exclusionary.

- Expand your knowledge base. As school psychologists seek to assist schools in becoming environments that value all students, there needs to be a recognition that schools with culturally diverse students are also vulnerable to disproportionality in discipline referrals, suspensions, and other exclusionary methods. To that end, school psychologists must understand the population of students by gathering data to examine discipline referral rates, suspensions, and expulsions. Policies and procedures should be reviewed to make sure they do not benefit one group at the expense of another. To promote socially just practice, school psychologists must be willing to ask the hard questions. Some of these hard questions are:

- Do certain groups receive harsher and more punitive discipline than others?

- Do teachers have classroom management strategies that are fair and equitable with all students?

- Is the school climate one that promotes a sense of community and encourages positive relationships between teachers and students?

- Do school personnel value the diversity that exists in their schools?

School psychologists need to be familiar with the literature on disproportionality and the detrimental effects it can have on students of color, including the zero tolerance policy. While school psychologists generally are experts in interventions, they must also be astute in developing a knowledge base about how issues of diversity may influence or impact interventions, and be prepared to make adjustments based on the context in which they are being implemented. For example, empirical research is emerging on the effectiveness of PBIS in urban schools (Lassen, Steele, & Sailor, 2006) including challenges encountered that need to be considered that are different than implementation in suburban schools (Warren et al., 2003).

## In-Service Training and Advocacy

School psychologists can hold in-services to aid teachers in understanding the importance of incorporating students' culture into classroom management strategies. Using the CRCM framework is one way to help guide discussions and provide teachers with strategies that are culturally responsive. A conscious movement towards socially just practice works to dispel the myth of unruly, out-of-control urban students in which teachers exert control over them, and move towards explicit instruction and modeling of prosocial skills that may improve behavior, self-esteem, and academic performance in the classroom (Lake, 2004). Although this may require more time, the teacher will be imparting valuable skills to the students, and will save time when students are exhibiting more pro-social behaviors allowing them to stay on-task and reduce disruptions (Lake, 2004). Social and emotional learning can also be a strategy that moves the school away from punishment to teaching challenging students who may lack the requisite skills to be successful behaviorally. In some ways, it forces the school to look at the students in its classrooms differently and examine how the teacher can be a contributor rather than an inhibitor in promoting socially acceptable behavior within a culturally responsive framework. Teachers should think of themselves as an external protective factor for many of their marginalized students with the goal of mitigating any risk-factors the students may bring to the classroom. Much of the research on culturally responsive approaches to classroom management and discipline has relationship building as a cornerstone. "As teachers develop greater connection with students, they are likely to better perceive the ecology of the classroom and larger environment that may be contributing to an adolescent's difficulties" (Gregory & Ripski, 2008, p. 349). Thus, school psychologists become advocates and work to find ways to engage and support the most behaviorally challenged students rather than "pushing them out" to a future that research clearly shows does not have a promising end (APA, 2008).

## Conclusion

The discipline gap that exists in schools between Whites and African Americans and other students of color (i.e., Latinos, Native Americans, and low-income students) is a social justice issue in that those students who experience disproportional discipline generally have dismal future outcomes both academically and behaviorally (APA, 2008). As demonstrated in this chapter, research suggests that the problem often begins in the classroom with a variety of factors contributing, including the lack of understanding of how issues of diversity play a role in how discipline is administered. In the past, the problems were mostly viewed as residing solely within the child. This chapter attempted to provide an alternate view that examines what happens in the classroom and in the school that may contribute to an over-reliance on discipline referrals that are very likely influenced by a lack of cultural competence. Approaches to classroom management that are sensitive to the needs of culturally diverse populations are presented as well as ways that school psychologists can be advocates in promoting socially just practices within schools.

---

**Case Study**

Majesty High School has been working with several consultants throughout the school year to help its faculty engage in more rigorous teaching and to develop a culture of academic achievement in the school. One afternoon, four of the consultants along with the principal conducted "walk throughs" to observe teachers in their classrooms. Outside of a science classroom sat an African American male who appeared sullen and slumped in his chair with a worksheet on his science book. The teacher opened the door to admit the group to the classroom. One member of the group asked the young man why he was sitting outside the classroom. Not letting the student answer, the teacher shared that he had not been to her class in some time. The teacher then asked him where was his pencil. He said he didn't have one. She asked what he did for his other classes. He said he borrowed one. She informed him that she doesn't give pencils and he better find one. She was clearly annoyed. One of the men in the group gave him a pencil. The group went into the classroom. Immediately a white female student said to the teacher that she did not have a pencil, to which the teacher replied "There is one right there" (a cup holder with pencils was in the middle of the table where the student was sitting). The female responded that she didn't like color pencils, to which the teacher chuckled. The door to the classroom was open so the student outside heard this exchange between the teacher and the female student.

## Questions to consider:

1. Was there inequitable treatment of this young man? If so, describe what it is.
2. How might the teacher's response be an example of racial micro-aggression?
3. How could the teacher respond differently?
4. What role does relationship play in this scenario?
5. What is the responsibility of the student?

## Observations from a Social Justice Perspective (Answers Could Vary)

There are several observations with respect to this scenario. First—and most obvious—is the treatment of the student by the teacher. This was an actual occurrence. The group conversed afterwards and was struck by how the teacher announced to strangers that the student was frequently absent and that this was his first day back in school after being absent for a week. It seemed clear to the group that she wanted to embarrass him. But a member of the group also suggested that her comments may have been to save face as she might have been embarrassed by the fact she had removed the student from her class at a time that visitors were observing her classroom. The group wondered why this student would want to even return to this teacher's classroom after such an interaction. There seemed to be little to no positive relationship between the teacher and the student and she seemed intent to engage in a power play which was to let it be known to the student that she was in charge. The last thing you would want to do with a student who has missed classes is to sit him outside the classroom when he does come. Second, there was clearly a double standard when it came to giving a student a pencil when requested. Not only that, the door was open so the student outside the door could clearly hear the other student asking for the pencil and the subsequent response by the teacher. The scenario for the young African American male could reinforce inequitable treatment in the classroom but more importantly send a clear message that his presence is not valued. This is the very type of student who is at risk for behavior problems and who most likely feels disconnected from the school community. This is a great example of how a teacher's actions are inconsistent both in terms of race and gender and of a lack of compassion.

# References

American Psychological Association Zero Tolerance Task Force. (2008). Are zero tolerance policies effective in the schools? An evidentiary review and recommendations. *American Psychologist, 63,* 852–862.

Bondy, E., & Ross, D. D. (2008). The teacher as warm demander. *Educational Leadership, 66,* 54–58.

Bradsaw, C. P., Mitchell, M. M., O'Brennan, L. M., & Leaf, P. J. (2010). Multilevel exploration of factors contributing to the overrepresentation of Black students in office disciplinary referrals. *Journal of Educational Psychology, 102,* 508–520.

Coalition for Psychology in Schools and Education. (2006). *Report on the Teacher Needs Survey.* Washington, DC: American Psychological Association, Center for Psychology in Schools and Education.

Collaborative for Academic, Social, and Emotional Learning (CASEL). (n.d.). Benefits of SEL. Retrieved August 31, 2012 from http://casel.org/why-it-matters/benefits-of-sel

Davidson, G. (1999). Cultural competence as an ethical precept in psychology. In Martin, P. R., & Noble, W. (Eds), *Psychology and society.* Armidale, Australia: University of New England.

Dinkes, R., Kemp, J., and Baum, K. (2009). *Indicators of school crime and safety: 2009* (NCES 2010–012/NCJ 228478). Washington, DC: National Center for Education Statistics, Institute of Education Sciences, U.S. Department of Education, and Bureau of Justice Statistics, Office of Justice Programs, U.S. Department of Justice.

Durlak, J. A., Weissberg, R. P., Dymnicki, A. B., Taylor, R. D., & Schellinger, K. B. (2011). The impact of enhancing students' social and emotional learning: A meta-analysis of school-based universal interventions. *Child Development, 82,* 405–432.

Eggleston, T., & Miranda, A. H. (2009). Black girls' voices: Exploring their lived experiences in a predominately white high school. *Race and Ethnicity, 2* (2), 259–285.

Ferguson, A. A. (2001). *Bad boys: Public schools and the making of Black masculinity.* Ann Arbor, MI: University of Michigan Press.

Gallup. (2005). *PDK/Gallup polls of the public's attitudes toward the public schools: PDK/Gallup poll resources.* Retrieved from www.pdkintl.org/poll/index.htm

Gay, G. (2000). *Culturally responsive teaching: Theory, research, and practice.* New York, NY: Teachers College Press.

Gonzalez, L. E., Brown, M. S., & Slate, J. R. (2008). Teachers who left the teaching profession: A qualitative understanding. *The Qualitative Report, 13,* 1–11.

Goldstein, S., & Brooks, R. B. (2007). *Understanding and managing children's classroom behavior: Creating sustainable, resilient classrooms.* Hoboken, NJ: Wiley.

Gorski, P. (2007). Savage unrealities: Classism and racism abound in Ruby Payne's framework. *Rethinking Schools, 21* (2), 16–19.

Gregory, A., & Mosely, M. (2004). The discipline gap: Teachers' views on the overrepresentation of African American students in the discipline system. *Equity and Excellence in Education, 37*, 18–30.

Gregory, A., & Ripski M. B. (2008). Adolescent trust in teachers: Implications for behavior in the high school classroom. *School Psychology Review, 37*, 337–353.

Higgins, K. M., & Moule, J. (2009). "No more Mr. Nice Guy": Preservice teachers' conflict with classroom management in a predominantly African-American urban elementary school. *Multicultural Perpectives, 11*, 132–138.

Hodgkinson, H. (2002). Demographics and teacher education: An overview. *Journal of Teacher Education, 53*, 102–105.

Kazdin, A. E. (1975). *Behavior modification in applied settings.* Homewood, IL: Dorsey Press.

Lake, V. E. (2004). Ante up: Reconsidering classroom management philosophies so every child is a winner. *Early Child Development and Care, 174*, 565–574.

Larrivee, B. (1985). *Effective teaching for successful mainstreaming.* New York, NY: Longman.

Lassen, S. R., Steele, M. M., & Sailor, W. (2006). The relationship of school-wide positive behavior support to academic achievement in an urban middle school. *Psychology in the Schools, 43*, 701–712.

Losen, D. J. (2011). *Discipline policies, successful schools, and racial justice. The civil rights project at UCLA.* Boulder, CO: National Education Policy Center.

Marshall, M. (2007). Classroom management vs discipline: Discipline and parenting without stress. Retrieved August 31, 2012 from www.marvinmarshall.net/classroom-management-discipline

Matus, D. (2001). Traditional classroom management revisited in the urban school. *American Secondary Education, 30*, 46–57.

McCoy, L. P. (2003, March 28). It's a hard job: A study of novice teachers' perspectives on why teachers leave the profession. *Current Issues in Education, 6* (7). Retrieved from http://cie.asu.edu/volume6/number7/index.html

McIntosh, P. (1990). White privilege: Unpacking the invisible knapsack. *Independent School,* Winter, 1–6.

Monroe, C. R. (2009). Teachers closing the discipline gap in an urban middle school. *Urban Education, 44*, 323–347.

Paine, C. K., & Cowan, K. C. (2009). Remembering Columbine: School safety lessons for the future. *Communiqué, 37* (6), 1–10.

Rimm-Kaufman, S. (n.d.). *Improving students' relationships with teachers to provide essential supports for learning.* American Psychological Association. Retrieved August 31, 2012 from www.apa.org/education/k12/relationships.aspx

Soodak, L. C. & Podell, D. M. (1994). Teachers thinking about difficult-to-teach students. *Journal of Educational Research, 88*, 44–51.

Skiba, R. J., Michael, R. S., Nardo, A. C., & Peterson, R. L. (2002). The color of discipline: Sources of racial and gender disproportionality in school punishment. *Urban Review, 34*, 317–343.

Skiba, R. J., & Rausch, M.K. (2006). Zero tolerance, suspension, and expulsion: Questions of equity and effectiveness. In C. M. Evertson & C. S. Weinstein (Eds.), *Handbook of classroom management* (pp. 1063–1092). Mahwah, NJ; Lawrence Erlbaum Associates.

Sue, W. S., Capodilupo, C. M., Torino, G. C., Bucceri, J. M., Holder, A. M., Nadal, K. L., et al. (2007). Racial microaggressions in everyday life. *American Psychologist, 62*, 271–286.

Tobin, T., Sugai, G., & Colvin, G. (1996). Patterns in middle school discipline records. *Journal of Emotional and Behavioral Disorders, 4*, 82–94.

Ullucci, K. (2009). "This has to be family": Humanizing classroom management in urban schools. *Journal of Classroom Interaction, 44,* 13–28.

US Department of Education, Office for Civil Rights, *OCR Elementary and Secondary School Survey,* 2002. Retrieved August 31, 2012 from www2.ed.gov/about/offices/list/ocr/data.html?src=rt

Vavrus, F., & Cole, K. (2002). "I didn't do nothin'": The discursive construction of school suspension. *Urban Review, 34,* 87–111.

Wald, J., & Losen, D. J. (2003). Defining and redirecting a school-to-prison pipeline. *New Directions for Youth Development, 99,* 9–15.

Warren, J. S., Edmonson, H. M., Griggs, P., Lassen, S. R., McCart, A., & Turnbull, A. (2003). Urban applications of school-wide positive behavior support: Critical issues and lessons learned. *Journal of Positive Behavior Interventions, 5,* 80–91.

Weiner, L. (2003). Why is classroom management so vexing to urban teachers? *Theory into Practice, 42,* 305–312.

Weinstein, C. S., Tomlinson-Clarke, S., & Curran, M. (2004). Toward a conception of culturally responsive classroom management. *Journal of Teacher Education, 55,* 25–38.

Wentzel, K. (1997). Student motivation in middle school: The role of perceived pedagogical caring. *Journal of Educational Psychology, 89,* 411–419.

Wentzel, K. R. (1998). Social relationships and motivation in middle school: The role of parents, teachers, and peers. *Journal of Educational Psychology, 90,* 202–209.

Wheldall, K., & Merrett, F. (1988). Which classroom behaviours do primary school teachers say they find most troublesome? *Educational Review, 40,* 13–27.

# thirteen
# Consultation and Collaboration

## Janay B. Sander

Consultation and collaboration are two important areas of competence for the role of a school psychologist (Ysseldyke, Burns & Rosenfield, 2009). Social justice and consultation are distinct, but related, terms relevant to the practice of school psychology (Brown, Pryzwansky & Schulte, 2011; Moe, Perera-Diltz & Sepulveda, 2010; Shriberg & Fenning, 2009; Vera & Speight, 2003). The use of consultation skills to facilitate social justice is not only compatible with the role of a school psychologist, it is also consistent with the ethical principles of this profession. Social justice is related to the principle of *respecting people's rights and dignity* in the National Association of School Psychologists (NASP, 2010) standards for ethical practice and the American Psychological Association's *Ethical Principles and Code of Conduct* (2010). The principle of *justice* within the APA (2010) code is also applicable to consultation. Psychological and school consultation encompasses a broad set of skills that make it possible to facilitate success for all students in terms of academic, social, behavioral, and emotional domains within the context of a school. Social justice could be infused into the roles of a school psychologist as a consultant throughout the system.

This chapter is intended to offer practical advice and tools to both recognize and capitalize on opportunities to effect changes to advance social justice within the role of consultation. Using the working definition provided in Chapter 1, social justice encompasses *access* to necessary resources and the experience of being *respected* and treated with *fairness* (Sander et al., 2011). The ideal goal would be for all members of a school community to have this experience, along with being psychologically and physically safe, regardless of race, ethnicity, culture, sexual orientation and gender expression/identity (Speight & Vera, 2009).

In this chapter, therefore, the focus will be on defining consultation and collaboration, followed by ideas about how to incorporate a social justice lens into school consultation. A brief description of several models of school consultation will be followed by case examples and questions for reflection and discussion. Schools are a type of organization, so systems theory as it applies to organizations will also be introduced. First, an overview of the essential vocabulary in consultation is necessary. Then we will cover some research about consultation, followed by a discussion to integrate and apply a social justice framework to a few of the consultation practice models.

## Terms and Definitions

The term "consultation" is typically defined as indirect service delivery—it is a classic and cornerstone skill within the profession of school psychology. The "consultant" is typically the school psychologist within this context, and the "consultee" would be the other party to whom or with whom the consultant is offering services; the services would be in order to benefit a third party, the client (student or child in school consultation situations). Direct services would be a program or intervention that a professional provides to the client, such as teaching a student, providing therapy to one child, or conducting an assessment of one student. Indirect services are when one party offers services, skills, or training to another party who then provides direct services to a third party, the client. For example, a school psychologist (consultant) might offer suggestions and support for alternative classroom discipline strategies to a teacher (consultee), and the teacher implements the plan to improve some element in the classroom (students are clients) (Erchul & Martens, 2010; Dougherty, 2009).

The concept of social power within the consultation literature is one area of considerable discussion (Erchul, Grissom & Getty, 2008). Social power refers to the interpersonal means of exerting influence that a consultant might use in order to produce behavior change in a third party, such as the consultee or the client. Some models of consultation adopt a hierarchical authority-based approach that is often more directive (Erchul, Raven & Wilson, 2004), others emphasize non-hierarchical relationships, a consultee-directed approach, equality and shared power (Pearrow & Pollack, 2009)—this is simply a distinction among different consultation methods. There is not a unified, accepted approach to consultation in terms of directiveness, hierarchy, social influence, or relationship power (Brown et al., 2011), but the terms and nuances among different models are relevant for understanding differences in consultation models. In all consultation approaches, the consultant would attempt to be helpful, respectful, and address the concerns of the consultee (Brown et al., 2011; Dougherty, 2009; Erchul et al., 2008).

Within the consultation literature, the term "stakeholder" is important to define. A stakeholder is someone within the system who has a vested interest in the process and outcome of the decisions and consultation activities. Some stakeholders have authority or power within the system; other stakeholders would have little power to effect changes. From a social justice perspective, it is important to consider all stakeholders, not just those in powerful positions (Pearrow & Pollack, 2009).

Using the definition of social justice in educational settings, as long as respect, fairness, and access are addressed for all parties, variations in consultant and consultee power would be acceptable, including collaboration, shared power, or hierarchical approaches. Would the situation influence how you might feel about your own role in terms of power? There is no clear "right answer" about using influence and social power, but knowing your personal comfort level and preferred style can help you navigate your role or different situations with more clarity.

## Systems Theory and Schools

School-based consultation is typically a systems-level form of practice, even in individual consultation meetings that may occur in a school setting with the purpose of creating change (Hazel, Laviolette, & Lineman, 2010). Although there are many variations and applications of organizational systems theory, a basic understanding of it is an essential tool for any consultant. There are several simple tenets of systems theory in its applications to school psychology (Brown et al., 2011; Dougherty, 2009; Kuhn & Beam, 1982; Thelen, 2005), as follows.

1. If you have at least two people you have a system.
2. Systems prefer homeostasis.
3. Systems can be described as being characterized as open or closed as one key quality. Openness refers to the degree to which a system incorporates changes, new ideas, and flexibility, and more closed systems tend to be more rigid, resist changes, and are more static in general.
4. All systems have a goal or purpose.
5. There is differentiation in roles for each member of the system.
6. In human organization systems, there is a leadership structure that guides the decision making processes, including formal and informal leadership subgroups.
7. The system will have some mechanism for dealing with internal and external input about the system's functions and goals.

In order to be considered *healthy*, a system must have (a) goals or a purpose that is clear to all members of the system—because they have a role in the system to support the goals in some way, (b) a mechanism to transmit feedback about whether it is meeting its goals, (c) a way to perceive outside information that would be important to the goals and survival of the system, and (d) a way to respond or adjust the system members' roles in response to that new information, which is related to a system being "open" to input, ideas, and adaptability. Too much change, or an inadequate process to cope with it, will lead to chaos and dysfunction, which sometimes causes so much stress that the organization disintegrates. On the other hand, too little change and influx of new ideas or energy, or a "closed" system, will lead to stagnation and obsolescence—a sort of death of the idea or organization. The rules of systems theory do not change, but the way a consultant will recognize and address them makes systems change possible (Dougherty, 2009; Thelen, 2005; Brown et al., 2011).

Even introducing small actions that would foster social justice may be a challenge to incorporate due to normal systems processes—changes to increase social justice may disrupt the homeostasis. Fortunately, there are many models, some of which are described below, that can help the consultant to think through a strategy regarding systems change via consultation. A description of the stages of consultation, the most common approaches and methods in consultation that have been empirically evaluated, as well as an overview of cultural considerations, will be provided in the following sections.

## Stages of Consultation

In consultation, there are several typical stages, or steps, along the way—from the initiation of a relationship to evaluation and concluding the job within that role. The stages are: entry, assessment, problem definition, goal setting, implementation, evaluation, and termination (Brown et al., 2011; Dougherty, 2008; Erchul & Martens, 2010). The stages of assessment, defining the problem, setting specific goals, implementing the plan, and evaluation of the outcomes are generally covered in other areas related to empirical-based practice, research design, and program evaluation. Entry is one of the most essential components within consultation specifically (Dougherty, 2009; Marks, 1995), and warrants some discussion here due to the opportunities to set the stage for a social justice oriented practice during this particular stage of a consultation relationship.

## Entry

The entry stage, the most crucial stage of consultation, is when a consultant's role is defined (Marks, 1995). This stage sets the stage for ensuring clarity of roles and also is consistent with the idea of informed consent, when a potential consultee could evaluate the situation for himself, herself, or hirself (for more on gender pronouns see American Psychological Association, n.d.) and decide to engage in that professional relationship activity. At this stage, it is helpful to be explicit in the goals of the role of consultant to avoid misunderstanding and build trust with a system or with individuals. In some situations, it may even be advised to use a written contract for engaging in consultation as a mental health activity (Brown et al., 2011), but in all cases it is important to communicate a clear definition of the role of consultant along with an opportunity to obtain informed consent from consultees.

At the stage of entry, social justice is important in terms of setting up the role of consultation in a way that respects all parties' rights and dignity, assures there is fairness, and considers all parties involved: the consultee, the student, parents, or the other individuals within the system that would be affected by the consultation activities. Establishing entry is essential for effective consultation, but there are many nuances to this stage, including: whether the consultant is internal or external to the system, the interpersonal skills of the consultant, the social power structure, the characteristics of the system and/or consultees in terms of openness to change, and opportunities for the consultee and consultant to interact and build trust (Brown et al., 2011; Erchul et al., 2008; Marks, 1995).

## Assessment, Problem Definition and Goal Setting

Assessment, problem definition and goal setting are all discrete stages, but for the purposes of this chapter as an overview of consultation within a social justice context, only some aspects will be highlighted. Again, there are numerous texts on these topics that provide more details and examples for the broad role of consultant (see Brown et al., 2011; Erchul & Martens, 2010; Dougherty, 2009; Erchul & Sheridan, 2008). First, assessment is necessary in terms of determining the general resources of a system, the consultant and consultee strengths and weaknesses, and consideration of the important aspects of the environment that may facilitate or impede changes in the area of concern (Brown et al., 2011). In some models of consultation, the assessment phase also would be related to collecting baseline data prior to implementing an intervention designed to change some specific measurable variable (Kratochwill & Bergan, 1990).

However, one important component from a social justice perspective is that the way in which the consultation assessment phase is carried out is respectful, fair, and inclusive in terms of access or in obtaining relevant and comprehensive perspectives on the areas of concern. It is important to consider the power structure, and obtain information from disempowered members of a system and not just from those in power (Pearrow & Pollack, 2009; Sue, 2008).

Problem definition and goal setting are also subject to the same potential for disempowering individuals or an inadvertent oversight in terms of respect, access and fairness of the consultee as well as the student or classroom. What is helpful in terms of ensuring that a sense of social justice is included within the consultation activity is to rely on behavioral and objective descriptions of the problem and of the goals. By offering definitions that ensure respect to all parties, this can facilitate fair and more objective solutions as the consultation progresses (Li & Vazquez-Nuttall, 2009).

## Consultation Models and Methods

This particular chapter is an overview of consultation—the skills and methods of consultation deserve an entire book, sometimes even an entire book about only one approach. There are many consultation models that have been evaluated in empirical investigations: behavioral consultation, conjoint behavioral consultation (Erchul & Sheridan, 2008), mental health consultation (Caplan, Caplan & Erchul, 1995), consultee-centered consultation (Lambert, Hylander, & Sandoval, 2004), multicultural consultee-centered consultation (Ingraham, 2000), instructional consultation (Rosenfield, 2002), solution-focused consultation (George, 2005), and a problem-solving model of consultation (Newell & Newell, 2011), among others. Given the space limitations, a very general overview of the most common consultation methods is presented here. Please also keep in mind that discussing only three models in limited detail here is no reflection on the importance of the other models that have not been discussed—I urge the reader to learn about them as well.

## Consultee-Centered Consultation

One contemporary model is consultee-centered consultation (CCC). This is based on earlier work described by Gerald Caplan, known as mental health consultation. Mental health consultation is a wellness approach (Lambert et al., 2004; Brown et al., 2011). The presumption is that the consultee has the capacity to move toward wellness with the right tools or assistance along the way. It is not a deficit model, where there is a clearly defined problem that warrants fixing *per se*; it is more of a facilitative model, to offer assistance for the consultee to accept or reject, according to the consultee's own needs and goals (Lambert et al., 2004). According to CCC, the consultee may be seeking consultation due to a need for (1) increased confidence, moral support or encouragement, (2) more accurate or deeper understanding of the psychological and/or social (cultural, economic, linguistic) factors related to the referral concern, (3) skills in order to handle the situation differently or more effectively, or (4) greater or renewed objectivity and clarity of perspective about the situation. Objectivity might be compromised, for example, when a teacher has experienced chronic frustration in dealing with a particular student's behaviors during class (Lambert et al., 2004).

As you can imagine, this particular model is challenging for experimental designs and controlled efficacy trials to establish a basis of empirical support (Brown et al., 2011; Knotek, Kaniuka & Ellingsen, 2008). Nonetheless, this model, when perhaps evaluated using research methods that allow for more of a constructivist approach, such as qualitative and mixed-methods approaches (Knotek et al., 2008), remains promising due to its overall appeal.

## Behavioral Consultation

Behavioral consultation, originally outlined by Bergan and Kratochwill (1990), has traditionally been the most widely researched and empirically tested model of consultation in the field of school psychology (Martens & DiGennaro, 2008). The main steps begin with the consultant working with the consultee to define the problem and operationalize the target behavior in clear, measureable terms. Next, the consultant helps the consultee (via interview or other direct or indirect assessment) identify the antecedents and consequences of the behavior—the function of the behavior is also important to include in this process. Then, the consultant would assist the consultee with brainstorming possible interventions to address the goals of reducing or increasing a specific target behavior. The consultant would then help the consultee select, then implement, the intervention. The consultee would collect data to evaluate its effect, and the consultant would check in with the consultee within a few days or a week to see how the plan worked. If the goal is not reached, the plan is revised and evaluated again, or monitored and faded out, until all parties are satisfied and the consultation can be concluded (Kratochwill & Bergan, 1990).

Contemporary behavioral consultation in its classic description (Bergan & Kratochwill, 1990) has evolved into a more widespread application of behavioral principles used in a variety of classroom settings with the increased adoption of functional behavioral analysis and assessment (FBA; Steege & Watson, 2009). The increase in the use of data-driven interventions in schools is a good partnership with the observable, measurable behaviors emphasis of the behavioral model that is used by more professionals than just school psychologists (i.e., special education teachers, behavior support specialists, school administrators). Even though a variety of professionals use behavioral approaches now—more so than when behavioral consultation first emerged—the role of the school psychology consultant in designing and offering ongoing staff support and training to implement empirically based and theory-driven behavioral plans remains important.

Conjoint behavioral consultation is similar in the theoretical behavioral underpinnings to classic behavioral consultation, but it is designed to include parents and teachers together as consultees in the process from start to finish (Sheridan, Kratochwill & Bergan, 1996). The consultant's role in this model is to facilitate the process as parents and teachers jointly engage in the process of behavioral consultation across settings. The goals of this model include process and outcome objectives. Process outcomes include objectives such as improving the interpersonal connections and relationships across home and school settings (Sheridan, Clarke, & Burt, 2008). In general, there is modest empirical support for this variation of behavioral consultation (Sheridan et al., 2008).

## Cultural Considerations within Consultation

There are two main approaches to cultural-specific considerations within a school consultation role. One is Ingraham's (2000, 2008) framework using a multicultural lens. This model explicitly describes the ways that cultural competency should be addressed within the role of consultation across several domains (see Table 13.1). Another consultation model is participatory culture-specific consultation, or the Participatory Intervention Model (PIM; Nastasi, Varjas, Bernstein & Jayasena, 2000a; Nastasi, Varjas, Schensul, Silva, Schensul & Ratnayake, 2000b). PIM is an approach to make the somewhat fluid and confusing process more explicit. The overall PIM goals include specifying a process to collaboratively design, implement, and evaluate some program or intervention that is relevant to the consultee. The route by which this is accomplished is somewhat non-traditional in terms of school psychology consultation training, and space does not permit elaboration here. For the interested reader, in brief, the PIM approach relies on participatory action research and incor-

**TABLE 13.1.** Five components of multicultural consultation framework

| | |
|---|---|
| I. Domains of consultant learning and development for multicultural school consultation competence | 1. Understanding one's own culture<br>2. Understanding the impact of one's own culture on others<br>3. Respecting and valuing other cultures<br>4. Understanding individual differences within cultural groups and multiple identities<br>5. Cross-cultural communication and multicultural consultation approaches for rapport<br>6. Understanding cultural saliency and how to build bridges<br>7. Understanding the cultural context for consultation<br>8. Multicultural consultation and intervention appropriate for the consultees and clients |
| II. Domains of consultee learning and development | 1. Knowledge<br>2. Skill<br>3. Perspective and decrease of:<br>filtering perceptions through stereotypes<br>overemphasizing culture<br>taking color-blind approach<br>fear of being called a racist<br>4. Confidence<br>Preventing paralysis<br>Avoiding reactive dominance |
| III. Cultural variations in the consultation constellation | 1. Consultant–consultee similarity<br>2. Consultant–client similarity<br>3. Consultee–client similarity<br>4. Three-way diversity: tricultural consultation |
| IV. Contextual and power influences | 1. Cultural similarity within a differing cultural system<br>2. Influences by the larger society<br>3. Disruptions in the balance of power |
| V. Methods for supporting consultee and client success | 1. Framing the problem and the consultation process<br>• Value multiple perspectives<br>• Create emotional safety and motivational support<br>• Balance affective support with new learning<br>• Build on principles for adult learning<br>• Seek systems interventions to support learning and development |

2. Potential multicultural consultation strategies for working with the consultees
   - Support cross-cultural learning and motivation
   - Model bridging and processes for cross-cultural learning
   - Use consultation methods matched with the consultee's style
   - Work to build consultee confidence and self-efficacy
   - Work to increase knowledge, skill, and perspective
3. Continue one's professional development and reflective thinking
   - Continue to learn
   - Engage in formal and informal continuing professional development
   - Seek feedback
   - Seek cultural guides and teachers

From: Ingraham (2000), p. 327.

porates qualitative approaches to understanding the overall situation and designing solutions (Nastasi, Moore & Varjas, 2004). Some especially important aspects of PIM include working with the values, culture and beliefs of the stakeholders, and to empower stakeholders. The goal of PIM is to foster, design, implement, and evaluate interventions that would be relevant and acceptable to the consultees in terms of culture, values, language, and beliefs. This model has been used in consultation projects on an international scale (Nastasi et al., 2000). Ingraham's approach and Nastasi and colleagues' model both address the ecological model, the system, and the cultural contextual influences on the consultant, consultee, and clients.

Within the organizational consultation literature, Sue (2008) offers a specific approach to consider social justice and the multicultural development of organizations as a system. The practice of multicultural organizational consultation would be highly applicable and relevant to school consultation in the ways that school policies, procedures, and hierarchy may inadvertently limit respect, access, and fairness for its disempowered members. Multicultural organizational consultation is a specific systemic perspective, broader than individual consultation models previously discussed. It is designed to address the culture of school administrative policies and procedures in terms of bias, power, and privilege that limit its members' success, and foster discrimination and disempowerment of members (i.e., teachers, students, or parents) within that system (Sue, 2008). Multicultural organizational consultation incorporates principles of a multicultural lens, including the consultant's own cultural competence and development, but is more of an advocacy orientation to consultation, rather than adopting and supporting the organizational culture that may be undermining its members' access, fairness, and respect. Given the organizational nature of schools, a systemic strategy for approaching consultation roles and relationships is helpful as a tool to effect social justice changes. Each individual consultation relationship offers an opportunity to move toward a culture- and school-wide value of social justice principles in action: access, fairness, and resources for all members of the system (teachers, parents, administrators, and students alike).

In addition, Chen-Hayes (2001) poses reflection questions that are useful in terms of school-based organizational consultation (see Table 13.2). These questions offer a way to consider system qualities, such as openness or resistance to change or new ideas. This perspective would be helpful in identifying the systemic influences on how social justice is represented (or not) in that school as a whole community. From there, a problem-solving approach could be used to address specific areas in the organization that may not be consistent with social justice. It would be challenging, if not impossible, to effect social justice changes at the system level without a clear representation, formal or informally assessed, of the system itself and the community-wide level of awareness or motivation to change in regard to social justice principles.

**TABLE 13.2.** Social justice strategic questions for consultation within organizations

Cultural/Institutional Social Justice Advocacy Skills

**Directions**: Answer the following questions to develop an action plan for change to promote greater social justice awareness, knowledge, and skills in your organization.

1. Who's excluded in your organization, including policies and procedures (clients, staff, administration) and who's not? How will this change in the future?
2. Who funds the organization? How much do funders influence the decision-making culture (i.e., the Board of Education, United Way, grantmakers, etc.)?
3. Whose ethnic/racial identities/world view/gender roles/sexual orientations/gender identities dominate your organization? How might this change in the future?
4. Who are your traditional healers/cultural consultants with clients/consultees whose cultural and language identities you don't have experience with? How do you find and collaborate with cultural consultants on their terms?
5. What issues of oppression are regularly addressed by those with power in your organization? Which ones are not? How could this change in the future?
6. How is good leadership defined/implemented in your organization? Are leadership and social justice/advocacy skills development offered? How are decisions made (collectively or hierarchically) in your organization?
7. Whom do you want as allies inside and outside the organization? What groups do you advocate for best in your family, community, or organization and what groups do you need to advocate for more openly?
8. What are the barriers and fears to cultural and systemic change in your organization? Who are the blockers? How can the blockers be neutralized or developed as allies?

From: Social Justice Advocacy Readiness Questionnaire (Chen-Hayes, 2001, p. 201).

# Resistance

There are two essential elements that consultants must address in order to build and maintain a successful consultative relationship with individuals or within a system: entry and resistance. Entry we discussed as part of the earlier section on stages of consultation. Resistance in some cases may actually be a "failed" entry, rather than resistance as such (Marks, 1995). Once entry has occurred, or when someone has called for consultation, this is a positive sign of openness to change, and that there is some need within the system. Yet it is sometimes the case that the person seeking consultation may not be the person who is volunteering to change—that person may wish for you to change someone else. This poses a predicament, since as consultants we seek to facilitate and support change in support of the consultee's goals, and is also related to resistance. While the basic tenets of good consultation presume that resistance is normal, and even healthy in some ways so that a system will not become stressed with too much change too quickly (Thelen, 2005; Marks, 1995), at other times, resistance is something more negative, even with a flavor of "dislike" or "anger" at having to participate in consultation. There are several ways to address this.

Diplomacy, respect, good interpersonal skills, and adherence to the professional role of a consultant can soothe the tension in this "I want you to change that other party but not me" scenario. For this situation, I cheerfully refer to an old joke. Question: How many school psychologists does it take to change a light bulb? Answer: One, but only if the light bulb wants to change. This can become a particular problem for a consultant who has been "assigned" to work with "a problem student," or "a low-performing teacher" who may or may not want to actually work with you. But, even in this case, if you realize that the administrator in power in a system has asked you to change someone else, you can always reframe the question for yourself to assist with seeking how that person might wish to change, or what change would be most beneficial to the system, stakeholders, *and* for social justice. What is really needed? What does the administrator need? What does the student really need? What might that teacher really need? And how does that serve the system's goals as well as social justice? What type of change is truly called for? Clarifying what part of the system is indicating (the feedback mechanism) that change is needed can help you develop a strategy that will be consistent with social justice, and move your practice away from simple task completion and to more advanced levels of systemic change and social justice.

## Social Justice in Consultation Literature

In general, the existing social justice component in consultation literature is sparse. As I was preparing this chapter, I did a search on the *PsycINFO* database using the terms "consultation" and "social justice." Thirty-eight publications showed up on the results screen. Using the *Academic Search Complete* (EBSCO) search tool, 52 results appeared using the same search terms—not all were relevant. Seven of the results (both databases) were from the same special issue of *Journal of Educational & Psychological Consultation* (2009, Vol. 19, Issue 1). It is clear that the literature is sparse, but the concepts are important nonetheless.

What is clear is that there is emphasis on understanding the role of power and privilege as a common component in training consultants from a social justice lens (Hazel et al., 2010; Sue, 2008). Communication and access are also important specific aspects within the school consultation literature. The students (adolescents and children) themselves need to be recognized as individuals with needs, given a voice, and encouraged to strive for their own self-determination—they need to be empowered to pursue their own needs using healthy mechanisms (Pearrow & Pollack, 2009). Consultants and school psychologists in consultation and collaboration roles are in key positions to facilitate these types of access to resources and power within schools as systems. Advocacy, the focus of chapter 16 in this book, was also a common discussion point in the social justice and school consultation. These concepts are also evident in the scenarios presented below.

## Case Examples

The following examples are based on actual cases, but names and some of the specific details have been disguised to protect the identity of all parties. Consider that you are the school psychologist in each case. Then, after reading the scenario, consider the questions in Table 13.3 that will highlight potential important aspects that may influence the success of consultation from a social justice perspective.

**TABLE 13.3.** Questions to consider prior to initiating consultation: José and Thai

1. What is the student's level of acculturation? What might his family's level of acculturation in the United States be? In what ways might level of acculturation influence this student's access to education and related services?
2. What is the student's parent's level of education? How might level of education influence access within the education system itself, or perhaps relate to respect the parent gives to or receives from the child's teachers?
3. What is the role of anxiety in what is viewed as "disrespectful" behavior in class? In what ways might anxiety or depression (how Jose or Thai conveys anxiety/depression) be interfering with how the student is treated with fairness?
4. What might be some teacher perceptions or misperceptions about the nature and roots of the student's rudeness? In what ways might teachers interpret or perceive his behavior that could be inaccurate?
5. How is the school's approach to address the student's rude behavior, and efforts to build positive relationships with each student, consistent (or inconsistent) with social justice?
6. Is it fair to teachers that students would be disrespectful to them?
7. Is it fair that teachers would exclude students from class or that administrators repeatedly send them to disciplinary settings due to the disrespectful behavior when it has no effect?

8. In what ways does each student perhaps feel he is respected by the school teachers and administrators? What about the child's parent: would a parent possibly feel respected by the school? Why or why not?

9. In what ways might this be similar or different based on culture, race, or ethnicity?

10. If a goal is to facilitate respect, access to services, and a sense of fairness to all parties, what are some creative solutions that might foster these outcomes for the student, his parent(s), and the teachers?

11. Based on the goals of: (a) facilitating respect, access, and fairness, as well as (b) measuring change in order to inform practice and intervention with each student, how would you (1) operationalize/define the problem and (2) measure the outcome?

---

## *"José"*

José is an 11-year-old boy in the fifth grade. His homeroom teacher, Mr Simms, is also his math teacher. Mr Simms is a second year teacher. Mr Simms seeks your consultation after a fifth-grade team meeting because he is worried about José failing fifth grade and he wants José to "show more motivation" in class. Mr Simms indicates that José is at risk of failing math due to poor test grades and missing homework, shows low motivation in school, and often puts his head down on his desk during math class and social studies. Mr Simms is very frustrated with José because of what he perceives as disrespectful non-participatory behavior and lack of effort, even describing José as "lazy." Mr Simms suggests to you that José probably has ADHD, and asks that you come do an observation in class so that you can see about formalizing a request for evaluation so that José might be able to "get motivated." You agree to engage in a formal consultation about José with Mr Simms, including a possible behavior plan if that seems indicated, and then (according to your state guidelines) you contact the mother for informed consent.

José's mother, Mrs Garza, was glad to hear that someone would be interested in helping her son. She shares with you that she immigrated from Mexico to the United States as a young girl and wants a better life for her children here in the United States—and she is very worried about José. Her family worked as farm laborers. She had around a seventh-grade education. José is her oldest child. José lives with his mother and step-father, and two younger half-siblings (a boy and a girl). His step-father is a farm worker who was a recent immigrant from Mexico and only speaks Spanish. As you discuss your concerns, you learn that José's mother has a history of depression, and her current relationship involves domestic violence. Mrs Garza cries several times on the phone with the school psychologist as she tells her story and her concerns about José.

During the classroom observation, you notice that Mr Simms seems focused on getting José to participate. José does appear lethargic, frustrated, and looks repeatedly for his materials at various times during the lesson as the teacher moves from topic to topic. The other students do not seem to have difficulty with the flow or organization, and Mr Simms seems firm with the class in general, but also focused on the lesson. You note that Mr Simms calls on José several times, but José does not know the answer because he seemed to be looking for his worksheet page while Mr Simms was asking a question for the class to answer. Each of the five times Mr Simms called on José, José is unable to provide the correct answer. José puts his head on his desk after he is unable to answer the fifth question from Mr Simms. As soon as that happens, Mr Simms calls José to the board to work a math equation in front of the class as an example of the classwork they are about to start that day. José complies, and you overhear him ask a nearby classmate to help make sure he writes it correctly. As soon as seatwork begins after the lesson, José appears to busy himself shuffling papers, he cannot seem to locate his math work and has to ask for another copy. Then he stares at the problems but does not write any more than his name in the 15 minutes allotted. José does not raise his hand or talk to any other students during that time. Several other students complete their worksheet in the time provided.

## "Thai"

A 14-year-old boy in ninth grade, Thai, has a history of truancy, disrespectful behaviors with teachers and staff at school, and has been sent to a disciplinary alternative education placement on several occasions. His teachers do not want him in their classes and will often send him out of class and down to the office with only slight provocation on his part, such as eye rolling. Even the school nurse, whom he visits regularly with complaints of stomach aches, has indicated that he can only come to her office with presence of a security escort due to his disrespectful behavior. Thai is considered intellectually capable by the teachers, is very articulate, and has excellent verbal communication skills, but he has very negative relationships with all adults at the school because of his extremely disrespectful behavior to authority figures. He has no real friends among his peers, and he mostly stays to himself during unstructured times when most of his classmates would be socializing with others.

   This school has a collaborative relationship with a nearby school psychology training program. You have available information from a practicum student who conducted an emotional screening with Thai as part of a class assignment. Thai suffers from social anxiety. His father is the sole income earner in the household, at a relatively low-paying job, and immigrated to the United States within the past 15 years. He speaks English, but is not fluent. Thai's parents are divorced and his mother lives in another state. His step-mother only speaks Vietnamese and has never attended any school meetings. The school administration is very frustrated and worn out with the repeated disciplinary actions necessary with Thai. They do not know what to do, and what they have tried is not working. Thai's father comes to some meetings, but often cannot attend meetings due to his work and fears of losing his job if he is absent too often. The school administration is predominantly White, and most of Thai's teachers are also White, but two of them are African American women.

## Follow up: The End of Each Story and Description of Consultant Roles

These are complex cases involving several consultation considerations. There are also several ways to address the concerns that facilitate social justice in both cases. The school psychologist functioned in the role of consultant and advocate in both cases.

In José's case the school psychologist adopted a consultee-centered approach. This entailed a conceptualization that the teachers needed (1) more information about depression in children in order to understand the psychological aspects in the classroom, as well as (2) skills, validation, and support to Mr Simms in particular about using more positive classroom management strategies. In addition, the school psychologist had excellent rapport with the mother, and was able to refer the family to an outside mental health clinic with a sliding fee scale that she could afford. Jose was evaluated and ended up getting services in school in special education under a serious emotional disturbance label for depression. He received counseling and resource room instruction in math.

In Thai's situation, there were several aspects to being a consultant that required strong conviction as an advocate for Thai's well-being and educational success—and several ingredients to being able to function in that role. The school psychologist was an internal consultant at the disciplinary campus Thai attended. She also functioned as an external consultant to Thai's home campus once his disciplinary placement concluded and he returned to his original school. The first step this consultant took was gaining trust with Thai via showing him *respect*. Even though the school psychologist was providing indirect services and advocacy via consultation, she had to form a direct relationship with Thai in order to accomplish the other goals. Given the role of consultation in terms of also being collaborative, this consultation situation necessitated the consultant to act as collaborative mediator in repairing relationships. In addition, Thai needed services to address his anxiety. His anxiety was indeed interfering with his ability to participate in classes and was eroding his relationships with peers and teachers, with his rudeness serving the function to escape the situation by being sent out of the class. There was a need to educate teachers about his anxiety, and there were repairs that needed to happen in order to foster better relations at the school. The father conveyed that he was traditional in his approach to parenting and family matters, was mistrustful of the school, and truly did have work constraints.

The school psychologist had to become involved and establish a relationship with Thai's father, always being mindful of the father's need to be perceived as the authority over his son and being very gentle with suggestions about parenting (i.e., setting limits, monitoring, and rewarding desired behaviors). With the help of a student therapist, whom the school psychologist enlisted, Thai, who was truly remorseful for his rudeness, wrote apologies to the teachers and the nurse. The father was willing to participate in some parenting help as part of the student training opportunity, but the school psychologist had to facilitate that bridge and attend the first session. As part of that complex intervention, which was facilitated by the school psychologist as a consultant, Thai ended up staying in school and nearly (but not entirely) eliminating his disrespectful behaviors toward teachers.

The school psychologist attended several disciplinary review hearings about Thai over a period of several months. It was necessary for the school psychologist to offer (1) validation and empathy for the teachers' frustration, (2) a clear plan of action to correct and address the rudeness with teachers, and (3) a consistent voice to advocate for appropriate interventions as opposed to punishment and continued ineffective disciplinary placements for Thai in a way that he would feel respected as an individual while he was also getting access to services he needed in order to cope with his social anxiety.

## Conclusions

This chapter is intended to offer practical advice and tools, and an overview of literature is essential as a starting point. There is a gap in knowledge (1) that schools are a social justice venue and (2) in practical ways to address social justice using skills in consultation. There is an even wider gap in how school psychologists, via consultation, could improve outcomes for students using evidence-based and socially just interventions and strategies.

In consultation there is always at minimum three parties, and therefore there is always a system: consultant, consultee, and target of the consultation (i.e., student in classroom). This chapter on consultation is deeply bent toward a systems approach. Systemic change is the whole point of consultation; the idea that making changes with one person or one procedure in that school (system) has the potential to impact dozens of students in a classroom or hundreds of people within that whole school over time. In this sense, systemic consultation is very consistent with the common aims of social justice.

The existing forms of consultation likely allow for a social justice approach, but they also may need to be modified. In many ways, if a consultant does not experience access to resources, respect by colleagues and supervisors, and fair treatment as a person or professional, it would be more difficult for that consultant to make changes or advocate using power-based approaches. Furthermore, it takes time and energy to change systems—particularly if the system is less open to changes and new ideas, or has limited resources and energy for changes to flourish. As a consultant, you may be in situations that require you to stand up for social justice repeatedly until the system itself is motivated to change. As a school psychologist you may make changes at the school administration level with broad policy changes, or you may make changes one teacher at a time, one meeting at a time, or with one child at a time.

My hope is that the reader will be able to understand system theory and consultation in terms of how change occurs: the system must want to change for some reason (internal or external pressure). Change takes time. Moderate levels of resistance are *normal* in a healthy system. Change does happen, and keeping a social justice agenda and systemic perspective in mind allows for addressing change in several areas once a system is making changes already, once the homeostasis is disturbed, at a time when the system is more open to change in general.

In conclusion, I will leave you with one of my favorite fables—it is about power, or at least can be interpreted to be about power. It's a fable attributed to Aesop, timeless and relevant in any century. I especially appreciate Aesop's fables in relation to social justice, as Aesop was reportedly a slave in the fifth century BC. This particular fable is about the sun and the north wind, and they had a competition between them about who was more powerful. The sun and north wind saw a man walking down on the earth, and agreed that whoever could get the man to take off his coat is the most powerful. The north wind went first, and blew as hard as possible. The man, of course, pulled his coat tighter around himself. Then the sun took a turn. The sun beamed down warmth. The man chose to take off his coat in the sunshine. It is possible that social justice oriented consultation can be more like the sun than the north wind in schools. The consultant has the simple but challenging task to find out what will help the system, the stakeholders, the powerful administrators, or the student who is acting out to be able to relax and take off their coats.

## References

American Psychological Association. (2010). *Ethical principles and code of conduct.* Washington, DC: APA.

American Psychological Association. (n.d.) *Answers to your questions about transgender people, gender identity, and gender expression.* Retrieved February 29, 2012 from www.apa.org/topics/sexuality/transgender.aspx#

Bergan, J. R., & Kratochwill, T. R. (1990). *Behavioral consultation and therapy.* New York, NY: Plenum Press.

Brown, D., Pryzwansky, W. B., & Schulte, A. C. (2011). *Psychological consultation and collaboration: Introduction to theory and practice* (7th ed.). Upper Saddle River, NJ: Pearson Education.

Caplan, G., Caplan, R. B., & Erchul, W. P. (1995). A contemporary view of mental health consultation: Comments on "Types of Mental Health Consultation" by Gerald Caplan (1963). *Journal of Educational and Psychological Consultation, 6,* 23–30.

Chen-Hayes, S. F. (2001) Social Justice Advocacy Readiness Questionnaire. *Journal of Gay & Lesbian Social Services, 13* (1–2), 191–203.

Dougherty, A. M. (2009). *Psychological consultation and collaboration in school and community settings.* Belmont, CA: Brooks/Cole Cengage Learning Publishers.

Erchul, W. P., Grissom, P. F., & Getty, K. C. (2008). Studying interpersonal influence within school consultation: Social power base and relational communication perspectives. In W. P. Erchul & S. M. Sheridan (Eds.), *Handbook of research in school consultation* (pp. 293–322). New York, NY: Lawrence Erlbaum Associates.

Erchul, W. P., & Martens, B. K. (2010). *School consultation: Conceptual and empirical bases of practice* (3rd ed.). New York, NY: Springer.

Erchul, W. P., Raven, B. H., & Wilson, K. E. (2004). The relationship between gender of consultant and social power perceptions within school consultation. *School Psychology Review, 33* (4), 582–590.

Erchul, W. P. & Sheridan, S. M. (Eds.). (2008). *Handbook of research in school consultation.* New York, NY: Lawrence Erlbaum Associates.

George, E. (2005). Consultation: A solution-focused approach. In A. Southall (Ed.), *Consultation in child and adolescent mental health services* (pp. 55–67). Abingdon, UK: Radcliffe.

Hazel, C. E., Laviolette, G. T., & Lineman, J. M. (2010). Training professional psychologists in school-based consultation: What the syllabi suggest. *Training and Education in Professional Psychology, 4* (4), 235–243.

Ingraham, C. L. (2000). Consultation through a multicultural lens: Multicultural and cross-cultural consultation in schools. *School Psychology Review, 29* (3), 320–343.

Ingraham, C. L. (2008). Studying multicultural aspects of consultation. In W. P. Erchul & S. M. Sheridan (Eds.), *Handbook of research in school consultation* (pp. 269–291). New York, NY: Lawrence Erlbaum Associates.

Knotek, S. E., Kaniuka, M., & Ellingsen, K. (2008). Mental health consultation and consultee-centered approaches. In W. P. Erchul & S. M. Sheridan (Eds.), *Handbook of research in school consultation* (pp. 127–146). New York, NY: Lawrence Erlbaum Associates.

Kratochwill, T. R., & Bergan, J. R. (1990). *Behavioral consultation in applied settings: An individual guide.* New York, NY: Plenum Press.

Kuhn, A., & Beam, R. D. (1982). *The logic of organizations.* San Francisco, CA: Jossey-Bass.

Lambert, N., Hylander, I., & Sandoval, J. (Eds.). (2004). *Consultee-centered consultation: Improving the quality of professional services in schools and community organizations.* Mahwah, NJ: Lawrence Erlbaum Associates.

Li, C., & Vazquez-Nuttall, E. (2009). School consultants as agents of social justice for multicultural children and families. *Journal of Educational and Psychological Consultation, 19,* 26–44.

Marks, E. S. (1995). *Entry strategies for school consultation.* New York, NY: Guilford Press.

Martens, B. K., & DiGennaro, F. D. (2008). Behavioral consultation. In W. P. Erchul & S. M. Sheridan (Eds.), *Handbook of research in school consultation* (pp. 147–170). New York, NY: Lawrence Erlbaum Associates.

Moe, J. L., Perera-Diltz, D., & Sepulveda, V. (2010). Are consultation and social justice advocacy similar? Exploring perceptions of professional counselors and counseling students. *Journal for Social Action in Counseling Psychology, 3* (1), 106–123.

Nastasi, B., Moore, R., & Varjas, K. M. (2004). Participatory culture-specific intervention: Formative (research) phases. In B. Nastasi, R. Moore, & K. M. Varjas (Eds.), *School-based mental health services: Creating comprehensive and culturally specific programs* (pp. 79–80). Washington, DC: American Psychological Association.

Nastasi, B. K., Varjas, K., Bernstein, R., & Jayasena, A. (2000a). Conducting participatory culture-specific consultation: A global perspective on multicultural consultation. *School Psychology Review, 29* (3), 401–413.

Nastasi, B. K., Varjas, K., Schensul, S. L., Silva, K., Schensul, J. J., & Ratnayake, P. (2000b). The Participatory Intervention Model: A framework for conceptualizing and promoting intervention acceptability. *School Psychology Quarterly, 15* (2), 207–232.

National Association of School Psychologists (2010). Principles for professional ethics. Retrieved February 29, 2012 from www.nasponline.org/standards/2010standards/1_%20ethical%20principles.pdf

Newell, M. L., & Newell, T. S. (2011). Problem analysis: Examining the selection and evaluation of data during problem-solving consultation. *Psychology in the Schools, 48* (10), 943–957.

Pearrow, M. M., & Pollack, S. (2009). Youth empowerment in oppressive systems: Opportunities for school consultants. *Journal of Educational and Psychological Consultation, 19,* 45–60.

Rosenfield, S. (2002). Best practices in instructional consultation. In A. Thomas et al. (Eds.), *Best practices in school psychology IV* (pp. 609–623). Washington, DC: National Association of School Psychologists.

Sander, J. B., Sharkey, J. D., Groomes, A., Krumholz, L., Walker, K., & Hsu, J. Y. (2011). Social justice and juvenile offenders: Examples of fairness, respect and access in education settings. *Journal of Educational and Psychological Consultation, 21* (4), 1–29.

Sheridan, S. M., Clarke, B. L., & Burt, J. D. (2008). Conjoint behavioral consultation: What do we know and what do we need to know? In W. P. Erchul & S. M. Sheridan (Eds.), *Handbook of Research in School Consultation* (pp. 171–202). New York, NY: Lawrence Erlbaum Associates.

Sheridan, S. M., Kratochwill, T. R., & Bergan, J. R. (1996). *Conjoint behavioral consultation: A procedural manual.* New York, NY: Plenum Press.

Shriberg, D., & Fenning, P. A. (2009). School consultants as agents of social justice: Implications for practice: Introduction to the special issue. *Journal of Educational & Psychological Consultation, 19,* 1–7.

Speight, S. L. & Vera, E. M. (2009). The challenge of social justice for school psychology. *Journal of Educational and Psychological Consultation, 19,* 82–92.

Steege, M. W., & Watson, T. S. (2009). *Conducting school-based functional behavioral assessments* (2nd ed.). New York, NY: Guilford Press.

Sue, D. W. (2008). Multicultural organizational consultation: A social justice perspective. *Consulting Psychology Journal: Practice and Research, 60* (2), 157–169.

Thelen, E. (2005). Dynamic systems theory and the complexity of change. *Psychoanalytic Dialogues, 15* (2), 255–283.

Vera, E. M., & Speight, S. L. (2003). Multicultural competence, social justice, and counseling psychology: Expanding our roles. *Counseling Psychologist, 31,* 249–252.

Ysseldyke, J., Burns, M. K., & Rosenfield, S. (2009). Blueprints on the future of training and practice in school psychology: What do they say about educational and psychological consultation? *Journal Of Educational & Psychological Consultation, 19* (3), 177–196.

# fourteen
# Mental Health Issues: Non-academic Barriers to Success in School

## Kisha M. Radliff and Jennifer M. Cooper

Once upon a time there was a town that happened to have a playground located at the edge of a cliff. Every so often a child would fall off this cliff and be seriously injured. At last the town council decided to take action but was immediately deadlocked on what to do. Should they put a fence at the top of the cliff or an ambulance at the bottom?

(Slavin, Karweit, & Wasik, 1994, p. ix)

The plight of addressing the mental health needs of youth in school presents a similar dilemma. Should efforts be focused on prevention for all students, or targeted and individualized to meet the needs of the students experiencing the most severe mental health issues, or a combination of the two? For argument's sake, let's agree that strategies to prevent and treat pre-existing mental illness among all school-age youth is the ultimate goal. The challenge is deciding who should provide such services and how districts should fund these programs. Although these are questions to which there are no easy answers, it is paramount that we address children's mental health in schools. Untreated mental health issues affect children's success in schools and represent a serious concern that is not going away. Mental health is a key aspect of every child's healthy development, and research has demonstrated that the public mental health service system remains largely ineffective in meeting the needs of children and adolescents (Biebel, Katz-Levy, Nicholson, & Williams, 2006; Budde et al., 2004; Cooper, 2008).

While we understand that countless youth experience mental health issues that impact their success at school both academically and socially, we often hit a roadblock as to how to best address their needs. Unfortunately, this frequently leads to a lack of services, particularly for those who are unlikely to receive mental health care outside of school due to various barriers (e.g., lack of insurance, cost, and transportation). While school districts may not have caused these inequities, failure to address them is tantamount to social injustice by perpetuating non-academic barriers to academic achievement for marginalized students. Consider bullying, a problem that is pervasive across schools, affecting approximately one in three youth and that can create or worsen mental health issues (Nansel et al., 2001). Silence or inaction only serves to exacerbate the problem and does not support an equal opportunity for learning for students with mental health issues. Schools have a responsibility to do more to help the children they serve. Research has demonstrated that mental health, learning, and academic achievement are irrevocably intertwined (Johnson, Malone, & Hightower, 1997) and that mental health has an impact on academic achievement and success in school (US Department of Health and Human Services, 1999). Students who are mentally healthy or are able to have their mental health needs addressed are more likely to experience academic success.

This chapter will provide a brief review of the history of addressing mental health issues in schools and the role of school psychologists in providing mental health services from a social justice perspective. We will discuss the prevalence of mental health issues among underserved populations, such as minority youth, students from impoverished families, and students with emotional/behavioral disturbances; the challenges and barriers that often prevent these youth from receiving services; and the need for school-based mental health services. Examples of school-based mental health models will be discussed. Finally, a case study will be provided along with important questions for practitioners to consider in moving toward adopting a more socially just school-based mental health service delivery model that addresses mental health issues across the tiers (e.g., prevention, screening, small group intervention, and individual intervention).

## Mental Health in the Schools: A Historical Overview

Schools began providing general health services at the beginning of the 20th century (Flaherty, Weist, & Warner, 1996). Research describes that youth who had poor health had difficulty learning, which led to nurses being placed in school to address students' general health needs. School nurses provided general services such as vision and hearing screenings and keeping track of student immunizations; children with more critical needs were referred for outside services (Lear, Gleicher, St. Germaine, & Porter, 1991). Around this same time (late 19th century, early 20th century), children's mental health services began to be provided to meet the needs of youth in schools and as an alternative to putting youth in prison with adult offenders (Pumariega & Vance, 1999). The first clinics were offered through a university setting and juvenile courts, with the University of Pennsylvania housing the first psychological clinic for youth (Witmer, 1907/1996). The early clinics used an interdisciplinary treatment approach through physicians, social workers, and psychologists. These clinics paved the way for the creation of "child guidance clinics" in the early 1920s, which maintained the interdisciplinary approach (Pumariega & Vance, 1999).

Services in the community sector continued to evolve, and in the 1970s and 1980s hospital settings began to offer more intensive mental health services to youth (i.e., psychiatric services). As this was occurring, Public Law 94–142 was created and eventually reauthorized as the Individuals with Disabilities Education Act (most recently reauthorized in 2004 as the Individuals with Disabilities Education Improvement Act; IDEIA). With the passing of PL 94–142 and reauthorizing of IDEA, schools have slowly been given increasing responsibility for addressing the mental health needs of youth in schools (Annino, 1999). In addition to federal mandates, the 1980s saw a push for school-based clinics due largely to concerns about adolescent mental health and the resulting impact of these issues on education (Dryfoos, 1988). Further, society began to recognize that youth from communities that lacked resources or were high in poverty were less likely to graduate from high school (Dryfoos, 1988). These factors all contributed to an increase in availability of mental health services in schools. In fact, school-based clinics increased from few available in the 1970s to almost 1300 in 2001 (Weist, Goldstein, Morris, & Bryant, 2003).

Since the 1980s, school-based mental health (SBMH) programs have continued to be developed across the nation and have been found to be effective in providing services that make a difference. Rones and Hoagwood (2000) conducted a review of research and found that SBMH programs demonstrated effectiveness in addressing several issues, including various emotional and behavioral problems. In a more recent review, Browne, Gafni, Roberts, Byrne, and Majumdar (2004) found that SBMH programs that included an ecological approach to services had large benefits for students.

## Where Do School Psychologists Fit in?

In a 1907 address to the American Psychological Association, Witmer stated that there was a need for "training of students for a new profession—that of the psychological expert, who should find his career in connection with the school system" (Witmer, 1907/1996, p. 249). This sets the stage for the field of school psychology, with training in both psychology and education. School psychologists were among the mental health professionals providing services in school-based clinics. However, since the passage of PL 94–142, school psychologists have been seen as the "gatekeepers" to special education with the primary role of assessment. Over time, the field of school psychology has integrated consultation and academic and behavioral interventions services into its repertoire. School psychologists address student mental health needs through assessment, consultation, and intervention. The National Association of School Psychologists' (NASP) Model for Comprehensive and Integrated School Psychological Services (or NASP Practice Model) serves as the organization's official policy regarding the delivery of school psychological services and includes at least two domains specific to the delivery of mental health services in schools (NASP, 2010a; NASP, 2010b). NASP endorses a comprehensive service delivery model and encourages school psychologists to provide psychological services beyond the traditional role of assessment. For example, school psychologists might provide direct services to students and/or their families including individual or group counseling and social–emotional assessment to examine non-academic barriers to learning. This emphasis on the provision of comprehensive services recognizes the connection between mental health issues and student learning and illustrates the importance of addressing mental health needs in schools.

Despite NASP's emphasis on providing comprehensive services, school psychologists do not always find themselves practicing in this way. Current school psychology practice sometimes affords school psychologists the opportunity to provide mental health services to youth and their families such as counseling; however, it seems that more often than not, school psychologists have a narrowly defined role and are expected to spend most of their time conducting assessments. In fact, some districts hire other school professionals (e.g., school counselors or social workers) to provide these services (Johnson et al., 1997) and may be unaware that their school psychologist is trained to provide these same services. Whether or not school psychologists provide counseling services is often determined by "the setting . . . their training, experience, and interest . . . their time and scheduling flexibility; and the presence or absence of other qualified professionals" (Fagan & Wise, 2007, p. 133). It is important that school psychologists take the initiative to inform others of their skillset and advocate for their role to include the provision of comprehensive services so that they more effectively act as a social justice change agent for children and adolescents.

## Mental Health Prevalence among Youth and Service Utilization

One in five school-age youth have a diagnosable mental disorder (New Freedom Commission on Mental Health, 2003; U.S. Department of Health and Human Services, 1999), and one in 10 has serious mental health problems that are severe enough to impact their functioning at home, in school, or in the community (New Freedom Commission on Mental Health, 2003). Despite this, it is estimated that 75–80% of children and adolescents in need of mental health services do not receive them (Kataoka, Zhang, & Wells, 2002). Unfortunately, ethnic minority children and adolescents in need of mental health care receive it even less frequently. More than 85% of African American and Latino youth who need mental health intervention receive no services (US Department of Health and Human Services, 1999).

Issues related to insurance also contribute to the lack of mental health services received by ethnic minority youth. Medicaid has increased funding towards children's services; however, most of the funding targets the most intensive services such as residential and inpatient treatment programs (Burns, Taube, & Taube, 1991). This is problematic because the majority of youth covered under Medicaid are from ethnically diverse, high poverty, and underserved populations and few of them receive services in inpatient or residential (Fox & Wicks, 1995). Compounding the problem is that many children and adolescents living in poverty and without insurance substantially underutilize services (Kataoka et al., 2002). Of those youth who do seek out and engage in mental health treatment, 40–60% terminate therapy prematurely (Peacock & Collett, 2010). Weist and Ghuman (2002) point out that the gap between needs and resources stems from youth not accessing services from "traditional" mental health sites, such as private offices and community-based mental health centers. Barriers to accessing services include stigma, transportation issues, payment difficulties, lack of awareness of treatment sites, and long waiting lists (usually a minimum of two months or longer). There has been increasing recognition of the importance of providing mental health services to children and adolescents in settings familiar to them, such as school- or home-based services (Weist & Ghuman, 2002).

Of the small percentage of children fortunate enough to receive mental health services, the majority receive those services in a school setting (Burns et al., 1995; Paternite, 2005), primarily from school psychologists or guidance counselors Burns et al., 1995). Very few of these youth received additional services elsewhere Burns et al., 1995). The unmet need for mental health services for diverse populations has a potentially detrimental impact on their academic success and speaks to the importance of school-based mental health services.

School-based mental health is vitally important given the mental health needs of our youth, and for our culturally and linguistically diverse youth in particular, and the ideal position that schools are in to provide those services. Hence, it is imperative that schools are provided with appropriately trained school-based mental health professionals (e.g., school psychologists), financial means, and other tangible resources in order to effectively address the mental health needs of students. School psychologists have an opportunity to serve as social justice change agents in the provision of mental health services for youth by engaging in culturally competent practices and using a social justice approach to service delivery.

## Addressing Mental Health in Schools: A Social Justice Approach

Community-based services integrate the Child and Adolescent Service System Program (CASSP) initiative which proposes specific guidelines for community-based services. Included within these guidelines is the provision of services in the least restrictive environment, which encourages the use of family and community resources; integrating the family into the treatment process; and the use of non-discriminatory and culturally sensitive services (Stroul & Friedman, 1986). In developing a model for a culturally competent system of care, Cross, Bazron, Dennis, and Isaacs (1989) reviewed several community-based systems and found that the most effective programs were compatible with the cultural values of ethnic minority populations and consistent with the guidelines listed above. These same principles are consistent with NASP's guidelines for the role of school psychologists in providing mental health services. More notably, these highlight the importance of the family and cultural beliefs and values being integrated into the treatment of culturally diverse youth and the importance of culturally competent clinicians to provide these services. In order to have a socially just approach to the provision of mental health treatment, it is important that those services are delivered in a culturally competent manner. This means that treatment should be individualized and should be sensitive to the needs of the student, their family, and their community (NASP, 2008).

## Role of the School Psychologist

The NASP Practice Model includes two domains that serve as guidelines of practice for school psychologists in the delivery of mental health services in schools. Domains four and six focus on interventions and mental health services to develop social and life skills and, preventive and responsive services. NASP has also developed position statements in support of school psychologists providing mental health services (e.g., NASP, 2008). In drawing specific attention to the connection between mental health issues and student learning, NASP endorses a comprehensive service delivery model and encourages school psychologists to provide psychological services beyond the traditional role of assessment in the areas of intelligence and achievement. One such area is counseling and social–emotional assessment to examine non-academic barriers to learning. The services that school psychologists provide both directly and indirectly impact the student's ability to experience success "academically, socially, behaviorally, and emotionally" (NASP, 2010a, p.1).

The school psychologist who acts as a change agent for social justice must develop cultural sensitivity and engage in culturally competent practice. Cultural competence can be defined as "a set of congruent behaviors, attitudes, and policies that come together in a system, agency, or amongst professionals and enables that system, agency, or those professionals to work effectively in cross-cultural situations," (Cross et al., 1989, p. iv). For the school psychologist who practices in a socially just way, it is important to be culturally sensitive, to engage in culturally competent practice, and to be mindful that cultural competence is an ongoing process. Cultural competency in no way implies mastery of diversity issues; the key to being a truly culturally competent practitioner is to dedicate oneself to a life-long journey of learning and integrating new knowledge and skills into one's practice in the best interest of one's clients. This process means engaging in ongoing self-reflection (e.g., of biases, beliefs, values) and training in cultural competency, and maintaining an openness to learning about the individual needs of youth and their families so that these needs can be integrated into effective services for the youth he or she serves.

Some common elements that are considered essential to developing cultural competence are highlighted by Nastasi (2005) as well as Cross and colleagues (1989). These elements have some overlap and emphasize the importance of culturally competent practice at the individual, group, and systems levels. First, we will present the elements discussed by Cross and colleagues, followed by a discussion of Nastasi's guiding principles that comprise common elements from diverse perspectives of cultural competence. Cross and colleagues (1989) suggest five essential elements important for becoming culturally competent. These are discussed as they would apply to the role of a school psychologist in addressing the mental health needs of children and adolescents.

1. *Acknowledge cultural differences and consider their impact in therapy.* This illuminates the importance of understanding the client's perspective, their view and approach to therapy, their view of mental health, and the role of the family.

2. *Recognize and acknowledge the influence of your culture on your thoughts, beliefs, and actions.* This is a process of self-reflection. For example, consider how you define family, appropriate classroom behavior, or important life goals. These are generally shaped by cultural norms and reinforced by those around us (family, peers, and social institutions).

3. *Understand that both you and the client will bring your own unique history influenced by your different cultures to the therapeutic relationship.* Your interactional styles, approach to problem-solving, and even view of appropriate manners or politeness may differ due to cultural differences. For example, consider the importance of eye contact in Western culture; it signifies respect and confidence. However, other cultures believe that lowering of the eyes is a sign of respect. It will be critical to consider values and biases that contribute to interpretations of your client's interactional style and engagement in therapy.

4. *Make every effort to understand your client's behavior within the context of their culture.* This contributes to a more truthful interpretation of the client's behavior and more effective and culturally appropriate interventions to address your client's needs. This helps you to avoid interpreting the client's behavior based on the norms of the dominant culture.

5. *Gather information about the cultural background of the clients you work with.* Because it is not realistic to have comprehensive knowledge of all cultures, know where you can obtain more information to better understand individual clients. This is a continual process in that you should gather new knowledge over time and integrate what you learn into the provision of

services with diverse clients. However, it is important to note that while knowledge of the cultural groups with which your client identifies is critical to the therapeutic alliance, the culture of the individual is paramount. For example, your experience with one 15-year-old, Somali male client may be very different from another client that shares cultural ties within the same group, but differs with respect to familial and/or individual cultural traits.

These elements are consistent with cultural competencies discussed within the school psychology literature. Nastasi (2005) summarized essential elements of cultural competence as including: (a) engaging in self-reflection; (b) being willing to reflect on others' viewpoints and learn from those; (c) understanding that culture plays a role in human development; (d) obtaining knowledge about different cultural groups; (e) skill-building that allows you to gather rich, qualitative information (beyond numbers); and (f) communicating in a way that allows others' perspectives to be considered and emphasizes collaborative decision-making.

Both Cross et al. (1989) and Nastasi emphasize that cultural competence is important at the individual (e.g., self-awareness and acknowledgement of the role of culture in one's own life), dyadic (e.g., specific cultural knowledge of individuals you work with, understanding your client's behavior within their cultural context), and systems levels (e.g., collaborative communication and decision-making, understanding the impact of cultural dynamics—your client's and your own—on the therapeutic process, and connecting the role of culture in human development). Cultural competency is the cornerstone of socially just practice; focusing on the ideals of social justice without engaging in the nuts and bolts of cultural competency will do little to advance the social justice agenda and improve mental health services for underserved populations. It is critical to be knowledgeable of the clients you work with (cultural knowledge) and engage in culturally sensitive and appropriate assessment, intervention and consultative practices (culturally competent practice) at all levels when approaching mental health service delivery from a social justice framework.

## School-Based Mental Health Services as an Ideal

So why address mental health issues in schools? Mental health issues need to be addressed in the schools because "children whose emotional, behavioral, or social difficulties are not addressed have a diminished capacity to learn and benefit from the school environment" (Rones & Hoagwood, 2000, p.236). The priority of schools is to educate all children; if children are not mentally healthy, this affects their ability to learn and to succeed academically. The National Association of School Psychologists (NASP, 2008) has developed a position statement on the importance of addressing mental health needs in schools, collaborating with outside agencies, and engaging school psychologists in the provision of services. School psychologists are in an ideal position to play a role in the provision of mental health services in schools.

Providing mental health services in the schools is a cost-effective and more efficient way to meet the needs of all youth (NASP, 2008). In the schools we have convenient access to children, not only convenient for mental health providers (e.g., school psychologists, social workers, school counselors), but also for those families who are unable to take their children to local community health care centers or are unable to afford services (Burns et al., 1995). This is particularly important for our ethnic minority youth who so frequently do not receive the services they need (Kataoka et al., 2002; US Department of Health and Human Services, 1999). The National Center for Children in Poverty (NCCP) developed policy recommendations which highlight the importance of providing early mental health prevention and intervention programming for African American boys (Aratani, Wight, & Cooper, 2011). The research consistently indicates that early prevention and intervention services are important for fostering the social–emotional health of all youth because these factors have been shown to be predictive of future academic performance (Aratani et al., 2011). This is consistent with the mission of schools to educate all youth. To effectively meet this mission, factors, such as mental health, that impact learning and academic success need to be addressed in schools.

## Barriers to School-based Mental Health

While legislative mandates and initiatives such as the New Freedom Commission on Mental Health, IDEIA, Public Health Service and the Patient Protection and Affordable Care Act of 2010 demonstrate a commitment of the federal government to address the mental health needs of children and adolescents, schools still face considerable challenges in effectively meeting those needs (Maag & Katsiyannis, 2010). Readers are encouraged to see Calfee (2004) for a thorough review of the barriers to funding school-based mental health services and examples of federal funding for mental health inservices. Maag and Katsiyannis (2010) present four challenges that are particularly germane to schools in obtaining funds for school-based mental health service delivery: (1) reducing the stigma associated with mental health issues, (2) forming interagency partnerships, (3) obtaining parental consent and ensuring privacy, and (4) building mental health service capacity.

Stigma and misconceptions about mental illness have long been a part of our social fabric, and efforts to raise awareness and reduce the stigma for individuals with mental health problems have existed since the deinstitutionalization movement (Grob, 2008). Doll (2008) suggests reframing the treatment of mental illness as part of the broader goal of psychological well-being for all students. The shift to a "wellness" model and use of terminology that focuses on the value of psychological well-being, similar to physical well-being, may help to reduce stigma associated with mental health disorders or emotional disturbances. Given our extensive training in consultation as school psychologists, we are well suited to lead professional development sessions for school staff, students, and their families about the importance of psychological well-being and to raise awareness regarding the stigma surrounding mental illness. Maag and Katsiyannis (2010) argue that schools should embrace and be proud of their role in providing quality mental health services to children and their families. In advocating for mental health services focused on social justice, we would argue that schools taking a proactive role to address the inequities in the mental health system, preventing future mental health issues among school-age youth, and meeting students' unmet mental health needs, especially among the most vulnerable groups, is precisely what advocacy and active engagement are all about.

Given the finite resources available to them, schools must work to form effective interagency partnerships to improve students' mental health. While there are many challenges inherent in working as part of a multidisciplinary, interagency team, these partnerships also hold the greatest potential for socially just practice. According to Maag and Katsiyannis (2010), the first step in addressing these challenges is the formation of a team. Given that mental health services are likely to be provided within the school setting, schools usually initiate this process and play an important role in considering who the key stakeholders are that should comprise the team. This presents an opportunity for school psychologists to work collaboratively as part of a multidisciplinary team and to advocate for needed services that promote their students' physical, social, emotional and intellectual well-being (e.g., translation services and culturally acceptable counseling services). To ensure productivity among the team, school psychologists and other school-based mental health professionals must strive to create and maintain a collegial environment. Ross and Reichle (2007) point to the importance of valuing each team member's contributions and being sensitive to their time in promoting a productive and collaborative team-based approach. Appropriately identifying key team members and engaging in a collaborative effort ensures that multiple perspectives are considered and allows each member to bring their unique resources to the group. The school psychologist can play a role in advocating for a social justice framework in the approach to mental health services and the provision of culturally competent services to meet the needs of culturally and linguistically diverse youth.

One of the greatest challenges for schools in delivering mental-health services to students is ensuring their clients' and families' privacy. Evans (1999) conducted a review of the literature in response to concerns regarding a lack of privacy safeguards and a common set of standards by schools and found that no research existed on consent procedures in school-based mental health, although he did find general consent procedures in mental health that could have implications for school-based settings. Further complicating the issue is the variation in state consent laws, with some states allowing children as young as 12 years old to consent to treatment (DeKraai & Sales, 1991). According to Maag and Katsiyannis (2010), the issue of consent may depend on the type of services in question (e.g., some early intervention programs are integrated in the district's curriculum and therefore may not require additional consent). Passive consent is a method where schools inform parents about a service that their child may be eligible for and explain that they have the right to object if they choose (Evans, 1999). This practice is probably sufficient to protect the right of most, but not all, parents (Esbensen et al., 1996; Severson & Biglan, 1989). Alternatively, active consent requires parental consent prior to administering treatment and is one of the best ways to demonstrate respect for parental rights (Evans, 1999). However, this approach may prevent children who need services from receiving them (e.g., when it is difficult to obtain consent). We would argue that passive consent does not consider cultural differences regarding views on mental health, how mental health issues should be addressed, or possible educational and/or language barriers that may inhibit a caregiver's understanding of what they are consenting to. Given that some families may need more information to determine if the services provided are consistent with their cultural beliefs and values, active consent is more consistent with socially just practice.

Another major barrier that schools face in providing quality mental health services to students is easiest to understand in the economic terms of supply and demand. In schools, the number of referrals is likely to far exceed the ability of school-based mental professionals to provide services to meet students' needs (Maag & Katsiyannis, 2010). To overcome this barrier, it is important for school psychologists, school counselors, social workers and others to prioritize the needs of students and work to implement evidence-based prevention approaches to reduce the number of referrals, as outlined in a Multi-Tier System of Supports (MTSS) [commonly referred to as Response to Intervention (RtI)] framework. Additionally, NASP (2008) encourages collaboration with outside agencies, which is important as a part of culturally responsive practice. Integrated models of service delivery such as those outlined in the sections on school-based health centers and full-service schools offer innovative strategies to establish community partnerships to meet the needs of students and their families.

## Potential Benefits to School-based Mental Health

Despite the challenges of addressing mental health needs in schools, there are many potential benefits. As indicated above, school-based mental health services are an efficient way to address the needs of all youth. For example, when students access services in the school setting it reduces their time out of school. Delivering mental health services during the school day allows the therapeutic process to have maximum impact on academics (Pumariega & Vance, 1999). Even if these services are delivered after school hours within the school, this allows for easy access to services for families at no cost.

Offering mental health services in school, a community-based setting that serves all youth and their families, provides a relatively stigma-free setting within which to deliver services (Dryfoos, 1994; Pumariega & Vance, 1999). This is important because, as stated above, many cultures view mental health issues as stigmatizing, which may be a contributing factor to underutilizing services. Although school-based service delivery may not entirely reduce stigma, practitioners can offer culturally sensitive approaches to treatment, such as school–community partnerships that respect the values of different cultural groups (e.g., the importance placed on natural supports/interventions and family involvement for Indigenous Americans). Providing mental health services in schools also emphasizes the importance of mental health as it relates to academic success. This fits well with a "wellness" model (as described earlier) that emphasizes the importance of psychological well-being as contributing to academic success. Addressing mental health issues in schools and framing them in the context of overall academic success could help increase service utilization among underserved populations, particularly ethnic minorities and those who are uninsured.

Another benefit to school-based mental health services is that within schools there is an opportunity to provide comprehensive services from an ecological perspective. Unlike a community agency or hospital setting, schools are a natural setting for youth where they spend much of their day. By engaging an ecological perspective, we consider not only individual characteristics, but also their environment in the treatment of mental health issues. Through this perspective we consider the multiple systems within which the child exists (e.g., family, school, peer relationships, community; Motes, Melton, & Waithe Simmons, 1999). An ecological perspective also encourages emphasis on a strengths-based approach by considering protective factors that can support effective treatment. This may be particularly salient when working with ethnically diverse youth who often are viewed through a deficit model with emphasis on risk factors (e.g., poverty). School-based mental health service providers can draw on protective factors that might exist within the school (e.g., social support through positive peer and teacher relationships), as well as external protective factors such as family and community supports to implement effective and culturally relevant treatment.

## School-Based Mental Health in Practice

As the push for schools to address children's mental health needs continues to permeate discussions at the state and federal levels, local school districts will look for service delivery models that have been successful in meeting students' mental health needs. This is no easy feat considering the fiscal, personnel, and other challenges (discussed in an earlier section) that schools face as they come into their own in this new and evolving role. The need for school-based mental health (SBMH) programs with a strong evidence base is at the core of this discussion as schools do not have the time or resources to implement ineffective approaches. Although a large number of evidence-based mental health interventions exist in the literature, further research is needed to investigate how to adapt these approaches to be effective within schools and with students from diverse backgrounds. The purpose of this section of the chapter is to provide practitioners, administrators, trainers, and students with practical examples of SBMH programs and related resources. While no two schools are exactly alike, it is our goal that by sharing the lessons learned by researchers and districts across the country, we will help to inform others considering implementation of such programs. Learning more about each of the models should also help readers to evaluate the pros and cons of contrasting approaches and assist them in determining how best to meet their students' needs (see Center for Community Solutions, 2008 and Price & Lear, 2008, for a detailed discussion of steps for implementation and best practices).

## Framework for Service Delivery

The pyramid or tiered model often used in public health and behavioral health initiatives provides a framework to discuss the delivery of school-based mental health services. MTSS, Positive Behavior Support (PBS), and Restorative Justice (RJ; see Chapter 6 for review) are three examples of school-based tiered models that many school psychologists should be familiar with and that can be adapted to apply to the provision of mental health services. A tiered model offers supports at varying levels of intensity to meet the individual needs of all students. In a mental health example, at tier 1 (universal level), programs that support the socio-emotional development of all students would be offered. Examples of these types of interventions could include character education, school-wide behavior and social skills development, and motivation initiatives (e.g., mentoring, student of the month). At the next tier (secondary or targeted tier), students who did not respond well to the tier 1 intervention or who require additional services would be offered targeted mental health and/or substance abuse services. Examples of evidence-based interventions at this tier would include Second Step, Promoting Alternative Thinking Strategies (PATHS), and the Peacemakers Program. At the intensive (or tertiary) tier, individual interventions would be offered to students who are referred by a multidisciplinary team or individual evaluations. Interventions at this level would be tailored to the individual and may include referrals to mental health day treatment or residential treatment, referrals for pharmacological services, and individual treatment using evidence-based therapeutic approaches (Center for Community Solutions, 2008). Crisis intervention services can also be included in the tiered mental health service delivery model. Often, these services are provided at tier 3; however, when there is a major crisis affecting many or all students (e.g., an incidence of school violence or a natural disaster), crisis intervention services may also be considered as part of the universal tier. NASP has developed a crisis intervention curriculum, PREPaRE, for implementation within a school-based setting (Brock et al., 2009; see www.nasponline.org).

Focusing on service delivery within a social justice framework, it is important to consider if the prevention and intervention strategies you intend to use have demonstrated effectiveness with children and adolescents similar to the students you will be working with. For example, does the intervention have demonstrated effectiveness in urban settings and/or with African American and Latino youth? If not, are suggestions for adaptions for use in urban settings or with diverse youth discussed in peer-reviewed journals? The Substance Abuse and Mental Health Services Administration's (SAMHSA) National Registry of Evidence-based Programs and Practices (available at: www.nrepp.samhsa.gov/search.aspx) is a useful tool for locating interventions based on specific search criteria (e.g., setting, race/ethnicity, presenting problem). A search of SAMHSA's national registry that focused on urban settings and students of color as 50% or more of study populations found 55 evidence-based interventions.

An alternative framework for discussing the delivery of SBMH services is categorizing programs into distinct perspectives or models. Kutash, Duchnowksi, and Lynn (2006) propose three major models that differ in their approach as well as in the services that they offer. This first model, labeled the Spectrum of Mental Health Interventions and Treatments, includes what would be considered by most as traditional mental health interventions applied within a school setting (Mrazek & Haggerty, 1994; Weisz, Sandler, Durlak, & Anton, 2005). This model could include interventions aimed at prevention, psychotherapy and other evidence-based mental health treatments, and psychopharmacology. The second model comprises three overarching systems targeting prevention, early intervention, and systems of care for children with serious impairments. These three systems are integrated to form a continuum of SBMH services for children (Adelman & Taylor, 2006; National Institute for Health Care Management, 2005). This model is referred to as Interconnected Systems for Meeting the Needs of All Children. The last perspective, The Application of Positive Behavior Supports to Reduce Challenging Behaviors in School, is focused primarily on the management of behaviors and uses positive behavior supports (PBS) and functional behavioral assessment strategies within school settings as methods of both prevention and intervention to address challenging behaviors (Horner, Albin, Sprague, & Todd, 1999).

Whether delivering school-based mental health services through a tiered service delivery model or within a distinct perspective, such as PBS, one thing is clear—schools across the United States are implementing SBMH programs in a variety of ways in response to the growing need to address children's mental health. According to Kutash et al. (2006), the diversity of SMBH programs can, in part, be attributed to the fact that policymakers have yet to receive clear guidance from the field on selection criteria and effective implementation. In fact, within the literature, there is consensus that the delivery of school-based mental health services is not guided by a particular conceptual model and can, at times, offer conflicting perspectives that drive contrasting policies and programs (Kutash et al., 2006). SBMH programs run the gamut; including everything from broad-based school reform (e.g., Adelman & Taylor, 2006) to the use of clinical psychology interventions in the schools (e.g., Armbruster & Lichtman, 1999; Weist, Myers, Hastings, Ghuman, & Han, 1999) and the implementation of positive behavior supports for students with emotional disturbances (e.g., Horner et al., 1999). Other examples in the provision of SBMH programs include school-based health centers, expanded school mental health services, and full service schools. The examples provided below are intended to give a brief overview of each of the most prominent types of SBMH programs. Regardless of the conceptual model chosen, school leaders need to consider which programs and services will best match their school's unique demographics, resources, and stage of development in the delivery of school-based mental health services while capitalizing on the strengths of the school community and its student body (Kutash et al., 2006). Readers are encouraged to consult the case study and guiding questions at the end of this chapter and begin a thorough needs assessment at their school before selecting the appropriate SBMH model and programs to meet their students' needs.

## School-Based Mental Health along a Continuum

In this section, we will examine varying types of school-based mental health approaches through a social justice lens. The first two levels, the restricted and limited access approaches, fall within the spectrum of mental health interventions and treatments which would be considered by most as traditional mental health interventions applied within a school setting (Mrazek & Haggerty, 1994; Weisz et al., 2005). The third level, the integrated approach, would be categorized as part of the interconnected systems model most clearly defined and advocated for by the Center for Mental Health in Schools at UCLA (Adelman & Taylor, 2006) and the Center for School Mental Health Assistance at the University of Maryland (Weist et al., 2003).

### Restricted Approach

Recognizing that mental health issues often affect academic success, schools may attempt to identify basic mental health needs and offer indirect services, such as referrals to community-based agencies, to children who may be experiencing or are at risk of developing a mental health disorder (Calfee, 2004). However, few offer direct services to address their students' immediate needs. Any funding for services provided by the schools would be for services offered off-site. This model has been referred to as the traditional school–community relationship, and most charter schools and private schools tend to fall in this category (Calfee, 2004). Given that this approach severely restricts access to mental health services within schools, we find it inconsistent with the guiding principles of socially just practice as it serves to perpetuate academic and behavioral problems stemming from service underutilization.

### Limited Access Approach

Another model, the school–community partnership, is where most public schools in this country would be categorized (Calfee, 2004). In this model, the connection between the school and outside mental health providers is closer and school-based services are available. However, only students with special needs may access those services. Under the IDEIA, school districts are required to provide special education services to children and adolescents whose disability interferes with their academic achievement. When students are classified with behavior disorders or serious emotional disturbances, schools are legally required to offer services such as counseling, behavior modification, or special schools to meet the child's individual needs. However, not all children, even those with serious mental health issues, qualify for special education.

Within this model, school psychologists have historically been viewed as "gate-keepers to special education" rather than as mental health professionals. However, two major shifts—the movement toward a more comprehensive service delivery model (NASP, 2010a) and the push for schools to address the mental health of their students—have the potential to forever change the landscape of school psychology and the roles and functions of its professional workforce. Socially just mental health service delivery requires school psychologists to act as advocates for students with mental health issues and to integrate culturally appropriate prevention services and interventions to effect change at the individual and systems levels. Successful implementation of many of the examples discussed below would require, at a minimum, role redefinition, creativity and flexibility from school administration, and systemic change. As students, trainers, and practitioners of school psychology, we encourage you to be a part of the change that you wish to see and know that we have the ability to be leaders within our schools and agents for meaningful change (see Nastasi, 2005 for further discussion).

## Integrated Approach

In this model, the school views children's mental health as a top priority within the context of education. These schools offer all of the "core" services in the limited access model, but go much further by offering additional mental health services tailored to meet the needs of that particular school and student body. SBMH programs within this model are known under different names including, but not limited to, full-service schools, expanded school mental health programs (ESMH), and school-based health centers. While some of the approaches within this model differ, they all have the commonality of providing a "true system of care" that includes three levels of services: prevention, intervention, and crisis services (Calfee, 2004). From a social justice perspective, integrated approaches that include wraparound services address traditional barriers to mental health service access and promote psychological well-being at the individual and system levels. By integrating culturally competent practice within this approach, we stand the greatest chance of effectively meeting the mental health needs of ethnically diverse and underserved populations. ESMH programs, specifically, aim to reach underserved children and adolescents with the goal of improving a host of outcomes important to children, their families, and schools. These programs have growing support based on studies demonstrating improved student functioning (Armbruster & Lichtman, 1999) and improved school climate (Walrath, Bruns, Anderson, Glass-Seigel, & Weist, 2004).

### *School-based health centers*

School-based health centers (SBHCs) provide a wide range of health services (including both physical and behavioral health) to students, and highlight one example of an integrated approach to service delivery. Many school-based health centers provide an array of services such as primary medical care, health education and promotion, substance abuse counseling, and mental/behavioral health care (Strozer Juszczak, & Ammerman, 2010). Schools often partner with a community health organization such as a local health department or hospital to operate school-based health centers (Strozer et al., 2010). From a social justice standpoint, the services that individual SBHCs provide would be determined by the needs of the students and available community resources. There are approximately 2000 school-based health centers operating nationwide, every day that school is in session (Strozer et al., 2010). While the services offered vary from site to site, mental health and counseling services available at SBHCs could include individual and family therapy, mental health assessments, crisis intervention, consultation with teachers, and case management.

SBHCs have diverse staffing arrangements, but most models fall within three types of service delivery. The primary care (PC) model is typically staffed by a nurse practitioner or physician assistant with the primary focus on students' physical health. Service delivery may be supplemented with dental health services, health education, and social services, but mental health services are typically not offered in this model. However, primary care providers may offer limited mental health services such as referrals, screening, and crisis intervention when there is no mental health staff at the SBHC. Approximately 25% of SBHCs fall into this model. The largest group of SBHCs (40%) is staffed by a primary care provider and a mental health professional in the Primary Care–Mental Health (PCMH) model. Mental health professionals may include a psychologist, social worker, or substance abuse counselor. The third model, Primary Care–Mental Health Plus (PCMH+), represents the most comprehensive service delivery model, offering a multidisciplinary approach to address students' physical and mental health, as well as providing case management and nutrition services. Approximately 35% of SBHCs across the country offer these types of services to school-age children. Strozer et al. (2010) report an increase in SBHCs with staffing models other than the three previously mentioned with the majority of these programs providing mental health services only.

An overwhelming majority (96%) of SBHCs are housed within the school building, with the majority (57%) located in urban communities. Providing services within school buildings in urban communities is critically important to overcoming barriers to access such as transportation, cost, and stigma (Calfee, 2004; Maag & Katsiyannis, 2010). SBHCs also offer a viable solution to the underutilization of mental health services by minority students and families without insurance. Strozer et al. (2010) report that students in schools with SBHCs are typically ethnically diverse youth who are under-insured, lack insurance, and experience other health disparities. For example, in the latest available national census of SBHCs (school year 2007–2008, $n = 1096$), Hispanic children and adolescents represented 36.8% of students in schools with SBHCs, African American students comprised 26.2%, Asian/Pacific Islander students represented 4.4%, and Native American students comprised 1.7%. In addition to serving historically underserved groups, SBHCs have been shown to have a positive effect on school attendance and academic achievement (Shaw, Kelly, Joost, & Parker-Fisher, 1995). Students in urban schools who received school-based mental health services had a 95% decrease in disciplinary referrals, a 31% reduction in failing course grades, and a 32% decrease in school absences (Jennings, Pearson, & Harris, 2000).

According to Strozer (2010), 36% of schools reported only serving their student population (a decrease from 45% in the 2004–2005 census), meaning that schools are providing services to other patient populations including students from other schools in the community (58%), out-of-school youth (34%), family members of students (42%), faculty and school personnel (42%), and other community members (24%). This indicates an important trend of SBHCs expanding their ability to provide access to quality, affordable health care to others in the community (Stozer et al., 2010). From a social justice perspective, caring for students holistically and acknowledging community and family factors that may impact a child's educational experiences is of paramount concern. Additionally, in opening their doors to others in the community, SBHCs provide a solution to addressing inequities in our health care system in high-need communities, which aligns with a socially just practice orientation of equality and fairness in service allocation. The federal government has backed the SBHC model as evidenced by the Affordable Care Act, appropriating a total of $200 million for 2010 through 2013 to support capital grants to improve and expand school-based health centers. The affirmation by Secretary of Education Arne Duncan that "If kids aren't healthy then kids can't learn" provides a strong argument for increasing school-based mental health services in schools to address non-academic barriers to educational success (US Department of Health and Human Services, 2011, p. 1).

## Full service schools

Another approach within an integrated service delivery model is the full service or "whole child" schools, which are based on the notion that no single magic bullet can substantially improve the lives of at-risk children and their families (Dryfoos, 1994). Full-services schools represent an educational approach that improves academic success by addressing students' overall physical, social, intellectual, and emotional needs (Santiago, Ferrara, & Blank, 2008). One example of a full-service community elementary school is in the urban neighborhood of Port Chester, New York. This school serves a largely poor, Latino immigrant population where 50% of students are English language learners. Many of the families struggle to find affordable housing, child care, health care, and nutrition in addition to the stressors that recent immigrants face such as acculturation, language barriers, and legal status (Santiago et al., 2008). In the late 1990s, administrators and teachers began to see the connection between outside-of-school factors and students' well-being and its impact on academic achievement. Students were frequently absent from school due to illness, and only 19% of the school's fourth graders were passing the state standardized assessment in English

Language Arts. In response to concerns regarding students' learning and families' expressed needs for child care, resources to address language barriers, and a desire for greater involvement in their child's schooling, the school began the journey of becoming a full-service community school. Today, this school offers school-based health care, therapy and family casework, parent enrichment and capacity building, and after-school enrichment. The model is dependent on support from partnerships with local universities and non-profit agencies. June 2007 marked the 10-year anniversary of the school and 93% of fourth-grade students passed the 2006 New York State Assessment in English Language Arts (Santiago et al., 2008). Additionally, 75% of families were participating in school events. The school credits its success to strong community-based partnerships that provide services on-site at the school and, in doing so, contribute to a strong sense of interagency cooperation and collaboration. By educating the whole child, all parties stand to benefit: children and families receive services that improve their lives; schools have more time for teaching and learning as a result of reducing non-academic barriers to learning; and community-based agencies are better able to reach families to provide needed services.

## Conclusion: Making School-Based Mental Health a Reality

Given the high prevalence of mental health issues experienced by youth in schools, the impact on academic and social success in school, and particular impact this has on culturally and linguistically diverse youth, it is imperative that school psychologists are at the forefront of prevention and intervention efforts. Integrated service delivery models offer the opportunity for school psychologists to increase the provision of mental health services to children and families. In the examples presented above, school psychologists can serve as an important link between clients, school staff, and community partners, "facilitating a collaborative system of care for students" (Brown & Bolen, 2003, p. 285). Creating and implementing school-based mental health programs is a process that can seem challenging and overwhelming at first; however, with the proper supports, framework and collaboration, the process is a worthwhile undertaking and can have a positive impact on the student body, their families, and school staff. While any approach must take into consideration the school's unique demographics, school climate, students' needs and strengths, and barriers, effective school-based mental health programs around the country equip and inspire us to become social justice advocates for improving access to mental health services and educating our children holistically. To help you as you embark on this important journey, a case study is now presented along with guided questions for discussion or for practitioners to use with their schools.

Appendix

Developing a Comprehensive Socially Just School-Based
Mental Health Model:

A Case Study

## Case Study: Developing a Comprehensive Socially Just School-Based Mental Health Model

A brief case study is presented below to use as an example for applying the questions that follow. While these questions are not an exhaustive list, they are intended to guide school-based mental health professionals in approaching mental health service delivery through a social justice lens.[1]

You are a school psychologist and this is your second year postgraduation. Your assignment was recently changed and you will begin the school year at a different elementary school this year. The school serves around 400 students, 91% of whom are students of color, and 99% received free and reduced lunch. Ten percent of the student body are English language learners (ELL) and 15% of students receive special education. The school is housed within a community that has high levels of violence and crime, and the majority of students enrolled in the school live in the surrounding community. The school has had a Department of Education rating of Academic Emergency for two consecutive years, and disaggregated data from standardized achievement tests indicate that almost all students are behind grade level in core content areas, with African American and Latino students lagging farthest behind. You have heard from the former school psychologist that external factors and poor social-emotional health significantly impact many students' abilities to do well academically. She also believes that a large number of students who should be receiving services are not due to unethical practices by the former administration. Despite these challenges, several positive factors exist: (a) a new principal has been brought on board to assist with school reform efforts, (b) while parent/guardian engagement has historically been low, they show a desire to work with the school for positive change, (c) perceived school climate as reported by students is higher than expected, and (d) several "master" teachers are committed to their students' success and are highly effective in the classroom.

## Important Questions to Consider

### Pre-Work Stage

Conduct preliminary research to assess the need of your student body (i.e., who are the students, what are their mental health needs, are they being served?), to determine if there are current school-based practices to address student

mental health needs and the effectiveness of these practices, to identify training needs of the school staff, to assess whether or not your school is engaging
in socially just practice with regard to these issues and what that looks like, and
to identify potential community partners. As a part of this stage, school-wide
assessment should occur to identify the unique needs of the student body.

- What are the demographics of the school? (Paying particular attention to historically marginalized groups, e.g., students of color, students
  with disabilities, and ELL.)
- What are the cultural demographics of your students? This is especially
  important information to consider in ensuring that culturally competent
  services are provided to youth and their families.
- What are the cultural demographics of the school staff? This is especially important information to consider in ensuring that culturally competent services are provided to youth and their families and identifying
  potential training opportunities around diversity, cultural competency,
  impact of culture on teaching and learning, impact of non-academic
  barriers on student achievement, etc.
- What are the identified mental health needs of the students? For example, what percentage of youth are identified for services through IDEIA,
  and who are these youth?
- What are the current practices in effect to address student mental
  health needs? How effective are these practices? It will be important
  to find evidence for the effectiveness of these services (e.g., outcome
  data from treatment that is in progress or completed).
- How are the services available to students being provided in a socially
  just way? Here you might consider over- or under-representation of
  diverse youth in certain programs (e.g., gifted programming, college
  prep or AP courses, special education).

## *Tier 1 Stage*

Focus on questions related to developing and implementing universal prevention efforts to meet the unique needs of your school and its students. As a part
of this stage, progress monitoring and/or follow-up assessments should be
conducted to identify students who are not responding to the universal intervention or who require additional intervention.

- Is there currently school-wide programming in place? If so, is it effectively meeting the needs of all students in my school? Is it an appropriate program given the demographics of the student body?
- What type of school-wide programming would best meet the need of
  the students in my school? Has this program been demonstrated to be
  effective with diverse youth?

- What type of training will school staff need in order to integrate this programming into their classes?
- What type of training will be needed to ensure that the programming is implemented in a socially just way?

## Tier 2 Stage

Focus on questions related to developing and implementing small group treatment programs and interventions for students who did not respond to tier 1 approaches. Examine evidence-based approaches that could easily be adapted for school-based service delivery such as cognitive behavioral treatment (CBT), in addition to interventions designed specifically for schools. As a part of this stage, progress monitoring and/or follow-up assessments should be conducted to identify students who are not responding to the targeted intervention or who require additional intervention.

- Why did these students not respond to the universal intervention? It will be important to determine if this was due to the student needing more intensive treatment or due to a lack of effective delivery of the intervention (e.g., not delivered consistent with a socially just approach).
- What types of targeted interventions are currently being implemented in my school? Are these programs effectively meeting the needs of the youth who are participating in them? Are the current programs culturally relevant for the students?
- What additional or new targeted interventions will need to be integrated into my school? Have these programs demonstrated effectiveness with diverse populations?
- Who will implement these targeted interventions? What can I do to ensure that others who implement small group interventions are trained in culturally competent practice?

## Tier 3 Stage

Focus on questions related to developing and implementing individualized treatment efforts for students that did not respond to tier two approaches. May include changes to special education referral process and examining ED criteria to be more inclusive.

- Why was the targeted intervention unhelpful for this student? It will be important to determine if this was due to the student needing more intensive treatment or due to a lack of effective delivery of the intervention (e.g., not delivered consistent with a socially just approach).
- What types of individualized treatments are currently available at my school? Are these treatments effectively meeting the needs of each individual student? Are the current treatments culturally relevant for the students participating in the treatment?

- What additional or new individualized treatments are needed to meet the needs of my students? Have these treatments demonstrated effectiveness with diverse populations?
- Who will implement the individualized treatment? What can I do to ensure that others who deliver individualized treatment are trained in culturally competent practice?

## Note

1 In each tier, it is important to consider the role of the school psychologist as a social justice change agent and implications for working with multiple stakeholders: school staff (e.g., professional development training), parents (parent support and/or psychoeducational groups); administration and organizational leadership (raising awareness of problem areas, connections to student learning); universities/training programs (integrating existing partnerships or creating new ones that are mutually beneficial; e.g., using interns to run groups is cost- and time-efficient for schools and provides meaningful learning opportunities for graduate students); partnerships with community health agencies (integrating existing partnerships or creating new ones that are mutually beneficial; e.g., streamlining the referral process for students with more severe behavioral/mental health concerns and inviting outside providers to IEP meetings, this helps with the goal of providing services to those in need and allows schools to provide case management or wraparound services that holistically care for students).

## References

Adelman, H. S., & Taylor, L. (2006). *The school leader's guide to student learning supports: New directions for addressing barriers to learning*. Thousand Oaks, CA: Corwin Press.

Annino, P. (1999). The 1997 amendments to the IDEA: Improving the quality of special education for children with disabilities. *Mental and Physical Disability Law Reporter, 23*, 125–128.

Aratani, Y., Wight, V. R., & Cooper, J. L. (2011). *Racial gaps in early childhood: Socio-emotional health, developmental, and educational outcomes among African-American boys*. New York, NY: National Center for Children in Poverty.

Armbruster, P., & Lichtman, J. (1999). Are school-based mental health services effective? Evidence from 36 inner city schools. *Community Mental Health Journal, 35* (6), 493–504.

Biebel, K., Katz-Levy, K., Nicholson, J., & Williams, V. (2006). *Using Medicaid effectively for children with serious emotional disturbance* (Draft), 1–55.

Brock, S. E., Nickerson, A. B., Reeves, M. A., Jimerson, S. R., Feinberg, T., & Lieberman, R. (2009). *School crisis prevention and intervention: The PREPaRE model*. Bethesda, MD: National Association of School Psychologists.

Brown, M. B. & Bolen, L. M. (2003). School-based health centers: Strategies for meeting the physical and mental health needs of children and families. *Psychology in the Schools, 40* (3), 279–287.

Browne, G., Gafni, A., Roberts, J., Byrne, C., & Majumdar, B. (2004). Effective/efficient mental health programs for school-age children: A synthesis of reviews. *Social Science & Medicine, 58*, 1367–1384.

Budde, S., Mayer, S., Zinn, A., Lippold, M., Avrushin, A., Bromberg, A., et al. (2004). *Residential care in Illinois: Trends and alternatives.* Chicago, IL: Chapin Hall Center for Children at the University of Chicago.

Burns, B., Taube, C., & Taube, J. (1991). Mental health services for adolescents. In U.S. Congress, Office of Technology Assessment (Eds.), *Adolescent health, Volume II: Background and effectiveness of selected prevention and treatment services* (OTA-H-466). Washington, DC: US Government Printing Office.

Burns, B. J., Costello, E. J., Angold, A., Tweed, D., Stangle, D., Farmer, E. M. Z., et al. (1995). Children's mental health service use across service sectors. *Health Affairs, 14,* 148–159.

Calfee, C. S. (2004). The basics of organizing and funding school-based mental health services. In K. E. Robinson (Ed.), *Advances in school-based mental health Interventions: Best practices and program models* (3-1-3-46). Kingston, NJ: Civic Research Institute.

Center for Community Solutions. (2008). School-based mental health tool kit for Cuyahoga County school districts. Cleveland, OH: CCS.

Center for Health and Health Care in Schools. (2008). *School mental health services for the 21st century: Lessons from the District of Columbia school mental health program.* Washington, DC: CHHCS.

Cooper, J. L. (2008). *Towards better behavioral health for children, youth and their families: Financing that supports knowledge.* New York, NY: National Center for Children in Poverty.

Cross, T., Bazron, B., Dennis, K., & Isaacs, M. (1989). *Towards a culturally competent system of care, Volume I.* Washington, DC: Georgetown University Child Development Center, CASSP Technical Assistance Center.

DeKraai, M. B., & Sales, B. D. (1991). Liability in child therapy and research. *Journal of Consulting and Clinical Psychology, 59,* 853–860.

Doll, G. (2008). The dual-factor model of mental health in youth. *School Psychology Review, 37,* 69–73.

Dryfoos, J. G. (1988). School-based health clinics: Three years of experience. *Family Planning Perspectives, 20* (4), 193–200.

Dryfoos, J. G. (1994). *Full-service schools: A revolution in health and social services for children, youth, and families.* San Francisco, CA: Jossey-Bass.

Esbensen, F., Deschenes, E. P., Vogel, R. E., West, J., Arboit, K., & Harris, L. (1996). Active parental consent in school-based research: An examination of ethical and methodological issues. *Evaluation Review, 20,* 737–753.

Evans, S. W. (1999). Mental health services in schools: Utilization, effectiveness, and consent. *Clinical Psychology Review, 19,* 165–178.

Fagan, T. K., & Wise, P. S. (2007). *School psychology past, present, and future* (3rd ed.). Bethesda, MD: National Association of School Psychologists.

Flaherty, L. T., Weist, M. D., & Warner, B. S. (1996). School-based mental health services in the United States: History, current models and needs. *Community Mental Health Journal, 32* (4), 341–352.

Fox, H., & Wicks, L. (1995). Financing care coordination services under Medicaid. In B. Friesen & J. Poertner (Eds.), *From case management to coordination for children with emotional, behavioral, or mental disorders: building on family strengths* (pp. 95–131). Baltimore, MD: Paul Brookes.

Grob, G. N. (2008). The transformation of American psychiatry: From institution to community, 1800–2000. In E. R. Wallace & J. Gach (Eds.), *History of psychiatry and medical psychology:With an epilogue on psychiatry and the mind–body relation* (pp. 533–554). New York, NY: Springer.

Horner, R. H., Albin, R. W., Sprague, J. R., & Todd, A. W. (1999). Positive behavior support for students with severe disabilities. In M. E. Snell & F. Brown (Eds.), *Instruction of students with severe disabilities* (5th ed., pp. 207–243). Upper Saddle River, NJ: Merrill–Prentice Hall.

Jennings, J., Pearson, G., & Harris, M. (2000). Implementing and maintaining school-based mental health services in a large, urban school district. *Journal of School Health, 70,* 201–206.

Johnson, D. B., Malone, P. J., & Hightower, A. D. (1997). Barriers to primary prevention efforts in the schools: Are we the biggest obstacle to the transfer of knowledge? *Applied & Preventive Psychology, 6,* 81–90.

Kataoka, S. H., Zhang, L., & Wells, K. B. (2002). Unmet need for mental health care among US children: Variation by ethnicity and insurance status. *American Journal of Psychiatry, 159,* 1548–1555.

Kutash, K., Duchnowski, A. J., & Lynn, N. (2006). *School-based mental health: An empirical guide for decision-makers.* Tampa, FL: University of South Florida.

Lear, J. G., Gleicher, H. B., St. Germaine, A., & Porter, P. J. (1991). Reorganizing health care for adolescents: The experience of the school-based adolescent health care program. *Journal of Adolescent Health, 12,* 450–458.

Maag, J. W., & Katsiyannis, A. (2010). School-based mental health services: Funding options and issues. *Journal of Disability Policy Studies, 21* (3), 173–180.

Motes, P. S., Melton, G., & Waithe Simmons, W. E. (1999). Ecologically oriented school-based mental health services: Implications for service system reform. *Psychology in the Schools, 36* (5), 391–401.

Mrazek, P. J., & Haggerty, R. J. (Eds.). (1994). *Reducing risks for mental disorders: Frontiers for preventive intervention research.* Washington, DC: National Academy Press.

Nansel, T. R., Overpeck, M., Pilla, R. S., Ruan, W. J., Simons-Morton, B., & Scheidt, P. (2001). Bullying behaviors among US youth: Prevalence and association with psychological adjustment. *Journal of the American Medical Association, 285* (16), 2094–2132.

Nastasi, B. K. (2005). School consultants as change agents in achieving equity for families in public schools. *Journal of Educational and Psychological Consultation, 16* (1&2), 113–125.

National Association of School Psychologists. (2008). *The importance of school mental health services* (Position Statement). Bethesda, MD: NASP.

National Association of School Psychologists. (2010a). *Model for comprehensive and integrated school psychological services.* Retrieved September 1, 2012 from www.nasponline.org/standards/2010standards/2_practicemodel.pdf

National Association of School Psychologists. (2010b). *Standards for graduate school preparation of school psychologists.* Retrieved September 1, 2012 from www.nasponline.org/standards/2010standards/1_graduate_preparation.pdf

National Institute for Health Care Management. (2005). *Children's mental health: An overview and key considerations for health system stakeholders.* Washington, DC: NIHCM.

New Freedom Commission on Mental Health. (2003). Achieving the promise: Transforming mental health care in America. Final Report (DHHS Pub. No. SMA-03-3832) Rockville, MD: US Department of Health and Human Services, Substance Abuse and Mental Health Services Administration.

Paternite, C. E. (2005) School-based mental health program and services: Overview and introduction to the special issue. *Journal of Abnormal Child Psychology, 33* (6), 657–663.

Peacock, G. G., & Collett, B. R. (2010). *Collaborative home/school interventions: Evidence-based solutions for emotional, behavioral, and academic problems.* New York, NY: Guilford Press.

Price, O. A. & Lear, J. G. (2008). *School mental health services for the 21st century: Lessons from the District of Columbia School Mental Health Program.* Washington, DC: Center for Health and Health Care in Schools.

Pumariega, A. J., & Vance, H. R. (1999). School-based mental health services: The foundation of systems of care for children's mental health. *Psychology in the Schools, 36* (5), 371–378.

Rones, M., & Hoagwood, K. (2000). School-based mental health services: A research review. *Clinical Child and Family Psychology Review, 3* (4), 223–241.

Ross, R., & Reichle, J. (2007). Forming interagency partnerships. In C. L. Betz & W. M. Nehring (Eds.), *Promoting health care transitions for adolescents with special needs and disabilities* (pp. 235–254). Baltimore, MD: Brooks.

Santiago, E., Ferrara, J., & Blank, M. (2008). A full-service school fulfills its promise. *Poverty and Learning, 65* (7), 44–47.

Severson, H., & Biglan, A. (1989). Rationale for the use of passive consent in smoking prevention research: Politics, policy, and pragmatics. *Preventive Medicine, 18,* 267–279.

Shaw, R. S., Kelly, D. P., Joost, J. C., & Parker-Fisher, S. J. (1995). School-linked and school-based health services: A renewed call for collaboration between school psychologists and medical professionals. *Psychology in the Schools, 32,* 190–201.

Slavin, R. E., Karweit, N. L., & Wasik, B. A. (Eds.). (1994). *Preventing early school failure: Research, policy, and practice.* Boston, MA: Allyn and Bacon.

Stroul, B. A. & Friedman, R. M. (1986). A system of care for children and youth with severe emotional disturbances (revised edition). Washington, DC: Georgetown University Child Development Center, CASSP Technical Assistance Center.

Strozer, J., Juszczak, L., & Ammerman, A. (2010). *2007–2008 National School-Based Health Care Census.* Washington, DC: National Assembly on School-Based Health Care.

US Department of Health and Human Services. (1999). *Mental health: A report of the Surgeon General.* Rockville, MD: US Department of Health and Human Services.

US Department of Health and Human Services (2001). *Mental health: Culture, race, and ethnicity*—A supplement to *Mental health: A report of the surgeon general.* Rockville, MD: US Department of Health and Human Services.

US Department of Health and Human Services (2011). *HHS announces new investment in school-based health centers* [Press release]. Retrieved September 1, 2012 from www.hhs.gov/news/press/2011pres/07/20110714a.html

Walrath, C., Bruns, E. J., Anderson, K. A., Glass-Seigel, M., & Weist, M. (2004). Understanding expanded school mental health services in Baltimore City. *Behavior Modification, 28,* 472–490.

Weist, M. D., & Ghuman, H. S. (2002). Principles behind the proactive delivery of mental health services to youth where they are. In H. S. Ghuman, M. D. Weist, & R. M. Sarles (Eds.), *Providing mental health services to youth where they are: School- and community-based approaches.* New York, NY: Taylor & Francis.

Weist, M. D., Goldstein, A., Morris, L., & Bryant, T. (2003). Integrating expanded school mental health programs and school-based health centers. *Psychology in the Schools, 40* (3), 297–308.

Weist, M. D., Myers, C. P., Hastings, E., Ghuman, H., & Han, Y. (1999). Psychosocial functioning of youth receiving mental health services in the schools vs. the community mental health centers. *Community Mental Health Journal, 35* (5), 379–389.

Weisz, J., Sandler, I., Durlak, J., & Anton, B. (2005). Promoting and protecting youth mental health through evidence-based prevention and treatment. *American Psychologist, 60* (6), 628–648.

Witmer, L. (1907/1996). Clinical psychology. *American Psychologist, 51,* 248–251.

# fifteen
# Family, School, and Community Partnerships

## Janine M. Jones

In the age of performance-based assessment and academic achievement, we have high expectations of our teachers and schools. Additionally, school personnel hold a significant amount of responsibility for the care and well-being of our children. However, over the past 20 years there has been an increased emphasis on the importance of partnering with families and communities to foster better educational outcomes for children in schools. Ecological systems theory (Bronfenbrenner, 1992) is among the perspectives that help researchers recognize the family and community as significant influences on the development of children and adolescents. This theory also provides a foundation for research and clinical work on cultural diversity, cultural competence, multiculturalism, and social justice. All of these constructs are directly connected. According to Shriberg et al. (2008), social justice is derived from the earlier scholarship on multiculturalism. As defined in North (2006) and also in Chapter 1 of this book, social justice is a framework that is based on the belief that all individuals and groups have a right to fairness and respect and are entitled to the same resources that are available to others. If school psychologists are to function using this framework, then it makes perfect sense for school psychologists to lead the efforts in advocating for and empowering families to seek equity in schools (Pearrow & Pollack, 2009). As such, school psychologists can attempt to identify "institutional and systemic obstacles" that inhibit opportunities for equity in schools (Shriberg et al., 2008, p. 465). By identifying barriers and advocating for families, communication can be reorganized in a way that optimally bridges the gap between schools, families, and communities and leads to a true "systems" perspective with opportunities for shared responsibility. As a result, the school can be restructured into a collaborative community that operates through a social justice framework. Thinking systemically then can be considered synonymous with acting as an agent of social justice (Shriberg et al., 2008).

This chapter will focus on how a social justice framework applies as an ideal foundation for collaboration between families, schools, and communities. In order to apply this framework to collaboration, we must recognize the historical context of collaboration in schools and how the philosophy has changed over time. Placed within the contemporary context, this chapter reviews barriers to collaboration such as fragmentation, poor infrastructure, lack of trust, and the lack of recognizing differences as strengths. Once common barriers are identified, the chapter shifts to identify key aspects of model collaboration programs, including understanding culturally embedded values, approaches to communication, and applying these characteristics to understand the sociocultural context. Using the characteristics of model collaboration programs, specific strategies are identified that can be used both at the systems level and the individual level. Systems-level strategies are targeted toward school administrators and team leaders who have responsibility for collaboration programs. Individual-level strategies are designed for all personnel within the school system including school psychologists, school counselors, teachers, and administrators as individuals. To begin, we will focus on how the construct of collaboration has changed over time.

## Historical Developments in Collaboration: A Shift in Thinking

Historically, teachers have been expected to be the experts in educating children. Teachers have been pressured to know everything about their content area for the developmental age they serve. When teachers struggle in teaching content to students, blame is often placed on external factors such as the child's social, economic, and/or cultural background (Dryfoos, 1994). The top-down bureaucratic nature of the educational system has perpetuated this perspective, so little investment has historically been made to solve problems collaboratively. The original paradigm of thinking was often referred to as the *separation* paradigm (Amatea, 2009). Policy-makers perpetuated the separation paradigm in the 1960s by making no provision or requirement for interacting with parents. In fact, in the Elementary and Secondary Education Act of 1965, educators were expected to provide "compensatory" education whereby the school environment was to mitigate the negative experiences of children from disadvantaged backgrounds (Amatea, 2009). This shift in thinking was referred to as a *remediation* paradigm. The remediation paradigm was the beginning of legislation that included the language for inclusive participation in programs designed for children with less-than-optimal educational opportunities. In the remediation paradigm, teachers are the leaders. They have the power and parents are passively involved in the school. Passive involvement includes activities such as responding to teacher requests, attending conferences, and sending notes back to school. The literature at this point was focused on parent "involvement", rather than "engagement" and the idea of collaborating with parents was nonexistent.

Now, we are in a new era—a third paradigm shift. As part of this shift, some of the more progressive school systems began to recognize the added value of shared leadership and the value of parents collaborating with schools. Although this shift has not translated fully to the practices of the majority of school systems, the shift in the literature is apparent. With the newest paradigm shift to *collaboration*, school staff members recognize the importance of seeing students and their families as collaborators in the educational process. In this model, teachers, parents, and students are all involved in decision making. Instead of taking an outsider's view of family life, educators now adopt a social justice perspective—they see the ways that family, schools, and communities collectively interact to influence the development of children. An example of a collaboration approach to interacting with families would be an environment where the families, teachers, and students are all involved at different levels. Take for example a teacher-guided activity such as a family math night. Using the separation model, the family math night might look like a traditional back-to-school night where parents are sitting in a cafeteria, auditorium, or classroom and teachers are instructing parents on how to do specific math activities at home. Then parents are left to try the skills out on their own. The collaboration model would be administered differently. Using the collaboration model, the students can be the experts in the math activity. While the teacher may guide and structure the activity, he or she can involve the children by having the children teach others the math skills at different workstations while the teacher and parents act as coaches. This approach engages parents and students in the process where active two-way communication and collaboration is at the core. In a socially just world, families are not just "involved" in schools, they are instead true collaborators with shared responsibility for outcomes.

By encouraging collaboration between stakeholders in the school community, equal emphasis can be placed on the three *spheres of influence*. Epstein (2001) proposed the spheres of influence model as a means for understanding the sociocultural factors impacting children in schools. The model depicts three overlapping circles with each circle representing the family, school, and community. According to Epstein, more overlap between the circles correlates with a higher level of achievement for students. Through her analysis of these spheres, Epstein was able to recognize that the overlap between the circles was usually smaller for ethnic minority families and those from disadvantaged backgrounds. Low overlap correlates with lower family involvement at the school and subsequent lower achievement. This is consistent with other studies that have shown that family involvement with schools is lower for families with high mobility, lower socioeconomic status, and from minority backgrounds (Kohl, Lengua, & McMahon, 2000). This means that significant effort must be made to increase the overlap between family, school, and community with families from diverse backgrounds.

There is a considerable amount of literature that addresses the factors associated with family involvement in schools. Henderson and Mapp (2002) critiqued the literature that indicated that minority and low-income families were less interested in being involved in schools. In fact, they noted that these families were reportedly more involved with their children at home than at school. Thus, the findings from studies that assessed family involvement were often limited by only assessing school-based activities. By not including home-based activities, an element of the overlap is missed. Epstein (2001) noted that some of the factors associated with lack of overlap were cultural differences, language barriers, time, and perception of influence.

## Barriers to Collaboration

School psychologists are usually trained to work as systems change agents and integrate the needs of families in all aspects of the school psychology practice. As part of training, programs should prepare trainees to identify and address the barriers to effective collaboration. Without this knowledge it is difficult to bring the goal of effective collaboration to fruition. Thus, with a realistic frame of reference for collaboration and an understanding of the contemporary context, a school psychologist or administrator will be able to prepare for and prevent barriers to collaboration from disrupting the development of a family–school collaboration framework.

There are often significant barriers that must be overcome to facilitate the process of integrating family, school, and community. Fragmentation, lack of infrastructure, failure to recognize differences as strengths, and differing expectations are among the barriers to collaboration. While these factors alone would not cause a collaboration initiative to fail, the lack of recognition that they are factors *is* problematic.

## Fragmentation

The problem of fragmentation occurs when the family–school collaboration is not well planned. An example of fragmentation is when there are policies in place that mandate collaboration, but there is no clear guide on roles and responsibilities, or how to do it. While schools may aspire to be inclusive of families and community, if there is only one individual devoted to the cause, the initiative is fragmented and will fail. To reduce fragmentation, a team approach should be implemented. The team should be inclusive of all stakeholders in the collaboration, including families. See the systems-level techniques that follow later in the chapter for more detail on appointing teams for the collaboration program.

## Lack of Infrastructure

Collaborative partnerships require significant investment from the system and all of its stakeholders. There is a need to have a vision for the collaboration. When creating the vision, it cannot be one leader within the organization designing the vision; it must be a community of people representing all of the spheres of influence. One way to develop the vision is to formulate a well-rounded steering committee that has representation from the family, school, and community. This committee would be charged with designing the vision, garnering support and perspectives from collaborators, translating the vision into policy, developing the strategic plan, and measuring outcomes during implementation of the plan (Adelman & Taylor, 2007). Once the infrastructure is in place, there is a community of individuals that are invested in moving the initiative forward and holding everyone accountable to positive outcomes.

## Failure to Recognize Differences as Strengths

There is a negative connotation associated with the word "difference." One usually thinks of solving a problem or the desire to "reconcile our differences." This is akin to the theory of color-blind racism (Carr, 1997), where the perspective of "sameness" is considered the path to equality. Along the same vein, using "school curricula that explicitly or implicitly promote a 'common community' view of U.S. society, which are based on an idealized Euro-American immigrant model of being, mask our racially and economically divided social reality" (North, 2006, p. 517). However, in the context of collaboration within a social justice framework, differences can enrich the outcomes for people by increasing the diversity of perspectives. According to Lynch and Baker (2005), equal respect and recognition is "about appreciating or accepting differences rather than merely tolerating them" (pp. 132–133). Common differences that may be misidentified as barriers are: sociocultural background characteristics, language spoken, time, and perception of influence. Sociocultural background differences include differences related to power, status, and orientation (Adelman & Taylor, 2007). There is a well-established culture of schools and many families and communities don't understand the culture. Similarly, individuals within the school culture may not understand all of the individual cultures of the families within the school. Thus, there is likely to be a disconnect between the parties and it is easier to stay within a comfort zone than to reach out and learn a different perspective.

## Different Expectations for Instructional Style and Child Behavior

Another barrier to success for collaboration programs is the lack of a shared worldview about styles of instruction and expectations of behavior. When worldviews are congruent, positive outcomes are easier to obtain—when incongruent, there is room for frustration and disappointment. Educators need to recognize that a shared worldview is unlikely in multicultural environments, thus alleviating the expectation that everyone will inherently be on the colloquial "same page." When one does not assume any common denominator in beliefs, the implication is that everyone within the system is open to learning from another perspective.

One of the classic areas of misunderstanding involves student behavior. For example, some ethnic minority children exhibit *verve*—a cultural style where expressiveness, movement, and seeking of high levels of physical stimuli are common characteristics (Stevenson, Winn, Walker-Barnes, & Coard, 2005; Tyler, Boykin, Miller, & Hurley, 2006). In school settings, researchers have measured verve by defining it as a preference for moving from one activity to the next, and the flexibility to move between activities as a way of learning new constructs simultaneously (Sankofa, Hurley, Allen, & Boykin, 2005). This behavioral style may be inconsistent with an instructor's teaching style and behaviors could be interpreted as a lack of readiness to learn or lack of interest in educational activities. When an educator interprets this behavioral style as a problem, parents may not understand why the behavior is a problem, or purport that the behavior is "not an issue at home." Educators with knowledge of verve would have a stronger ability to communicate the concerns or interpret the behavior with less miscommunication.

Similarly, in other ethnic minority communities, "speaking up" in class is not a shared value. There is a belief in some cultures that talking interferes with your ability to learn new information (Li, 2005). Talking is not seen as a process for understanding new content—rather, talking should be reserved for communicating after the new material is understood. The following case example demonstrates how this cultural misunderstanding can affect a student in school.

---

Min is a student of Chinese descent whose family immigrated from China two years ago. She speaks both Mandarin and English while her parents and grandparents all speak Mandarin. In school, Min is a quiet yet high-performing student. Her progress reports consistently include high grades academically, but low participation grades. The comment on every progress report is consistent, "Min is a wonderful student, but she never raises her hand, or speaks up in class. I would like to hear her voice more and would like her to be more confident."

In this example, Min is being penalized for her lack of participation, despite the fact that she is a fantastic student academically. Not only is there a lack of understanding of the cultural context, but also a misinterpretation of why Min is not speaking up in class. If a school psychologist was consulting with teachers, they could provide information about the cultural context for Chinese Americans and advise the teacher to give Min a participation grade relative to her cultural context rather than comparing to American peers.

---

For educators who operate under the assumption that class participation is best measured by those who speak up the most, cultural misunderstandings are likely for students whose families do not share the same worldview. Thus, developing an understanding of expectations and meaning of behavior is crucial to collaboration efforts.

## Lack of Trust

There is a well-researched literature base revealing that families of ethnic minor-ity cultural backgrounds report feeling misunderstood, disenfranchised, and that their cultural values are not respected in schools (Cross, 2003; Freng, Freng, & Moore, 2006). Due to denigration of educational opportunities, discrimination, and/or lack of integration of cultural values into the mainstream school setting, some ethnic minority families have developed mistrust of the educational system. In order to break down the pattern of mistrust, numerous healthy interactions must occur for families to "unlearn" mistrust and re-establish trust.

## Key Characteristics of Successful Collaboration Programs

Although there are numerous perceived barriers to successful collaboration, edu-cators and systems that are prepared for potential barriers and recognize why they exist will be in the best position to develop a sustainable model for a social justice model of collaboration. Authentic family–school collaborations are grounded in respectful alliances among school personnel, families, and community groups that include open communication, sharing of power, and relationship building as core values (Auerbach, 2010). Figure 15.1 describes essential components and strategic approaches to successful collaboration programs.

Clarke, Sheridan, and Woods (2010) outline three key elements for healthy family–school relationships: *trust, sensitivity, and equality.* Trust between the indi-viduals within the system is a core element that helps sustain healthy relationships. Within a social justice framework, there is an inherent value for mutual respect

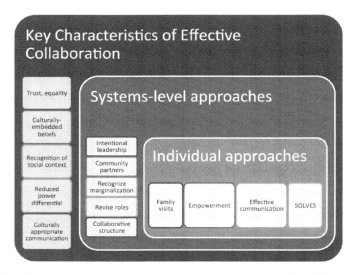

**FIGURE 15.1.** Essential components and strategies for successful collaborations.

and fairness, so trust is one way to operationalize socially just relationships. The trust between parents and teachers has been directly linked with favorable outcomes including student attendance and student achievement (Byrk & Schneider, 2002). Sensitivity to cultural beliefs and values is a second important element to healthy family–school relationships. As included in the definition of social justice offered in Chapter 1, families should feel respected. One way to demonstrate respect for family cultural beliefs is to acknowledge and integrate the social, cultural, historical, and linguistic experiences families bring into the school setting (Harry, Kalyanpur, & Day, 1999). Building bridges across cultures is critical to making a difference in the lives of children in schools. Finally, when equality is collectively sought in school systems, there is less conflict among families and school personnel. In fact, Lake and Billingsley (2000) found that when there is an imbalance of power, there is increased conflict in family–school relationships. Even though families enter the school with less power than the school personnel, the way that the school structures communication and collaboration can help reduce the power differentials. From a social justice perspective, one must recognize the power difference, acknowledge the differences overtly with families, and challenge the structures that sustain the power differential.

## Culturally Embedded Beliefs and Values

Successful family–school collaborations recognize the culturally embedded beliefs and values that exist. Not only do children and families bring cultural values to the school setting, but there are also cultural values that influence the operation of schools. For instance, institutions of education have the expectation that teachers lead every child through academic progress and their guidance is tied to educational goals and outcomes for the grade. Students who are not progressing successfully are compared to those other students who are succeeding in academic settings. This comparative view of students is the foundation for the "deficit" approach to thinking about students and learning outcomes. In the culturally responsive education realm, the comparison of one student's progress to another is the operationalization of individualism—a Eurocentric worldview. If educators recognize that the culture of most schools includes this paradigm, they may move closer to true collaboration.

As a principle for family support in schools, Grant and Ray (2010) noted that successful family involvement requires programs that affirm and strengthen families' cultural, racial and linguistic identities. Similarly, Hill (2010) indicates that the way the family and school develop a mutual understanding is a process of socialization. Similar to the construct of acculturation (the process by which a person changes after exposure to a different culture), shared beliefs and understandings can lead to positive changes in the family–school interactions. When parent/family and school beliefs intersect, positive socialization occurs (Hill, 2010).

One culturally embedded belief that is consistent across many communities of color is the *collectivistic* cultural worldview (Amatea, 2009). Collectivism is a way of thinking, knowing, and interacting with others. This belief is common among many ethnic minority groups such as people who are Asian, Latino/a, Native American/American Indian, and of African descent (Jones, 2009; Paniagua, 2005). The ideals of this orientation include operating with a sense of "we" rather than an emphasis on the self. In Trumbull, Rothstein-Fish, Greenfield, and Quiroz (2001), the authors identify the significant level of contrasting values between individualistic and collectivistic cultures. A core individualistic value is competition whereas a collectivistic value is cooperation. In the same way, people with an individualistic worldview value assertiveness while people with a collectivistic worldview value modesty and patience. Additionally, in collectivistic cultures, hierarchy, rank, and status are important variables for determining how to interact with others, while in individualistic cultures egalitarianism is most important. Collectivism may be a foundational value and a key influence for the family's perspective of their role in education. The following case example highlights how cultural values can create a barrier to collaboration that is based on a misinterpretation of meaning.

Javier, a student from Ecuador, has been in the US for four years. His family is traditional and align closely with Latin American cultural values. Javier has been receiving frequent notes home that indicate that he is putting minimal effort into his assignments. His teacher is sending assignments back with the note "redo" at the top of the page with no instruction on how to complete it again. The parents review the teacher's comments and sit Javier down each night and tell him to redo the assignment, but Javier says that he thought he did the assignment correctly and doesn't know what his teacher wants him to do differently. His father replies, "It doesn't matter what you think. Your teacher knows best. Just do what she says."

Here, Javier's father recognizes teachers as authority figures and holds the perspective that the "teacher knows best." With this belief, he will not challenge any of the statements that the teacher presents to them, nor will he allow Javier to do so. Javier's father is deferring to the teacher as an authority and as a form of respect. The teacher, on the other hand, may be seeking assistance from the parent indirectly. This lack of interaction may lead to misunderstandings and misinterpretations of the parent's values. Often a lack of feedback from a parent is interpreted as a lack of investment. A school-based professional who is operating within a social justice framework will recognize the cultural value and attempt to empower the parent by acknowledging the parent as an equal contributor because they, too, have expertise and knowledge about their child. Along the same lines, if the teacher is to criticize the child, a parent from a collectivistic culture may experience shame because the child is a representative of the family system, not just themselves. In both interactions, the teacher must be attuned to the cultural factors that may influence how the parent perceives the teacher's role.

A desire for harmony and conflict-avoidance guide the behavior of people from collectivistic cultures, but conflict is accepted in individualistic cultures as part of the process of survival. With these differences, it is clear that intentional behavior is required to build shared responsibility for educational outcomes. Schools in the United States are typically operating from an individualistic cultural framework. There is emphasis on competition, individual achievement, and independent success. However, during the past 15 years, culturally responsive instruction has become a more prevalent trend in education (Banks & Banks, 2004). With this contemporary model of instruction, collectivism is integrated into the dissemination of information. When a model of culturally responsive instruction is adopted, this is consistent with a social justice framework. Culturally responsive instruction is an example of an intentional effort to respect core cultural differences. This type of instruction has the potential to lead to successful, socially just family–school collaborations.

## Communication: Structure and Timing

In collectivistic cultures, the personal relationship is far more important than time. Thus, collaborative communication between school and families should occur intentionally and with the ultimate goal of preserving the relationship. As a result, the timing of the interaction is important. When school officials (including administrators and teachers) approach a parent with criticism and/or advice on managing a child's behavior, a common response is defensiveness. Receiving unexpected information at a time that communication is not expected can lead to anxiety, frustration, and defensiveness. In this situation, the family member is potentially being given information that they did not request and there may be a limited opportunity for dialogue and context. Hill (2010) explains that the timing of information is important because families are more receptive to information when it is received in context. Thus, discussions that are initiated by a family member and linked to the context of the communication are more likely to be understood and responded to in a productive way. Information should be encapsulated within two-way communication and not only provided in the language the parent speaks, but also in a form that it can easily be received (telephone or in person). For example, some educators have initiated the habit of making positive phone calls to the family about their students. Imagine if these conversations were facilitated in a collaborative fashion. A one-way communication would include the teacher informing the family that their child is doing well in school and perhaps share a story about something positive that has happened. However, a collaborative approach to communication might include the teacher asking the family member how they are feeling about the school year so far, how they see the child changing and growing in the new year, and adding additional positive feedback to the family's knowledge about the child's success in the classroom. In this same conversation, the educator can directly inquire about ways to ensure that the family's culture is recognized in the child's behavior, and academic and social experiences. Through cultural sharing (Miller, Arthur-Stanley, & Lines, 2012), two-way communication can occur between the family and teacher. This inter-action will allow the family to see that their opinion is not only encouraged but valued and that the teacher is noticing the "whole" child and the family system.

## Understanding the Sociocultural Context

As discussed previously, individualism and collectivism are contrasting world-views that may be operating simultaneously in a family–school collaboration. By adopting the collectivism perspective, family–school collaborations make sense! Collaborations fit the frame of the collectivistic worldview and offer room for shared decision-making and mutual understanding. There is more focus on favo-rable outcomes for the collective (the group) rather than for independence and autonomy. Trumbull et al. (2001) describe the challenge of collectivism as a con-flict for Latino(a) families when individualism and competitiveness are empha-sized in schools. As described, inherent to the design of American education is independence and individual personal achievement rather than group-oriented success. When a child enters the school where the "good of the group" is a higher value than individual achievement, the success of that particular child may be hin-dered by sacrifices that they make. For example, on a group project, a child from a collectivistic culture may not strive to lead the group if they feel that their talents may outshine the abilities of others. The cultural value of collectivism could over-ride the child's desire for personal achievement so that others in the group could shine equally.

## Systems-Level Approaches to Collaborative Partnerships

With an understanding of key components of collaboration partnerships, school psychologists can be key players on leadership teams who aspire to develop strong family–school partnerships. Such collaborative partnerships cannot be developed in isolation. The entire system needs to be structured around the model—a way of integrating all stakeholders in successful outcomes. Thus, systems-level approaches must be employed in addition to individuals having responsibility for components within their professional roles. Since many of the systems-level approaches involve management-level decisions, school psychologists can coach administrators on these processes. This section addresses the systems-level approaches and is fol-lowed by individual-level strategies within a collaboration framework.

## Starting with a Collaborative Structure

The first contact with families should be structured in an inclusive way. Often a back-to-school night is the first point of contact between the school and families.

Although holding such events is common practice, the design and implementation of the event sends a message to families about how the school anticipates parent participation to occur.

A traditional back-to-school night may include parents attending the event without their children. Parents may be sitting in the cafeteria, auditorium, or a large room with chairs facing the leadership and teachers. At the front of the room, the school administrators and teachers may be seated facing the parents and doing presentations about the goals, curricula, and plans for the academic year. This is an excellent model for disseminating information to parents and for showing families the expertise of the school staff. For some parents, this model builds their confidence in the school that they have chosen for their children. It also shows that the family can expect the school personnel to "do their job." This model does not, however, do anything to build shared responsibility for educational outcomes. It models the expectation for parents to rely on the decisions of the school personnel (the experts) to ensure that their child will succeed.

A collaborative back-to-school night would be structured differently—from the physical setup to the facilitation of dialogue among its participants. Imagine a round table set up for all participants where every table includes a combination of school personnel and parents and the leadership at the front of the room includes an administrator, teacher, and parent. The leaders of the back-to-school night could act as facilitators rather than individuals to disseminate information. They could model for the "table teams" the expectations for open communication and shared vision. In their teams, teachers, parents, and staff could discuss goals and expectations of the child/family/school. These expectations can include operationalizing roles, goals, and processes for decision-making. The small group discussions could be documented and compiled for all stakeholders, with all ideas placed for a vote within the larger school community. Since this process can be time-consuming, the majority vote likely will have to apply, but the message that will be given to families is that they have a voice and can influence the process. This also gives school systems a way to learn about the cultural values of all constituents within the school community. A similar process could be facilitated with the students to help give them ownership over the rules and regulations of the school.

For example, in a multicultural private school in the Northwest, the students were required to wear uniforms. The uniform policy was particularly stringent, with only one color option for shirts and pants. After years of rumblings from the students about the uniform, the administration asked the students in the middle school to come up with a process for gaining feedback from all students and determine a solution that would be satisfactory to everyone. The students were given the time and resources to lead an all-school discussion, collect data from fellow students and their parents, analyze the results, and present the findings to the administration of the school. The end result of the process was a revised uniform design that included five color options for shirts, two options for outerwear, and several styles of pants and skirts. The students were proud of the outcome and took ownership of the new uniform policy. The school leadership provided an opportunity for students to work collectively to identify opinions, talk with their families, and have their desires considered. They demonstrated respect for the students and their families, and the process for discussion alone modeled a cultural value—collectivism. As a result, this exemplifies how collaboration through a social justice framework can lead to favorable outcomes and increased engagement.

## Appoint an Intentional Leader or Leadership Team

Successful collaboration programs cannot be effective without leadership. The leadership of the initiative should be knowledgeable regarding the potential barriers, the culturally embedded values of the community, school, and families, and the goals of the organization. All processes should occur intentionally with family, school, and community input at every level. All individuals involved should strive to develop and maintain a school environment that is conducive to collaboration. The individuals may begin with principles of social justice and guide school personnel through true collaboration—a leadership approach that is literally built on shared power and equality at all levels. The leader or leadership team can hold individuals within the system accountable for implementation of family-centered processes as well. As a leader of the collaboration, administrative support should be provided for the leadership team and this support can be a contact point for all individuals within the collaboration collective.

## Effective Engagement with Community Partners

There are community-based organizations that have clear understandings of community and family needs. Many of these organizations are designed to provide resources to families as well as schools. If the leader of the collaboration initiative is effectively engaging with the community partners, they will have immediate awareness of how to connect with diverse communities and to demonstrate respect for cultural values. An example of effective engagement with the community is building a team of cultural brokers—individuals from diverse backgrounds that can be contacted as community partners to consult on issues of culture (Jones, 2011). Cultural brokers, also referred to as cultural ambassadors (Banks & Banks, 2004; Christenson & Sheridan, 2001), can be resources to the school by having knowledge of cultural values that are in conflict with traditional school roles. They can assist the school in designing a culturally inclusive environment where families feel connected and respected. Cultural brokers may also assist the school personnel in accessing resources in the community for the specific population that is served in the setting. Visible community partners send the message to families that the school personnel are seeking to support not only the child but also the system that the child lives within.

## Recognizing Parent Marginalization

Traditional approaches to family engagement may seem optimal to school personnel, but from the family's perspective, the opportunities may perpetuate the cycle of marginalization and may not feel like collaboration. Cooper, Riehl, and Hasan (2010) noted that activities such as "open houses, parent teacher conferences, and fundraisers" may feel condescending to families when all other interactions with the school are in the context of accepting feedback and recommendations from teachers regarding their child's behavior. This pattern of interaction is an example of a "delegation model of school family relationships" (Swap, 1993). The delegation model perpetuates the top-down approach to leadership where schools reign at the top of the hierarchy. This model privileges upper middle-class families who share the values of the American educational system and have the skills needed to effectively navigate the bureaucratic structure of such schools (Cooper, 2009). If school personnel are using a social justice lens to design family–school engagement, they will recognize the structures that are in place which inhibit connections and foster further marginalization.

## Revising Roles and Responsibilities

Ladwig (2009) wrote about the structure of interactions between families and school personnel in the context of educational planning for students with special needs. However, the foundational principles of her work apply to all culturally diverse settings. As shown in Table 15.1, she compares family-centered roles versus traditional roles for families in schools.

In the family-centered model, parents are seen as experts with respect to the needs of their child and family. As an expert, parents can identify priorities for helping support the child with other team members. Parents are considered an asset to the team in this model because they are not simply providers of information for others to make determinations regarding the needs of the child. Parents are expected to be decision makers. Based on their knowledge and experience with the child, the

**TABLE 15.1** Family Roles and Responsibilities

| Family-Centered Roles | Traditional Roles |
|---|---|
| • Parents as experts<br>• Decisions are informed by experience<br>• Parents are partners with equal status<br>• Parents are advocates | • Parents are resources to school personnel<br>• Parents make decisions based on options presented<br>• Parents are trainees<br>• Parents are therapeutic agents<br>• The child or family can be the source of the problem |

Adapted from Ladwig (2009).

family-centered model relies on the parent's ability to decide what is best for the child and family in all areas. This is in contrast to the traditional model where parents are encouraged to make decisions, but only to make a choice based on options offered by other professionals. Parents in the family-centered model are equal partners and have equal status on the team. In this model, there is no power hierarchy that assumes that some individuals have to compromise their values for the preservation of the child in the school setting. Thus, parents are not on the team as "trainees"—rather they are full-fledged meaningful participants in the process at every level. Finally, with a family-centered model, parents are advocates for their children. They participate at all levels, including influencing school policy.

## Individual Approaches to Foster Collaboration

The preceding section focused on approaches that can be used by administrators to structure the school interactions with family and community in a collaborative way. Changes to the structure should occur not only at the systems level, but also at the level of the individual. Individual personnel must take personal responsibility for integrating collaborative strategies in their everyday roles. School psychologists, for example, can utilize individual collaboration techniques in providing counseling services, assessments, and consultation with teachers and administrators. School psychologists can also hold teams accountable for being collaborative. Similarly, teachers individually should also interact with families in a collaborative fashion. The following are some approaches that school personnel can use for better family–school collaboration.

### Family Visits

Getting to know families can be a challenge with the start of the school year and the responsibility of navigating numerous new relationships all at once. Family visits have increasingly become a standard of practice for teachers in diverse communities. Teachers should avoid referring to family visits as "home visits" (Kyle, McIntyre, Miller, & Moore, 2002) due to the negative association with Child Protective Services. If families perceive a family visit as potentially punitive, they will avoid participation.

Conducting family visits allows for the school personnel to initiate a collaborative process within the family context. The appointment can be scheduled at the convenience of the family and all members of the family system can participate. For multigenerational families, this approach is extremely respectful of the cultural context. School personnel can go to the family with questions rather than answers. They can learn about the student's personal characteristics from the parent's perspective and through dialogue rather than a one-way questionnaire. One way to structure the dialogue and make room for learning the cultural values of the families and external community is through "cultural sharing conversations" (Lines, Miller, & Arthur-Stanley, 2011). Cultural sharing conversations may include learning about customs, beliefs, rituals, and daily routines that contribute to a collective "fund of knowledge" (Gonzalez & Moll, 2002). These conversations can help build insights into the values of the members within the system and result in bridge building. As part of the family visits, school personnel can begin to gather basic knowledge about the cultural dynamics that govern the everyday lives of the families within the school. This model provides the perfect opportunity for asking about the strengths, resources, areas of concern, and interests (Amatea, 2009).

School psychologists can also use family visits as a way to work collaboratively with families. For example, it is sometimes challenging to include families in counseling and assessments that school psychologists provide. The nature of working in schools creates a context that implies that families are not to be included because they are at work during the day. Thus, school psychologists should make efforts to be inclusive that go beyond getting a parent's permission for their child to participate in counseling or an assessment. Through family visits, a school psychologist can hold occasional family counseling sessions, ensure that families are aware of their rights and roles in an assessment process, and use the contact to develop a relationship with the family and offer support for other non-academic needs.

## Empower the Family

When teachers initiate relationship building with the family visits, the implication is that the family can be encouraged to advocate for themselves throughout the academic year. The social justice framework allows the teacher to recognize that there may be differing perspectives on the responsibility of the parent and the parent's role. Thus, the encouragement to express opinions and advocate for the child's needs may be the opposite viewpoint. The teacher can share with the family processes for communication and the desire for an open door policy (Jones, 2011). When the expectation for open communication is outside of the cultural norm, it is crucial for school personnel to be responsive to the feedback. For some families, stepping outside the cultural norm is a risk, so when that occurs, school personnel should listen carefully and incorporate ideas in ways that demonstrate the family's leadership in the school setting. This includes giving credit to the families for the ideas, posting and marketing ideas publicly, and implementing the plans in a collaborative way (e.g., including other families in the implementation of new ideas). Using this style, families will be encouraged to participate and connect at all levels of the organization. Empowerment can most easily occur through open and effective communication.

## Open and Effective Communication

As a primary component of empowerment, open communication is necessary. Through the use of active listening skills and bidirectional communication, collaborative relationships can develop and be maintained. Using active listening skills, facilitating bidirectional communication, and conducting collaborative family–school meetings all provide opportunities for open communication to occur.

## Active listening skills

Active listening skills include techniques where a person makes intentional efforts to "hear" another person. Active listening can take the form of nonverbal signals such as nodding in agreement, shaking one's head in disagreement, smiling, or hand gestures. Nonverbal communication occurs in a variety of ways. For example, eye contact and proximity are two very important aspects of nonverbal communication. These may vary from culture to culture. Thus, there should be awareness of cultural communication styles and this awareness should guide teachers into styles of communication with families. If a teacher has awareness of cultural styles for nonverbal communication, it is less likely that there will be misunderstandings and misinterpretation of meaning. For instance, if a teacher is attempting to do the active listening technique of offering direct eye contact with a family member while they are speaking, in the dominant culture—this is clearly communicating, "I am listening to you." However, to expect the same in return may not be appropriate. In some communities of color, direct eye contact when listening is considered rude and disrespectful (Sue & Sue, 2008). Thus, a family member looking away while the teacher is speaking is a culturally appropriate way to show active listening.

Similarly, there are culturally guided rules to proximity. In some cultures, interacting with another person by close physical contact is a sign of connecting and valuing the interpersonal relationship. In other cultures, physical distance between people is a way to honor and respect the other person's cultural values. Take for instance the values in some religious communities where men are prohibited from touching women who are not their wives. This includes handshakes and other impersonal physical contact. To replace the familiar with the unfamiliar (e.g. bowing the head, placing hands together in honor of the other person) would be an appropriate way to communicate with the family in a culturally responsive way. These are just a few examples of ways that school personnel can demonstrate respect for others through nonverbal communication.

## Bidirectional communication

While using active listening in one-to-one interactions facilitates open and effective communication, another goal that should be addressed is to encourage bidirectional communication. By opening with family visits and empowering parents, school personnel are structuring the environment for good bidirectional communication. This type of communication encourages open dialogue between families and schools. Families are encouraged to initiate contact, request meetings, participate in decision-making, and grow in the school community. To make this happen, school personnel should seek family input frequently and at nontraditional times. Traditional times for communication include parent–teacher conferences or curriculum nights, but nontraditional can take a variety of forms. Newsletters are an excellent way of distributing information from the school to the families; however, that is a one-way form of communication. As a way to change from one-way communication to two-way, families could be encouraged to contribute to the newsletter and share information about family roles in the school. Using this approach, families can present issues for discussion and make invitations for feedback from other parents. Feedback must be requested through multiple forms. Feedback cannot be limited to coming to a meeting at the school, but must also include numerous opportunities for written communication that families can choose from (e.g., email, paper ballot, online surveys). In addition to written communication, verbal communication can be used (e.g., voice mail messages, direct phone calls, school meetings). Having multiple methods for collecting information increases the likelihood of participation and the subsequent shared ownership of outcomes.

## SOLVES Family–School Meeting

It should be expected that collaboration efforts will be impacted by conflict at times. Given that conflict will arise, how it is resolved is crucial to maintaining the collaborative environment. Amatea, Daniels, Bringman, and Vandiver (2004) developed a model for problem solving by modifying the format of the family–school meeting. The SOLVES model assumes that a problem-solving meeting is not the first interaction between the family and school and that the collaborative environment has already been established. For school personnel who are viewing families through a social justice lens, each step of the SOLVES model provides an opportunity to respect and demonstrate awareness of the family culture. They may also integrate the culture of the family at every step. Thus, within the context of the socially just collaborative environment, six steps are required to implement a SOLVES family–school meeting. The steps are aligned with the acronym: S—setting up the meeting, O—orienting to the purpose and process, L—listening to concerns and blocking blame, V—validating concerns and creating consensus, E-expanding solutions, and S—setting up and implementing a plan.

### *Setting up the meeting*

The initial contact about the meeting must be carefully planned and implemented. Families who have participated in schools where collaboration may not have been a priority are likely to be used to punitive phone calls. Such phone calls may include threats of punishment for their child, or informing the family of a punishment that was established for their child. The SOLVES approach includes the family in the decision-making process rather than informing the family of the decision after it has been made. When setting up the meeting, ask the parent who they would like to include in it and where and when they would like it to be held. Then the school personnel can talk with the family about the structure of the meeting—a place for all to present concerns and solutions.

## Orienting to the purpose and process

Amatea et al. (2004) recommend having a form to guide the discussion. This form includes the initial concern, a description of the perspectives of all members of the problem-solving team, and an action plan. It is best to start and end the meeting with an acknowledgment of strengths of the child and family. Recognizing the strengths allows for a positive tone to be set and for the family to offer information from a cultural perspective. It is also helpful for a staff member to offer the first positive input to the group, such as a strength of the child. This will model for the family that the strengths can be specific and an honest appraisal of the child's characteristics.

## Listening to concerns and blocking blame

As the meeting proceeds, active listening skills should be modeled for the family. School personnel should also pay attention to the nonverbal communication of the family. For example, do they appear uncomfortable or worried? If nonverbal signals suggest that the family is not fully able to engage in the process comfortably, the meeting should revert to the initial step of focusing on strengths and outlining the meeting as a mutual goal-setting process. All participants should have a voice in the meeting and should have the opportunity to express concerns without blaming. The lead facilitator should listen carefully for any instances of blaming and be prepared to reframe the statements to include a positive statement along with a reflection of the concern. Amatea (2009) offers excellent examples of statements that imply blame by parents and teachers and techniques for blocking blame. Interruptions should not occur, so a volunteer from the group should record the thoughts without revision or criticism.

## Validating concerns and creating consensus

The goal of this stage is to determine common characteristics of the concerns that were presented. The facilitator should highlight all points where there was consensus. They should also frame the concerns using change-inducing language (Amatea, 2009). Change-inducing language includes speaking in the past tense about a problem, avoiding the use of definitive words such as "always" or "never," and talking about the problem independently of the student. One way to make sure this language occurs is to have the student present for the entire meeting. School personnel are typically sensitive to the emotional needs of children, so discussing concerns in this context can be communicated with sensitivity for them as children.

## Expanding solutions

Once the group has consensus on a concern, the entire group (including the student) can brainstorm solutions. All solutions should be seen as viable options and none should be criticized. The list should be generated so that all can see the ideas together. Then the group can mutually select from the list of options a potential action plan that would be effective.

## Setting up and implementing a plan

The final step of setting an action plan allows all participants to take ownership over some aspect of the solution. Each member should be given the opportunity to select a task to complete as part of the action plan. The plan should be documented in writing and a plan for a follow-up meeting to discuss progress should occur.

## Conclusion

Schools, families and communities need to become partners in the educational process. As educational policy has evolved, schools have increasingly recognized the importance of collaborating with all stakeholders in the educational community. The process does not occur automatically and requires significant effort and a commitment to eliminating barriers, resolving conflict, and developing sincere relationships that integrate parents and neighboring communities into the operation of the school. The social justice framework encourages school personnel to recognize that families are assets to the educational environment and as a result healthy collaborations can be established so that responsibility for positive educational outcomes can be shared across all members of the educational community. The elements of this chapter integrate culture into all aspects of collaboration and if implemented will enhance the system's ability to provide socially just family–school collaboration.

## Resources

- Center for Family, School, and Community (FSC) (www2.edc.org/fsc). This center was designed to strengthen schools to foster learning and development for all students. It works with agencies and provides technical assistance, program design, and consultation to enhance the leadership capacity of district and school administrators
- Center for Family Involvement in Schools (CFI) (www.centerforfamily-involvement.org). This center provides equity-focused professional development programs and resources to help strengthen family–school–community partnerships and encourage schools and districts to address the academic, intellectual and social development of *all* children.
- Center for Schools and Communities (www.center-school.org). This center provides technical assistance, training, program evaluation, research,

and resource development for improving outcomes for schools in the context of the community.

- Center on School, Family, and Community Partnerships (www.csos.jhu.edu/p2000/center.htm). This center conducts and disseminates research, programs, and policy analyses for schools. It strives to produce new and practical knowledge to help parents, educators, and members of communities work together to improve schools, strengthen families, and enhance student learning and development.
- Children, Youth and Families Education and Research Network (CYFERnet) (www.cyfernet.org). Cyfernet is a network of universities that provide practical, research-based resources for entities that seek to address the educational needs of children and families.
- Coalition for Community Schools (www.communityschools.org). This coalition provides resources and tools for creating "community schools." Members of the coalition recognize schools to be a hub for the community and have an integrated focus on academics, health and social services, youth and community engagement.
- Communities in Schools (www.cisnet.org). CIS is a network or professionals that work in public schools to determine the needs of students and establish partnerships with local community agencies and business to provide resources that address student needs.
- Family Involvement in Children's Education (www.ed.gov/pubs/faminvolve/index.html). This resource is a federal report on the status of family involvement in education. It provides ideas for successful partnerships and describes model programs.
- National Center for Culturally Responsive Educational Systems (NCCREST) (www.nccrest.org). This center provided technical assistance and professional development to close the achievement gap between students from culturally and linguistically diverse backgrounds and their peers, and reduce inappropriate referrals to special education. The Center's initiative is continuing through the work of the Equity Alliance at ASU (www.equityallianceatasu.org).
- SEDL National Center for Family and Community Connections with Schools (www.sedl.org/connections). This center conducts research to improve education outcomes for children and families. Their research has led to the development of toolkits that support developing school, family, and community connections.
- National Coalition for Parent Involvement in Education (NCPIE) (www.ncpie.org). This organization advocates for the involvement of parents and families in their children's education, and fosters relationships between home, school, and community to enhance the education of all students. It serves as a visible representative for strong parent and family involvement initiatives at the national level. It also conducts activities such as national conferences and luncheon seminars, and provides resources and legislative

information to help member organizations promote family involvement.
- National Network for Collaboration (www.uvm.edu/extension/community/nnco). This website is a collection of resources for building successful collaborations. Faculty at the Ohio State University and the University of Florida host the collaboration network and provide resources for other organizations through the website.
- National Network of Partnership Schools (www.csos.jhu.edu/p2000). NNPS is a network of partnerships that encourage schools, districts, states, and organizations to join together and use research-based approaches to organize and sustain excellent programs of family and community involvement that will increase student success in school.
- National PTA (www.pta.org). The National PTA is a volunteer child advocacy association that provides parents and families with a mechanism for working with schools to speak on behalf of children. The organization offers tools empowering families to help their children be safe, healthy, and successful in school and in life.

# References

Adelman, H., & Taylor, L. (2007). *Fostering school, family, and community involvement: Effective strategies for creating safer schools and communities.* Washington, DC: The Hamilton Fish Institute on School and Community Violence & Northwest Regional Educational Laboratory.

Amatea, E. (Ed.). (2009). *Building culturally responsive family–school relationships.* Upper Saddle River, NJ: Pearson Education.

Amatea, E., Daniels, H., Bringman, N., & Vandiver, F. (2004). Strengthening counselor–teacher–family connections: The family–school collaborative consultation project. *Professional School Counseling, 8,* 47–55.

Auerbach, S. (2010). Beyond coffee with the principal: Toward leadership for authentic school–family partnerships. *Journal of School Leadership, 20,* 728–757.

Banks, J., & Banks, C. (Eds.). (2004). *Handbook of research on multicultural education* (2nd ed.). San Francisco, CA: Jossey Bass.

Bronfenbrenner, U. (1992). Ecological systems theory. In R. Vasta (Ed.), *Six theories of child development: Revised formulations and current issues* (pp. 187–249). London, UK: Jessica Kingsley.

Byrk, A., & Schneider, B. (2002). *Trust in schools: A core resource for improvement.* New York, NY: Russell Sage Foundation.

Carr, L. (1997). *Colorblind racism.* Norfolk, VA: Sage.

Christenson, S., & Sheridan, S. (2001). *Schools and families: Creating essential connections for learning.* New York, NY: Guilford Press.

Clarke, B. L., Sheridan, S. M., & Woods, K. L. (2009). Elements of healthy school–family relationships. In S. L. Christenson & A. L. Reschly (2010). *Handbook of school–family partnerships.* New York, NY: Routledge.

Cooper, C. (2009). Parent involvement, African American mothers, and the politics of educational care. *Equity and Excellence in Education, 42* (4), 379–394.

Cooper, C., Riehl, C., & Hasan, A. (2010). Leading and learning with diverse families in schools: Critical epistemology amid communities of practice. *Journal of School Leadership, 20* (6), 758–788.

Cross, W. (2003). Tracing the historical origins of youth delinquency and violence: Myths and realities about black culture. *Journal of Social Issues, 59* (1), 67–82.

Decker, L., & Decker, V. (2003). *Home, school, and community partnerships.* Lanham, MD: Scarecrow Press.

Dietz, M., & Whaley, J. (1997). *School, family and community: Techniques and models for successful collaboration.* Gaithersburg, MD: Aspen Publishers.

Dryfoos, J. (1994). *Full service schools: A revolution in health and social services for children, youth, and families.* San Francisco, CA: Jossey-Bass.

Epstein, J. (Ed.). (2001). *School, family, and community partnerships: Preparing educators and improving schools.* Boulder, CO: Westview Press.

Freng, A., Freng, S., & Moore, H. (2006). Models of American Indian education: Cultural inclusion and the family/community/school linkage. *Sociological Focus, 39* (1), 55–74.

Gonzalez, N., & Moll, L. (2002). Cruzando el puente: Building bridges to funds of knowledge. *Educational Policy, 16* (4), 623–641.

Grant, K., & Ray, J. (2010). *Home, school, and community collaboration: Culturally responsive family involvement.* Thousand Oaks, CA: Sage.

Harry, B., Kalyanpur, M., & Day, M. (1999). *Building cultural reciprocity with families: Case studies in special education.* Baltimore, MD: Brookes.

Henderson, A., & Mapp, K. (2002). *A new wave of evidence: The impact of school, family, and community connections on student achievement.* Austin, TX: Southwest Educational Development Laboratory.

Hill, N. R. (2010). Culturally-based worldviews, family processes, and family–school interactions. In S. L. Christenson et al. (Eds.), *Handbook of school–family partnerships* (pp. 101–127). New York, NY: Routledge.

Jones, J. (Ed.). (2009). *The psychology of multiculturalism in the schools: A primer for practice, training, and research.* Bethesda: National Association of School Psychologists.

Jones, J. (2011). Culturally diverse families: Enhancing home–school relationships. In A. Canter, L. Paige, & S. Shaw (Eds.), *Helping children at home and school* (3rd ed.). Bethesda, MD: NASP.

Kohl, G. O., Lengua, L. J., & McMahon, R. J. (2000). Parent involvement in school: Conceptualizing multiple dimensions and their relations with family and demographic risk factors. *Journal of School Psychology, 58* (6), 501–523.

Kyle, D., McIntyre, E., Miller, K., & Moore, G. (2002). *Reaching out: A K-8 resource for connecting families and schools.* Thousand Oaks, CA: Corwin Press.

Ladwig, C. N. (2009). Making decisions and plans with families of students with special needs. In E. S. Amatea (Ed.), *Building culturally responsive family–school relationships.* Upper Saddle River, NJ: Pearson Education.

Lake, J., & Billingsley, B. (2000). An analysis of factors that contribute to parent school conflict in special education. *Remedial and Special Education, 21,* 240–251.

Li, J. (2005). Mind or virtue: Western Chinese beliefs about learning. *Current Directions in Psychological Science, 14,* 190–194.

Lines, C., Miller, G., & Arthur-Stanley, A. (2011). *The power of family–school partnering (FSP): A practical guide for school mental health professionals and educators.* New York, NY: Routledge.

Lynch, K., & Baker, J. (2005). Equality in education: The importance of equality of condition. *Theory and Research in Education, 3,* 131–164.

Miller, G., Arthur-Stanley, A., & Lines, C. (2012). Family–school collaboration services: Beliefs into action. *Communiqué, 40* (5), 1, 12–14.

North, C. (2006). More than words? Delving into the substantive meaning(s) of "social justice" in education. *Review of Educational Research, 76,* 507–536.

Paniagua, F. (2005). *Assessing and treating culturally diverse clients: A practical guide* (3rd ed.). Thousand Oaks, CA: Sage.

Pearrow, M., & Pollack, S. (2009). Youth empowerment in oppressive systems: Opportunities for school consultants. *Journal of Educational and Psychological Consultation, 19* (1), 45–60.

Sankofa, B., Hurley, E., Allen, B., & Boykin, A. (2005). Cultural expression of black students' attitudes toward high achievers. *Journal of Psychology, 139* (3), 247–259.

Shriberg, D., Bonner, M., Starr, B., Walker, A., Hyland, M., & Chester, C. (2008). Social justice through a school psychology lens: Definition and applications. *School Psychology Review, 37*, 453–468.

Stevenson, H., Winn, D., Walker-Barnes, C., & Coard, S. (2005). Style matters: Toward a culturally relevant framework for interventions with African American families. In V. McLoyd et al. (Eds.), *African American family life: Ecological and cultural diversity* (pp. 311–334). New York, NY: Guilford.

Sue, D., & Sue, D. (2008). *Counseling the culturally diverse: Theory and practice*. Hoboken, NJ: Wiley.

Swap, S. (1993). *Developing home–school partnerships: From concepts to practice*. New York, NY: Teachers College Press.

Trumbull, E., Rothstein-Fish, C., Greenfield, P., & Quiroz, B. (2001). *Bridging cultures between home and schools: A guide for teachers*. Mahwah, NJ: Lawrence Erlbaum Associates.

Tyler, K., Boykin, A., Miller, O., & Hurley, E. (2006). Cultural values in the home and school experiences of low-income African American students. *Social Psychology of Education, 9*, 363–380.

## sixteen
# The School Psychologist as Social Justice Advocate

## Alissa Briggs

The field of school psychology is in the midst of two related shifts. The first is the movement from a medical model that focuses on individual deficits to a public health model that focuses on prevention (Ysseldyke et al., 2006). In addition, the field of school psychology is grappling with conceptualizing its practice within a social justice framework (Speight & Vera, 2009). Conceptualizing service delivery in terms of a public health model and adopting a social justice framework for practice are a natural pairing (Prilleltensky, 2005). A public health model requires an ecological-systems perspective and a social justice framework requires a consideration of how school psychology practice can promote fairness and respect by addressing the school ecology, from the individual to systems (Prilleltensky, 2005; Rogers & O'Bryon, 2008; Shriberg et al., 2008; Speight & Vera, 2009). Both the public health model and a social justice framework focus on promoting well-being as opposed to ameliorating deficits (Prilleltensky, 2005).

As the field of school psychology moves from a deficit-oriented framework toward a prevention-oriented framework, the school psychologist's role includes that of a change agent. School psychologists guide the redefinition and reorganization of systems in schools so that prevention is possible. The National Association of School Psychologists' (NASP; 2010a) *Model for Comprehensive and Integrated School Psychological Services* explicitly states that "school psychologists function as change agents" (p. 5). In transforming systems, school psychologists must think critically about the presence of social justice and how transforming systems could further social justice. Otherwise, school psychologists risk supporting the continued institutionalization of injustice. Therefore, it is critical that the shift towards a public health model and a shift towards conceptualizing school psychology practice within a social justice framework occur together.

Social justice advocacy is a strategy that combines public health and social justice frameworks. The purpose of this chapter is to define social justice advocacy as it applies to current school psychology practice and provide a guiding framework for how to conduct social justice advocacy. In the first part of the chapter, a conceptualization of the school psychologist's role as a social justice advocate will be provided. Critical skills school psychologists must develop as well as skills school psychologists have that are essential to social justice advocacy will also be discussed. The second part of the chapter will discuss social justice advocacy as it applies to the public health model. Examples of what social justice advocacy could look like at each tier will be provided.

## Defining Social Justice Advocacy

School psychologists' role as child advocates has roots throughout the history of the profession. Discussions regarding the school psychologist's role as an advocate date back to the 1970s when the Education for All Handicapped Children Act (Public Law 94–142, 1975)[1] was passed (McMahon, 1993). In fact, it was with the passing of Public Law 94–142 that school psychologists' role obtained legal legitimacy. Discussions regarding school psychologists' role as child advocates calmed in the 1980s, but were soon rekindled with the United Nations Convention on the Rights of the Child in 1989 (McMahon, 1993). Then, in 1992, NASP published ethical guidelines organized around the idea that school psychologists are child advocates. More recently, NASP (2010a) highlighted advocacy as a foundation for service delivery. In addition, NASP (2010b) stated in its *Principles for Professional Ethics* that:

> School psychologists consider the interests and rights of children and youth to be their highest priority in decision making, and act as advocates for all students. These assumptions necessitate that school psychologists "speak up" for the needs and rights of students even when it may be difficult to do so. (p. 2)

What "speaking up" looks like depends on the issue at hand. How school psychologists can "speak up" for the needs and rights of children will be conceptualized and illustrated later in the chapter. However, the commitment to children, even when not the easy choice, is central to the advocate role (Mearig, 1974).

Speaking up will be difficult at times, especially if the psychologist is in a position of limited power (e.g., intern or new employee) or has less power than the individual(s) who transgressed the rights of the child(ren) (e.g., an administrator). People, including school psychologists, are influenced by social power. Social power can have origins in authority, expertise, or a desire to please others (Raven, 1993). The younger the school psychologist, the more likely it is that others have more authority and expertise. The school psychologist may also desire to make a favorable impression on others at a new job. However, a school psychologist can utilize other areas of social power in advocating for a child or children. He/she could highlight specific knowledge and build relationships with others in a way that makes the school psychologist one whose thoughts are valued (Raven, 1993). Indeed, Wilson, Erchul, and Raven (2008) found that school psychologists find these strategies to be most effective in consultation with teachers.

Another way to increase social power is to join with others in working towards social justice. School psychologists could work with families, colleagues, and even children themselves. By definition, an advocate is one who joins with an individual or group in order to work for the individual or group's due (Conoley, 1981, p. 158). What is "due" to a particular individual or group is rooted in social justice theory (Prilleltensky, 2012). Recent literature within the field of school psychology indicates that what is due to children is respect, access, and equity within a multicultural context (Sander et al., 2011; Shriberg et al., 2008; Shriberg, Wynne, Briggs, Bartucci, & Lombardo, 2011). In order to work with children and families in order to secure their due, school psychologists could collaborate with them prior to an individualized education program (IEP) meeting so that they are prepared to be part of a team that advocates for their needs. Some school psychologists have gone so far as to sit down with children and help them create a Power Point of their needs that they can use to guide the meeting. By being empowered to advocate for themselves, families and children are given the opportunity to access a system in a more equitable manner, which is social justice in action.

That being said, sometimes social justice advocacy occurs beyond children and families. The policies and practices that guide schools can perpetuate injustice. Intervening at the level of systems of operation is often preferred, if possible, because it is a proactive and efficient (once the long process of designing and implementing them is achieved) way to protect the needs and rights of children. Indeed, NASP's (2010b) *Principles for Professional Ethics* states that school psychologists assume "a proactive role in identifying social injustices that affect children and schools" and "strive to reform systems-level patterns of injustice" (pp. 11–12). In order to be proactive in identifying injustice, school psychologists must seek to understand the diversity of human life in which they practice and how individuals, groups, and cultures in their setting relate to one another. As Mary Clare eloquently stated, "social justice is the aspiration; advocacy . . . is the strategy; and . . . human diversity is the context" (2009, p. 9). In striving for systems-level reform once injustices are identified, school psychologists will need to call on their collaboration skills and align with key stakeholders in initiating and implementing change.

In order for school psychologists to understand the context for their social justice advocacy work, they must develop a critical consciousness. They must be critically reflective so that they understand their positions and the positions of others in the context in which they work (Prilleltensky, 2012; Vera & Speight, 2003). The development of a critical consciousness entails developing an understanding of one's own privilege, culture, and biases, developing an understanding of other cultures and positions in society, and critically examining policies and practices so as to identify those that may perpetuate injustice (Prilleltensky, 2012; Vera &

Speight, 2003). The development of a critical consciousness is particularly important for the majority of school psychologists who have at least one privileged position in society: whiteness (see Sabnani, Ponterotto, & Borodovsky, 1991 for a discussion of white privilege and identity). According to the 2009–2010 NASP demographic statistics reported by Castillo, Curtis, Chappel, and Cunningham (2011), about 91% of school psychologists identified as White/non-Hispanic. A critical consciousness is imperative for those with privilege because they do not naturally encounter the barriers presented to those without the privileged position. They lack the experiences that would facilitate them in defining and describing oppression (Clare, 2009; Sabnani et al., 1991).

School psychologists can develop a critical consciousness in a variety of ways. They can actively engage in reflection—on their own or through dialogue with others—on their personal histories as compared to the personal histories of those with whom they work. They can reflect on how these histories relate to how they experience the school context. Contact and dialogue with diverse groups is recommended (Prilleltensky, 2012). A few high schools in the Chicago area, with the active support of their school psychologists, that have significant White, Black, and Hispanic populations have implemented *Courageous Conversations about Race* (see Singleton & Linton, 2006) as a way to engage in critical reflection together. However, not all school settings are open to such a formal approach, so school psychologists could engage in reflection on their own or informally with colleagues. Such dialogue may be a good starting point for building relationships that could result in collaborative relationships for social justice advocacy. They may also be a venue to advocate for the culturally respectful treatment of children in classrooms.

In addition to engaging in self-reflection and reflective dialogue with others, school psychologists must listen to the perspectives of others, especially those most impacted by school systems—children who attend them and their families. Listening is critical because those at the margins of a system and those who are the recipients of the system's services, such as children, are more likely to be able to identify and describe aspects of the system that are dysfunctional and perpetuate situations in which their needs are unmet (Clare, 2009). Listening to those who are the recipients of services or at the margin of society can be challenging since their position may suggest that they lack the expertise to critique the system (Raven, 1993). However, the school psychologist must work to recognize the unique perspective that children and those on the margin of society have to offer and trust them to define and describe their concerns (Conoley, 1981). Actively soliciting and listening to their perspectives could involve surveys, focus groups, meetings, and even casual dialogue with children, their families, and community members.

At this point, the reader may be saying to himself or herself, "Developing a critical consciousness and actively listening sounds like it takes hard work, and these are only prerequisites for social justice advocacy. Social justice advocacy is going to be very challenging." The reader would be correct. However, competent school psychologists also have many skills that will facilitate social justice advocacy. So, while challenging, it is not impossible! Specific skills that warrant particular attention are collaboration and data-based decision-making. These skills permeate all aspects of school psychology service delivery according to the NASP practice model (2010a).

The National Association of School Psychologists (2010a) states that part of the school psychologist's job is to create linkages between the school, family, and community so that services can be coordinated to meet children's needs. Coordinating services so that children have access to needed resources is one way to advocate for social justice. However, in advocating for social justice, school psychologists might consider going above and beyond coordination to building connections with community agencies or to support children and their families. For example, school psychologists could collaborate with police and the local hospital to support children and families in crisis, or work with local health care providers to open a clinic in the school.

In addition to collaboration, data-based decision-making is another competency that permeates all aspects of service delivery (NASP, 2010a) and is critical to social justice advocacy. According to NASP, school psychologists are skilled in developing data collection tools, well versed in different methods of data collection, and skilled in gathering, interpreting, and communicating multiple sources of data (2010a). These skills translate to identifying needs, calling school stakeholders to action, and evaluating whether or not interventions developed in collaboration with alliances are effective in meeting the needs identified. Needs and outcome assessments can be developed and used as a guide for affecting change that the school community members view as meeting their needs. Needs and outcome assessments are essential tools for social justice advocacy because they empower stakeholders to define their needs and solicit their perspectives as to whether or not those needs have been met. School psychologists are also skilled in gathering, interpreting, and presenting data on student performance. Sharing school-wide data on student performance as a whole or by group can inspire action and monitor the impact of action taken. In sum, data are essential in highlighting injustice and calling others to action, as well as in identifying advocacy needs and monitoring the impact of advocacy efforts. How school psychologists can conceptualize the challenging task of developing systems, programs, and interventions to address needs is addressed in the next section.

## Conducting Social Justice Advocacy

Specific guidelines put forth by organizational bodies governing school psychology practice regarding how school psychologists could conceptualize or approach advocacy from a social justice perspective do not exist. However, the public health model, also known as the "three-tiered model" in school psychology literature, is accepted as best practice and provides a framework for conceptualizing points at which school psychologists could advocate for social justice. The three-tiered model includes three levels of service delivery: universal, targeted, and individual (Ysseldyke et al., 2006). At the universal level, tier 1, school-wide systems of prevention are in place so as to promote the well-being of all students (Ysseldyke et al., 2006). For groups of students who need moderate support, interventions are in place at the targeted level, tier 2. For individual students who need significant support, individual interventions are designed to meet their unique needs at tier 3 (Ysseldyke et al., 2006). Thus, school psychologists could advocate for social justice through systems change, developing group interventions, or advocating for the individual child. At all of these levels, school psychologists will need to access their critical consciousness and listening skills in order to help develop interventions that match the ecological context of the school, groups of children, and child.

While the three-tiered model is useful in outlining multiple points of intervention, an additional level is necessary when thinking about social justice advocacy. The American Counseling Association's (ACA) advocacy competencies (Lewis, Arnold, House, & Toporek, 2003) are divided into levels, much like the three-tiered model, but they include a level of intervention in the public realm. This level, the macro level, includes legal and political action. NASP is very active in advocacy at this level (visit www.nasponline.org/advocacy for information on NASP's public policy advocacy efforts), but does not explicitly conceptualize these efforts as part of a service-delivery model. Since NASP is active in the legal–political realm, the addition of a "zero level" or "tier 0" to the public health model as it applies to school psychology may be helpful when thinking about the school psychologist's role as a social justice advocate. A zero level would include legal and political support for the universal, targeted, and individual school interventions. A zero level is a natural fit for the three-tiered model given that the NASP's practice model (2010a) highlights legal practice as a foundation of school psychology practice. Please see Figure 16.1 for a visual representation of the public health model with the zero level incorporated.

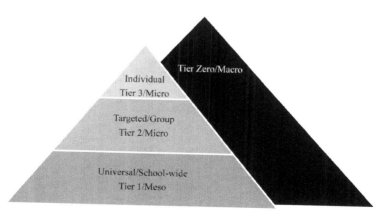

**FIGURE 16.1.** The public health model as it applies to schools (Ysseldyke et al., 2006), with a tier reflecting work in the public domain.

Another useful way in which to conceptualize social justice advocacy, as outlined in the ACA competences, includes distinguishing between advocacy with others and advocacy on behalf of others (Lewis et al., 2003). Advocacy with others involves empowerment, collaboration, and the provision of information (Lewis et al., 2003). Advocacy on behalf of others involves coordination, leadership, and legal action (Lewis et al., 2003). In general, acting with others is preferred to acting on behalf of others because acting with others empowers individuals or groups to change their lives in a manner that is deemed valuable and contextually appropriate to them. Acting with others upholds social justice by demonstrating respect for diverse contexts, by providing for diverse methods, and by shifting power so that oppressed individuals or groups are the advocates rather than the recipients of advocacy. That being said, sometimes individuals or groups need an advocate to act on their behalf because they may not have the power or skills to effect the necessary change at the necessary time. What will be challenging for advocates is to determine when acting with others is not possible and acting on behalf of others is required. Below are some reflection questions that the advocates might ask themselves in order to ascertain whether they should act with others or on behalf of others.

1.   Am I acting on behalf of others because it is easier or because it is necessary? Will acting with others produce similar results but simply take more time and effort?
2.   Is immediate change critical in order to prevent harm, or can I take the time to empower others to advocate for themselves?
3.   If I advocate on behalf of others, what will happen when I am not around to lead advocacy efforts? Will change be institutionalized; will the process continue, or will my efforts disappear with me?

What follows is a discussion of what social justice advocacy (both "with" and "on behalf of") at tiers 0, 1, 2, and 3 might look like. The goal is to provide general guidelines, because school psychologists' roles vary depending on the school, district, city/town, and state. The guidelines are summarized in Table 16.1 for tier 0, Table 16.2 for tier 1, and Table 16.3 for tiers 2 and 3 along with guiding questions. Examples are provided in text to give an idea of what social justice advocacy could look like. Please note that the examples are not intended to prescribe what every school psychologist should do. Each school has its own unique contextual factors that need to be evaluated and considered when applying social justice advocacy, which is why developing a critical consciousness and listening to others is critical.

## Zero-Level Advocacy

At the zero level, competent school psychologists are knowledgeable about laws and policies in place, in revision, or in development that affect their practice (NASP, 2010a) and how to advocate for legal and policy change (Conoley, 1981). In order

**TABLE 16.1.** Social justice advocacy steps and guiding questions—zero level

| Type | Steps | Guiding Questions |
|---|---|---|
| Overall | • Critically evaluate laws and policies for their ability to promote social justice. | • What laws and policies affect educational practice in my community?<br>• Do these laws and policies promote equity, access and respect? What evidence do I have to support my conclusions? |
| With | • Call stakeholders to action in a contextually appropriate manner. | • How can I call stakeholders to action in a manner that will be heard? |
| On behalf | • Gather evidence.<br>• Present concerns and evidence to legislators and/or policy makers.<br>• Work with legislators to effect change. | • Do I feel that action on my part is critical to effecting change?<br>• Who are my legislators and/or policy makers and how can I get them on board? |

**TABLE 16.2.** Social justice advocacy steps and guiding questions—tier 1

| Type | Steps | Guiding Questions |
|---|---|---|
| Overall | • Critically evaluate school-wide systems and practices.<br>• Identify needs and priorities for change.<br>• Assemble or identify a team representative of the school.<br>• Develop an action plan.<br>• Communicate regularly. | • Do school curricula align with the diverse needs and lives of students?<br>• Do data highlight discrepancies in access and achievement?<br>• What are the perspectives of school stakeholders regarding how the school as a whole is supporting the healthy development of children? What do they identify as needs and priorities?<br>• What systems and/or practices need to be developed or modified? Who needs to be involved in this process? What steps need to be taken?<br>• How can communication be facilitated in order to ensure the action plan is acted upon? |
| With | • Identify allies who have common concerns.<br>• Meet with allies and discuss common concerns and goals.<br>• Identify strengths and resources all allies have to offer. | • Who in the school is working towards similar goals?<br>• How can we work together?<br>• What is our timeline?<br>• How are we progressing? Does our action plan need revision? |

**TABLE 16.2.** *Continued*

| Type | Steps | Guiding Questions |
|---|---|---|
| On behalf | • Develop an action plan.<br>• Monitor progress and problem-solve along the way.<br>• Synthesize and share data—call others to action.<br>• Gather a team of school stakeholders and develop a mission.<br>• Develop an action plan.<br>• Communicate regularly about progress and problem-solve when needed. | • What data highlights priorities for change and how can I share this so that others will be inspired to act?<br>• Who needs to be at the table in order for change to occur?<br>• Are action items being completed on time, and if not, why not? What can be done to help move the process forward? |

**TABLE 16.3.** Social justice advocacy steps and guiding questions—tiers 2 and 3

| Type | Steps | Guiding Questions |
|---|---|---|
| Overall | • Identify groups and individuals who may experience oppression or who may need extra support. | • Is there a group of students that is experiencing bullying or discrimination or students who need specific types of support? |
| With | • Support children in identifying their strengths and resources.<br>• Support children in identifying barriers to their well-being.<br>• Create an action plan with children that will support them in using their strengths and resources to address, and be resilient in the face of, barriers to their well-being. | • What are the sources of resilience in this child or these children?<br>• What societal, cultural, political, and/or economic factors are preventing this child or these children from developing?<br>• How does the child or children respond to barriers to their progress?<br>• What can the child or children do in order to advocate for his/her/their development?<br>• How can I support the child or children without taking over the process? |
| On Behalf | • Identify or develop intervention(s).<br>• Implement intervention(s).<br>• Monitor progress and modify or change intervention(s) as necessary. | • Do research-based interventions exist for the issue of concern? If not, what research can I draw from in developing an intervention?<br>• Are the interventions respectful of the context of the child/children and do they support him/her/them in making decisions for and/or advocating for himself/herself/themselves? |

to advocate for social justice, school psychologists first need to evaluate whether or not laws and policies are shaping practice and service-delivery in schools in a manner that respects diversity and promotes equity and access. Most often, these laws and policies will be in place at the federal or state level. Thus, school psychologists may find that their advocacy efforts are most effective when done in collaboration with state and national organizations. As aforementioned above, there is an advocacy action center on NASP's website that provides information on current advocacy efforts and resources to enable school psychologists to get involved.

Districts may also have policies that shape the practice of school psychologists that are unjust. In this case, school psychologists may want to provide key stakeholders at the district level with information assembled by their state association or NASP. They may highlight how the recommendations outlined by professional organizations are similar and different from policies and practices in their districts. The benefit of providing information assembled by professional organizations is that they carry the power of authority of numbers, so school psychologists are not alone in advocating for change. School psychologists may also want to consult and collaborate with colleagues and/or community agencies that serve children in advocating for change at the district level. Advocating for change with others gives power to the message through the numbers behind it and the depth of different perspectives. School psychologists can advocate with school stakeholders by organizing them to act with the school psychologists to effect legal and policy change.

For example, school psychologists could research the implementation of a law or policy of interest, such as high stakes testing, and the ways in which it has or has not promoted social justice in their school district. Research regarding impact could range from quantifiable student data to interviews with students, parents, and teachers. They could also gather research from NASP's advocacy website (see above), which addresses a variety of topics. School psychologists could then share the information at a school or district leadership meeting, at an institute day, at a board meeting, through a newsletter, or at a parent–teacher organization meeting. Information can be shared in a variety of ways, and school psychologists will need to share information in a manner that is appropriate for their context. The forms of support school psychologists gather depend on the change necessary and the preferences of the stakeholders. Most often, support comes in the form of contacting legislators or school officials regarding community concerns about a law or policy.

While school psychologists respect stakeholders by giving them the choice to respond to calls to action, they may also be compelled to uphold social justice by being active in the legal and political landscape on behalf of others. In order to be effective in this, school psychologists should be familiar with the legal and political change process, know who their representatives are, and approach their representatives in a way that will inspire these political figures to work with them to change, drop, or add laws and policies. School psychologists should be prepared to share data to support their case. In general, face-to-face meetings are more likely to inspire collaboration. If a meeting is not possible, personal phone calls, emails, and letters are a start, and these should also include clear evidence in support of the position as well as provide suggestions for next steps.

For example, recommendations on the part of several school psychologists, along with research conducted and disseminated by many school psychologists, helped lead to the inclusion of *Response to Intervention* (RtI) as a possible method of determining whether or not a child has a specific learning disability (SLD) in the IDEIA (2004; Kovaleski & Prasse, 2004). The inclusion of RtI as a method for diagnosing SLD upheld social justice by prompting schools to consider, develop, and implement practices that would prevent children from falling significantly academically behind their peers before they accessed the support they needed. That being said, it would be naïve to argue that RtI as it is currently understood is sufficient to uphold social justice in schools, or even implemented in a socially just way in all settings. Social justice is an aspiration and thus the social justice advocacy work of school psychologists must continue at the zero level.

## Tier 1 Advocacy

Social justice advocacy work is also necessary at tier 1, where school-wide systems and practices are implemented. At tier 1, school psychologists must evaluate current school-wide systems and practices for their ability to uphold children's rights identified by laws and policies, promote respect, and provide access to the resources and benefits of the school. In order to do this, school psychologists can reflect on how the curricula align with the diverse context of the school, gather and examine existing data in order to identify needs, and listen to the goals and perspectives of school stakeholders. For example, school psychologists could examine the curriculum for its ability to meet the diverse needs of students as well as for its representation of diversity in its content. They could examine academic, behavioral, and engagement data. They could solicit the perspectives of others through surveys, interviews, and focus groups. Then, school psychologists can use these data to inform the further development or implementation of systems and/or practices.

In order to advocate with others for school-wide changes to systems and/or practices, school psychologists should identify potential allies who desire change. In advocacy with others, these allies will most likely be those most impacted by the school-wide systems and/or practices. School psychologists could meet with these allies, listen to their concerns and goals, and highlight common concerns and goals. When meeting with allies, school psychologists should work to identify the strengths and resources of the group and how they can utilize these strengths and resources to support school-wide systems and/or practices that will promote social justice. This should eventually result in the creation of an action plan where responsibilities are designated to individuals depending on the resources they have to offer.

For example, school psychologists may advocate with others to address a common headache in schools—negative student behavior. Negative student behavior impairs the well-being of school stakeholders by demanding teacher and administrator time for discipline, by creating negative interactions, and by occasionally leading to the exclusion of children from school. Exclusionary discipline, such as suspensions and expulsions, is unjust because it does not teach students what they need to know—how to demonstrate positive behavior—and restricts access to education opportunities.

In order to truly advocate *with* those most affected by discipline, school psychologists could align with children. Before aligning with children, school psychologists will need to ensure that their administrators support students being part of the change process and are willing to support recommendations made by the students. It would be disempowering for school psychologists to align with students only for administrators to ignore or reject their efforts, and students will likely feel disempowered if they work to collect data, develop a report, and present the data and nothing is done. If school psychologists are supported in advocating with children, they could support students in researching discipline practices and involvement of students in discipline. Support from school psychologists might include helping them develop research questions, think through data collection methods, determine how to analyze the data, and determine how best to present their findings and recommendations. Students could present their data and recommendations to a team of administrators, at a staff meeting, or even to the school board. After students share the data and recommendations, it must be acted upon. In order to move forward, a team of key school stakeholders could be formed or an existing team could be charged with addressing the recommendations. Regardless, the team should include students who worked on researching the concerns and providing recommendations. The students could help the team develop their mission and think through action steps.

However, not all adults are open to working with children. When it is clear that students would be disempowered by working with the school psychologist to impact school-wide change, school psychologists will need to advocate on their behalf. However, school psychologists can certainly solicit and listen to the perspectives of children in order to inform how they guide systems to change. In order to advocate for systems-change, school psychologists could synthesize and share the data that indicate a need for change with critical allies. These allies will most likely include administrators and teachers, as administrators hold the power of authority and teachers have the power of the majority. Allies could also include counselors, social workers, support staff, board members, and parents. Data school psychologists could share with key allies might include disparities between groups of students in rates of suspension and expulsion. School psychologists could highlight concerns about how inequitable engagement in discipline may relate to inequitable achievement on high-stakes tests due to disparities in access to classrooms. Once critical allies are called to action, a team should be assembled that is representative of these allies.

As the team's efforts unfold and practices are implemented to address social injustices highlighted by data, school psychologists could work with the team and/or students to monitor progress—using the same data that called them to action and perhaps more. In monitoring progress, school psychologists should use data to ensure that the school-wide change is promoting social justice. Even the most well-intentioned efforts can fail in promoting social justice. For example, if problem behavior decreases as a result of the team's efforts but the same group of students who were more likely to be excluded from school as a result of problem behavior are still more likely to be excluded from school as a result of problem behavior, changes to systems and/or practices did not address that particular social justice concern and thus the efforts must be revised. That being said, if school psychologists work to develop a critical consciousness, they minimize the risk that they will be an active part of school-wide change that fails to promote social justice.

## Tier 2 and Tier 3 Advocacy

While changing school-wide systems and practices is a proactive way to advocate for social justice for all students, groups of students and individual students will still need social justice advocacy at tiers 2 (groups) and 3 (individuals). The social justice advocacy process at both tiers is similar. Children who may need advocacy at tiers 2 and 3 could be those who are experiencing bullying, discrimination, and/or who are involved in gangs. These students can be identified through surveys, discipline reports, or by school psychologists actively listening to the concerns of various school stakeholders, especially children.

If it is possible to support children at tiers 2 and 3 by advocating with them, school psychologists could focus on empowering them to advocate for themselves. In order to effectively empower children, school psychologists would need to support them in identifying their strengths, barriers to well-being, and resources they need in order to address or be resilient in the face of barriers to their well-being (adapted from Lewis et al., 2003). After strengths, barriers, and resources are identified, school psychologists can support children in determining what they need in order to achieve well-being and how they can access these resources by helping them develop and carry out an action plan (adapted from Lewis et al.). School psychologists can provide this support by guiding the children in developing their plan, evaluating their progress, and identifying next steps.

Children who may benefit from school psychologists empowering them include those who identify as lesbian, gay, bisexual, transgender, or questioning (LGBTQ). A survey of middle and high school students in 2009 conducted by the Gay, Lesbian, and Straight Education Network (GLSEN, 2010) found that 84.6% of lesbian, gay, bisexual, and transgender (LGBT) youth experienced harassment at school in the past year because of their sexual orientation. More likely than not, students who identify as LGBTQ would benefit from advocacy efforts that promoted their rights to respect and access to a safe school environment.

School psychologists could advocate with LGBTQ students by working with a Gay–Straight Alliance (GSA) club or conducting a LGBT support group. What venue school psychologists use to advocate with LGBT students may depend on the political climate of the school. Creating a situation in which a school or community reacts in a hateful way may do more harm than good. Regardless of the venue, school psychologists could support these students in identifying their strengths as individuals and resources they can access for social, emotional, and political support. In terms of identifying strengths as individuals, one high school group the author has worked with noted that they could find their own source of power when they could find pride in what they had to offer the world as individuals. In terms of identifying resources for support, this same group found inspiration in campaigns such as *It Gets Better*[2] (see www.itgetsbetter.org) and by collaborating with a local teen center in order to make the center a safe space for them.

However, children do not always have the skills, power, or resources to advocate for themselves with the support of school psychologists. When empowerment is not possible, school psychologists must advocate on behalf of children. When advocating on behalf of children, school psychologists must first identify or develop interventions that are designed to meet these students' needs in a way that is respectful of their context and right to self-determination. If interventions must be developed, school psychologists should aim to develop interventions that are supported by research and sensitive to the social, political, economic, and cultural factors affecting the children.

A group of children who may need school psychologists to advocate on their behalf are children who are involved in gang activity. Children involved in gang activity, if identified, elicit strong reactions from staff and administration because their behavior threatens the safety of the school community and thus threatens adults in positions of authority. A common consequence for gang-related activity may be suspension or expulsion. Adults may want these children out of the school due to perceived safety risks. However, these consequences threaten children's access to an education and fail to provide students with the support they need in order to process the consequences of their involvement and develop a plan for exiting a gang. Thus, when and if students return to school, they are likely to still be in a gang and to receive more exclusionary discipline for gang-related activity. Moreover, suspensions and expulsions send students back to the very streets where the barrier to their healthy development exists—gangs.

School psychologists could advocate for gang-involved children by working with administrators to implement an alternative to suspension—group intervention. Students and parents can elect participation in such a group in lieu of a suspension. An example of such an intervention is Gang Avoidance Intervention Now (GAIN; Pesce, 2008). Implementation of GAIN requires collaboration with community law enforcement, who must have representative members actively involved in the group. The GAIN curriculum includes nine sessions and two field trips designed to support youth in reconsidering gang involvement (J. Sterling Morton High School District, 1999). Towards the end of the curriculum, students develop an exit plan and identify supports they will need in order to carry out the plan (J. Sterling Morton High School District, 1999). After the group is over, students continue to receive support through an after-care program and alliances developed with school and community members (such as police officers) who were involved in conducting the group. In the end, the program moves from an intervention developed and implemented on behalf of students to an intervention developed with students during the action planning phase of the group.

## Conclusion

Not all advocacy efforts will clearly be advocacy with others or advocacy on behalf of others or fit cleanly into one tier or another. Not all advocacy efforts will result in changes within a day, a month, or even a year. Advocacy will likely take time and involve multiple steps. However, conceptualizing advocacy within a modified public health model and distinguishing between two categories of advocacy can provide guidance as to how a school psychologist can use advocacy as a strategy to work towards a social justice aspiration over his or her tenure.

How school psychologists approach advocacy within their own settings will depend on the context of their practice. Developing a critical consciousness and listening to the perspectives and concerns of others will help school psychologists in understanding the context for their advocacy efforts. Administrators' beliefs and buy-in are often an important contextual factor, as their support of advocacy efforts that require implementation of interventions is often a prerequisite to their implementation. Thus, school psychologists may find themselves advocating first by calling others to act with them. Therefore, the social justice advocacy model presented in this chapter is a guide that may need to be adapted to fit the varied settings school psychologists encounter.

That being said, there are concrete principles that can be applied to guide school psychologists in social justice advocacy. As social justice advocates, school psychologists aspire to ensure that children have equitable educational opportunities, access to the resources they need, and are respected. When advocating for children, school psychologists employ a critical consciousness, listen, collaborate with others, and use data. Whenever possible, school psychologists advocate with others, using the resources and skills they have to empower children, families, and communities to advocate for themselves. In sum, when engaging in social justice advocacy efforts, school psychologists should ask themselves the following questions.

1. Am I engaging in critical self-reflection?
2. Am I listening to the perspectives of others?
3. Am I always critically evaluating and questioning laws, policies, systems, and practices?
4. Am I using data to identify social injustice and monitor the impact of advocacy efforts?
5. Am I developing alliances and working with them?
6. Am I simply doing things on behalf of others because it is easier or am I empowering others?

## Notes

1 Several reauthorizations later, Public Law 94–192 is what we now call the Individuals with Disabilities Education Improvement Act (IDEIA, 2004).
2 *It Gets Better* and the *It Gets Better Project* are trademarks owned and licensed by Savage Love, LLC. Copyright © 2010–2011 Iola Foundation dba It Gets Better Project.

## References

Castillo, J. M., Curtis, M. J., Chappel, A., & Cunningham, J. (2011, February). *School psychology 2010: Results of the national membership study.* Paper presented at the annual meeting of the National Association of School Psychologists, San Francisco, CA.

Clare, M. M. (2009). Decolonizing consultation: Advocacy as the strategy, diversity as the context. *Journal of Educational and Psychological Consultation, 19* (1), 8–25.

Conoley, J. C. (1981). Advocacy consultation: Promises and problems. In J. C. Conoley (Ed.), *Consultation in schools: Theory, research, procedures* (pp. 157–178). New York, NY: Academic.

Gay, Straight and Lesbian Education Network. (2010). 2009 national school climate survey: Nearly 9 out of 10 LGBT students experience harassment in school. Retrieved September 3, 2012 from www.glsen.org/cgi-bin/iowa/all/library/record/2624.html?state=research&type=antibullying

J. Sterling Morton High School District. (1999). *Gang Avoidance Initiative Now curriculum.* Cicero, IL: J. Sterling Morton High School District.

Kovaleski, J. F., & Prasse, D. P. (2004). Response to instruction in the identification of learning disabilities: A guide for school teams. *Helping Children and Families at School II: Handouts for Families and Educators.* Bethesda, MD: National Association of School Psychologists.

Lewis, J., Arnold, M. S., House, R., & Toporek, R. (2003). *Advocacy competencies.* Retrieved September 3, 2012 from: www.counseling.org/Resources/Competencies/Advocacy_Competencies.pdf

McMahon, T. J. (1993). On the concept of child advocacy: A review of theory and methodology. *School Psychology Review, 22* (4), 744–755.

Mearig, J. S. (1974). On becoming a child advocate in school psychology. *Journal of School Psychology, 12* (2), 121–129.

National Association of School Psychologists. (2009). *Appropriate behavioral, social, and emotional supports to meet the needs of all students* (Position Statement). Bethesda, MD: NASP.

National Association of School Psychologists. (2010a). *Model for comprehensive and integrated school psychological services.* Bethesda, MD: NASP.

National Association of School Psychologists (2010b). *Principles for professional ethics.* Bethesda, MD: NASP.

Pesce, R. C. (2008). *Executive summary: Gang Avoidance Intervention Now.* Report submitted to the Illinois State Police.

Prilleltensky, I. (2005). Promoting well-being: Time for a paradigm shift in health and human services. *Scandinavian Journal of Public Health, 33,* 53–60.

Prilleltensky, I. (2012). Wellness as fairness. *American Journal of Community Psychology, 49,* 1–21.

Raven, B. H. (1993). The bases of power: Origins and recent developments. *Journal of Social Issues, 49,* 227–251.

Rogers, M. R., & O'Bryon, E. C. (2008). Advocating for social justice?: The context for change in school psychology. *Psychology, 37* (4), 493–498.

Sabnani, H. B., Ponterotto, J. G., & Borodovsky, L. G. (1991). White racial identity development and cross-cultural counselor training: A stage model. *Counseling Psychologist, 19* (1), 76–102.

Sander, J. B., Sharkey, J. D., Groomes, A. N., Krumholz, L., Walker, K., & Hsu, J. Y. (2011). Social justice and juvenile offenders: Examples of fairness, respect and access in education settings. *Journal of Educational and Psychological Consultation, 21* (4), 309–337.

Shriberg, D., Bonner, M., Sarr, B. J., Walker, A. M., Hyland, M., & Chester, C. (2008). Social justice through a school psychology lens. *School Psychology Review, 37* (4), 453–468.

Shriberg, D., Wynne, M., Briggs, A., Bartucci, G., & Lombardo, A. C. (2011). School psychologists' perspectives on social justice. *School Psychology Forum, 5* (2), 37–53.

Singleton, G. E., & Linton, C. W. (Eds.). (2006). *Courageous conversations about race: A field guide for achieving equity in schools.* Thousand Oaks, CA: Corwin Press.

Speight, S. L., & Vera, E. M. (2009). The challenge of social justice for school psychology. *Journal of Educational and Psychological Consultation, 19,* 82–92.

Vera, E. M., & Speight, S. L. (2003). Multicultural competence, social justice, and counseling psychology: Expanding our roles. *Counseling Psychologist, 31,* 253–272.

Wilson, K. E., Erchul, W. P., & Raven, B. H. (2008). The likelihood of use of social power strategies by school psychologists when consulting with teachers. *Journal of Educational and Psychological Consultation, 18,* 101–123.

Ysseldyke, J., Burns, M., Dawson, P., Kelly, B., Morrison, D., Ortiz, S., et al. (2006). *School psychology: A blueprint for training and practice III.* Bethesda, MD: National Association of School Psychologists.

## seventeen
# Graduate Education and Professional Development

## David Shriberg

Throughout this book, different authors have described different topics germane to school psychology practice through the lens of social justice. These chapters provide terrific suggestions on ways in which school psychology students, practitioners, and/or researchers can act in ways that promote and sustain social justice.

In this chapter, the goal is to consider "best practices" towards preparing school psychologists to engage in these sorts of "pro social justice" actions. Of course, the very notion that social justice is something that can and should be taught in graduate education and professional development activities is contested. From my perspective, the goals of social justice and the goals of school psychology (namely to help facilitate an environment where ALL children can learn) go hand in hand. How can all children learn if some, or even most, of the children in any given school are on the receiving end of injustice? For example, is it likely that a male student who is being verbally and physically bullied because he is gay (or is perceived to be gay) will achieve at the same level as he would have if he was not bullied? Thus, while individual interpretations of what social justice means and how this concept translates to practice vary, it is my position that well-developed social justice training and professional development activities not only will leave participants with an expanded toolbox towards becoming an agent of social justice, but also will speak to the reasons why the vast majority of school psychologists enter the field—namely, to support ALL children. Thus, social justice has the potential to be an organizing framework from which a student or practitioner can analyze the scene around her/him and from which individuals can gauge their own performance.

As noted by several authors (e.g., Burnes & Singh, 2010; Goodman et al., 2004; Shriberg, 2009; Speight & Vera, 2008), scholarship documenting "the best of" social justice training in psychology is just emerging. However, as will be described, there are several emerging resources available to persons interested in developing psychologists as agents of social justice. Drawing upon multicultural theory and from the practices of scholars and educators actively engaged in "teaching for social justice," this chapter can be thought of as a sort of "starter set" towards framing and leading social justice education initiatives.

This chapter is organized around two primary theme areas: "foundations" and "implementation". In the "foundations" section, the context from which teaching for social justice is being practiced is explored. For example, in some cases the facilitator or teacher may be teaching a course as part of a graduate program that explicitly emphasizes social justice. In other cases, the facilitator or teacher may be teaching for social justice in a university or applied context where the very notion of social justice, as defined by leading thinkers and researchers in psychology and education, is a novel concept. Or perhaps social justice is being taught as the focus of a professional development session for practitioners. Another consideration is the background of the facilitator or teacher in terms of whether this person primarily comes from a privileged background or perhaps from a background where he or she has been on the receiving end of oppression (most of us have parts of both in our background). The first section explores topics such as these as part of framing social justice education.

In the "implementation" section, drawing from both the school psychology literature and literature from related fields, several models and perspectives on implementing social justice education are provided. The chapter closes with a case example from the author's own experience utilizing service learning as an outlet for teaching for social justice.

## Frameworks

## Context in which Training Takes Place

Whether you are approaching social justice education from the vantage of graduate training or professional development, an important consideration is the framework and context from which this effort is springing forth. For example, I have the luxury of approaching social justice education as a tenured faculty member in an institution that is organized around a social justice mission. This context provides me with certain freedoms that I would not have in many—if not most—other settings. For example, in talking with colleagues, I can openly state that my research and teaching interests revolve around issues of social justice and not only am I not penalized or otherwise made to feel ashamed of this, but rather this interest is nearly universally viewed as a positive, including by persons who were involved in hiring me as a professor and by persons who were in positions of authority and influence when I came up for tenure. Similarly, the school psychology graduate program in which I teach makes it plain to all applicants that the program has a social justice focus, so as a result the vast majority of entering students (if not all of these students) come into the school psychology graduate program with some expectation that social justice will be discussed and valued. Clearly, this type of context provides a different opportunity for social justice education than would working in a university environment where social justice was not so explicitly and implicitly valued by all, including persons in positions of power.

Thus, in training geared towards school psychology graduate students, the university context is important. Also important is the training model from which the course, experience, or perhaps set of courses and experiences takes place. One line of demarcation is how issues of social justice are framed within the program. Whereas some programs may take an "infusion" approach, where issues of social justice are seen as part and parcel of many courses and training experiences, other programs may confine social justice to one course or to one unit within a course. There are potential pros and cons to each approach. While an infusion model is generally viewed as more desirable than not having multicultural content in the curriculum at all, what exactly is meant by "infusion" is not clear and there is the danger in some cases that "infusion" may simply mean that statements reflecting social justice are included in course syllabi but otherwise it is not discussed or that social justice topics are covered in only a very superficial way. For this reason, having at least one course devoted to social justice content is desirable. However, the potential "con" to this approach is that if a graduate program has one course dedicated to social justice content, there can be a sense that social justice content is not needed in other courses because "that is already covered in the social justice course" and thus the "infusion" component does not occur. This is why the most common best practice recommendation is for programs to have both one or more courses dedicated to social justice and infusion of social justice-related ideas and experiences throughout the curriculum (Radliff, Miranda, Stoll, & Wheeler, 2009). In an analysis of research that examined the practices of "exemplary" multicultural training in psychology, Rogers (2005) reports that 96% of these programs utilize an "infusion" model, 96% offer at least one course about diversity issues, and 89% of these programs considered this course a requirement.

While at present there is very limited analysis of social justice training in school psychology, Ratts (2011) noted that social justice can be viewed as directly connected to the multicultural psychology movement. Ratts used the terminology that social justice and multiculturalism can be viewed as "two sides of the same coin." He argued that multicultural awareness and responsiveness is a precursor to social justice action. However, applied social justice involves an advocacy and questioning of the status quo that is not necessarily implied in multicultural competence. As an example, suppose I am a school psychologist who has been asked to consult in a case where an African American male has received many disciplinary referrals. From a multicultural perspective, I might interact with this student and his family in a way that others might judge to be culturally responsive in terms of my knowledge, attitudes, and behaviors. However, given what we know from decades of research on the intersection of race, gender, and discipline referrals (see Chapter 6), if I did not raise the obvious questions and investigate whether this situation had a racial component, I would not be engaging in social justice advocacy.

Thus, social justice competency can be viewed as built upon a multicultural foundation. However, to date there is little to no research on specific social justice frameworks that might be clearly defined either in a graduate course or in providing professional development activities to school psychology practitioners. From my anecdotal experiences presenting on the topic of social justice to practitioners, I have found that if I do not connect this topic to practice early and often, invariably the first question I will receive goes something like, "How does this relate to my day-to-day work?" As such, an important consideration when providing professional development to practitioners around topics related to social justice is the manner in which this training is framed. Is "social justice" being positioned by the persons who organized the training as a "new development?" Is social justice seen as something outside of "mainstream" school psychology? Or is social justice being positioned as part and parcel of school psychology practice (e.g., a framework a practitioner can draw from when thinking through an anti-bullying/pro-wellness initiative)? In my travels to date, I have found this distinction to be quite important and, if it is not clear from the setup that my presentation will relate to "mainstream" school psychology practice, I strive to make this connection quite evident (often through applied examples) at the outset before getting into social justice theory. As Burnes and Singh (2010) note, terms such as "social justice" may come across as "too academic" or "too eggheady" in applied settings unless efforts are made by facilitators to understand what is valued at the applied site and to seek to make connections regarding what "applied social justice" might look like in terms of specific skills and/or activities.

## Assumptions of and Opportunities Afforded the Instructor/Trainer

A final important framework consideration is the social justice educator as an individual, both in terms of her or his personality and strengths and also in terms of the extent to which this educator's identity and life experiences reflect privilege and oppression. For example, while I can seek out, listen, and learn from diverse people and sources and while I can strive to obtain diverse experiences, including experiences quite different from the culture in which I was raised, in the end as a social justice educator I must recognize that I am a straight White male who, while not affluent, has never lived in poverty. This position likely has some strengths and limitations. On the positive side, since the vast majority of my students are also While, straight, and/or come from middle to higher SES backgrounds, perhaps the typical content of social justice training experiences—content that is often quite disquieting to persons from privileged backgrounds—is more easily heard and processed when initiated by someone the students view as similar to them culturally. For example, perhaps it is easier for White students to process and have a discussion on White privilege led by a White instructor than it might be if I were not White, and thus these students are more likely to become allies in cross-racial dialogue and healing. It is also possible that my privileged status opens some doors for me to model a particular form of ally behavior based on mutual respect and dialogue that would not be as easily accomplished if I were from a different background. On the other hand, being from a privileged background (in most respects—being Jewish, I do have some experience with being a member of an oppressed group) surely limits my capacity to fully understand and appreciate the perspective of those in the class who are not straight, middle to higher SES White men.

In terms of privileges, it is important to recognize that as a White male, I am able to teach courses—be they "social justice courses" or courses designed primarily to cover other content (e.g., counseling theories) through a social justice lens—without having the burden of the negative attributions that may be applied to faculty of color teaching the exact same courses in a similar fashion. As one participant in a survey of faculty who teach multicultural counseling courses stated,

> As a White male teaching multicultural courses, White students initially see me as 'selling out' while students of color aren't sure they trust my motivations. My faculty colleagues of color are often victims of harsh criticism and 'up risings' by resistant (mostly White) students. My being White and male seems to unfairly buffer me from these angry expressions. (Reynolds, 2011, p. 172)

In a poignant and powerful study of African American faculty, Constantine, Smith, Redington, and Owens (2008) document several forms of microaggressions. For example, as noted in the preceding comment, participants in this study often stated that they were treated with less respect by students and colleagues, including colleagues undervaluing their research and teaching agenda if this agenda related to multicultural topics. For example, whereas as a White male my interest in multicultural school psychology may be viewed favorably by some without consideration to my own race or gender, these same individuals might view these same topics as "too personal" for women and/or faculty of color to pursue. Additionally, Constantine et al. report that faculty of color are often pulled into more extensive service and mentoring roles based on a lack of faculty of color at their university, a situation that I have never encountered as a White male.

As these findings highlight, as a White male it is very likely that my privileges outweigh the obstacles in terms of how I might be treated by students and evaluated by colleagues. In particular, I can teach courses related to social justice without persons linking this interest to my race, gender, sexual orientation, religion, or any other component of my identity (no one says, "there goes that White guy again talking about diversity!"). However, my experiences thus far have led me to believe that there are some inherent disadvantages to being a White male engaged in teaching for social justice. For example, as a White male I am aware that I am simultaneously attempting to teach a message that unearned power and privilege should be challenged, yet I represent and surely on some level replicate these inequities. Additionally, as the course instructor, while I strive to be as empowering and egalitarian as possible, in the end it is not the students who arrange the course meeting time and requirements, it is I as the course instructor. I am not dependent on the students to give me a good grade in order to advance my career; they are dependent on me. No matter how one divides it, there is always an inherent power differential between faculty and student, particularly in school psychology programs where faculty tend to know every student in the program and the student does not have the option of fully avoiding a faculty member that they find to be oppressive. Thus, while hopefully my students do not find me to be oppressive, they are essentially stuck taking a social justice course with a straight White male who has never known poverty and who likely can never see certain issues of oppression as clearly as some of his students can because they have lived these struggles and he has not. This does not mean, at least in my opinion, that a straight White male of a higher SES status is incapable of teaching a social justice class, or even, as described previously, that there are no potential positives to this situation. Rather the point is that if one is going to be putting himself or herself out there as some sort of model or impetus for developing agents of social justice, one must be attentive to his or her own biases and privileges that affect one's knowledge base and credibility. To teach a social justice class as a straight White male of higher SES status without personally reflecting upon and then overtly recognizing the likely limitations and strengths of my perspective is to undermine my credibility and potential impact as an instructor.

## Implementation

What then would be considered "best practices" in social justice education for school psychologists? At a certain level, at this stage of the game the honest answer is, "we don't fully know," as scholarship aimed at examining social justice education through the specific prism of school psychology training and practice is quite limited. However, there are several promising examples, as well as several models from other fields that can help guide the current or aspiring school psychology social justice educator.

Within school psychology, "Teaching for Social Justice in School Psychology" was the focus of a special topic issue of *Trainers' Forum* (a journal focused on graduate education topics in school psychology) in 2009 (Shriberg, 2009). In this issue, there were three articles coauthored by school psychology graduate students and faculty describing their respective programs' efforts to embed social justice into their training model and practice.

In the first piece, faculty and students affiliated with the school psychology program at The Ohio State University (Radliff et al., 2009)—a program that focuses on urban school psychology—identify five key areas central to infusing social justice into their program. These key areas are: mission statement, student body, program courses and experiences, community partnering, and community-based projects. Similarly, in the second piece of this special topic issue, faculty and students associated with the school psychology program at Northeastern University in Boston (Li et al., 2009) describe a three-pronged approach to teaching for social justice. These prongs are: (1) integrating social justice into courses, (2) engaging students in social justice scholarship and research, and (3) faculty and students collectively acting in concert with their core values and ethical standards for the purpose of improving the lives of others in real world settings. In the final article in this special topic issue, students and faculty at Loyola University Chicago (Briggs, McArdle, Bartucci, Kowalewicz, & Shriberg, 2009) present the results of a focus group with school psychology graduate students regarding how they experienced this program's social justice education. Among the primary findings was that the students identified service learning as an activity that significantly advanced their capacity to be an agent of social justice. Based on this finding, a new social justice course with service learning as the primary assignment was created. The details of this course are described in the case example at the close of this chapter.

Numerous fields related to school psychology, particularly counseling psychology, have also made notable contributions towards a model of social justice training. In a seminal work as part of a special topic issue in *Counseling Psychologist*, Lisa Goodman and her colleagues (Goodman et al., 2004) identify six core components of social justice training: ongoing self-examination, sharing power, giving voice, facilitating consciousness-raising, building on strengths, and leaving clients the tools to work towards social change. Additionally, teaching for social justice in the psychology practicum experience was the theme of a 2010 issue of the journal *Training and Education in Professional Psychology* (*TEPP*). In the first article in this special topic issue, Lewis (2010) describes the importance of placing social justice training within a theoretical framework, encompassing and distinguishing between multiple forms of justice (e.g., procedural justice, distributive justice, and interactional justice). This author concludes with five primary recommendations.

1. The program should make a clear statement related to its commitment to social justice, including placement of this commitment in the program's mission statement.
2. Early in training (and prior to practicum) students should be provided with the program's working definition of social justice, as well as exposure to pertinent scholarship outlining different theoretical approaches to social justice.
3. Desired competencies to be obtained in practicum should be spelt out clearly.
4. Evaluation and processing of progress towards these competencies in practicum should be anchored through the social justice model and theoretical framework provided early in training.
5. Advanced training in higher level systems change should be provided as part of the practicum experience.

In the second article in this series, Burnes and Singh (2010) provide several recommendations related to making psychology practica an impactful social justice training experience. Reiterating advice outlined in more detail in a previous work published by one of these same researchers (Burnes & Manese, 2008), they emphasize the importance of developing a working definition and mission statement related to social justice. They also describe three primary elements for integrating social justice into practicum courses: examination of literature and readings, self-examination learning activities, and examination of systems learning activities. These authors also highlight the importance of engaging in dialogue with field sites as to the program's social justice mission and how this mission might reflect specific desired skills and experiences to be obtained on practicum. They encourage dialogue with students regarding their conception of social justice.

In a seminal article involving school psychology and other graduate students associated with a college of education, McCabe and Rubinson (2008) present data indicating that student attitudes regarding an oppressed group (in this case, GLBTQ youth) may not always translate to ally behavior in support of this group in the field. In the third article in the *TEPP* series, Caldwell and Vera (2010) present the results of interviews with 36 counseling psychologists or counseling psychology doctoral students—all of whom met criteria as social justice experts based on their professional activities. The questions posed to this expert group related to critical incidents that cultivated a social justice orientation. Participants' responses yielded five primary categories: (1) influence of significant persons (e.g., mentors, parents/family, peer support), (2) exposure to injustice (either personal direct experience or witnessing injustice), (3) education/learning (coursework, readings and scholarship, graduate training philosophy), (4) work experiences, and (5) religion/spirituality. When asked to rank-order which of these five categories were most impactful towards developing a social justice orientation, exposure to injustice was the top ranked category.

## Summary of Recommendations

In reviewing this literature, several trends/overlapping themes seem apparent. Based on this research, the following recommendations are offered as guides to persons leading college courses or professional development opportunities related to social justice in school psychology.

## Engage in dialogue related to why this content is important

Whether you are teaching a "social justice" course, a course that has social justice elements, or leading a professional development session or consultation that relates to social justice, context matters. Particularly if social justice content is new to your graduate program or professional audience, it is important to have discussions as to why this content is vital to school psychology training. In the particular case of the graduate program in which I teach, we have a faculty retreat (typically in the summer) at least once a year and our program's social justice philosophy and curriculum is typically a discussion item for this retreat, as well as a discussion item for faculty meetings held regularly during the school year. Several years ago, as part of a broader discussion of why our program values social justice and based on student feedback (see case example below), the program decided not only to create a new social justice course, but to make this course a required first semester course for all incoming school psychology graduate students. Previously, our program had a social justice course, but this was seen as more of a capstone experience. The rationale for the creation of the new course was that if the program was going to recruit incoming students based on a social justice mission, we needed a course during the student's first semester that provided them with an opportunity to explore what social justice means to them and to have an applied experience centered on social justice ideas.

As an individual faculty member, it is possible that I might have been able to propose this same course on my own and obtain the necessary approvals for the course to be created. However, this would be a different (and, in my opinion, a much less effective) path than first engaging in a dialogue with all of the core faculty in the school psychology program about why it is important to all of us to have social-justice related coursework, with this course emerging as a natural result of this discussion.

## Develop a Mission Statement/Core Training Goals Related to Social Justice

While ongoing dialogue is critical, several authors (e.g., Burnes & Manese, 2010, Lewis, 2010, Radliff et al., 2009) note the importance of this dialogue being linked to a mission statement and core operational goals. These can provide an important core framework from which individual and systemic decisions can be made. Similarly, in doing a professional development offering, particularly around a topic such as social justice that can be quite abstract and have multiple meanings, it is important to begin with some core goals and/or assumptions to frame the content and experiences that you have organized.

## Embed meaningful experiences that help make "social justice" a real thing, not simply a theoretical construct or aspiration

Is social justice a noun or a verb? Is the goal of "social justice training" to obtain a clearer sense of what a "just" society might look like as it relates to school psychology practice, or is social justice more about obtaining hands-on experience? Whether the meaningful experiences come from individual class assignments or programmatic requirements such as service learning, practicum, and internship, a recurring theme (e.g., Briggs et al., 2009) relates to the importance of making the social justice experience "real." This suggestion is particularly important given the knowledge that attitudes consistent with social justice principles do not necessarily translate to behaviors consistent with social justice, as McCabe and Rubinson (2008) found with their graduate student participants who reported non-prejudiced attitudes towards GLBTQ students but whose attitudes did not appear to translate to ally behavior.

Keeping in mind Caldwell and Vera's (2010) finding that "exposure to injustice" was rated as the most impactful way that students developed a 'social justice orientation", in the context of graduate education in school psychology "applied social justice" might take the form of seeking "traditional" (e.g., schools) and "non-traditional" (e.g., homeless shelters) sites for students to obtain meaningful experiences. In the context of professional development, focusing on the specific experiences of session attendees—particularly as relates to sharing power, leaving clients with the tools for change, and other core social justice training concepts described by Goodman et al. (2004)—can help bridge the gap from social justice as an aspiration to social justice as a practice.

## Provide a safe and supportive forum for eliciting voice and constructive dialogue

While several didactic approaches to teaching social justice are likely to be effective, it is very difficult to imagine an impactful social justice course where the course instructor did all the talking and multiple viewpoints were not considered. In particular, Burnes and Singh (2010), Goodman et al. (2004), and many others speak to the importance of creating an educational space and opportunity to explore what social justice might look like from different perspectives, including the individual perspective of every student in a course or of every participant in a professional development session. For this reason, a common recommendation for social justice instruction is to be sure to provide one or more forums (e.g., verbal, written) for reflection (O'Brien, Patel, Hensler-McGinnis, & Kaplan, 2006). For example, some individuals may put into writing thoughts that they might not share verbally with the group. Others may arrive to a professional development session very keen to publicly share a particular impactful experience. Reflection can be an extremely powerful conduit for eliciting voice and sharing ideas. Instructors play a critical role in this process, both as individual models and as facilitators of challenging yet supportive dialogue where students/attendees feel safe to express their feelings and opinions. None of us are perfect social justice beings (whatever that means), and when facilitators are able to speak to their own self-perceived limitations that can help provide a space for students to do the same.

Additionally, in a qualitative study of social justice educators in counseling education, Odegard and Vereen (2010) found that in a well-designed social justice course students are likely to experience several "awakenings" and/or paradigm shifts. In my personal experience, these awakenings can take several forms. For example, many students may state or write that they realize that they have been acting in ways that they now consider to be "unjust." For others, there may be a strong educational component, where they state or write that they "didn't know what I didn't know" until exposed to specific readings, discussions, and/or experiences in the course. Additionally, some students may feel inspired towards action on a larger scale, such as community advocacy and/or working to change school psychology practices. There are many models of multicultural competence that speak to these kinds of awakenings and most of these models take a stage approach where different students may be at different stages of awareness at different points in time. Invariably, students and the course instructor(s) may feel some discomfort, anger, and/or embarrassment as part of this type of course. There likely will be times when students and the instructor say or do something that others may experience as a poorly phrased statement or action at best or as a microaggression at worst. How these types of situation are handled is a challenge to all instructors, but the core element repeated again and again in the literature is that social justice growth experiences in education require that the student voice is valued and that a safe and respectful class atmosphere is created. Typically this requires the creation of groundrules developed by the students/session attendees and instructor together at or near the start of a course, as well as a commitment in word and deed by the instructor that what students/attendees have to say truly matters and that the goal is not for students/attendees to agree with the instructor's views on any particular topic, but for there to be an atmosphere where divergent opinions are valued and respected. Relatedly, it is critical that mechanisms for ongoing (in the case of a course or multi-week professional development session) and summative feedback from students/attendees regarding the course, the instructor, and the intended outcomes are put into place and utilized.

Although all of the above suggestions are applicable to both graduate courses and professional development sessions, it is recognized that the amount of time available and the context of the interaction between instructor and facilitator plays an important role. In general, the more time one has available (it is of course extremely difficult to do all of the above with much depth in a three hour workshop, although each element can be touched upon) and the more encounters one will have with the participants over time (e.g., a semester-long course), the better the opportunity to make a lasting impact. If you only have one or two sessions with participants and/or limited hours to do all of the above, it is recommended that you focus on ways to highlight the relationship of social justice ideas to practice and work with participants on ways that they can tap into their personal and professional potential (e.g., through self-exploration exercises and goal setting) as an agent of social justice. In my experience, while it is important to define "what" social justice is, it is the "why" of social justice that is most likely to spur individuals to action, particularly if this "why" is connected with why the person entered the field and how she/he can impact justice positively and realistically in her/his professional setting.

In graduate courses, one has the opportunity to really embed social justice into the "what" and "why" of school psychology ideas of emerging professionals, as highlighted in the following case example.

## Case Example: Service Learning as a Mechanism for Teaching for Social Justice in School Psychology

For the facilitator seeking to lead a course or professional development work related to social justice, a critical goal and challenge is to facilitate the application of social justice principles to practice. One mechanism to achieve this goal is service learning. Service learning is an approach commonly associated with social justice training due to its emphasis on providing students with the opportunity to engage in and reflect on socially relevant real-life experiences intended to make a positive difference in the community (Cuban & Anderson, 2007). In this case example, I will describe my experience teaching an introductory social justice course where service learning is the primary course requirement.

As described, I am a core faculty member in a school psychology graduate program that is housed within a university (Loyola University Chicago) and College of Education centered on a social justice mission. As such, faculty within our program share a common commitment to teaching for socially just school psychology practice, but are continuously grappling with the best mechanisms to bring this aspirational goal to practice.

During the 2008–09 academic year, a group of school psychology doctoral students set upon the task of systemically evaluating our program's efforts in this regard through a series of focus groups that they led with the then current school psychology doctoral and specialist level students at Loyola. Specifically, they led three focus groups—one for first year students, one for second year students, and one for third year and above students—with Loyola graduate students. In these groups they asked questions related to how these students understood social justice, whether they viewed social justice as relevant to school psychology practice (and, if so, in what ways), and their feedback on what the training program did well and what could be improved as related to its "social justice curriculum."

These focus groups were repeated over the course of three academic years. A pilot study, featuring the findings from third year and above Loyola graduate students in 2009, has been published (Briggs et al., 2009) and the remaining data is being prepared for publication review at the time this chapter is being written. One of the primary findings from this research was that Loyola students consistently identified the program's service learning requirements as a potent (many said service learning was the most potent) social justice learning experience and cited a lack of an outlet for processing their service learning experiences as they occurred as a gap in the program's instruction.

Based on this data, the program created and approved an "Introduction to Social Justice" course as a required fall course for all first year school psychology specialist and doctoral students, with service learning the primary course requirement. Prior to the initiation of this course, all students had been required to complete 100 hours of service learning as a free-standing (not tied to any course) master's degree requirement. This requirement was originally put into place as a result of a shift in the common background experiences prior to entry in Loyola's school psychology graduate program. Whereas at one point in time most Loyola graduate students had previous experience either as teachers or in other professional capacities in the school setting, for the past several years the vast majority of our students were not education majors and/or professional educators, but rather typically were psychology majors as undergraduates and/or had little experience in the school setting prior to their entry as school psychology graduate students.

Over the years, the number of required hours and the parameters of the work that could be counted towards these service learning hours has shifted for various reasons, but the core idea has been to ensure that all students obtain a rich experience either directly in the school setting or in a setting directly relevant to school psychology practice (e.g., tutoring in a community clinic). Additionally, over time, as part of the program's social justice mission, students have been encouraged to move outside of their personal cultural comfort zone in their service learning work.

Accordingly, beginning in Fall 2010 all first year school psychology graduate students enrolled in an "Introduction to Social Justice in School Psychology" style course with this author as the primary course instructor. Three school psychology doctoral students served as course TAs and one of these students received university funding to serve as the program's graduate "service learning coordinator." This student has primary responsibility for keeping connection with the field sites, helping students to find appropriate placements, and working with the university professor to monitor, support, and problem-solve as needed during the course of the semester as students volunteered at their site.

In this course, a number of structural and process elements have been put into place (if you are interested in a copy of the course's syllabus, please contact the author at dshribe@luc.edu). In terms of core content, the course begins with an overview of social justice theory, focusing on introducing concepts such as "power," "privilege," "oppression," and "ally." At the start of the third class meeting, students are required to turn in two documents related to social justice. The first is a photo journal depicting "social justice" as they understand the concept. The second document is a personal biography reflecting their multicultural history and their current perspective on social justice.

During approximately weeks 4–11, each week focuses on a different dimension of diversity, such as race/ethnicity, gender, sexual orientation, transgendered oppression, religious oppression. These topics are based on the primary text used in this course, Adams et al.'s (2010) *Readings for Diversity and Social Justice*. One adaptation is that, rather than following the book chapters in order, we have chosen to start this section of the course with topics—ableism, adultism, and sexism—where it is believed that students have more common ground in terms of their opinions and life experiences. We then build off these initial discussions as we move into topic areas (racism, classism, religious oppression) later in the course that can be seen as touchier and riskier to talk about.

While ally development is discussed throughout the course, the final three class sessions are devoted specifically to developing action strategies as agents of social justice. First, we read about and discuss ways that school psychology as a profession can be more engaged in social justice, including discussion of what practitioners might do at the individual level. Second, we focus on each individual student in terms of his or her personal growth and ways in which he or she might leverage his or her personal talents and passions to be an agent of social justice.

On the service learning front, during the second week of the course the community partners come to the course to introduce themselves and their setting. Prior to these presentations, the course instructor states to the entire group the two primary objectives of service learning (these objectives were based on student and field supervisor feedback, as well as the instructor's beliefs). These objectives are: (1) to be as helpful as possible to the site, and (2) to utilize service learning as a mechanism for personal and professional growth as an agent of social justice.

Regarding the first objective, prior discussions are held with field sites regarding the nature of the work desired, and then students and field supervisors (students are free to choose whatever site best suits their interests and availability) work together to write out a basic agreement stipulating in general the type of work to be done by the student. Students are also required to work with partner sites to take the lead on an "original contribution," meaning an additional activity and/or project that would not have occurred had the student not volunteered at that site.

Regarding the second goal of utilizing service learning as a mechanism for personal and professional growth, on the service learning agreement that is signed by the student, the field supervisor, and the university supervisors (the graduate student coordinator and myself), the student outlines some goals in this area. These goals are then discussed extensively (and also at times with the field supervisor, although this is not required) during small group supervision meetings that take place nearly every week of class once the service learning placements have been made (typically these placements are finalized within a month of the start of class). Students also blog about their service learning experiences weekly, as well as turn in a final revised photo journal on social justice and a final written paper describing their views on social justice (this paper includes reflection on their personal goals, an analysis of the impact of their service learning experience on their conception of social justice, and a social justice action plan moving forward).

This description is intended as an example of one program's attempt to bring social justice ideas to practice through a required course that integrates social justice theory, analysis of key social justice concepts, self-reflection and goal setting, and applied work connected to these ideas. While this course and related features (e.g., we have an annual celebration with service learning partners at the end of the year, pre and post service learning surveys are completed by students and field supervisors, there are ongoing student focus groups on social justice) are something that I feel proud to be associated with, by no means is this example intended as a "best practice," but simply as a description of one way to go about this type of training.

## Conclusion

As social justice achieves increased prominence as an aspiration and expected practice for school psychologists, there is a need for courses, professional development materials, and program models for what "teaching for social justice in school psychology" might look like. This chapter highlighted several considerations and potential key features of teaching for social justice. As the reader continues to develop his or her own understanding of and commitment to social justice, it is hoped that she or he will contribute to this knowledge base by creating new teaching and professional development structures that expand this literature.

## References

Adams, M. A., Blumenfeld, W., Casteñeda, C. R., Hackman, H. W., Peters, M. L., & Zuñiga, X. (2010). *Readings for diversity and social justice* (2nd ed.). New York, NY: Routledge.

Briggs, A., McArdle, L., Bartucci, G., Kowalewicz, E., & Shriberg, D. (2009). Students' perspectives on the incorporation of social justice in a school psychology graduate program. *Trainers' Forum, 28* (4), 35–45.

Burnes, T. R., & Manese, J. E. (2008). Social justice in an accredited internship in professional psychology: Answering the call. *Training and Education in Professional Psychology, 2,* 176–181.

Burnes, T. R., & Singh, A. A. (2010). Integrating social justice training into the practicum experience for psychology trainees: Starting earlier. *Training and Education in Professional Psychology, 4,* 153–162.

Caldwell, J. C., & Vera, E. M. (2010). Critical incidents in counseling psychology professionals' and trainees' social justice orientation and development. *Training and Education in Professional Psychology, 4,* 163–176.

Constantine, M. G., Smith, L., Redington, R. M., & Owens, D. (2008). Racial microaggressions against Black counseling and counseling psychology faculty: A central challenge in the multicultural counseling movement. *Journal of Counseling & Development, 86,* 348–355.

Cuban, S. & Anderson, J. B. (2007). Where's the justice in service-learning? Institutionalizingservice-learning from a social justice perspective at a Jesuit university. *Equity &Excellence in Education, 40,* 144–155.

Goodman, L. A., Liang, B., Helms, J. E., Latta, R. E., Sparks, E., & Weintraub, S. R. (2004). Training counseling psychologists as social justice agents: Feminist and multicultural principles in action. *Counseling Psychologist, 32,* 793–837.

Lewis, B. L. (2010). Social justice in practicum training: Competencies and developmental implications. *Training and Education in Professional Psychology, 4,* 145–152.

Li, C., Kruger, L., Mulé, C., Lippus, K., Santora, K., Cicala, G., et al. (2009). Including social justice in the training of school psychologists. *Trainers' Forum, 28* (4), 24–34.

McCabe, P., & Rubinson, F. (2008). Committing to social justice: The behavioral intention of school psychology and education trainees to advocate for lesbian, gay, bisexual, and transgendered youth. *School Psychology Review, 37,* 469–486.

O'Brien, K. M., Patel, S., Hensler-McGinnis, N., & Kaplan, J. (2006). Empowering undergraduate students to be agents of social change: An innovative service learning course in counseling psychology. In R. L. Toporek et al. (Eds.), *Handbook for social justice in counseling psychology* (pp. 59–73). Thousand Oaks, CA: Sage.

Odegard, M. A., & Vereen, L. S. (2010). A grounded theory of counselor educator integrating social justice into their pedagogy. *Counselor Education & Supervision, 50*, 130–149.

Radliff., K. H., Miranda, A. H., Stoll, S., & Wheeler, A. (2009). A conceptual framework for infusing social justice in school psychology training. *Trainers' Forum, 28* (4), 10–22.

Ratts, M. J. (2011). Multiculturalism and social justice: Two sides of the same coin. *Journal of Multicultural Counseling and Development, 39*, 24–37.

Reynolds, A. L. (2011). Understanding the perceptions and experiences of faculty who teach multicultural counseling courses: An exploratory study. *Training and Education in Professional Psychology, 5*, 167–174.

Rogers, M. R. (2005). Multicultural training in school psychology. In C. L. Frisby & C. R. Reynolds (Eds.), *Comprehensive handbook of multicultural school psychology* (pp. 993–1022). New York, NY: Wiley.

Shriberg, D. (2009). Teaching for social justice in school psychology graduate programs: Strategies and lessons learned: Introduction to the special topic issue. *Trainers' Forum, 28* (4), 5–9.

Speight, S. & Vera, E. (2008). Social justice and counseling psychology: A challenge to the profession. In S. D. Brown & R. W. Lent (Eds.), *Handbook of counseling psychology* (4th ed., pp. 54–67). New York, NY: Wiley.

# eighteen
# **Moving Forward**

## David Shriberg,
## Samuel Y. Song,
## Antoinette Halsell Miranda,
## and Kisha M. Radliff

Over the past 17 chapters, 25 different authors have provided their thoughts and expertise on a range of school psychology topics. Reflecting the broad scope of social justice, some authors focused more on micro- or meso-level topics whereas others focused on macro-level themes. Many chapters did both. In the aggregate, we are left with the first comprehensive book for school psychologists where social justice is the organizing theme.

Now that we have reached the final chapter, what are the primary take-aways and suggested next steps? The most relevant answers to these questions are the take-aways and next steps that you as a reader have determined. As mentioned in the opening chapter, if this book has been helpful in advancing your personal capacity as an agent of social justice in school psychology, then it has been a success from our perspective as book editors. However, in the spirit of helping you as a reader to determine some of your own take-aways from this book and also as an aid to individuals who may be motivated to get involved in furthering social justice advocacy and scholarship at multiple levels within school psychology, each editor provides reflections based on her or his involvement in this book specifically and with social justice efforts more generally. Going in alphabetical order, we begin with Antoinette Halsell Miranda.

## Antoinette Halsell Miranda's Reflections

I found that I was continually challenged in writing my chapter to think about what socially just practice is and what it looks like. It is easy to have the words "social justice" roll off your tongue. Writing about it forced me to really delve into the issue of social justice as it related to the topic of behavior in a much deeper, more meaningful way. I had to really think about how practice with the most marginalized students should look if it was done in the right way. It was most helpful to return to the definition articulated in the first chapter. Thus, writings from a best practice perspective must also include some aspect of an advocacy-related construct. It was interesting because almost all authors were asked to be more specific about social justice as it related to their topic area in their chapter in the second draft. They tended to write from a best practice perspective but with little to no inclusion about social justice. All authors returned chapters that were more thoughtful and specific about how social justice should look as a part of practice or in the foundational topic. Thus, it was interesting that many of the authors were not initially as explicit about social justice in their writings. This was not surprising given that we as editors too had to think in deeper, more intentional ways about socially just practice.

The writing of the chapter(s) required a thoughtful and intentional process regarding how social justice is practiced in school psychology. Social justice requires an understanding of cultural competence and societal variables that impact marginalized students in sometimes negative ways. It also requires us to examine and explore writings from different disciplines, as school psychology is often lacking in this area. In reviewing chapters, it became clear that best practice is not equivalent to social justice. While most wrote from a best practice perspective, it was clear that it was something more. If social justice was simply best practice, then we wouldn't need this book. The authors had to be challenged to think beyond best practice because with marginalized students best practice also has to incorporate an advocacy-related construct which was often absent.

Going forward, it is clear that writings in school psychology regarding social justice have to be done in a more intentional and explicit way. If we, who are committed to social justice, initially "struggled" to write about it in an explicit fashion, it stands to reason that the practitioner too may not be sure what it looks like. It is hoped that this book will provide that explicit look at social justice in practice so that marginalized students will experience educational success and psychological well-being.

## Kisha M. Radliff's Reflections

As an early career school psychology trainer, social justice has become a more salient part of what I do and who I am. Engaging in the process of developing this book has helped me to look critically at, and to understand and embrace more fully, what it means to be a social justice advocate. I really enjoyed the process of writing a chapter and reviewing the chapters of other authors. Specifically, throughout the process I realized that examining issues through a social justice lens wasn't as simple as attaching the words "social justice" or integrating "diversity" into the language. Rather, one has to really consider what social justice means, and more specifically, what it means within the context of the issue being addressed. It was initially easier to recognize this as I reviewed other chapters. Like Antoinette, I felt that it was easy to integrate "best practice" into chapters, but it was more difficult to emphasize how social justice advocacy goes above and beyond best practice. I found myself going back to my chapter, rereading and asking myself if it emphasized social justice, and revising it in attempts to make a socially just approach more explicit.

One word that kept coming to mind throughout this process was *purposeful*. I began to recognize that we had to be purposeful, or intentional, in describing school psychology practice from a social justice perspective. This meant reviewing and rereading the material to ensure that we were explicitly emphasizing socially just practice. Oftentimes, I found that examples or case studies were helpful in illustrating what socially just practice could look like. It also became apparent that engaging in socially just practice could sometimes be challenging and seem overwhelming. To me, this emphasized the value of colleagues, collaboration, and building support networks of like-minded individuals (both within and outside of our field). For us to be social justice advocates and to continually engage in socially just practice it is optimal to collaborate with others who have similar ideas and can support our efforts.

I am glad that we had a mix of "seasoned" authors as well as "newer" (early career) authors. The challenge of integrating a social justice approach to practice, for example, was not just a challenge for early career authors, but to almost all authors. To me, this emphasized the importance of internalizing a social justice perspective so that it becomes the lens through which I approach my role as a school psychologist. In this way, social justice more fully permeates my practice. For example, as a trainer, my approach to teaching, research, and service would be advanced through a social justice lens influencing cases that I integrate into course materials, the design of my research studies, and the service activities I select. I realize that this is an ongoing practice and that I will need to continually examine my practice to determine if I am being purposeful with integrating social justice within my practice.

## Dave Shriberg's Reflections

One of the primary reasons for creating this book was our belief that social justice considerations permeate *every* component of social justice practice. Now that all of the chapters have been completed, I feel even more strongly that this is true. While, as both Antoinette and Kisha have pointed out, it is a challenge for many of us—if not all of us—to conceptualize fully what applied social justice in school psychology might look like, I believe that it is equally challenging to make a case that social justice does *not* apply to any area of school psychology practice. Put another way, for every chapter in this book, I felt that if we had the time and space (and if readers wanted to read a 1000-page book—come on, I know you want a 1000-page book!) we could have come up with two or three more chapters that would cover pertinent and related areas of practice. In this sense, I really hope and believe that this book can be a springboard for additional works and advocacy on a variety of topics. As we do this, as a field we will build on the foundational works described in Chapter 1 regarding defining and creating a model of social justice in school psychology that has strong support and is understandable and relatable to practice.

While I also agree with Antoinette and Kisha that for most authors—myself certainly included—there was a tendency in the first draft to have a "best practice" focus where the link to social justice was not always very often or very clearly made, I also felt that many authors appeared to enjoy the opportunity to write and think in a bigger picture context. Speaking only for myself, I find that writing about social justice can be very liberating in this sense. As a reader of school psychology journals, I feel that peer-reviewed journals tend to bias towards studies with high internal validity and a very narrow focus. As such, I often wonder if and how some of this information can translate to practice and whether this information typically inspires the reader. The chapters in this book have the potential not only to provide some guidance on specific action steps, but also to *inspire* the reader to view practice through social justice goggles. In this sense, social justice can become a way of looking at the world that taps directly into why we all entered the field—to make the world a better place for children and families. As more research builds upon these foundational chapters, it is my belief that this kind of writing—even reports of empirical work—can both instruct *and* inspire school psychologists around the noble reasons why we all entered the field.

Regarding next steps, as mentioned I feel that this book can serve as a platform for all kinds of additional books, research, and advocacy related to social justice. If this occurs, I concur with Kisha in that I strongly believe that we can accomplish more working together than any of us can working alone. This is true both within school psychology and across disciplines. Within school psychology, I hope we use structures such as NASP's Social Justice Interest Group and Division 16's Workgroup on Children's Rights and Social Justice to meet and advocate with other school psychologists who are committed to social justice. Similarly, within every state there are school psychology organizations one can get involved with and through which a social justice agenda may be advanced. So, I urge the reader to get involved locally, regionally, nationally, and internationally to build community and forward social justice.

Finally, while it will always be important to link social justice to school psychology practice, it is my hope and recommendation that school psychologists who engage in these efforts work hard to find common ground and to learn from individuals in related fields who face similar social justice struggles and have similar social justice goals. We are in an era of academic and applied specialization, whereas achieving social justice almost certainly requires much collaboration across professional disciplines and between educators, children, families, and other community members. Who better than school psychologists to be boundary-crossers?

## Sam Song's Reflections

I have learned that I am not alone. Social justice work, whether it is practice, scholarship, or living it out in the rest of one's life, can be lonely. Perhaps this is one reason why both Kisha and Dave emphasized community building. While many will agree with social justice ideals and values, not as many will be explicit about it in their work in schools, the academy, or how they live their life. A reason for this phenomenon may be that the work of social justice is risky for an individual. It is risky because of the misperceptions people hold of social justice and because it requires advocacy disrupting the status quo. For example, on a job interview for a school psychologist position, some applicants have not received offers because they are perceived to be too strong an advocate for children rather than a "team player." In the academy, social justice scholars' and researchers' work is viewed by some as less rigorous or not scientific, leading to unfavorable and prejudicial reviews. In the social arena, one may lose friendships or become less popular at work because one lives out social justice in one's life.

The future of social justice, then, may rely to some extent on how well we can address the problem of riskiness for individuals. While I am not suggesting that other ways are not as important, one way to accomplish this is through more focused scholarship. One research question to pursue is how social justice might lead to enhanced practice in school psychology. It is assumed that social justice practice is "better" than the status quo practice. How is social justice practice better compared to the status quo and even best practice? It may be that social justice practice leads to improved outcomes and intervention fidelity and sustainability, enhanced relationships, the empowerment of marginalized groups, or less burnout on the job, for example. As more models of social justice practice are delineated for school psychology practice, the data needs to be there to support these models. As this happens *over time*, social justice practice may become less risky to individuals because it has become more accepted as "best practice."

Contributing to scholarship is the job not only of academics, but also of practitioners. Practitioners may consider collaborating with university groups to conduct research in their schools on social justice practice (e.g., community-based research models), which may lessen the burden of doing research alone. Another option could be to conduct action research in schools working with school personnel to collaboratively collect data to support social justice practice. Finally, students may be the most important in this effort. If you are reading this book as a student, then you have a great opportunity to learn all of the new social justice practice ideas in our field that did not exist even three years ago. You may bring these social justice practice models into the schools, disseminate them, and collaborate on research to support them empirically. While this of course is easier said than done, remember that you are not alone.

> Never doubt that a small group of thoughtful, committed people can change the world. Indeed, it is the only thing that ever has. (Margaret Mead)

# Index

Locators in **bold** refer to tables and case studies

ACA (American Counseling
  Association) 299–300
academic success: ecological model 194–6;
  family 194–5. *See also* barriers to
  academic success
acculturation **237–40**
achievement gap 144–5, 190–4
ADHD. *See* Attention Deficit Hyperactivity
  Disorder
advocacy, social justice 294–5, **308**,
  328–30; conduct 298–308; culturally
  responsive practice 297–8, 313–14;
  definition 295–8; discipline 306;
  guidelines 294–5, 298–9; policy 303–4;
  tiers 300–8, **301–2**
Aesop's fables 241
African Americans 95–100, 110–11, 119,
  147, 211
agenda 15; historical development 16–19;
  preventative discipline 94–5;
  promotion 24, 92, 99
American Counseling Association
  (ACA) 299–300
American Psychological Association
  (APA) 16, 225; mental health 246–7;
  promotion of globalized approach 30
apartheid. *See* segregation

assessment 64, 124, 173–6, 185; case
  study 182–5; consultation 229;
  continuum 177–8;
  individual 181–5; language 178–9;
  nondiscriminatory 174–6,
  178–9, 182–5; principles 176–9;
  school psychologist 179–82, 185;
  systemic 179–81; theory and
  practice 175–6, 179–85
Attention Deficit Hyperactivity Disorder
  (ADHD) 142, **237–8**
attitudes 53; changing 15–16;
  prosocial 16, 311, 319–20; racial 18;
  western-centric 32–3

barriers to academic success 145–7,
  189–94, 203; consultation services
  00–1; ecological model 194–6;
  process 196–201; systemic
  intervention 201–3
barriers to collaboration 273–6
behavioral issues 8, 106–8, 304–5:
  assessment 181; consultation
  230–1; control 107–8; equitability 16;
  psychosocial behaviors 142–3; respect
  for diversity 16. *See also* bullying,
  classroom behaviour; discipline

best practice 54, 160–3; discipline 93; moving beyond 327–31; prosociality 311; public health model 298–304; school culture and climate 155–60

bias 121–2, 199–200; confirmation 182–3; cultural 178–9, 250–1; ethnocentric 214–15; psychometric testing 174; responsive practice 109–10; special education 77–82; Western centric 109–10

blame 21–2, 123; parents 150; poverty 144; teachers 271–3

Brown v. Board of Education (1954) 18, 125, 147–8

bullying 20, 43–4, 156–60, 164–6. *See also* behavioral issues; discipline

caregivers 17, 19, **38**. *See also* family; parents; teachers

Carroll, D. W. 150–1

case studies **86–7**, **100–2**, 182–5; consultation **236–40**; cosmopolitan resilience **131–2**; mental health **263–6**; Pink Power 157–61, 165–7; professional development **322–4**; race **220–2**; underachievement 189–90, 192–3

Casella, R. 97

CCC (Consultee-Centered Consultation) 230

changing attitudes 15–16

Child and Adolescent Service System Program (CASSP) 248–9

child development 155, 189–90; environmental factors 138–40; institutional barriers 140–1

child rights 29–30, **36**; advocacy 295–8; Convention on the Rights of the Child 33; liberty 34

children: childhood experiences 16; crime 91–2, 143, 207–10; exploitation 33–4; poverty 139–41; preschool 17; as target population 16–17

city schools. *See* inner-city schools

Civil Rights Act (1974) 75

Civil Rights Movement 18, 62–3, 74, 147. *See also* Brown v. Board of Education (1954)

class distinctions 54. *See also* privilege

class sizes 123–4, 126

classroom behavior 206–8, 220; cultural 214–18; management 208–13; school psychologist role 218–20; teachers role 209–13

CLD (culturally and linguistically diverse learners) 73–84, 98

cognitive testing 64, 83–5

collaboration 225–8, **275**, **278**, 330–1; advocacy 298, 300; barriers to 273–6; family 17, **283**, 283–6; family, school, and community partnerships 270–1, 289–91; historical perspectives 271–3; individual approaches 284–9; programs 276–80; systems-level approaches 280–4

collectivism 281–2

color. *See* race

communication: caregivers 19; culturally responsive practice 285–6; family-school 286–9; SOLVES model 287–9

community 18, **38**, 159, 330–1: Child and Adolescent Service System Program 248–9; global 30–1, **31**; homophobia 21; mapping 129. *See also* collaboration

compulsory schooling 93, 207

confirmation bias 182–3

consultation 64, 225–9, **234**, 240–1; assessment 229; behavioral 230–1; case studies **236–40**; Consultee-Centered Consultation 230; culturally responsive practice 228–34, **232–3**; definition **38**, 226–7; entry 228–9; goal setting 229; guidelines 225; models and methods 229–34; motivation 236, **237–40**; multiculturalism 233–4; Participatory Intervention Model 231–3; resistance 235; scholarship 235–6; services 19–20, 200–1; systems theory 227–8, 240–1

Consultee-Centered Consultation (CCC) 230

continuum, in assessment 177–8

control-driven tactics 107–8. *See also* punitive discipline

Convention on the Rights of the Child (CRC) 33

conventional scholarship 55–6

corporal punishment 93. *See also* punitive discipline

cosmopolitan resilience 118–22, 130–3: case study **131–2**; rural schools 122–8; school psychologist 128–30; suburban schools 122–6; urban schools 122–4. *See also* resiliency

CRC (Convention on the Rights of the Child) 33

credit crunch 138–40

crime 123, 143; school to prison pipeline 91–2, 207–10

crisis, economic 138–40
Cronbach, L. J. 198
Cross, T. 250–1
cultural construction 40–6, 61; responsive practice 109–10; stakeholders 42–4; subjectivity 60; terminology 42
cultural minorities 160–2, 315–16
culturally and linguistically diverse (CLD) learners 73–84, 98
culturally responsive practice 98, 109–10, 162, 178–9, 250–1; advocacy 297–8, 313–14; classroom management 214–18; collaboration 274–9, 284–6; communication 285–6; consultation 228–34
culture: acculturation **237–40**; cultural transformation 162–3, 165–7; heteronormativity 157, 164–5; individualism 157; norms and values 211–12, 214–18. *See also* environmental factors; meta-culture
curriculum 124, 126, 129, 133

Darling-Hammond, L. 145–6
data collection. *See* evidence-based practice
decision-making, schoolwide data focus 102–5
definitions 2, **5**, **36–9**, 61–5; advocacy 295–8; consultation and collaboration 226–7; cultural construction of 42; poverty 138–9; resiliency 119; school culture and climate 156; social justice 8, 60–1, 137, 175, 327–31; stakeholder 226
delivery, mental health services 256–8
deprivation 29–30, 33–5. *See also* poverty
detention, preventative 97
development. *See* child development; professional development
disability. *See* learning disability, mental health
discipline 8, 103–4, 206–8; advocacy 306; disproportionality 92, 94–8, 111–12, 193, 211; history 93–5; negative 208; preventative 94–5, 97, 110–11; punitive 91–4, 143; social climate 105; statistics 95–6; zero tolerance 94
discrimination 1–2, 6, 18, 61–3, 161: assessment 178–9; gender 55–8; as perceived cause of peer violence 43–4; prevention 295–8, 306–7; race 144–5; special education 73–8. *See also* bullying; marginalization
disenfranchisement 161–2
disproportionality 6–7, 92, 94, 124, 139, 192–3, 199: African American students 95–100, 211; consultation 233–4; disciplinary 92, 93, 94–8, 111–12, 211; gender 55–9; intervention 100, **100–2**; schoolwide database 102–3; special education 73–81. *See also* equal opportunity; equality; equity; race
diversity 16, 40, 124, 274
dominant culture 61–5, 126, 250–1

ecological model 20–2, **37–8**, **40**, 149, 161–2, 270, 294; academic success 194–6; mental health 255
economic crisis 138–40
education 15–19; institutional barriers 143–9; as metaphor 19; policy 158; professional. *See* professional development; public health crisis 22–4; statistics **22–3**
Education for all Handicapped Children Act 63–4
emic model 40–5
empowerment, family 285–6
entry stage, consultation 228–9
environmental factors 190, 196–7. *See also* culture
Epstein, J. 272–3
equal opportunities 143–5, 147, 176
equality/inequality 16, 18, 21, 55–60
equity: in assessment 174–6; institutional barriers 270–1. *See also* disproportionality
ethics: relational 59–60; White expectations 98
ethnic composition 41–2. *See also* race
ethnocentrism 78, 214–15
etic model **36–40**, 40–5. *See also* meta-culture
European bias 109–10
evidence-based practice 46, 173–5, 331; advocacy 297–8, 305–6; classroom management 212–13; confirmation bias 182–3; consultation 230–1; restorative justice 108–9; schoolwide data focus 102–5
exclusionary discipline 91–3, 97, 103–4, 110–11, 207–8
exosystem 138, 158, 177–8, 195, 202
expectations. *See* values and norms
exploitation, children 33–4
external control 107–8

fables, Aesop's 241
family **38**, 159–60; academic

success 194–5; collaboration **283**, 283–6; empowerment 285–6; enhancing resiliency 120–1, 183–5; expectations 124–5; fragmentation 273; mental health 253–4; in poverty 139–42; school-family communication 284–9

financial difficulties 183. *See also* poverty

freedom of expression 34

full service schools 261

future directions 45–7, 327–31

Gaines, A. D. 46

gays. *See* Lesbian Gay Bisexual Transgender and Questioning

gender 55–8; inequality 59; special education 77

gender neutral restrooms 159, 165

Gilligan, C. 59–60, 66

global: citizenship 123, 131; community model **35**. *See also* international perspective

Golden Rule 162

Goodman, L. A. 317, 320

Gorski, P. C. 151–2

graduate education. *See* professional development

guidelines: advocacy 294–5, 298–9; assessment 176–9; consultation 225; mental health 246–7, 249–50; National Association of School Psychologists 2–3, 294–8; professional conduct **37**; school 158; special education 85

health, individual 141–3. *See also* public health

heteronormativity 157, 164–5

historical perspectives 6, 15–19, 24; collaboration 271–3; consultation services 19–20; discipline 93–5; ecological model 20–2; international 29; mental health 245–7; public health **22–3**, 22–4

homeostasis 227

homophobia 21, 157

homosexuality. *See* Lesbian Gay Bisexual Transgender and Questioning (LGBTQ)

human capital 120–1, 123, 126

humiliation 93–4

identity 183; ethnic 120–1

individual assessment 181–5

individualism 157

Individuals with Disabilities Education Act (IDEA) 75

inequality/equality 16, 18, 21, 55–60. *See also* disproportionality

information age 23–4

Ingraham, C. L. 231–3, **232–3**

injustice 318–21. *See also* discrimination; disproportionality

inner-city schools 103–4

institutional barriers 7, 128, 137–40, 150–2, **234**: poverty; to equity 270–1; expectations 274–5; school psychologist 149–52. *See also* barriers to academic success

instructors 314–16; privilege 312–15

integrated approach to mental health 259

interdisciplinary approaches 30

international perspective 6, 29–35, **36–40**, 47; cosmopolitan resilience 118–22; future directions 45–7; history 29; local context 40–5; meta-culture 32; Zeitgeist 45

intervention: academic success 201–3; children and youth 16; disproportionality 100, **100–2**; education 17; parents and caregivers 19; public health 23; school 160; special education 82–3

intimidation, of teachers 211–12

Justice, Loving 161–4, 167–8

justice, restorative 108–9. *See also* social justice

Kleinman, A. 40

language 53–4, 66; in assessment 178–9; barrier 165; theory and praxis 63–5; vocabulary 146

Latino Americans 97, 106, **278**

law: advocacy 303–4; education 158; Education for all Handicapped Children Act 63–4; Individuals with Disabilities Education Act 75; special education 75–6

learning disabilities 24, 180

Lesbian Gay Bisexual Transgender and Questioning (LGBTQ) 159, 165

Lewis, T. J. 317

limited access to mental health 258–9

local contexts, international perspective 41–2

Locke, John 155

Loving Justice 161–4, 167–8

macrosystem 195–6, 299. *See also* institutional barriers

malnutrition 141–2
marginalization 283; academic 191; disciplinary approach 92–3. *See also* discrimination; stigmatization
medical model 64, 138, 176–7, 294
mental health 8, 31, 244–5, 262; case study **263–6**; culturally responsive practice 250–1; ecological model 255; guidelines 246–7; history 245–7; as model 41, 257–8; prevalence 247–8; stigmatization 252–4
mental health services, school-based 251–62, 255–6; barriers 252–4; benefits 254–5; continuum of approaches 258–62; delivery 256–8; as ideal 251–2; School-Based Health Centers 259–61
mesosystem 195. *See also* relationships
meta-culture 32, **36**
metapsychology 30
microaggression 321; racial 211–12, 215, **220–2**, 315–16
microsystem 194: discipline 207; fostering collaboration 283–9; mental health 253–4. *See also* community, family
Millenium Development Goals (MDGs) 33–5; in local context 42–5
minorities 18, 21, 24, 110–11; acculturation **237–40**; assessment 178–9; enhancing resiliency 32, 119–21; poverty 139–40; special education 74–9; suburban schools 124–6. *See also* race
minors. *See* children
models: consultation 229–34; Consultee-Centered Consultation 230; country-specific 32; emic 41–5; etic **36–40**, 40; global community **35**; medical 64, 138, 294; mental health 41, 257–8; outdated 32; Participatory Intervention Model 231–3; Practice Model 249–50; public health 294–5, 298–304, **299**; punitive discipline 92; SOLVES 287–9; support 95. *See also* ecological model; paradigms
motivation, consultation 236
Mpofu, E. 174
multiculturalism 122–3, 150–1, **232–3**; consultation 233–4; training courses 312–14
multi-tiered model: advocacy 298–9; case study **263–6**; mental health 256–8
multi-tiered support 95, 102–5

National Association of School Psychologists (NASP) 8, 150, 198, 225, 251–2; current practice 32–3; mental health 247; official guidelines 2–3, 294–8; Practice Model 249–50; public health model 298–304
Nastasi, B. 250–1
Native Americans 107
nature vs. nurture 155
negative discipline 208. *See also* punitive discipline
No Child Left Behind 195–6
nondiscriminatory assessment model 184–5
norms. *See* values/norms

Obama, President Barack 143
opportunity gap 144–5, 147
Ortiz, S. 174, 177–9
outreach programs 130
outwardness 161–2, 164–6
overrepresentation. *See* disproportionality

paradigms: collaboration 271–3; ecological 20–2; pathology 17, 20–2, 176–7; public health 22–4; remediation 271–3. *See also* models
paradox of school psychology 19
parents **38**, 124–5, 129–30; collaboration 17, **283**, 283–6; intervention 19; in poverty 139–40
participation 34, 80–1
Participatory Intervention Model (PIM) 231–3
partnerships. *See* collaboration
pathology, as paradigm 17, 20–2, 176–7. *See also* blame; medical model
personal relationships 59–60
Participatory Intervention Model (PIM) 231–3
Pink Power case study 157–61, 165–7
Platinum Rule 162
policy: advocacy 303–4; education 158; No Child Left Behind 195–6
positive psychology 176–7
poverty 123, 137–40, 152: academic skills 145–7; child development 139–41; education 143–5; health 142–3; implications for school psychology practice 149–52; psychosocial behaviors 142–3; resegregation 147–8; special education 77–9; teaching 148–9. *See also* deprivation

Power, T. J. 3
praxis and theory 63–5, 318–20
preschool children 17
preventative discipline 94–5
principles, assessment 176–9
privacy issues, mental health 253–4
privilege 56–8, 61–7, 92–3; cultural
    embedding 174; of instructors 312–15;
    as obstacle 150–1; special
    education 80–1; White 99–100, 144–5,
    314–16
professional conduct 37; culturally
    responsive practice 109–10, 112; special
    education 79–87
professional development 311–12, 325;
    case study **322–4**; context 312–14;
    course structure 318–19,
    **322–4**; foundations 312–16;
    implementation 316–18; instructor, role
    of 314–16; recommendations 317–21;
    training 219–20
professionalism **37**, 58–60
prosociality 16, 319–20; of school
    psychologists 311
protective factors 119
psychometric testing 173–5
psychosocial behaviors 142–3
public health crisis **22–3**, 22–4
public health model 294–5, 298–9, **299**;
    tiers 300–8, **301–2**
punitive discipline 91–4, 143

qualitative/quantitative research 46,
    229–33

race 18, 24, 56–7, 124–6: achievement
    gap 190–3; case study **220–2**;
    discipline gap 92, 94, 95–6, 211; ethnic
    composition 41–2; health 141–2;
    identity 120–1; of instructors 314–
    16; microaggression 211–12, 215,
    **220–2**, 315–16, 321; poverty 138–9,
    144–5; psychosocial behaviors 142–3;
    resilience 119; special education 74–9,
    86–7; teaching 148–50. *See also* African
    Americans; Latino Americans; Native
    Americans
reading: assessment 180; learning
    disability 24
redistribution of resources 99
referral practices 82–3, 103, 191–2, 198
relational ethics 59–60
relationships 119–20, 126, 129, 132, 138;
    school-family 284–9
religion 126, 130, 162

remediation 271–3
research, qualitative/quantitative 46. *See
    also* evidence-based practice
resegregation 147–8
resilience 7, 32, 119, 142. *See also*
    cosmopolitan resilience
resistance to consultation and
    collaboration 235
resource allocation 5, 140, 177–8,
    191–6, 199–200, 203; race 144–5;
    redistribution 99; special education
    78–81; urban schools 123–4
restorative justice 108–9
restricted approach to mental health 258
rhetoric 66
rights. *See* child rights
rural schools 126–8

scholarship 53–63, 155–60;
    consultation 235–6; in context 55–6;
    convention 55–6; future directions
    327–31; informing practice 45–6;
    language 63–5; limitations 316–17;
    qualitative and quantitative research 46
school culture/climate 155,
    167–8; implementation 163–7;
    outwardness 161–2, 164–6; status
    quo 155–60; transformation 165–7;
    vision 160–3
school psychologist 18, 19–20; as advocate.
    *See* advocacy; as agent of social justice 9,
    15, 92, 99, 110–11, 131, 150–2, 197–203;
    aspirations 1–2, 9; assessment 179–82,
    185; classroom behavioral issues 218–
    20; collaboration 284–5; cosmopolitan
    resilience 128–30; definition 2;
    poverty 149–52; race 149–50;
    training 219–20
school to prison pipeline 91–2, 207–10
School-Based Health Centers
    (SBHCs) 259–61
schooling: compulsory 93; effective 23–4,
    270–1
schools: as arena for promoting social
    justice 16–17; inner-city 103–4; norms
    and values 156–7, 274–9; rural 126–8;
    suburban 124–6; uniform 281–2;
    urban 122–4, 208–9
schoolwide data focus 102–5, 177–8,
    179–81, 298
schoolwide positive behavior support
    (SWPBS) 106–8
segregation (resegregation) 147–8
sexism 57, 59
sexuality 157, 159, 164–5

single parent households 139
slavery 195, 241
social capital 121–9; as theory 118, 120–1, 130
social engineering 15–17
social justice 2–6, 327–31; agenda 15; definition 4–5, **5**, 8, 137, 175; perspective 2–3, 9, 18–19; as theory 120–1; in training 3, 9; as verb 9, 319–20; Zeitgeist 122. *See also* advocacy
socialization 57–8
SOLVES model 287–9
special education 73–9, **131–2**; addressing inequities 79–81; case study **86–7**, 189–90; gender 77; guidelines 85; intervention 82–3; poverty 142; professional conduct 79–87; race 74–9; referral practices 82–3; stakeholders 84; stigmatization 74
stakeholders 42–5, 106, 271–3; cultures and contexts 42–3; definition 226; intervention 160; special education 84; working with 44
standards. *See* values and norms
statistics: defining social justice **5**; discipline gap 95–6; education **22–3**; poverty 138–40, 143–5; School-Based Health Centers 259–61
status quo 155–61
stereotypes 128
stigmatization 74; mental health 252–4; poverty 141–2
strengths-based assessment 176–7; mental health 255
subjectivity: offenses 96, 105; special education 76
suburban schools 124–6
support, multi-tiered model 95
survival and development 33–4, **37**
suspension. *See* exclusionary discipline
sustainability 45
systemic assessment 179–81
systemic school discipline 91–3, 111–12; culturally responsive practice 109–10; disciplinary disproportionality 95–6; history 93–5; intervention 100–2, **100–2**; restorative justice 108–9; schoolwide database 102–5; schoolwide positive behavior support 106–8; social climate 105; and social justice 97–8; societal/historical/cultural issues 97–8

systems theory 227–8, 240–1

*tabula rasa* 155
target population 16–17. *See also* children; schools
teachers 20, 271–3; approaches to discipline 208; classroom management 209–13; intimidation 211–12; leaving the profession 206
teaching 148–9. *See also* schooling
teenage pregnancy 142
terminology. *See* definitions
testing 64, 124; special education 77–8, 83–5
theory and praxis 63–5, 318–20
three-tiered model. *See* advocacy; public health model
training 3, 9, 219–20, 312–14. *See also* professional development
transformation, cultural 162–3, 165–7
treatment. *See* intervention

underachievement. *See* achievement gap
unemployment 138–9
uniform, school 281–2
United Nations (UN) 33–5, 42–5
urban schools: classroom management 208–9; cosmopolitan resilience 122–4. *See also* inner-city schools

values/norms 160–1; culture 211–12, 214–18; schools 156–7, 274–9; White 98
verb, social justice as 9, 319–20
verve 275
victims. *See* blame
violence 42, 43–4, 142–3; in schools 206–7

walking the talk 61–5; theory and praxis 63–5
western-centric outlook 32–3, 109–10
White privilege 98–100, 144–5, 314–16
World Health Organization (WHO) **37**

youth, mental health 247–8. *See also* children

Zeitgeist: international perspective 45; social justice 122
zero tolerance 94, 207–8

Made in the USA
San Bernardino, CA
08 September 2016